The Digest of Social Experiments
Second Edition

DAVID GREENBERG
AND MARK SHRODER

with the assistance of
Matthew Onstott

The Digest of Social Experiments

Second Edition

THE URBAN INSTITUTE PRESS
Washington, D.C.

Library of Congress Cataloging in Publication Data

The Digest of Social Experiments / David Greenberg, Mark Shroder.—
2nd ed.

   1. United States—social policy. 2. Evaluation research (social action programs)
—United States. 3. Public welfare administration—United States. 4. Human
Services—United States. I. Shroder, Mark. II. Title.

HN59.2.G74	1997	97-3224
361.6'1'0973		CIP

ISBN 0-87766-648-2 (cloth, alk. paper)

Printed in the United States of America

Distributed in North America by
University Press of America
4720 Boston Way
Lanham, MD 20706

THE URBAN INSTITUTE is a nonprofit policy research and educational organization established in Washington, D.C., in 1968. Its staff investigates the social and economic problems confronting the nation and public and private means to alleviate them. The Institute disseminates significant findings of its research through the publications program of its Press. The goals of the Institute are to sharpen thinking about societal problems and efforts to solve them, improve government decisions and performance, and increase citizen awareness of important policy choices.

Through work that ranges from broad conceptual studies to administrative and technical assistance, Institute researchers contribute to the stock of knowledge available to guide decision making in the public interest.

Conclusions or opinions expressed in Institute publications are those of the authors and do not necessarily reflect the views of staff members, officers or trustees of the Institute, advisory groups, or any organizations that provide financial support to the Institute.

TO ORDER THE *DIGEST* ON DISK

The text of this volume is available in an ASCII disk package, for class use only, upon proof of purchase of one hardback copy. The price is $20.00, including shipping and handling. To order, send check or money order, with hardback receipt, to:

Publications Sales Office
P.O. Box 7273
Department C
Washington, D.C. 20044

202-857-8687

ACKNOWLEDGMENTS

ASSISTANCE.   Matt Onstott collected and summarized the new reports in this edition of the Digest and is responsible for several improvements in organization. We take this opportunity to express our appreciation for his exceptionally able and conscientious work.

FUNDING.   Three grants made this book possible. Two of them were in the Small Grants Program administered by the Institute for Research on Poverty of the University of Wisconsin at Madison on behalf of the Office of the Assistant Secretary of Planning and Evaluation of the U.S. Department of Health and Human Services. A third was from the graduate school of the University of Maryland–Baltimore County.

CONSULTATION.   In learning about the demonstrations summarized here, we consulted with hundreds of people. Many are listed in the index. The authors appreciate this assistance more than this brief and collective acknowledgement can properly express. The following persons were in positions where their help was particularly needed and were kind enough to be responsive to our requests: Dick Saul, Peter Germanis, Girley Wright, Bill Dickenson, Michael Wiseman, James Zimmer, Marcy Gross, William Weissert, Jeanne Brooks-Gunn, Robert Schoeni.

COMMENTS.   Two anonymous referees read the Introduction. Their comments were uncommonly constructive, and resulted in significant improvement in the text. Three leading evaluation organizations were also asked for comments on summaries of experiments in which their groups had been involved. The authors thank Larry Orr of Abt Associates, Judy Gueron of Manpower Demonstration Research Corporation, and Chuck Metcalfe of Mathematica Policy Research for coordinating this review process in their respective firms.

OMISSIONS AND OTHER ERRORS.   The authors regret that it was not practical to extend the same opportunity to other evaluators. We ask persons with knowledge of omitted social experiments, or of other errors or omissions, to inform the corresponding author, David Greenberg, Department of Economics, University of Maryland–Baltimore County, Baltimore, MD 21228 (telephone—301/455-2167; email—DHGREENBERG@UMBC2.UMBC.EDU).

EDITING AND PUBLICATION.   It is a pleasure to thank two sets of editors for their efforts to improve the accuracy and clarity of the text we brought them. The Institute for Research on Poverty brought out the first edition of the Digest as Special Report #52 in May 1991; the responsible IRP staff were Betty Evanson and Paul Dudenheffer. The current edition owes its existence to Felicity Skidmore, the director of the Urban Institute Press; Molly Ruzicka did the copy editing and Scott Forrey shepherded production.

DISCLAIMERS.   The authors take full responsibility for all errors and omissions. Opinions expressed in this book should not be attributed to any other agency, organization, or individual. Specifically, the authors' opinions are not necessarily shared by policymakers in the U.S. Department of Housing and Urban Development or the U.S. Department of Health and Human Services.

CONTENTS

PART TWELVE: SINGLE/TEEN PARENT

PART THIRTEEN: UNEMPLOYED

FOREWORD

The Urban Institute Press is pleased to publish *The Digest of Social Experiments*, a comprehensive reference work on all known evaluations that have used or are using social experimentation to measure the impact of a social program. The fundamental challenge facing any analyst endeavoring to measure what a social program has caused to change is to measure what would have happened if the program had not existed. This is no easy task because measured outcomes can be affected by factors that have nothing to do with the program. Differing personal characteristics of program beneficiaries and changes in the program environment during the evaluation period are the main dangers.

Social experimentation using random assignment and control groups is the most powerful methodology available to isolate the impacts of social programs. It is also the only social science measurement tool that resembles the methods used by the natural sciences.

Random assignment is the strategy of assigning members of some relevant population (such as program eligibles) by a coin toss or equivalent randomizing procedure to one of two groups—a "treatment" group that receives program services and a "control" group that does not. Because chance alone determines who receives the service, the treatment and control groups can be assumed to be similar in all characteristics that might affect the outcomes of the program. This means, in turn, that any differences between treatment and control groups can be interpreted with confidence as impacts of the program. For every known social experiment, *The Digest* gives the cost, time period, treatment(s) tested, outcomes of interest, sample sizes and target population, major findings, design issues encountered, and methodological limitations.

Unfortunately, social experimentation, although the most rigorous evaluation strategy for measuring program impacts, is often impossible in the real world. The particular type of service may make withholding that service to create a control group ethically unacceptable.

The context of the service (an ongoing entitlement program, for example) may make withholding the service from a potential control group legally prohibited. The evaluation budget may make random assignment, which is a very expensive evaluation strategy, financially impossible. Where such experiments are not possible, all is not lost. Valuable information can be gained by applying statistical techniques to program data to correct for nonprogram differences among program beneficiaries or over time that could affect measured outcomes. *The Digest's* first chapter sets the stage for the rest of the book by discussing what social experiments can do, what they cannot do, and the issues the evaluator needs to consider in deciding whether to use social experimentation in a particular instance.

It is my hope that this book will be useful, not only to seasoned social experimenters interested in learning from previous experience in their efforts to design a better experiment, but also to undergraduate and graduate students learning about social experimentation for the first time. For the latter group the Press is making specially priced classroom copies of *The Digest of Social Experiments* available on disk.

William Gorham

Part One

INTRODUCTION

AN OVERVIEW OF SOCIAL
EXPERIMENTATION AND THE DIGEST

David Greenberg and Mark Shroder

This book testifies to the breadth and depth of a distinctive modern form of social research activity—the randomized social experiment. Such experiments have been conducted since the late 1960s to evaluate proposed changes in program or policy. Some experiments have been large and highly publicized—among them the "Seattle-Denver Income Maintenance Experiment," the "RAND Health Insurance Study," and the recent experimental evaluation of programs run under the Jobs Training Partnership Act of 1982; others have been small and obscure. Some have "pilot tested" major innovations in social policy; others have been used to assess incremental changes in existing programs. A few have provided the basis for evaluating the overall efficacy of major existing programs. Most have been used to evaluate policies targeted at disadvantaged population groups.

This *Digest* contains brief summaries of 143 known social experiments conducted in the United States, 1 from Canada, and 1 from the Netherlands. To the best of our knowledge, no other countries have conducted social experiments. In addition, for purposes of contrast, we also provide summaries of 3 quasi experiments. Each summary, typically two or three pages long and presented in a standardized format, outlines the cost and time frame of the demonstration, the treatments tested, outcomes of interest, sample sizes and target population, research components, major findings, important methodological limitations and design issues encountered, and other relevant topics. The experiments summarized are those for which findings were available by fall 1996. Brief outlines of 75 experiments still in progress at that time are provided in Appendix II, at the end of the *Digest*.

This introduction provides background information for readers regarding social experiments. Rather than attempting to comprehensively discuss social experimentation—a topic that would require an entire book of its own[1]—we touch upon a number of areas pertinent to interpreting the *Digest's* summaries. We begin by defining social experiments, discussing the concepts of internal and external validity of experimental findings and the categories into which experiments tend to fall. We then briefly describe quasi experiments, noting their strengths and weaknesses.

Next we examine the reasons for conducting social experiments, we provide an overview of ethical issues, and we describe nonexperimental methodologies that have been proposed as substitutes. Some common threats to the external validity of social experiments are then reviewed, as well as "optional" features often found in experiments. A discussion of the uses of social experiments in the policy process follows.

We then present a brief history of social experiments and discuss types of past experiments as well as trends in social experimentation. The final section of this introduction explains the uses and organization of this volume, so that readers can make optimal use of the summaries.

WHAT IS A SOCIAL EXPERIMENT?

The summaries in this *Digest* focus on field studies of social programs in which there was random assignment of individuals, households, or (in rare instances) firms or organizations to two or more alternative treatments. The primary research objective of the experiments was to measure impacts of the alternative treatments on market behavior (such as the receipt of earnings) and corresponding government fiscal outcomes (such as the receipt of transfer benefits). Thus, a social experiment has at least the following features:

- *Random assignment*: Creation of at least two groups of human subjects who differ from one another by chance alone.
- *Policy intervention*: A set of actions ensuring that different incentives, opportunities, or constraints confront the members of each of the randomly assigned groups in their daily lives.
- *Follow-up data collection*: Measurement of market and fiscal outcomes for members of each group.
- *Evaluation*: Application of statistical inference and informed professional judgment about the degree to which the policy interventions have caused differences in outcomes between the groups.

Random assignment involves neither choice nor discretion. Whereas human subjects may or may not have the right to choose to participate in the experiment, they do not have the right to decide which group within the experiment they will join. Similarly, persons administering the policy intervention may restrict eligibility for participation in the experiment, but once a person is admitted, program staff cannot determine the group in which that subject is enrolled, except by using randomization.

Social experiments test policy interventions: they are attempts to influence the endowments of, and the incentives and disincentives facing, human subjects. Thus, in most social experiments, one of the randomly assigned groups, the control group, represents the status quo and is only eligible for benefits and services under the existing policy regime. The remaining group or groups, the treatment group(s), are subjected to the policy innovation or innovations being tested. Comparisons of the control group with the treatment group(s) indicate the impacts of the tested innovations.

Social experiments are designed to determine whether (or how much) the policies being tested would affect the market behavior of individuals (e.g, their employment and earnings; consumption of food, energy, housing, and health care services; receipt of government benefits). Taken together, the second and third features of our definition exclude random-assignment experiments in medicine, psychology, economics, criminology, and education that are not designed to measure changes in subjects' transactions in their daily environment in response to policy innovations. For example, we exclude randomized clinical trials of prescription drugs intended to affect health status; we also exclude randomization of students to competing school curricula intended to improve scores on standardized tests.

Although outcome data may be collected by a variety of means, readers of this *Digest*'s summaries will notice that over time social experimenters have relied increasingly on administrative data, rather than surveys. Once collected, outcomes among the groups of randomly assigned individuals are compared. Outcome differences between the groups provide estimates of the impacts of the tested policy interventions. However, the data do not speak for themselves. Analysts must decide what data transformations are appropriate; what, if any, nonexperimental factors should be considered; what statistical techniques to use; and what results do and do not make sense.

Internal and External Validity

If implemented properly, the results of social experiments generally are *internally valid*, that is, they provide unbiased impact estimates for targeted people subject to different treatments at the particular time and place they were administered. However, evaluation, including that based on random assignment designs, requires considerable care, and is often expensive. Some of the experiments summarized here were done "on the cheap" and hurriedly. These experiments tended to be poorly designed and implemented, and as a result, a few of them either produced findings that lacked internal validity or did not produce findings at all.

Even when carefully implemented, the extent to which social experiments possess *external validity*—applicability to other individuals, places, and times—may be controversial and is always problematic. For example, differences in timing imply that social attitudes, government institutions, the business cycle, the relative demand for unskilled and skilled labor, the rate of inflation, and other factors may vary from what they were when the experiment was conducted. Different locations may result in dissimilarities in age, sex, racial, or ethnic mixes; social attitudes; state and local government institutions; industrial structure; and many other factors.

Categories of Social Experiments

Several of this volume's social experiments—notably the four income maintenance experiments, the "Housing Allowance Demand Experiment,"and the "RAND Health Insurance Study"—were designed to estimate "response surfaces"—that is, their designs allowed two or more continuous parameters of the program being tested to vary within wide ranges. For example, tax rates and guarantee levels in the income maintenance experiments varied greatly across treatment groups. Estimates of responses to program parameters can, at least in principle, be used to project the effects of any program that has the basic features of the one tested, even if the specific values of the program parameters differ.

In contrast to response-surface experiments, most social experiments permit only "black box" assessments of whether the tested intervention "works." That is, they provide different randomly selected groups of individuals with different "packages" of services and incentives (for example, job training, child care assistance, and job search assistance) and then determine whether outcomes (for example, postprogram earnings) differ among the groups. Only limited information is typically provided on the degree to which these impacts can be attributed to specific components of the service packages or on the effects of changes in program design. Findings from the response-surface technique are in some ways more flexible for projecting the effects of future policy, but it may not be possible in practice to carry out intervention(s) in the form of variations in the values of two or more continuous variables.

A second important distinction is between experiments that are "mandatory" and those that are "voluntary." An experiment is "mandatory" if the individual cannot enjoy certain benefits without participating. Many unemployment insurance and welfare experiments in this volume have been mandatory. The Minnesota Income Tax Compliance Experiment, in which certain taxpayers were randomly selected for a higher probability of audit, was mandatory in a broader sense, because the individuals had not applied for any specific benefits.

Individuals must in some way apply to enter a voluntary experiment. Experimental evaluations of training programs and electric-rate experiments have usually been voluntary. As demonstrated later, the fact that individuals chose to enter an experiment may complicate the evaluation of the outcomes.

Government agencies often consider themselves legally and ethically justified in conducting mandatory experiments if the alternative treatments are within the agency's ordinary administrative discretion. For example, randomly selecting certain taxpayers for audits is a necessary function of a tax office. Voluntary experiments generally require some type of informed consent by the subject.

WHAT ARE QUASI EXPERIMENTS?

In addition to summarizing randomized social experiments, this book also contains outlines of quasi-experimental demonstrations. Scholars and evaluation professionals have attached several conflicting meanings to the term quasi experiment; to keep the scope of this book manageable, we have limited the term to policy demonstrations in which potential sites are randomized to treatment or control group status. An example illustrates.

Say six sites are considered for a demonstration, and some 1,500 individuals will be subjects of the experiment at these sites. On some prior basis, the evaluators determine beforehand that site A is most like site B, site C most similar to site D, and site E is best matched with site F. By flipping a coin (or using a more sophisticated random process), the evaluators determine whether the innovative treatment will occur at site *A* and the control at site *B* or vice versa; at site *C* versus site *D*; and so on. For concreteness, let the treatment sites be *A*, *D*, and *F*, and the control sites be *B*, *C*, and *E*. The intention is to compare the *ADF* outcomes with the *BCE* outcomes, and, if they are significantly different, to attribute that difference to the policy intervention.

Significant theoretical and practical reasons may exist for choosing site randomization over randomizing individuals within a site. For example, an innovation may be intended to change "the culture of the welfare office" or "the culture of public housing projects"; for this cultural change to occur, the innovation must affect all similarly situated individuals who are members of the culture. Feedback and information processes, which may be crucial (and are treated at greater length later in this introduction), might only function if an innovation is adopted on a sitewide basis. The responses on "the other side of the market" from employers or landlords may also be important, and randomization within sites might attenuate these responses. For any number of reasons, it also may be simply impractical to administer randomly different treatments within the same site.

The most serious problem with the site randomization concept is that there may be too few sites for effective randomization to occur. Although the sites have been assigned to treatment and control status by chance, the people within the sites have not been randomized. People do not randomly choose whether to live at site *A* or at site *B*; they choose purposefully, and their choices create both observed and unobserved differences between sites subject to the different treatments.[2] Economic and social conditions in the two sets of sites will vary at the outset of the demonstration, and these conditions may change in the course of the demonstration for reasons unrelated to the demonstration itself. In short, both observed and unobserved differences will occur in the initial conditions as well as in the changes in those conditions.

If, at the close of the quasi experiment, *ADF* outcomes are significantly different from *BCE* outcomes, the evaluators and the readers of the evaluation must decide whether the difference in outcome is due to the difference in treatment or to one or more of the sources of unobserved difference noted earlier here.[3] They may find this decision very difficult (see Hollister and Hill 1995). If there were 1,500 randomized sites, rather than 6, the problem of unobserved random differences across sites would have no particular importance, but experimentation on such a vast scale is unlikely to be attempted.

REASONS FOR CONDUCTING SOCIAL EXPERIMENTS

The motives for undertaking a social experiment invariably differ from one experiment to the next. We begin with the most cynical motive—that the social experiment is conducted to replace difficult political decisions with symbolic action. This charge, which was leveled against the income maintenance experiments, will always have surface appeal, for many legislative and administrative actions have greater symbolism than content. Indeed, some groups often gain a political advantage by delaying a decision, and evaluations with any pretension to scientific standards do take time.

Despite the superficial attractiveness of this argument, we believe such a motive can be easily dismissed. A demonstration may serve as a symbol of a policymaker's sympathies, but no political logic requires an objective assessment of that demonstration. The usual purpose of delaying tactics is to make the issue go away. If that were the goal, an objective evaluation based on random assignment would act like a bomb with a very slow fuse, detonating years later, perhaps with embarrassing consequences for the policymaker's career.

Policymakers seem well aware of this. Egregiously pork-barrel or purely symbolic "demonstrations," or transparently political "programs" often seem deliberately designed to make future evaluations of any sort impossible. To the cynics, we suggest that policymakers have many other useful pretexts for delay that present fewer risks.[4]

We turn now to less-cynical explanations. First, an experiment may be intended for a specific policy decision. Feldman (1989: 80) has contended that if research were intended to influence a specific policy decision, both the timing of the decision and the alternatives to be considered would have to be known in advance. Otherwise, the research would probably not be available when the decision is made or would not be pertinent to the decision. Indeed, these conditions are seldom met in practice.

A less-demanding explanation of why social experiments are initiated is that policymakers plan to use the information gained whenever it becomes available. Therefore, if a social experiment demonstrates convincingly that an idea really works, it will help to generate the political support required to place it on the policy agenda.

A final possibility is that the experiment is intended to create an inventory of information for future policymaking (Feldman 1989: 92–96). The implied intention is for the experiment to contribute to a stock of knowledge, reducing uncertainty should a relevant issue reach the policy agenda.

All but the cynical explanation for social experiments suggest that such demonstrations are intended to generate information relevant to the policy process. Almost without exception, social experiments test the power of particular policies to solve or mitigate serious social problems—long-term welfare recipiency; rising health care costs; inadequate or unaffordable shelter for low-income families; long-term unemployment; the clouded future for former offenders, substance addicts, and at-risk youth. Experiments are funded when disagreement over appropriate policy interventions is caused, at least in part, by uncertainty over their potential consequences. If policymakers knew the outcomes, there would be little justification for sponsoring experiments. It is useful to keep this apparently banal idea in mind when considering whether social experiments are ethical, and whether they are the best form of research for assessing policy choices.

ARE EXPERIMENTS ETHICAL?

Policy interventions are intended to change people's lives; it strikes many people as wrong, or at least strange, to change them randomly.

A social experiment is ethical if the treatment received by each group of human subjects is ethical. The experiment is unethical if one or more of the treatments are unethical. The loudest critics of certain experiments have alleged either that the innovation being tested was unethical or that the status quo—the existing laws and regulations governing some aspect of society—was unethical. Random assignment itself is ethically neutral.

In practice, there is usually some restriction on the availability of benefits or services tested (because of budgetary limitation, for instance). If such restrictions exist, then the fact that assignment between treatment and control groups is random is a matter of ethical indifference. A first-come, first-served approach may be more convenient for the program staff, but has precisely the same moral value. Shutting the door on people who apply after 4 P.M. Tuesday is just as arbitrary as shutting the door on people who were born on an odd-numbered day or for whom the last two digits of their Social Security number add up to 12.

If we knew in advance that all members of a population would benefit or suffer from the application of a policy toward them, would an experiment on some fraction of them be unethical? Perhaps. Under the principle of horizontal equity, similarly situated individuals should be similarly treated, and singling out some members of a class for arbitrary rewards or punishments not applied to others is, in general, unjust.

When the effects of a policy are unknown, however, the same generalization cannot apply. Many treatments summarized in this book were expected (or at least were intended) to make the individuals subject to them better off, but failed to do so; sometimes they made at least some of them worse off. Individuals who were assigned to control groups and, hence, were randomly denied access to those treatments often seem to have lost nothing important. The state of honest ignorance required to justify disparate treatment existed at the time the experiment began.

In other instances, we may believe a priori that members of a target population will be better off, on average, as a result of an innovation (e.g., the income maintenance experiments). However, we may also believe that people outside the target population will be worse off (e.g., taxpayers). We do not know a priori whether the benefits are larger than the costs.[5] Not knowing the trade-off, some policymakers will refuse to institute the innovation until the benefits and costs are better measured, and this is the ethical justification for the experiment.

ALTERNATIVES TO SOCIAL EXPERIMENTATION

Given honest ignorance, it does not follow that random assignment is always the optimal form of evaluation. Social experiments can be quite costly, because they require extensive follow-up data on both treatment and control groups, and some types of policy interventions are better evaluated using nonexperimental methods. We now examine those methods, and consider their advantages and disadvantages relative to experimentation.

The most obvious feasible alternative to random assignment is to compare persons who participate in a particular program with persons who do not participate; the participants then constitute the "treatment group" and the nonparticipants the "comparison group." The least-sophisticated version of this approach consists of selecting the comparison group from among persons who initially applied for program benefits, but for one reason or another did not actually participate. A more-sophisticated version involves drawing a comparison group from among persons sampled in national micro-data sets (for example, the Current Population Survey [CPS]) by statistically matching these persons with members of the treatment group to make the two groups as comparable as possible.

Other approaches are feasible when a program is carried out in some geographic locations, but not in others. A treatment group, for example, might comprise individuals who live at the sites that have the program, and a comparison group might consist of similar individuals living at other sites. Alternatively, one might compare outcomes in the same set of sites before and after an innovation has been introduced.

An obvious problem with the geographic and chronological comparison groups is that economic and social circumstances differ from place to place and change over time; it is very difficult to control for these factors in a manner that allows the effects of the innovation to be isolated. The superiority of a randomly assigned control group over the "nonparticipant" comparison group alternatives may be less obvious.

There is essentially one reason for social experimentation: random assignment is the only known means of eliminating *selection bias*. If an individual can choose whether a policy intervention will or will not apply to himself, then people who choose treatment *A* will differ from those who choose treatment *B* in both observable and unobservable ways. The same is true if program administrators make the choice for individuals, rather than having the individuals choose for themselves. Selection factors will also bias comparisons across sites that have and have not implemented an innovation, if, as is usually the case, the decision as to whether to adopt the innovation was made locally.[6] For example, the sites may differ in terms of local economic conditions and in population characteristics.

If individuals in treatment and comparison groups differ only in observable ways, then the analyst can, in principle, adjust for them when researching outcomes.[7] However, absent random assignment, individuals in treatment groups are also likely to differ from those in comparison groups in unobservable ways. The unobserved factors that infuence which group they enter are also likely to influence outcomes.

For example, it has been well known since the 1970s that workers who volunteer for training have often experienced a sharp drop in their recent earnings. They cannot properly be compared with workers who have the same observable characteristics but no such dip. Earnings fluctuation may also be permanent or transitory; workers with the same observable dips as training participants will not be comparable if their dips have dissimilar causes.

In one common scenario, workers who have suffered short-term setbacks realize that their careers will recover without additional training, whereas others recognize their old careers have hit a dead end. The latter then try to enter a new path through training, sometimes unsuccessfully. In comparing workers who have temporary dips and do not enter training with those who have had lasting setbacks and do enter training, we may find that the trained have lower earnings than the untrained. We may then falsely attribute the lower earnings to poor training programs.

In this example, selection bias is negative—it makes the program being evaluated look worse than it is. Selection bias can be either positive or negative, and usually neither policymakers nor analysts know with certainty which is the case. Findings from numerous studies have suggested that selection bias, in whatever direction, can be very large (Bell, Orr, Blomquist, and Cain 1995; Fraker and Maynard 1987; Friedlander and Robins 1995; LaLonde 1986; LaLonde and Maynard 1987). These studies used the presumaby unbiased estimates of program impacts from experiments to assess impact estimates obtained by matching treatment groups with carefully drawn nonexperimental comparison groups. The selection bias associated with the nonexperimental estimates was often larger than the true program impact. Selection bias proved large enough to affect the statistical significance in most cases, the direction of the impact (positive or negative) in far too many cases, and any benefit–cost analysis in nearly all cases.

Bias of unknown sign and unknown but possibly critical magnitude must reduce the usefulness of nonexperimental forms of evaluation. Attempts have been made to develop techniques using nonexperimental data that would have the same degree of internal validity as experimental data (see, for example, Dehejia and Wahba 1995; Heckman and Hotz 1989; Heckman, Ichimura, et al. 1995). So far, unfortunately, there is little evidence that these techniques can consistently do so.

For example, Bell et al. (1995) have argued that selection by program staff might generate a comparison group with correctable bias if the criteria for selection are documented and consistently exercised. In principle, the analyst could then control for the observed selection factors. However, the one test of this hypothesis reported in their monograph fails. This might have been because the selection process was not, in fact, fully documented and consistent; this could occur, for example, if program staff select people who are more likable, attractive, persistent, or literate than those screened out or if the staff selection process effectively allows potential participants to screen themselves in or out.

Most experts in social program evaluation would probably agree with Burtless (1995) and Hollister and Hill (1995) that no alternative method can produce impact estimates that have as much internal validity as a social experiment with random assignment can. This is, however, a reluctant majority. Social experiments are subject to important limitations of their own. Most of these shortcomings concern threats to the external validity of social experiments. The next section lists the most important of these limitations.[8] These shortcomings are not unique to randomized evaluations; they also apply to most forms of nonexperimental evaluation.

THREATS TO EXTERNAL VALIDITY OF IMPACT ESTIMATES

Whether evaluated by random assignment or by nonexperimental methods, innovations to social programs are often tested on small-scale demonstration or pilot basis.[9] Manski and Garfinkel (1992) and Garfinkel, Manski, and Michalopoulos (1992) have suggested that an important component of some policy innovations intended for widespread adaptation is that they cause changes in community attitudes and norms; these, in turn, result in feedback effects that influence the innovation's success. These authors further suggested that program success depends on information diffusion to potential participants. They arued that feedback effects and information diffusion will not occur unless the innovation is adopted on a large scale, and that these effects will be missed by small-scale tests.[10]

Potentially important marketwide effects may also not occur in small-scale tests. For exampe, training programs could affect the level of wages in a community. They might also affect the number of employers in a community, if enough workers receive the training to induce firms to move into the area. Little is usually known about the importance of such effects. One can only speculate as to whether small-scale tests of social policies are seriously biased by their absence.

In arguments that are also applicable to nonexperimental evaluations of small-scale demonstrations, Heckman (1992), Heckman and Smith (1995), and Manski (1995) have contended that participants in small-scale experiments may not be representative of individuals who would participate in ongoing, full-scale programs. This could occur because of a lack of information diffusion, the relucatance of some individuals to subject themselves to random assignment, resource constraints in full-scale programs that result in program administrators restricting participants to persons meeting certain criteria, and numerous other reasons.[11]

One approach for eliminating biases caused by testing innovations on a small scale is to incorporate them on a site-wide basis in some locations and use other sites (perhaps statistically matched) that have not adopted the innovation for comparison purposes. For example, the effect of housing subsidy on rents in a housing market can only be learned through "saturation" of the community—that is, by providing the subsidy to all eligible households (see Lowry 1983). A saturation design, however, does not allow feedback effects, the effects of information diffusion, and market effects to be measured separately from other types of program impacts. Moreover, as previously discussed, such a design will produce biased impact estimates if the treatment and comparison sites differ in ways that are inadequately controlled for in the evaluation.

Social experiments are always limited to relatively few geographic areas. This is also true of many nonexperimental evaluations, especially those that rely on saturation designs. Because these sites are rarely selected randomly,[12] the external validity of the evaluations can be questioned (see Heckman 1992; Heckman and Smith 1995; Hotz 1992). Difficulties in obtaining a representative sample of program sites are especially acute in cases where the cooperation of local administrators is essential. However, the degree to which site selectivity translates into bias in the results of an impact analysis has not been proved empirically.[13]

Another potential shortcoming of social experiments concerns entry effects (Manski and Garfinkel 1992; Moffitt 1996). For example, if only unemployed persons or persons with incomes below certain thresholds are eligible for a training program that is being evaluated experimentally, and the services provided by this program are perceived as beneficial, some ineligibles may leave their jobs or otherwise reduce their incomes to qualify. In welfare-to-work programs that are mandatory for transfer recipients, and perceived by them as burdensome, some individuals who might otherwise have entered the welfare rolls may decide not to do so to avoid participating. Measuring entry effects in a random-assignment context requires that ineligibles be included in the evaluation sample; because of cost considerations, this is seldom done.[14]

A few experiments stand out as exceptions to this rule. In the Self-Sufficiency Project evaluation, a random assignment experiment currently being conducted in Canada (Card and Robins 1996), only persons who have been on welfare for at least one year qualify for the substantial increase in transfer payments made available through the tested program. The experimental sample, by design, includes transfer recipients who have been on welfare for less than one year—to see if some of them extend their stay on the rolls in order to qualify for the new benefit schedule. Similarly, the income maintenance experiments included households whose earnings at intake were too high to qualify for program benefits—to see if some of these households would reduce their earnings to qualify.

In both experimental and nonexperimental evaluations, members of the control or comparison group may, in practice, receive many of the same services as those received by members of the treatment group. For example, in the case of training programs, training of many types may already be available through community colleges and adult schools, and members of control or comparison groups can often obtain financing for these activities through existing nondemonstration sources. Consequently, estimates of program effects on participants do not measure impacts of the receipt of service against the nonreceipt of services. Rather, such estimates represent the *incremental* effect of the program services over the control services.

The existence of alternative services in the community and the measurement of incremental effects are not necessarily detrimental to an evaluation, depending upon the evaluation's goal. Commonly the goal is to determine the effect of an innovation relative to the actual environment, rather than relative to the complete absence of alternative services. Nonetheless, in interpreting impact estimates from social experiments and other evaluations, one should keep in mind that these estimates usually pertain to incremental effects, rather than to a control environment in which no services are available. Naturally, this limits the extent to which findings may be generalized from one environment to another.

The summaries in this digest give the reader some sense of the ambiguities that even the best experiments can create. We have also included a few outright failures, where the demonstration never answered and, in hindsight, never could have answered the policy questions asked. Social experimentation is a specialized research tool, suitable for some inquiries and not for others—a chisel that cannot substitute for a screwdriver, but the best instrument yet developed for many purposes.

ARE EXPERIMENTS UNDULY EXPENSIVE?

Social experiments have also been criticized for their cost (Levitan 1992).[15] Experimental costs fall into three basic categories:

- Implementing the innovative treatments;[16]
- Collecting data on the different groups; and
- Analyzing the data.

There are two perspectives on these costs. The first compares costs with benefits: Will the experiment be likely to generate information sufficiently valuable to the political or institutional process to justify the costs? There are three facets to this question: it must be answered *prospectively*, before the information exists; it involves the value of information provided by social scientists in a democracy; and it must be explicitly answered affirmatively by decision makers before the experiment can take place.

A somewhat different perspective looks at the experiment's opportunity cost,[17] weighing the net benefits of the experiment against the net benefits of the most probable alternative use of the resources. If the funds are federal, the most probable alternative use is another project at the same agency or agencies.[18] Perhaps, for example, the funds would be better spent on:

- A nationally representative in-depth survey, of, say, 50,000 households (at a 1995 annual cost of between $10 million and $12 million, depending on design choices);
- Demonstrating the feasibility of implementing a program change, rather than (or at least prior to) attempting to measure its impact (at an evaluation cost of between $20,000 and $20 million, depending on scale and number of sites);
- Improving program management information systems (costs vary too much to provide a range).

From either perspective, sponsoring a social experiment requires complex resource allocation decisions. The social experiments conducted to date were authorized by many different politicians, political appointees, and foundation directors, representing a wide spectrum of political views. Some of these persons were professional social scientists who could readily evaluate the technical merit of a proposed experiment on the basis of their own training and experience; the rest usually had as much access to expert opinion as they wished. It is striking that many very different individuals decided that this type of investigation is worth its costs. Nevertheless, controversy over the use of experimental techniques continues.

WHAT "OPTIONAL FEATURES" CAN EXPERIMENTS HAVE?

All social experiments are intended to provide impact estimates of the tested policy or policies. These estimates have already been discussed at some length. In addition to impact analyses, social experiments also commonly, but far from universally, feature two other types of analyses.

One of these, "process analysis," goes by sundry other names, and has a number of purposes. For example, an experiment's sponsor may desire third-party verification that the treatments were administered as planned. The sponsor may wish to know how many persons received the treatment and the nature and intensity of the services received. The sponsor may want to know the character of the environment in which the services were delivered and whether subjects understood the incentives provided to them by the experiment. The process analysis may also attempt to convey participants' and the program staff's subjective reactions to the experiment, or may speculate about whether certain identifiable subgroups would be likely to experience a greater or lesser impact than the sample as a whole.

An experiment without a process analysis is not necessarily useless. One may test the performance of a machine without any knowledge of the internal components. The lack of attention to "how it all really works" need not invalidate the findings, but the analysts may have greater difficulty interpreting the data and may be more prone to err in attempting to do so. Lack of attention to nonexperimental factors can lead to a "type-two" statistical error—the finding of no policy impact when in fact an impact exists. For one thing, a process analysis may reveal that an innovation was never really implemented,[19] and therefore data analysis is (probably) pointless; or that the assignments were not really random, so that internal validity is questionable.

A more subtle contribution of process analysis is in discovering relevant subgroups. These may only become clear to people who spend time in the field observing and interviewing. If two groups in an experiment really do differ only randomly, then a simple test comparing the mean outcome in one group with the mean outcome in the other yields an unbiased estimate of policy impact. Analysis by subgroup, however, may show that the treatment has significant impact for subjects of one type but not another. For the same reason, process analysis may turn up nonexperimental variables that should be controlled for in a regression analysis.

A second common, but far from universal, feature of social experiments is a benefit–cost analysis. Even policies with positive benefits for the target population are unjustified, if the cost to the rest of society is too high. A benefit–cost analysis aggregates benefits of the tested policy over time, both to participants and to society at large, and compares them to costs. Such analyses have greater value for some demonstrations than others. There is no need to compare benefits with costs, for example, if there are no demonstrable benefits.

Benefit–cost analyses encounter numerous difficult problems: what value to place on the loss of leisure to participants in training and welfare-to-work programs; how much future benefits and costs should be discounted; how to extrapolate experimental impacts beyond the period over which data were collected. These are all areas of significant controversy. The value to nonparticipants of changes in the behavior of program participants may be especially difficult to quantify. There is little evidence, for example, on the dollar value that nonparticipants place on seeing welfare recipients go to work; or on low-income persons enjoying increased consumption of health care, food, or housing; or on reductions in criminal offenses.

HOW MIGHT SOCIAL EXPERIMENTS BE UTILIZED?

Frequently, it is anticipated that results from a given social experiment will lead to a yes or no decision on the policy being tested. However, the relationship between experimental findings and policy decisions often does not appear to be so direct. Findings from social experiments are used in many ways, some of them unanticipated.

For example, it is unlikely that findings from the income-maintenance experiments had any major role in the failure to adopt the policy tested, the negative income tax (Greenberg and Mandell 1995).[20] However, the experiments did demonstrate that certain innovations used in administering the transfer programs (monthly reporting and retrospective accounting) could be successfully implemented. Partly as a result, these innovations were adopted nationally in existing welfare programs.

Findings from the income maintenance experiments also altered the commonly held pre-experimental view that extending cash assistance to intact families would enhance their marital stability. The experiments suggested that this did not occur. In addition, the income maintenance experiments provided useful information about the effects of transfer programs on hours of work by different types of adults. These findings were in turn used to guide decisions about other transfer programs—for example, Food Stamps and Aid to Families with Dependent Children.

There are at least three different dimensions on which utilization of findings from an experiment (or any other types of evaluation) might be mapped (Greenberg and Mandell 1995). First, findings may either influence specific policy decisions or may address unresolved scientific or intellectual issues. In our previous example, the finding that monthly reporting and retrospective accounting were operationally feasible affected the everyday administration of welfare programs, a policy effect. Both the unexpected findings on marital stability and the expected findings on the relative inelasticity of male labor supply had broader intellectual impacts.

Second, findings that are used may be more or less central to social policy. On the one hand, research findings may influence core policy decisions or general intellectual orientations; at the other end of the continuum are elaborative or peripheral uses—cases in which research findings influence relatively narrow elements of policy and its implementation. The income maintenance experiments demonstrated that male heads of household did not cut back much on hours of work when an income guarantee was available; this finding was a major intellectual contribution. The same experiments showed that retrospective accounting was feasible; this finding was elaborative or peripheral (which is not the same as unimportant).

A final dimension of utilization distinguishes between predecision and postdecision utilization (see Majone 1989: chap. 2). An old joke informs us that some people use statistics the way a drunk uses a lamppost—not for illumination but for support. If the positions of policymakers are established, at least in part, on the basis of research findings, we can say the research was used for illumination (utilization is predecision). Postdecision utilization refers to the use of research findings to advocate already-established positions. Findings on retrospective accounting seem to have changed the minds of key administrators; findings on male labor supply seem to have changed nobody's mind, but were used to support previously determined positions (see Greenberg and Mandell 1995, for further discussion).

WHAT IS THE HISTORY OF SOCIAL EXPERIMENTS?

The idea of a control group was firmly established by 19th century pioneers of medical and biological research. For example, in one classic experiment, Louis Pasteur divided a flock of sheep into two groups. In one group he injected attenuated material from other animals that had died of anthrax, so that they could develop an immunity; the second group did not receive this injection. Both groups were then injected with anthrax-infected matter. None of the treatment sheep became sick, but all of the control sheep died.

If Pasteur's results had been less dramatic, critics would certainly have claimed that for some reason the control group was more anthrax-vulnerable than the treatment group. Over time, the charge that controls were "inadequate" became commonplace, without any rigorous idea of adequacy being developed, since no treatment group was ever *identical* to the control group.

The concept of randomization, like many other fundamental statistical tools, was conceived by Ronald Fisher.[21] The concept appeared initially in a 1925 book by Fisher, *Statistical Methods for Research Workers*, and then was fully elaborated in his 1935 book, *The Design of Experiments*. Fisher pointed out that no two groups could ever be identical because every organism, test tube, soil sample, and so forth would vary slightly from every other. Therefore, the researcher's task was to design the difference between groups in such a manner that the mechanism for allocating cases to one group or another could not be related to the issue being studied. Allocation by pure chance (a coin flip, a table of random numbers) did exactly that.

Social experimentation, however, did not come about until much later. It is usually traced to the New Jersey Income Maintenance Experiment, which was initiated in 1968.[22] The idea of conducting an income maintenance experiment is attributed to Heather Ross, who in 1966 was a Massachusetts Institute of Technology graduate student in economics.[23] In that year, Ross was beginning work on her dissertation as a fellow at the Brookings Institution in Washington, D.C. Ross was frustrated that inferences about the responses of low-income persons to transfer payments could not be readily drawn from existing data. She was also concerned by the use of unsubstantiated anecdotes about welfare recipients by politicians. She wished to collect data that could be used to determine what poor people would actually do if they were provided money. Would they work less? Would they quit work altogether? How would they spend the additional money? To answer such questions, she proposed to conduct a random assignment experiment.

To fund this project, Ross wrote a proposal in 1967 to the U.S. Office of Economic Opportunity, which had a staff of social scientists. Ultimately, as Ross puts it, she ended up with a "$5 million thesis," which at the time was an extraordinary sum of money for a single social science research project.

Her proposal germinated in the New Jersey Experiment. Its importance as a landmark in social science research is hard to overstate.[24] Although the technique of randomly assigning individuals for purposes of clinical health trials and educational innovations had been utilized for years, the New Jersey Experiment was the first prominent study to use this technique to test social programs. Other social experiments, including additional income maintenance experiments, followed fairly quickly.

Like the income maintenance experiments, most social experiments have tested treatments targeted at disadvantaged groups. For example, a substantial fraction of social experiments have tested policies pertaining to the welfare population, especially recipients of AFDC. Other important target groups include the unemployed, disadvantaged youth, persons with mental impairment, persons charged with or convicted or crimes, and substance abusers.

From the time the New Jersey Experiment was launched until the mid-1970s, most social experiments were designed to test the feasibility of major reform measures. Thus, in addition to the income maintenance experiments, early social experiments measured the effects of a national housing allowance for the low-income population, major changes in the provision of health insurance, and an innovative training program for disadvantaged workers. These treatments were usually administered through field offices set up by government contractors for that purpose. As the summaries of the early experiments indicate, they tended to be large-scale and expensive to conduct.

Experiments launched between the mid-1970s and the early 1980s differed markedly from the earlier ones, in that they were smaller in scale and much less costly. Moreover, they tested policy changes that were more incremental in scope. That is, rather than test major new policy initiatives, as did the earliest social experiments, they were more likely to test small new programs that would be confined to narrow subsets of the population or to test modifications to existing programs. In keeping with this, these experiments were usually administered through existing state and local government agencies. Moreover, they were all "black box" in nature. Virtually all the response-surface experiments that have been conducted began before 1976.

New social experiments have become increasingly common since 1980. Some of the newer ones are considerably larger in scale and more expensive than those initiated between the mid-1970s and the early 1980s, but unlike the pre-1975 social experiments, they seldom test new social programs. Instead, they typically test the feasibility of achieving improvements in existing programs.

The recent experiments also rarely approach the earliest social experiments in terms of costs. Costs are controlled by using administrative records rather than surveys, and by using existing agencies rather than establishing special organizations solely for the demonstration. The more recent experiments often make extensive use of data obtained through computerized management information systems (e.g., payment files maintained by welfare agencies; wage data collected in administering unemployment compensation). With only a few exceptions, more recent experiments continue to be administered through existing state and local government agencies.[25]

WHAT IS THE FUTURE FOR SOCIAL EXPERIMENTS?

As demonstrated in Appendix II at the end of this Digest, numerous experiments are still in progress, and therefore cannot be fully summarized. We expect many more to be initiated in the future. Intractable social problems, unfortunately, show no sign of vanishing; substantial uncertainty clouds debate over proposed solutions; and the selection problem remains. The movement to return money and power to the states and to the private sector, if it persists, may reduce federal funding for experiments; but states and foundations have sponsored social experiments before, and the pressure to test new policies probably will not ease[26]—the resources, authority, and desire will invariably surface to determine whether a policy proposal will really make a difference.

However, certain types of social experiments will probably not be conducted in our lifetime, even when technically feasible. One such area is community development, where the appropriate unit of analysis is neither the individual nor the household, but the neighborhood or city.

An example illustrates. Suppose it is hypothesized that a $5 million investment of a particular type will generate more than $5 million in benefits in an average community of 10,000 people. However, the benefits are expected to be sufficiently modest—say $5.3 million—that 250 treatment communities and 250 control communities would be required in order to have an 80 percent probability of detecting the benefits with 95 percent confidence. Therefore, testing the hypothesis requires distributing a total of $1.25 billion to 250 randomly selected communities throughout the country. Such a test would allow one community to enjoy a benefit denied another, not because of some formula in law, and not because of the personal and political influence of their representatives in Congress, but because of the impersonal operation of a lottery. The aggregate appropriation and the number of communities not funded would make the program difficult to ignore or to gloss over. It seems highly unlikely that any Congress would countenance this experiment or anything like it.

Other policy controversies do not seem to be technically amenable to the experimental evaluation. A topical example might be the sensitivity of taxpayer savings and investment behavior to the tax rate on capital gains. Suppose one group of taxpayers were randomly assigned to a capital gains tax rate lower than the rate for other taxpayers, in order to evaluate the effects of rate reduction on the national economy. Members of the treatment group could obtain arbitrage profits by getting other taxpayers to sell property to them at below-market prices, permitting the sellers to avoid (evade) much of the capital gains tax that would otherwise be levied on them. (The arbitrage profit would be split with the sellers through a side payment.) Obviously, this would bias the estimated impact of the experiment.

The general point is that the feasibility of the experiment may depend on the ingenuity and deviousness of the target population. On the other hand, the people who design and implement the experiment may also have ingenuity, expertise, resources, and perhaps a little deviousness of their own. In the previous example, the detection of tax arbitrage activity is a constant pursuit of the tax authorities; we merely doubt that they would be willing to devote the substantial resources that an adequate capital gains tax experiment would require.

The first edition (1991) of this Digest listed no social experiments outside the United States. As stated earlier, aside from one Canadian and one Dutch experiment cited in the current volume, the social experiment apparently remains an exclusively U.S. phenomenon. We are unaware of any similar demonstrations in the Pacific countries or of experimental evaluations of aid programs in developing nations.

Although there is nothing specifically American about the experimental methodology, the separation of powers under the U.S. Constitution may be especially conducive to policy conflict and, therefore, to policy testing. When a Senate committee insists on one policy and its House of Representatives counterpart insists on another, they may temporarily maintain the status quo and authorize an experiment to compare the effects of the two proposals; similarly, an experiment can result from a conflict between Congress on the one hand and the executive branch on the other. Many social experiments in the welfare area have resulted from the desire of individual states to innovate in ways that deviate from federal policy (federal officials have insisted that the innovation be tested through random assignment). Nations with more centralized governments and parliamentary systems, in which policy conflicts are resolved within the cabinet or, more generally, the ruling coalition, may lack some of the political tensions that produce social experiments.

Alternatively, there may be more ideological polarization within the American polity than in other developed countries. This could foster controlled experimentation in two ways. First, policymakers in the United States may be under greater pressure than their foreign counterparts to demonstrate that their ideas are rational. Second, polarization stresses the political system, giving rise to a greater variety of consensus-building strategies: among the latter is a demand for objective technical information.

USES AND ORGANIZATION OF THIS BOOK

This volume is intended to serve as an archive, a reference, an "armory," and a textbook supplement:

- *Archive.* Social experiments deliver credible evidence on the responsiveness of human behavior to policy, but the findings from most social experiments have been only narrowly disseminated. We want to increase awareness of and access to this material, much of which may eventually become inaccessible in its current form.
- *Reference.* We hope to provide a one-stop guide to all experimental findings on particular interventions, which can be used as a first step in developing literature reviews, options papers, and the like.

- *"Armory."* The idea and practice of social policy experiments remain controversial. We expect that this book will suppply all sides of the debate with weapons and ammunition.
- *Textbook supplement.* We hope that these experiments can give students in a variety of courses—in public policy and administration, economics, social work, education, vocational rehabilitation, sociology, statistics, political science, metropolitan planning, and other fields—an appreciation for the interaction of theory, policy, statistics, and daily life.

To develop the list of social experiments summarized in this volume, we began with the 37 compiled by Greenberg and Robins (1986). We learned of a few additional older social experiments from a lengthy bibliography by Boruch, McSweeny, and Soderstron (1978). About a dozen experiments in the early childhood intervention literature came from a literature review by Benasich, Brooks-Gunn, and Clewell (1992). Names of additional experiments were obtained in response to written as well as telephone and E-mail requests both to academics and employees of prominent social science research firms. Still other experiments were acquired from various reports disseminated by research firms and the government and from journal articles. Finally, we used "snowballing" techniques: when interviewing persons associated with experiments with which we were familiar, we asked if they knew of any others. We may have overlooked some smaller social experiments, but we do not believe we have missed any large ones.

The information contained in the experiment summaries came from two major sources. First, we reviewed at least one research report on each experiment. Second, information not available from the research reports was obtained from telephone interviews with staff members of the organizations that conducted the evaluations and the government agencies that sponsored them. Often one interview was sufficient, but sometimes several telephone calls were necessary.

Most items appearing the summaries for each social experiment are self-explanatory, but a few require a brief comment.

Cost. Of all the information about social experiments that we attempted to collect, cost data were the most difficult, for a number of reasons. Sometimes the information once existed, but the necessary records could no longer be located. When an experiment was administered by an existing government agency, it was often difficult to separate the incremental cost of administering the experimental treatment from other costs incurred by the agency. Sometimes the total cost was available, but administrative costs could not be separated from the evaluation cost. In other cases, the experiment was part of a larger research project, and costs were not separately allocated to the experimental and nonexperimental parts of the research.

Number of Treatment Groups. The number of treatment groups always includes groups used for control purposes.

Major Findings. Information on findings reported in the summaries was typically obtained from the final reports we reviewed. For a few experiments, alternative sets of findings have been produced by a methodological approach different from that used in the final report. We usually ignored such findings. There are also some experiments for which a large volume of results exists. To keep the summaries brief and the reported numbers manageable, we have concentrated on those findings that pertain as directly as possible to the major experimental outcomes of interest.

Design Issues. Numerous issues arise in selecting treatment and control groups, administering experimental treatments, collecting data on outcomes, and so forth. Decisions concerning these issues can have a major influence on findings from social experiments, sometimes rendering the findings invalid. For each experiment, we attempt to alert readers to the most important design issues.

Treatment Administrator. The treatment administrator is the organization responsible for rendering the treatment. As stated earlier, treatments tested in early social experiments were often administered by separate offices set up by the evaluator expressly for that purpose; since 1975, the treatments tested in most social experiments have been administered through existing agencies.

Enabling Legislation. Federal and state legislation have often mandated that social programs, especially those tried on a pilot basis, be evaluated. Some of the experiments that we reviewed began as a result of legislative mandates for evaluation.

Information Sources. Each summary indicates at least one source for more detailed, written information (usually a final report) on the experiment described. In some cases, the report has been published in a journal or book, but more typically it can only be obtained from the research firm that conducted the evaluation or the government agency that sponsored it.

Finally, in a number of instances the findings of an experiment appear to have directly influenced the direction of policy, and we say so. As with all other elements of the summary, we admit the possibility of errors of omission and commission in these conclusions.

We have sorted the experiments by their target populations: welfare recipients, unemployed, and so on. Within each target population, experiments appear in approximately chronological order.

There are two indexes. The first lists persons and organizations who either were associated with particular experiments or acted or commented on these experiments. The second index references uses of specific interventions across populations.

Notes

1. Such a work is being prepared by Larry Orr and is tentatively entitled *Evaluating Public Programs with Experimental Methods*. In a series of essays, Hausman and Wise (1985) also discuss specific social experiments and issues that have arisen in conducting them.

2. Moreover, people may move from site A to site B, and vice versa, during the demonstration; and these moves may or may not be related to differences in the treatment. If people move because of differences in the treatment, then the validity of the evaluation will probably be compromised.

3. Observed differences across sites typically cause less serious problems than unobserved differences because they often can be controlled for statistically.

4. In the specific case of the income maintenance experiments, the fact of an ongoing income maintenance experiment was not used to delay action. On the contrary, premature, and eventually contradicted, data from the experiment were used in an attempt to push forward an income maintenance proposal by the Nixon administration that was similar to the one tested.

5. In poverty programs, some would argue that the social welfare evaluation is more complex: perhaps current benefits do long-range harm to recipients, whereas the reduction of poverty may raise the well-being of nonpoor taxpayers. These are valid concerns, but are tangential to this issue.

6. As previously discussed, quasi experiments involve using random processes to assign sites to treatment or control status. However, quasi experiments are relatively rare. One reason for this is that program administrators at local sites are generally very reluctant to relinquish their prerogative to decide whether or not to adopt particular innovations.

7. In practice, even observable differences may interact nonlinearly with treatment, and the analyst may fail to adjust for them correctly.

8. Burtless (1995) assessed most of the problems associated with conducting social experiments and vigorously defended the usefulness of the technique.

9. There is no inherent reason why social experiments must always be small-scale. For example, in some experiments, all members of the target population within a particular geographic area, but a small group of randomly selected controls, are eligible to receive program services.

10. Whereas the lack of feedback and information diffusion can threaten external validity, the presence of such effects can threaten internal validity. A notable example of this recently occurred in New Jersey, where the state instituted a "family cap" on welfare benefits—a rule that if a child was conceived while the family head was receiving Aid to Families with Dependent Children (AFDC), there would be no increase in welfare benefits when the child was born. To determine the effects of the innovation, the state randomly selected a relatively small control sample of the welfare population for whom the family cap did not apply. However, the policy change had already been widely publicized, and the state could not control the information that the control group received from sources other than program administrators. Subsequent studies have shown that the members of the control group believed that the family cap applied to themselves, and the results of the experiment, when completed, are likely to prove anomalous. (A summary of the New Jersey study is not included in this volume because it was not completed by mid-1996.)

11. Note that the main problem is whether small-scale demonstration results generalize to large populations. Randomization per se is a relatively unimportant element here. If the pilot program has limited slots, the target population necessarily self-selected in applying and not applying whether the allocation mechanism is random or nonrandom.

12. Note that this refers to selecting sites randomly from the population of potential sites, not to a saturation design in which sites are assigned randomly to program and control status. Choosing sites randomly has been attempted only recently.

13. The standard argument is that only sites operating superior programs will acquiesce to an evaluation. However, there may be only minimal correlation between local operators' self-appraisals and the results of a rigorous third-party evaluation. Indeed, even when sites are self-selected, estimated impacts are typically modest, suggesting that any site selection bias is not large enough to lead to an unwarranted expansion of a program in response to inflated impact estimates. Nevertheless, biases of unknown magnitude may arise from management difference among self-selected sites.

14. In nonexperimental evaluations, it is sometimes possible to estimate entry affects by using a site saturation design (Johnson, Klepinger, and Dong 1994; Marcotte 1992; Schiller and Brasher 1993; Wolf 1990).

15. We report some information about costs in the summaries of the individual experiments.

16. Costs associated with administering innovative treatments are typically counted as part of total experimental costs when the experimental treatment is administered through special offices set up expressly for the purpose, but are rarely counted if the experiment is administered through an existing government agency.

17. Orthodox benefit–cost theory holds that projects should be funded whenever benefits exceed costs, but it is widely recognized that real-world constraints (limited "control areas") may require the valuation of both benefits and costs at other than market prices (Sen 1972). In these circumstances, "benefits" and "costs" might be policy choices, rather than facts. The opportunity cost approach asks which of two competing projects should be funded if both have benefits greater than costs and there is not enough money for both.

18. The cost of the experiment will typically be a fraction of the rounding error in the appropriation for any major program of the agency, but this does not justify suboptimal use of the agency's research budget.

19. The more one knows about bureaucracy, the less surprising this news would be.

20. The most potentially damaging findings came from the Seattle-Denver Income Maintenance Experiment, which seemed to indicate that a negative income tax program

would cause family splitting. When these findings first became available, the Carter administration was attempting to promote a negative-income-tax-like program in Congress. The only members of Congress known to have reacted strongly to the findings was Senator Daniel Patrick Moynihan of New York, who said: "We were wrong about a guaranteed income! Seemingly it is calamitous" (quoted in Demkovich 1978). Although Moynihan was an influential authority on welfare, for many other reasons the administration's legislation never got out of committee in the U.S. House of Representatives and thus never reached the Senate. It is not clear that even Moynihan's opposition was primarily motivated by marital stability findings; the driving force may have been fiscal relief for New York state. See Greenberg and Mandell (1995) for greater detail.

21. Randomization also seems to have been conceived independently of Fisher, and slightly earlier, by W. A. McCall (1923).

22. The *Digest* provides summaries of six social experiments that preceded the New Jersey Income Maintenance Experiment. The earliest of these, the Perry Preschool Project, was initiated in 1962. These very early experiments were all very small relative to the New Jersey Experiment and their design did not require the same level of technical innovation. With the possible exception of the Perry Preschool Project, they never captured the attention of social scientists and policymakers. The Perry Project did receive considerable attention, but not until adult earnings data were available for the preschool children in the study sample. This did not occur until many years after both the Perry Project and the New Jersey Experiment were initiated. Thus, the New Jersey Experiment is almost universally considered the first social experiment.

23. The information in this paragraph is based on a telephone interview with Heather Ross and has been confirmed by several other persons who were involved in social experimentation in its early stages.

24. For classic early statements of the rationale, see Orcutt and Orcutt (1968) and Rivlin (1971: 86–119).

25. One reader of an earlier version of this introduction asked if the earlier experiments were not more tightly focused than the later ones. Recent U.S. welfare experiments have tended to include a cluster of innovations that are at best very loosely related to each other, because of developments peculiar to the AFDC waiver process (Wiseman 1993, 1995). For non-AFDC experiments, however, we do not sense any general loss of coherence over time.

26. Two experiments in this book—those of Southern California Edison Company and Niagara Mohawk Power Corporation—were funded by power companies for their own purposes. We have not discovered other examples of social experiments funded by for-profit companies, nor have we turned up any instances of social experimentation by the military.

References

Bell, Stephen, Larry L. Orr, John D. Blomquist, and Glen G. Cain. 1995. *Program Applicants as a Comparison Group in Evaluating Training Programs*. Kalamazoo, Mich.: W. E. Upjohn Institute for Employment Research.

Benasich, April Ann, Jeanne Brooks-Gunn, and Beatriz Chu Clewell. 1992. "How Do Mothers Benefit from Early Intervention Programs?" *Journal of Applied Developmental Psychology* 13: 311–62.

Boruch, Robert F., A. John McSweeny, and E. Jon Soderstron. 1978. "Randomized Field Experiments for Program Planning, Development, and Evaluation: An Illustrative Bibliography." *Evaluation Quarterly* 2 (November): 655–95.

Burtless, Gary. 1995. "The Case for Randomized Field Trials in Economic and Policy Research." *Journal of Economic Perspectives* 9 (2, Spring): 63–84.

Card, David, and Philip K. Robins. 1996. *Do Financial Incentives Encourage Welfare Recipients to Work?: Initial 18-Month Findings from the Self-Sufficiency Project.* Vancouver, British Columbia: Social Research and Demonstration Corporatin, February.

Dehejia, Rajeev H., and Sadek Wahba. 1995. "Causal Effects in Nonexperimental Studies: Re-Evaluating the Evaluation of Training Programs." Howard University. Photocopy, November.

Demkovich, Linda E. 1978. "Good News and Bad News for Welfare Reform." *National Journal*, December 30: 2061.

Feldman, Martha. 1989. *Order without Design: Information Production and Policy Making.* Stanford, Calif.: Stanford University Press.

Fisher, Ronald. 1925. *Statistical Methods for Research Workers.* London: Oliver and Boyd.

———. 1935. *The Design of Experiments.* London: Oliver and Boyd.

Fraker, Thomas, and Rebecca Maynard. 1987. "Evaluating Comparison Group Designs with Employment-Related Programs." *Journal of Human Resources* 22(2, Spring): 194–227.

Friedlander, Daniel, and Philip K. Robins. 1996. "Evaluating Program Evaluations: New Evidence on Commonly Used Nonexperimental Methods." *American Economic Review* 85 (4, September): 923–37.

Garfinkel, Irwin, Charles F. Manski, and Charles Michalopoulos. 1992. "Micro Experiments and Macro Effects." In *Evaluating Welfare and Training Programs,* edited by Charles F. Manski and Irwin Garfinkel (253–73). Cambridge, Mass.: Harvard University Press.

Greenberg, David H., and Marvin Mandell. 1991. "Research Utilization in Policy Making: A Tale of Two Series (of Social Experiments)." *Journal of Policy Analysis and Management* 10 (4, Fall): 633–56.

———. 1995. "The Income Maintenance Experiments." Baltimore, Md.: University of Maryland Baltimore County. Photocopy, October.

Greenberg, David H., and Philip K. Robins. 1986. "The Changing Role of Social Experiments in Policy Analysis." *Journal of Policy Analysis and Management* 5 (Winter): 340–62.

Hausman, Jerry, and David Wise, eds. 1985. *Social Experimentation.* Chicago: University of Chicago Press for National Bureau of Economic Research.

Heckman, James J. 1992. "Randomization and Social Policy Evaluation." 1992. In *Evaluating Welfare and Training Programs*, edited by Charles F. Manski and Irwin Garfinkel (201–30). Cambridge, Mass.: Harvard University Press.

Heckman, James J., and V. Joseph Hotz. 1989. "Choosing among Alternative Nonexperimental Methods for Estimating the Impact of Social Programs." *Journal of the American Statistical Association* 84(408, December): 862–74.

Heckman, James J., and Jeffrey A. Smith. 1995. "Assessing the Case for Social Experiments." *Journal of Economic Perspectives* 9 (2, Spring): 85–110.

Heckman, James J., Hidehiko Ichimura, Jeffrey Smith, and Petra Todd. 1995. "Nonparametric Characterization of Selection Bias Using Experimental Data: A Study of Adult Males in JTPA." University of Chicago. Photocopy.

Hollister, Robinson G., and Jennifer Hill. 1995. "Problems in the Evaluation of Community-Wide Initiatives." In *New Approaches to Evaluating Community Initiatives: Concepts, Methods, and Contexts*, edited by James P. Connell, Anne C. Kubisch, Lisbeth B. Schorr, and Carol H. Weiss (127–72). Washington, D.C.: Aspen Institute.

Hotz, V. Joseph. 1992. "Designing an Evaluation of the Job Training Partnership Act." In *Evaluating Welfare and Training Programs*, edited by Charles F. Manski and Irwin Garfinkel (76–114). Cambridge, Mass.: Harvard University Press.

Johnson, Terry R., Daniel H. Klepinger, and Fred B. Dong. 1994. "Caseload Impacts of Welfare Reform." *Contemporary Economics Policy* 12 (January): 89–101.

LaLonde, Robert J. 1986. "Evaluating the Econometric Evaluations of Employment and Training Programs with Experimental Data." *American Economic Review* 76 (4, September): 604–20.

LaLonde, Robert J., and Rebecca Maynard. 1987. "How Precise Are Evaluations of Employment and Training Programs? Evidence from a Field Experiment." *Evaluation Review* 11 (4, August): 428–51.

Levitan, Sar A. 1992. *Evaluation of Federal Social Programs: An Uncertain Impact.* Washington, D.C.: George Washington University, Center for Social Policy Studies, June.

Lowry, Ira S., ed. 1983. *Experimenting with Housing Allowances: Final Report of the Housing Allowance Supply Experiment.* Cambridge, Mass.: Oelgenschlager, Gunn, and Hain.

Majone, Giandomenico. 1989. *Evidence, Argument, and Persuasion in the Policy Process.* New Haven, Conn.: Yale University Press.

Manski, Charles F. 1995. "Learning about Social Programs from Experiments with Random Assignment of Treatments." Institute for Research on Poverty Discussion Paper 1061-95. Madison: University of Wisconsin, Madison, March.

Manski, Charles F., and Irwin Garfinkel. 1992. "Introduction." In *Evaluating Welfare and Training Programs*, edited by Charles F. Manski and Irwin Garfinkel (1–22). Cambridge, Mass.: Harvard University Press.

Marcotte, John. 1990. "Effect of Washington State FIP on the Caseload Size." Washington, D.C.: Urban Institute. Photocopy.

McCall, W.A. 1923. *How to Experiment in Education*. New York: MacMillan.

Moffitt, Robert A. 1996. "The Effect of Employment and Training Programs on Entry and Exit from the Welfare Caseload." *Journal of Policy Analysis and Management* 15 (1, Winter): 32–50.

Orcutt, Guy H., and Alice G. Orcutt. 1968. "Incentive and Disincentive Experimentation for Income Maintenance Policy Purposes." *American Economic Review* 58 (September): 754–73.

Rivlin, Alice M. 1971. *Systematic Thinking for Social Action*. Washington, D.C.: Brookings Institution.

Schiller, B.R., and C. Nielsen Brasher. 1993. "Effects of Workfare Saturation of AFDC Caseloads." *Contemporary Policy Issues* 11 (April): 39–49.

Sen, Amartya. 1972. "Control Areas and Accounting Prices: An Approach to Economic Evaluation." *Economic Journal* 82 (March, Suppl.): 486–501.

Whiteman, David. 1985. "Reaffirming the Importance of Strategic Use: A Two Dimensional Perspective on Policy Analysis in Congress." *Knowledge* 6 (March): 203–4.

Wiseman, Michael. 1993. "Welfare Reform in the States: The Bush Legacy." *Focus* 15(1, Spring): 18–36.

———. 1995. "Fixing Welfare Waiver Policy." *Public Welfare* 53(1, Winter): 10–16.

Wolf, Douglas A. 1990. "Caseload Growth in the Evaluation Sites: Is There a FIP Effect?" Washington, D.C.: Urban Institute. Photocopy.

Part Two

PUBLIC ASSISTANCE RECIPIENTS—AFDC

WIN LABS EXPERIMENTS

INTRODUCTION

The U.S. Department of Labor (DOL) financed a group of demonstrations at WIN (Work Incentive) program offices at different sites. Some of these demonstrations were experiments. The Manpower Demonstration Research Corporation (MDRC), New York, coordinated these projects, known as the "WIN Labs." The "WIN Labs" collectively, including the nonexperimental projects, cost $2.5 million (1979); costs of separate experiments are not available. The key DOL personnel were Howard Rosen, Merwin Hans, and Gordon Berlin.

LOUISVILLE IMMEDIATE JOB SEARCH ASSISTANCE EXPERIMENT

SUMMARY: This demonstration, conducted from 1978 to 1980, tested the efforts of immediate employment-assistance services and a counselor-directed job search program on a large sample of new female WIN registrants. Subjects were followed for one year.

COST: See introduction to "WIN Labs Experiments."

TIME FRAME: Demonstration period, November 1978–January 1980; data collected, November 1978–Summer 1980; final report, June 1981.

TREATMENTS TESTED:

1. Controls received "the regular services offered to WIN clients under normal procedures." Service delivery delays of 2 to 10 weeks under these procedures were common while approvals for welfare and other social services were pending.

2. Experimentals received services immediately on registering with WIN. The effect of this was to make them immediately eligible for reimbursement of child care, transportation, and lunch expenses and to provide an incentive payment for going to counseling sessions and job interviews.

The most important counseling technique was a counselor-directed, individual job search for four hours a day; participation in this was voluntary (it did not affect the AFDC grant). Those who found employment continued to be eligible for child-care services for up to 90 days, even if they still had not been found eligible for welfare.

At the initiation of the experiment, staff were randomly assigned between controls and experimentals. Subsequent personnel changes could not be kept random, but were not deliberately biased.

OUTCOMES OF INTEREST: (1) Employment; (2) Earnings; and (3) AFDC payments.

SAMPLE SIZE: Experimentals, 811; controls, 808.

TARGET POPULATION: New female WIN registrants (AFDC recipients and applicants). Clients already committed to a job, school, or training could refuse to participate.

NUMBER OF TREATMENT GROUPS: Two (with one control group).

NUMBER AND LOCATION OF SITES: One—Louisville, Kentucky.

RESEARCH COMPONENTS:
    Process analysis: Analysis of factors influencing willingness to participate in counseling programs.
    Impact analysis: Comparison of means, linear regression, and logit.
    Benefit–cost analysis: Data needed for such an analysis are reported.

MAJOR FINDINGS:
    (Data are regression adjusted.)
    1. Percentage Employed:

Quarter of Follow-up	Experimentals (%)	Controls (%)
First (includes month registered)	35.9	30.0
Second	39.1	33.6
Third	37.4	32.9
Fourth	34.7	28.8
Fifth	35.9	30.6

Note: All differences are statistically significant.

2. Average Earnings:

Quarter of Follow-up	Experimentals ($)	Controls ($)
First	218.93	163.59
Second	327.63	261.10
Third	381.20	346.23
Fourth	388.72	340.39
Fifth	408.14	338.48
Total	1,724.62	1,449.88

Note: Differences are statistically significant in the first, second, fifth, and last rows.

3. Average AFDC Payments:

Quarter of Follow-up	Experimentals ($)	Controls ($)
First	443.02	448.73
Second	452.84	469.65
Third	402.07	418.41
Fourth	372.92	385.13
Fifth	351.05	376.37
Sixth	337.47	356.75
Total	2,359.37	2,455.03

Note: Differences are statistically significant in the second, fifth, and last rows.

4. Sample is too small to reliably test the relative success of the experimental treatment on subgroups of the target population.

5. Estimated incremental administrative costs were about $77–$115 per experimental. The experimental treatment may be marginally cost-effective in terms of AFDC payment reductions. Earnings impacts are two to three times the administrative cost, so the experiment would pass a social benefit–cost test.

TIME TRENDS IN FINDINGS: Displayed above.

DESIGN ISSUES:

1. Although participation in job search counseling was voluntary, the WIN staff involved in the experiment were under considerable pressure to get experimentals to enroll in it, and this may have affected the way they communicated the fact of its being voluntary: "any inferences about likely participation rates should recognize that participation is likely to be influenced by the type and intensity of encouragement received by the potential participants" (Goldman 1981). About half of the experimentals were either considered unemployable at intake and therefore were not offered the intensive counseling service or did not participate when offered it.

2. Site self-selection bias possible. Most state WIN programs were not anxious to participate in the experiments.

REPLICABILITY: Treatments are documented.

GENERALIZABILITY: Generalization might be affected by the relative generosity of welfare benefits in other states and the relative employ-ability of those states' WIN populations.

FUNDING SOURCE: See introduction to "WIN Labs Experiments."

TREATMENT ADMINISTRATOR: Kentucky Department of Human Resources. Key personnel: Geralynne Clements.

EVALUATOR: Manpower Demonstration Research Corporation. Key personnel: Barbara S. Goldman.

ENABLING LEGISLATION: None.

INFORMATION SOURCES: Barbara S. Goldman, "Impacts of the Immediate Job Search Assistance Experiment," Manpower Demonstration Research Corporation, June 1981.

PUBLIC-USE ACCESS TO DATA: Public-use access does not exist.

WIN SERVICES TO VOLUNTEERS

SUMMARY: These two demonstrations, conducted from 1978 to 1979, tested the efforts of a special recruitment effort and enriched employment-assistance services in a large sample of female recipients of Aid to Families with Dependent Children (AFDC) whose children were five years of age or younger. Subjects were followed for one year.

COST: See introduction to "WIN Labs Experiments."

TIME FRAME: Demonstration period, October 1978–March 1979; data collected, October 1978–December 1980; final report, June 1981.

TREATMENTS TESTED: There were two experiments, A and B, as follows.

A. Effect of Recruitment

A random sample of AFDC recipients with children aged five or younger and not already voluntarily enrolled (volunteers) in WIN.

1. Controls were not subject to a special recruitment effort.
2. Experimentals received letters inviting them to recruitment meetings in their neighborhoods, at which WIN services were

described. They were paid $5 if they attended. To register for the services, they still had to go to the WIN office.

B. Effect of Special Services

A random sample of walk-in volunteers who were not in either group A1 or A2 was randomly assigned to:

1. Regular WIN services.
2. Special enriched services. Features: (1) Orientations were not focused on AFDC sanctions for nonparticipation; (2) information sessions included day-care choices; (3) training was available at a larger number of educational institutions; (4) on-the-job training wages were 75 percent (rather than 50 percent) subsidized; and (5) the social services and employment services staff were better integrated to improve service delivery.

OUTCOMES OF INTEREST: (1) Number of volunteers; (2) Employment; (3) Earnings; and (4) AFDC payments.

SAMPLE SIZE: A1, 1,003; A2, 1,003; B1, 114; and B2, 110.

TARGET POPULATION: Female AFDC recipients with children five years old or younger.

NUMBER OF TREATMENT GROUPS: Four (with two control groups).

NUMBER AND LOCATION OF SITES: One—Denver, Colorado.

RESEARCH COMPONENTS:

Process analysis: Interviews with volunteers and nonvolunteers were conducted.

Impact analysis: Conducted as a difference in means.

Benefit–cost analysis: Cost-effectiveness analysis (budgetary point of view).

MAJOR FINDINGS:

Experiment A	Experimentals	Controls
Volunteer WIN registrants	160	20
Incremental cost per recruit	$27.27	—

Note: Employment, earnings, and AFDC payment differences are all statistically insignificant.

In experiment B, the finding is a statistically significant, upward impact on AFDC payments to experimentals. As the pre-enrollment experimentals' earnings in this fairly small sample were significantly higher than those of the controls, the most likely reason is that a much higher percentage of experimentals were provided with institutional training than was the case with controls. The training reduced experimental earnings in subsequent quarters by reducing the time available for work. After registration, there are no significant differences in earnings.

TIME TRENDS IN FINDINGS: In B, significant reductions in AFDC payments to experimentals occurred in the third, fourth, and fifth quarters after registration.

DESIGN ISSUES: The sample in B was too small and many of the enhancements in services were too subtle to expect statistically significant differences to emerge.

REPLICABILITY: Experiment A is replicable; experiment B is a rather diffuse experiment, and aspects of it might not be replicable.

GENERALIZABILITY: The most frequent reason for registering with WIN was to get help in finding a job. The Denver labor market at this time had very low unemployment, and, therefore, subjects may have felt little need for WIN services.

FUNDING SOURCE: See introduction to "WIN Labs Experiments."

TREATMENT ADMINISTRATOR: Colorado Department of Social Services. Key personnel: Unknown.

EVALUATOR: Center for Social Research and Development, University of Denver. Key personnel: Ellen L. Slaughter and Edward C. Baumheier.

ENABLING LEGISLATION: None.

INFORMATION SOURCES: Ellen L. Slaughter, Paulette Turshak, Gale G. Whiteneck, and Edward C. Baumheier, "Final Report on WIN Services to Volunteers: Denver WIN Research Laboratory Project," Manpower Demonstration Research Corporation, June 1981.

PUBLIC-USE ACCESS TO DATA: Public-use access does not exist.

MADISON AND RACINE QUALITY EMPLOYMENT EXPERIMENT

SUMMARY (FROM INFORMATION SOURCE):   This experiment sought to place women from the Madison and Racine, Wisconsin, WIN programs into better-paying, nontraditional jobs. The centerpiece of the strategy was an employer subsidy, with up to a 100-percent reimbursement for on-the-job training through the first third of a contract (maximum length 50 weeks), declining first to 75 percent and then to 50 percent over the remaining term, provided the wage offered was over $4 an hour. The program also offered a peer support group for women adjusting to on-the-job problems. New registrants were randomly assigned to either the treatment or the control group.

> Wisconsin's main problem was the small size of the registrant pool, compounded by the fact that it was very slow to get the marketing and job development efforts underway. The result was a substantial shortfall in the number of women finding employment through the experimental program, so substantial that three-quarters of the way through the project, it was clear that there would be very little probability of seeing any impact from the demonstration. There was also little possibility of increasing the numbers, given the small registrant pool. . . . A decision was therefore made in the fall of 1979 to phase down the demonstration before its scheduled end, and also to discontinue the Madison/Racine complex as a Lab.

INFORMATION SOURCE: Joan M. Leiman, "The WIN Labs: A Federal/ Local Partnership in Social Research," Manpower Demonstration Research Corporation, July 1982.

PUBLIC-USE ACCESS TO DATA: Public-use access does not exist.

DENVER POSTPLACEMENT SERVICES PROJECT

SUMMARY: This demonstration, conducted from 1980 to 1982, tested the effects of postplacement case management on a medium-sized sample of AFDC recipients who had recently found employment. Subjects were followed for six months.

COST: See introduction to "WIN Labs Experiments."

TIME FRAME: Demonstration period, April 1980–May 1982; data collected, same period; final report, December 1982.

TREATMENTS TESTED: Experimentals were telephoned seven times over a six-month period, whether still receiving AFDC or not. Counselors inquired about job-related problems and offered to help. If a job was lost, help was offered in finding a new one. Controls were not telephoned. They were still eligible for WIN services (principally, child-care subsidies for 90 days).

OUTCOMES OF INTEREST: (1) Employment; (2) Earnings; (3) Recipiency; and (4) AFDC payments.

SAMPLE SIZE: Experimentals, 270; controls, 281.

TARGET POPULATION: WIN-mandatory AFDC recipients who had recently found full-time, permanent employment.

NUMBER OF TREATMENT GROUPS: Two (with one control group).

NUMBER AND LOCATION OF SITES: One–Denver, Colorado.

RESEARCH COMPONENTS:

Process analysis: Conducted principally through client interviews. The project report authors found that the average experimental had 8.3 contacts with WIN staff and that the average control had 6.6, in both cases mostly connected with the mandatory WIN job search after loss of the initial job. Concerning WIN staff intervention, participants mostly reported that "they talked with [us] about how to solve" a problem. Experimentals were more likely to receive child-care subsidies, whereas controls were more likely to either leave children with older siblings or leave them unattended. Controls were more likely to leave their jobs because of child-care conflicts, but experimentals were more likely to leave their jobs because of conflicts with supervisors and coworkers.

Impact analysis: Comparison of means.

Benefit–cost analysis: Cost-effectiveness only.

MAJOR FINDINGS:
1. No impact on job retention beyond one month.
2. Experimental/control differences in earnings, AFDC payments, and recipiency status were statistically insignificant.
3. Costs per experimental were $320 higher than costs per control, and thus the project was not cost-effective.

TIME TRENDS IN FINDINGS: Experimental/control job retention rates are significantly different (at the 10 percent level) in the first month, and insignificantly different thereafter.

DESIGN ISSUES: None apparent.

REPLICABILITY: Replicable.

GENERALIZABILITY: There is no obvious reason why this approach should work elsewhere when it did not work in Denver.

FUNDING SOURCE: See introduction to "WIN Labs Experiments."

TREATMENT ADMINISTRATOR: Denver Department of Social Services. Key personnel: Unknown.

EVALUATOR: Center for Social Research and Development, University of Denver. Key personnel: Ellen L. Slaughter and Edward C. Baumheier.

ENABLING LEGISLATION: None.

INFORMATION SOURCES: Ellen L. Slaughter, Gale G. Whiteneck, and Edward C. Baumheier, "Postplacement Services to WIN Clients: Final Report of a Denver WIN Laboratory Project," Manpower Demonstration Research Corporation, December 1982.

PUBLIC-USE ACCESS TO DATA: Public-use access does not exist.

LOUISVILLE GROUP JOB SEARCH EXPERIMENT

SUMMARY: This demonstration, conducted from 1980 to 1981, tested the effects of immediate employment-assistance services and incentive payments on a medium-sized sample of female WIN registrants. Subjects were followed for one year.

COST: See introduction to "WIN Labs Experiments."

TIME FRAME: Demonstration period, October 1980–May 1981; data collected through December 1981; final report, November 1983.

TREATMENTS TESTED: Experimentals received essentially the Job Club treatment, incentive payments of $1.50 per day, and transportation and child-care payments. These services were available immediately on registration. Controls received "the usual WIN services"; these might have included intensive counseling, on-the-job training, or classroom instruction, but the great majority of controls actually received no services. Controls who were given services received them after the usual administrative delays, sometimes up to 10 weeks.

OUTCOMES OF INTEREST: (1) Employment; (2) Earnings; and (3) AFDC payments.

SAMPLE SIZE: Experimentals, 376; controls, 374.

TARGET POPULATION: Female WIN registrants who were not already employed or in training or school, who did not have medical or personal problems preventing them from working, and who volunteered to participate.

NUMBER OF TREATMENT GROUPS: Two (with one control group).

NUMBER AND LOCATION OF SITES: One—Louisville, Kentucky.

RESEARCH COMPONENTS:

Process analysis: Conducted through observations and interviews. Job search techniques taught were fewer than in the Azrin model (see "Carbondale Job-Finding Club" and "Job Club Behavioral Supervision Test," in Part XIII, "Unemployed")—apparently the only one taught was cold calls from the Yellow Pages. An important finding is that "job-readiness" ratings, a major WIN criterion, were inherently subjective; consequently, job readiness could be affected by changing personal circumstances and group experience. In fact, 32 percent of non-job-ready experimentals found jobs.

Impact analysis: Comparison of means, ordinary least squares (OLS) regression, and logit.

Benefit–cost analysis: Cost-effectiveness only.

MAJOR FINDINGS:

Over two quarters of follow-up:

	Experimentals	Controls	Difference Significant?
Percentage ever employed	49%	34%	Yes, at 1%
Total average earnings	$550	$406	Yes, at 5%
AFDC payments	$1,680	$1,710	No

Employment impacts were largest for WIN volunteers; they were generally insignificant for WIN mandatories. Impacts were much larger for those who had not been recently employed than for those who had. The incremental cost was $195 per experimental. This is not cost-effective in budgetary terms, because the AFDC savings are insignificant. However, the Louisville experiment was clearly overstaffed compared to Azrin's, which had similar employment results.

TIME TRENDS IN FINDINGS: Earnings and employment in the second quarter increased over earnings and employment in the first quarter.

DESIGN ISSUES:

1. Roughly the first half of the sample's findings (covering the first six months of intake) were discarded because of dissatisfaction with the initial implementation of the treatment. Treatment procedures were revised, and findings are for the later sample only.

2. Because the program was voluntary, AFDC savings from one possible source in the Azrin WIN Job Club experiment could not have occurred. Azrin believed that some recipients had employment

that they concealed from welfare officials; since holding a job and going to daylong, supervised workshops and job search simultaneously would be difficult, he speculated that savings even from nonparticipants were possible if the Job Club were mandatory. Even without concealed employment, mandatory attendance would be a disincentive to recipiency. The MDRC report, on the other hand, emphasizes the importance of group reinforcement and solidarity in the frustrating telephone job search, and questions whether a mandatory program would have these elements.

3. Job retention is not reported.

REPLICABILITY: This is a replication.

GENERALIZABILITY: The project report authors argued that the impact estimates were not very different from Azrin's WIN Job Club impact estimates, when adjusted for differences in sample characteristics and job markets.

FUNDING SOURCE: See introduction to "WIN Labs Experiments."

TREATMENT ADMINISTRATOR: Kentucky Department of Human Resources. Key personnel: Geralynne Clements and Ruth Harvey.

EVALUATOR: Manpower Demonstration Research Corporation. Key personnel: Barbara S. Goldman.

ENABLING LEGISLATION: None.

INFORMATION SOURCES: Joanna Gould-Stuart, "Welfare Women in a Group Job Search Program: Their Experiences in the Louisville WIN Research Laboratory Project," Manpower Demonstration Research Corporation, April 1982; Carl Wolfhagen with Barbara S. Goldman, "Job Search Strategies: Lessons from the Louisville WIN Laboratory," Manpower Demonstration Research Corporation, November 1983.

PUBLIC-USE ACCESS TO DATA: Public-use access does not exist.

THE STATE WELFARE-TO-WORK
INITIATIVES

INTRODUCTION

In 1981 the Omnibus Budget Reconciliation Act (OBRA) authorized states to employ policies of mandatory unpaid work experience for recipients of Aid to Families with Dependent Children (AFDC) under certain circumstances, and to streamline the administration of the Work Incentive (WIN) program.

A series of demonstrations tested how effectively states used these new policies. Most of the evaluations were performed by the Manpower Demonstration Research Corporation (MDRC) with partial funding from the states, the U.S. Dept. of Health and Human Services (DHHS), and the Ford Foundation. The key officer at DHHS was Howard Rolston; at the Ford Foundation, key officers were Gordon Berlin and Prudence Brown.

Manpower Demonstration Research Corporation representatives made more than 100 presentations of their findings in 1986 and 1987. They testified before Senator Daniel Patrick Moynihan's Subcommittee on Social Security and Family Policy, as well as the full Senate Finance Committee, in 1987; and before the Moynihan subcommittee in 1989 on regulations to implement the Family Support Act (FSA). MDRC findings were prominently reported in the media.

The Manpower Demonstration Research Corporation reports were frequently cited in Congress during the framing of the Family Support Act (FSA) of 1988. In a 1991 article, Erica Baum, who was the principal staff support for Senator Moynihan, stated that MDRC's program evaluations were essential to the passage of the FSA because they were "germane . . . timely . . . unambiguous . . . not subject to challenge on methodological grounds," consistent across sites, and disinterested. Her account is confirmed by lobbyists and other congressional staff members in " 'The Remarkable Quango': Knowledge, Politics and Welfare Reform," a paper by Peter Szanton.

Total research expenditures by MDRC were $7.9 million (1985). Some states themselves undertook certain research-related activities, costs for which are not included in that figure.

BALTIMORE OPTIONS PROGRAM
(Maryland Employment Initiatives)

SUMMARY: This demonstration, conducted from 1982 to 1985, tested the effects of education, training, job search, and work experience on a large sample of AFDC recipients. Subjects were followed for two years.

COST: $1,000 per experimental for the program costs, or $1.4 million (1983).

TIME FRAME: Demonstration period, November 1982–December 1983; data collected, November 1982–March 1985; final report, December 1985.

TREATMENTS TESTED:
1. The experimental treatment consisted of a packet of options to enhance the employability of the subject, depending on her own perceived needs. The options included training programs, general equivalency diploma (GED) tutoring, job search (both group and individual), and work experience with on-the-job training funded in part by diversion of the AFDC grant.
2. Controls received regular WIN services. In fact, few of them received any formal services.

OUTCOMES OF INTEREST: (1) Employment; (2) Earnings; and (3) Welfare receipt.

SAMPLE SIZE: Experimentals, 1,362; controls, 1,395.

TARGET POPULATION: New WIN mandatories (mostly AFDC recipients with no children under six years old) and new applicants for AFDC who were in WIN-mandatory categories.

NUMBER OF TREATMENT GROUPS: Two (with one control group).

NUMBER AND LOCATION OF SITES: Baltimore County, Maryland.

RESEARCH COMPONENTS:
   Process analysis: Conducted. Operation of the program components is extensively reported.

Impact analysis: Used ordinary least squares (OLS) regressions.

Benefit–cost analysis: Conducted from taxpayer, recipient, and social perspectives.

MAJOR FINDINGS:

1. Average earnings per control for the three-year follow-up were $6,595, compared with $7,638 for experimentals. The 16 percent difference is statistically significant.
2. The experimental treatment produced persistent increases in earnings for sample members who lacked recent work experience (over half the sample).
3. The earnings gains of experimentals were not accompanied by aggregate reductions in welfare incidence or grant expenditures.
4. From a budgetary perspective, the experimental treatment cost more than it saved in AFDC payments.

TIME TRENDS IN FINDINGS: Employment impacts declined slightly over time; earnings impacts increased slightly. Insignificance of treatment for welfare receipt was lasting.

DESIGN ISSUES:

1. The Baltimore Job Training Partnership Act agency "is nationally recognized and locally influential . . . and had lobbied vigorously to run the new Options program (Friedlander et al. 1985)." Possible site self-selection bias.
2. The authors suggested several reasons for the paradox of higher earnings without lower benefits. First, Baltimore was somewhat more generous than other areas in counting work-related expenses. Second, some of the differential occurred among individuals who would have moved off welfare in any case. Third, information about earnings was often not communicated to the income maintenance workers either by the Options staff or by the recipients.

REPLICABILITY: Package of options is replicable.

GENERALIZABILITY: There is no obvious limitation on the generalizability of the demonstration.

FUNDING SOURCES: See introduction to "State Welfare-to-Work Initiatives."

TREATMENT ADMINISTRATOR: Maryland Department of Human Resources. Key personnel: Alvin Truesdale.

EVALUATOR: Manpower Demonstration Research Corporation. Key personnel: Daniel Friedlander.

ENABLING LEGISLATION: OBRA. See introduction to "State Welfare-to-Work Initiatives."

POLICY EFFECTS: See introduction to "State Welfare-to-Work Initiatives."

INFORMATION SOURCES: Daniel Friedlander, Gregory Hoerz, David A. Long, and Janet Quint, *Maryland: Final Report on the Employment Initiatives Evaluation*, Manpower Demonstration Research Corporation, December 1985; Daniel Friedlander, *Maryland: Supplemental Report on the Baltimore Options Program*, Manpower Demonstration Research Corporation, October 1987; Janet Quint with Joseph Ball (deceased), Barbara S. Goldman, Judith M. Gueron, and Gayle Hamilton, *Interim Findings from the Maryland Employment Initiatives Program*, Manpower Demonstration Research Corporation, February 1984; Maryland Department of Human Resources, "Final Evaluation of Maryland's Grant Diversion/OJT Demonstration Program," Office of Welfare Employment Policy, August 28, 1987.

PUBLIC-USE ACCESS TO DATA: Public-use file exists; contact MDRC about *Welfare Employment Studies 1 through 4*.

SAN DIEGO JOB SEARCH AND
WORK EXPERIENCE DEMONSTRATION

SUMMARY: This demonstration, conducted from 1982 to 1985, tested the effects of mandatory job placement assistance and work experience on a large sample of AFDC recipients. Subjects were followed for two years.

COST: See introduction to "State Welfare-to-Work Initiatives." For the second treatment, administrative costs of $636–$727 per experimental; for the first treatment, $562–$587 per experimental, or about $2.8 million total (1983).

TIME FRAME: Demonstration period, October 1982–August 1983; data collected through March 1985; final report, February 1986.

TREATMENTS TESTED: Random assignment occurred at the time of application for AFDC. Impacts per applicant therefore include those who were found ineligible for AFDC (and were therefore ineligible for programs).
1. Experimental group 1: Job placement assistance on day of AFDC application, followed by three weeks of Job Club.

2. Experimental group 2: Same treatment as group 1, but if still unemployed at the end of 3 weeks, required to hold an unpaid work experience job at a public or nonprofit agency for up to 13 weeks. The hours of unpaid work were set by the family's welfare grant divided by the minimum wage.
3. Controls: Minimal WIN services.

OUTCOMES OF INTEREST: (1) Employment; (2) Earnings; and (3) AFDC recipiency and payments.

SAMPLE SIZE: AFDC-R: group 1, 856; group 2, 1,502; controls, 873. AFDC-U: group 1, 831; group 2, 1,376; group 3, 813.

TARGET POPULATION: AFDC and AFDC-U applicants who were WIN-mandatory. Excluded were refugees, persons with language barriers, and applicants with children under age six.

NUMBER OF TREATMENT GROUPS: Three (with one control group).

NUMBER AND LOCATION OF SITES: San Diego County, California, countywide.

RESEARCH COMPONENTS:
  Process analysis: Conducted.
  Impact analysis: Conducted with ordinary least squares (OLS) regressions.
  Benefit–cost analysis: Conducted.

MAJOR FINDINGS:
1. Work experience supervisors found the productivity of their assigned subjects roughly comparable to those of regular entry-level employees.
2. Sanctions were applied to from 4 percent to 8 percent of experimentals, but to 1 percent or less of controls.

Findings for AFDC-Regular:
1. Both experimental groups had significantly higher rates of employment (61 percent to 55 percent) over six quarters than the controls, but the group 1 (no Workfare) differential faded to insignificance after the third quarter.
2. The Workfare group had $700 more in earnings per subject over six quarters than the control; the non-Workfare group had $251 more in earnings, but this was not significant.
3. Neither treatment had much effect on AFDC recipiency.
4. Over six quarters, the AFDC payments per Workfare experimental were $288 less than those per control; payments to Job-Club-only experimentals were $203 less than those per control, but this difference was not significant.

5. Program gains were largest among those in the sample who had no previous employment experience.

Findings for AFDC-U:

1. "For both program models, there were statistically significant and substantial reductions in welfare payments, but no significant impacts on the employment and earnings of AFDC-U applicants." The Workfare subjects received on average $530 less in AFDC payments over six quarters than did controls; the job-search-only subjects received $470 less.

2. "Sanctioning rates were higher for experimentals than for controls, and those sanctioned faced larger grant reductions than did AFDC's (regulars)."

3. "In general, mandating (Workfare) for AFDC-U's did not improve program outcomes compared to those found for the Job Search program." The benefit-cost analysis findings are that there were consistent, large net gains to taxpayers and government budgets for both programs and for both applicant groups. AFDC-R applicants also benefited financially from the Workfare treatment; the job-search-only treatment did not always have positive benefits. AFDC-U applicants were made worse off by the treatments, because they reduced their benefits without increasing their earnings.

TIME TRENDS IN FINDINGS: AFDC-R welfare savings from the Workfare treatment declined over time. AFDC-U welfare savings from the two treatments seem to decline gradually over time.

DESIGN ISSUES:

1. Site self-selection. Workfare is not politically acceptable everywhere.

2. The San Diego job market tightened over the course of the experiment. This affected the applicant mix. The study attempts to compare earlier with later cohorts to examine this.

3. The work experience programs seem to have been unusually well run, without any sense of makework or strong client resentment detected in the process analysis. It is not clear that other counties could replicate that success.

REPLICABILITY: Replicable, but see above.

GENERALIZABILITY: Generalization to the full AFDC population tested in the Saturation Work Initiative Model (SWIM) experiment.

FUNDING SOURCES: See introduction to "State Welfare-to-Work Initiatives." Key personnel: For California, Virginia Hamilton.

TREATMENT ADMINISTRATOR: State Employment Service Agency and the County Welfare Department. Key personnel: Ray Koenig and Joan Zinser.

EVALUATOR: Manpower Demonstration Research Corporation. Key personnel: Barbara S. Goldman.

ENABLING LEGISLATION: OBRA.

POLICY EFFECTS: See introduction to "State Welfare-to-Work Initiatives." Also led to the SWIM experiment.

INFORMATION SOURCES: Barbara S. Goldman, Daniel Friedlander, and David A. Long, *California: Final Report on the San Diego Job Search and Work Experience Demonstration*, Manpower Demonstration Research Corporation, February 1986.

PUBLIC-USE ACCESS TO DATA: Public-use access does not exist.

WASHINGTON COMMUNITY WORK EXPERIENCE PROGRAM

SUMMARY: This demonstration, conducted from 1982 to 1983, tested the effects of work experience and job search assistance on a small sample of AFDC recipients. Subjects were followed for one year.

COST: Administrative cost, $85,565 (1982).

TIME FRAME: Demonstration period, October 1982–May 1983; data collected through August 1983; final report, June 1984.

TREATMENTS TESTED:

1. Community Work Experience Program (CWEP): Workfare placement with public or nonprofit agencies for four months. Child-care and transportation reimbursement were provided. "Persons assigned to CWEP who refused to work were counseled by the CWEP coordinator and if a reasonable settlement was not achieved, these persons could be sanctioned. The sanction discontinued the client's portion of support from her grant for three months" (Nelson 1984).
2. Employment and Training (E&T): A Job-Club-based model, with three or four days of group job preparation, followed by five or six days in a phone lab, followed by individual job search.
3. Controls: No treatment. Presumably eligible for some WIN services.

OUTCOMES OF INTEREST: (1) Employment and (2) AFDC case closures and savings.

SAMPLE SIZE: CWEP, 64; E&T, 66; controls, 42.

TARGET POPULATION: WIN-mandatory AFDC recipients. Exclusions for persons deemed more or less unemployable.

NUMBER OF TREATMENT GROUPS: Three (with one control group).

NUMBER AND LOCATION OF SITES: Spokane County and Pierce County (which includes Tacoma), Washington.

RESEARCH COMPONENTS:
    Process analysis: Not conducted.
    Impact analysis: Comparison of means. No tests of statistical significance.
    Benefit–cost analysis: Budgetary perspective only.

MAJOR FINDINGS:
1. Thirty percent of CWEP clients found unsubsidized employment after participating in it, as did 39 percent of E&T clients; 14 percent of controls "were employed at some time during the one-year study period."
2. The author found evidence that CWEP was more useful than E&T to clients with less than a high-school education.
3. Program expenditures exceeded AFDC payment reductions during the study year.

TIME TRENDS IN FINDINGS: Only one year of data.

DESIGN ISSUES:
1. The sample sizes, which are substantially smaller than planned in the research design, are too small for useful analysis. Sample sizes were kept low by failure of the welfare staff to refer clients to WIN (which is run by Employment Security, a separate agency) and by discretionary removal of 63 clients from the treatment samples, either by the program staff or the evaluators. The discretionary removal of 37 percent of the sample appears to open the door to selection bias either by the clients themselves or by others. Much of this was caused by reliance on client follow-up interviews as the primary data source on outcomes.
2. No follow-up interviews were conducted with controls, so the data sources used for experimentals and controls do not match. In fact, it is not clear what data source was used for controls.

REPLICABILITY: Replicable.

GENERALIZABILITY: None. Sample is too small.

FUNDING SOURCES: U.S. Department of Health and Human Services, Social Security Administration. Key personnel: Unknown.

TREATMENT ADMINISTRATOR: Washington Department of Social and Health Services. Key personnel: Gladys McCorkhill and Judith Merchant.

EVALUATOR: Washington Department of Social and Health Services, Office of Research and Data Analysis. Key personnel: Hal Nelson.

ENABLING LEGISLATION: OBRA.

INFORMATION SOURCES: Hal Nelson, "Evaluation of the Community Work Experience Program," Washington Department of Social and Health Services, Division of Administration and Personnel, Office of Research and Data Analysis, Program Research and Evaluation Section, Report #06-23, June 1984.

PUBLIC-USE ACCESS TO DATA: We have no information about a public-use file for this demonstration.

ARKANSAS WORK PROGRAM

SUMMARY: This demonstration, conducted from 1983 to 1985, tested the effects of mandatory job search and work experience on a medium-sized sample of AFDC recipients. Subjects were followed for one year.

COST: See introduction to "State Welfare-to-Work Initiatives." Administrative cost of $158 per experimental, or about $92,000 (1983).

TIME FRAME: Demonstration period, June 1983–March 1984; data collected through January 1985; final report, September 1985.

TREATMENTS TESTED:

1. Experimentals received a fixed sequence of services, beginning with group job search (Job Club model), followed by individual job search, followed by work experience (i.e., Workfare). Few people ever participated in work experience, which was limited to 12 weeks and 20 to 30 hours per week. The most job-ready individuals could skip the Job Club.
2. Controls received virtually no services.

OUTCOMES OF INTEREST: (1) Levels of program participation; (2) Employment; (3) Earnings; (4) Welfare recipiency; and (5) Welfare payments.

SAMPLE SIZE: Experimentals, 583; controls, 570.

TARGET POPULATION: AFDC applicants and WIN-mandatory recipients. This included recipients with children between ages three and six, but in practice those with severe employment barriers were excluded from the research sample.

NUMBER OF TREATMENT GROUPS: Two (with one control group).

NUMBER AND LOCATION OF SITES: Pulaski County (Little Rock) and Jefferson County (Pine Bluff), Arkansas.

RESEARCH COMPONENTS:
   Process analysis: Conducted with emphasis on program participation.
   Impact analysis: Conducted with ordinary least squares (OLS) regressions.
   Benefit–cost analysis: Conducted from taxpayer, recipient, and social perspectives.

MAJOR FINDINGS:
1. Thirty-eight percent of the experimentals actually participated in at least one part of the program; 5 percent were sanctioned.
2. Employment rates increased by about 5 percentage points.
3. Earnings also improved.
4. There were substantial reductions in the incidence of welfare and in the amounts of welfare receipts. For example, in the third and last follow-up quarter, welfare receipts were reduced by about 15 percent.
5. The program resulted in modest positive net benefits from the social, budgetary, and taxpayer perspectives. There were net losses from the recipient perspective. Budgetary expenditures in running the program were small (about $250 per participant).

TIME TRENDS IN FINDINGS: Short follow-up.

DESIGN ISSUES:
1. A high priority was placed on treating the most job-ready clients first. With less creaming, the apparent effectiveness of the program might be lower.
2. It is not clear that the Workfare program can be expanded to treat the entire population.
3. As with most employment programs, private-sector displacement bias is a possibility.

4. Local staff were given considerable discretion to give participation exemptions and to decide which recipients were suitable for which components.
5. Staff turnover in Jefferson County probably reduced the treatment impact, because the Job Club component was less well run.

REPLICABILITY: Replicable.

GENERALIZABILITY: This experiment can be compared to the Job Club experiments, which generally found larger effects. The level of unemployment was high in both counties: 7.7 percent in Pulaski and 10.5 percent in Jefferson.

FUNDING SOURCES: See introduction to "State Welfare-to-Work Initiatives." In addition to the Ford Foundation, the U.S. Department of Health and Human Services, and Arkansas State, this study received funding from the Winthrop Rockefeller Foundation.

TREATMENT ADMINISTRATOR: Arkansas Department of Human Services. Key personnel: Jerry Evans.

EVALUATOR: Manpower Demonstration Research Corporation. Key personnel: Daniel Friedlander.

ENABLING LEGISLATION: OBRA. See Introduction. Special federal waiver obtained to mandate WIN status for some parents of children between the ages of three and six.

POLICY EFFECTS: See introduction to "State Welfare-to-Work Initiatives."

INFORMATION SOURCES: Daniel Friedlander, Gregory Hoerz, Janet Quint, and James Riccio, *Final Report on the WORK Program in Two Counties*, Manpower Demonstration Research Corporation, September 1985.

PUBLIC-USE ACCESS TO DATA: Public-use file exists; contact MDRC about *Welfare Employment Studies* 1 through 4.

MAINE TRAINING OPPORTUNITIES IN THE PRIVATE SECTOR (TOPS)

SUMMARY: This demonstration, conducted from 1983 to 1987, tested the effects of vocational training and work experience on a medium-sized sample of unemployed single AFDC recipients. Subjects were followed for two years.

COST: About $2,600 per experimental, or $770,000 (1984).

TIME FRAME: Demonstration period, October 1983–June 1985; data collected, October 1983–September 1987; final report, April 1988.

TREATMENTS TESTED: Experimentals received the following prescribed treatment sequence: Prevocational Training lasted two to five weeks, stressing personal growth and job-seeking and job-holding skills. Work Experience consisted of 20 hours per week of unpaid work in public or nonprofit sectors for up to 12 weeks. Those who demonstrated motivation and skills acquisition were eligible for on-the-job training (OJT) positions, preferably in the private sector. The training period was limited to a maximum of six months, and the employer subsidy was set at 50 percent of wages; the subsidy was funded by grant diversion. Controls could receive other WIN services from the treatment administrator.

OUTCOMES OF INTEREST: (1) Earnings; (2) Employment; and (3) AFDC payments.

SAMPLE SIZE: Experimentals, 297; controls, 147.

TARGET POPULATION: The experiment was open only to applicants. Applicants who met the program criteria were then randomly assigned an experimental or a control status. Applicants had to meet the following criteria: (1) single heads of households, (2) AFDC recipients for at least six months, (3) not currently employed, and (4) able to read at the level of the materials used in Prevocational Training. In addition, the intake staff used their discretion to screen out women who had (a) child care, transportation, health, or other problems that could interfere with participation, (b) low motivation, or (c) unrealistic ambitions. About 3 out of 10 applicants were considered inappropriate and were screened out prior to random assignment.

NUMBER OF TREATMENT GROUPS: Two (with one control group).

NUMBER AND LOCATION OF SITES: Statewide.

RESEARCH COMPONENTS:
   Process analysis: Conducted.
   Impact analysis: Conducted as a difference in regression-adjusted means.
   Benefit–cost analysis: Conducted.

MAJOR FINDINGS:
1. TOPS had sustained positive impacts on earnings over the entire follow-up period (2nd through 11th quarters). Experimentals had earnings of $7,344 on average, controls had $5,599 average earn-

ings, and the difference is statistically significant. However, differences in employment, AFDC recipiency, and AFDC payments were in general insignificant.

2. The project report authors speculated that the discrepancy between the earnings increase and the nonreduction in AFDC payments may be the result of three factors: (1) relatively generous allowances for work-related expenses; (2) substantial numbers of participants were already working—thus, at some point their earnings exceeded the AFDC break-even level and further earnings would not result in further benefit reductions; and (3) experimentals were trained in how to become "your own best advocate" within the welfare system.

3. Because there were no AFDC payment reductions, there was no positive budgetary impact. However, TOPS raised the income of experimentals about $3,000 each at a cost of about $1,100. "TOPS can be viewed as a much more efficient means of transferring income to this group than simply raising their AFDC benefits."

TIME TRENDS IN FINDINGS: The earnings effect grew stronger over time.

DESIGN ISSUES: A high degree of selectivity in the initial screening of the research sample makes it difficult to generalize the results.

REPLICABILITY: Replicable.

GENERALIZABILITY: The Maine AFDC population is unrepresentative of the U.S. AFDC population as a whole. It is mostly white, and historically many recipients worked, often full-time. A well-run OJT program funded by grant diversion in a state with low unemployment could be an effective but very limited part of the overall welfare strategy in other states as well.

FUNDING SOURCES: See introduction to "State Welfare-to-Work Initiatives."

TREATMENT ADMINISTRATOR: Maine Department of Human Services. Key personnel: Tomie McLean.

EVALUATOR: Manpower Demonstration Research Corporation. Key personnel: Patricia Auspos.

ENABLING LEGISLATION: OBRA. See introduction to "State Welfare-to-Work Initiatives."

POLICY EFFECTS: See introduction to "State Welfare-to-Work Initiatives."

INFORMATION SOURCES: Patricia Auspos, George Cave, and David A. Long, Maine: Final Report on the Training Opportunities in the Private Sector Program, Manpower Demonstration Research Corporation, April 1988.

PUBLIC-USE ACCESS TO DATA: Public-use access does not exist.

VIRGINIA EMPLOYMENT SERVICES PROGRAM

SUMMARY: This demonstration, conducted from 1983 to 1985, tested the effects of mandatory job search and work experience on a large sample of AFDC recipients. Subjects were followed for one year.

COST: See introduction to "State Welfare-to-Work Initiatives." Administrative cost of $388 per experimental, or about $920,000 total (1984).

TIME FRAME: Demonstration period, August 1983–September 1984; data collected through August 1985; final report, August 1986.

TREATMENTS TESTED:
1. Job Search/Work Experience. Participants were required to provide proof of three contacts with potential employers. If these contacts were unsuccessful, participants were then offered job search assistance, either individual or group, and community work experience, but in practice these were not mandatory. Group job search did not include a telephone bank for supervised employer contacts.
2. All Employment Services Program (ESP) Services. In addition to the above treatment, it was intended that these experimentals would have available greater education or training options. In fact, there were no additional resources for education or training for this group, so there was in fact no separate treatment.
3. Controls were not subject to either treatment.

OUTCOMES OF INTEREST: (1) Participation in services; (2) Employment; (3) Earnings; and (4) AFDC recipiency and payments.

SAMPLE SIZE: Job Search/Work Experience, 1,061; all ESP Services, 1,077; controls, 1,046.

TARGET POPULATION: WIN-mandatory female clients who did not fall into the following excluded categories: parents of children under six, those already in education or training programs, WIN volunteers, and those already assigned to nonexperimental treatment.

NUMBER OF TREATMENT GROUPS: Three (with one control group).

NUMBER AND LOCATION OF SITES: 11 Virginia counties: Fairfax, Newport News, Hampton, Chesapeake, Henry, Martinsville, Carroll, Grayson, Galax, Campbell, and Pittsylvania.

RESEARCH COMPONENTS:

Process analysis: Conducted. Emphasis on what treatments were actually received.

Impact analysis: Conducted with ordinary least squares (OLS) regressions.

Benefit–cost analysis: Conducted.

MAJOR FINDINGS:

Because treatments in the two experimental groups did not in fact differ, findings reported concentrate on differences between experimentals and controls.

Outcome	Experimentals	Controls
Ever employed, second to fourth quarters after random assignment	43.8%	40.5%
Average total earnings, those quarters	$1,119	$1,038
Received any AFDC payment, those quarters	86.0%	86.1%
Total payments received, including quarter of assignment	$1,923	$2,007

Note: Differences are significant in the first and fourth rows.

Differences were larger in urban than in rural areas, although sample sizes in rural areas would make it difficult to find an impact. The project report authors found increasing, long-term employment gains among applicants and short-term, temporary welfare savings among recipients.

From the subjects' perspective, the treatment resulted in income gains. From the perspective of government budgets, the treatment produced net positive benefits within five years for applicants; costs and benefits were roughly equal for recipients.

TIME TRENDS IN FINDINGS: Employment gains from the treatment among applicants were concentrated in later periods.

DESIGN ISSUES:
1. An element of site self-selection may bias the findings.
2. Treatments varied across sites, and it is impossible to determine whether this caused the impacts to vary as well.
3. The project report authors noted that Virginia is a relatively low-benefit state, and that employable individuals would be less attracted to AFDC than would be the case in higher-benefit states.
4. Virginia also has a highly decentralized welfare system. Treatment-standardization problems encountered in this experiment would be characteristic of policy-implementation problems in decentralized systems.
5. It is not clear why this treatment should be producing long-term rather than short-term employment gains. Benefit–cost analysis based on projections to 5 years from 18 months of data may not be robust.

REPLICABILITY: Replicable.

GENERALIZABILITY: Doubtful; see "Design Issues."

FUNDING SOURCES: See introduction to "State Welfare-to-Work Initiatives."

TREATMENT ADMINISTRATOR: Virginia Department of Social Services. Key personnel: Local agency heads listed in report.

EVALUATOR: Manpower Demonstration Research Corporation. Key personnel: James Riccio.

ENABLING LEGISLATION: OBRA.

POLICY EFFECTS: See introduction to "State Welfare-to-Work Initiatives."

INFORMATION SOURCES: James Riccio, George Cave, Stephen Freedman, and Marilyn Price, Virginia: Final Report on the Virginia Employment Services Program, Manpower Demonstration Research Corporation, August 1986.

PUBLIC-USE ACCESS TO DATA: Public-use file exists; contact Manpower Demonstration Research Corporation about Welfare Employment Studies 1 through 4.

WEST VIRGINIA COMMUNITY WORK EXPERIENCE DEMONSTRATION

SUMMARY: This demonstration, conducted from 1983 to 1986, tested the effects of mandatory work experience on a large sample of AFDC recipients. Subjects were followed for two years.

COST: $277 per experimental, or about $513,000 (1983).

TIME FRAME: Demonstration period, July 1983–April 1984; data collected through January 1986; final report, September 1986.

TREATMENTS TESTED: Experimentals: Mandatory Workfare in return for AFDC benefits, with no time limit on the obligation. Controls were excluded from the Workfare program.

OUTCOMES OF INTEREST: (1) Level of participation; (2) Earnings; and (3) AFDC recipiency and payments.

SAMPLE SIZE: Experimentals, 1,853; controls, 1,841.

TARGET POPULATION: All female WIN-mandatory AFDC recipients and both new registrants and prior registrants. As elsewhere, this excludes parents of children under age six. Also excluded were recipients already enrolled in full-time school or training, people who were already employed, and WIN volunteers.

NUMBER OF TREATMENT GROUPS: Two (with one control group).

NUMBER AND LOCATION OF SITES: 21 counties in West Virginia.

RESEARCH COMPONENTS:
   Process analysis: Conducted. Major emphasis on clients' attitudes toward jobs and supervisors' attitudes toward clients.
   Impact analysis: Conducted with ordinary least squares (OLS) regressions.
   Benefit–cost analysis: Conducted.

MAJOR FINDINGS:
1. Negligible effect on earnings.
2. Small reductions in transfer payments.
3. Net social benefit of the program is positive, because the cost of running it is small and the output of experimentals was large. (In fact, the productivity of experimentals was rated slightly higher than that of regular employees.)

TIME TRENDS IN FINDINGS: Participation rates were higher in the first six months.

DESIGN ISSUES:
1. The possible differential bias from experimentals migrating out of state to avoid the Workfare obligation while controls remain in-state is not addressed.
2. The difficulty (or lack thereof) of job finding or creation or both is not addressed in the report.
3. West Virginia had (and continues to have) a high unemployment rate, which may affect the findings and might imply a displacement effect.

4. Sanctions for refusal to participate in Workfare were rare.

5. Valuation of program output may be problematic.

REPLICABILITY: Replicable.

GENERALIZABILITY: The West Virginia AFDC population is not representative of the U.S. AFDC population as a whole, nor is its level of unemployment. Also, the state's fiscal distress results in a large number of readily identified community needs for which Workfare is not only appropriate but is the only affordable source of labor that can meet them.

FUNDING SOURCES: See introduction to "State Welfare-to-Work Initiatives." In addition to the Ford Foundation, funding was provided by the U.S. Department of Health and Human Services, West Virginia State, and the Claude Worthington Benedum Foundation.

TREATMENT ADMINISTRATOR: West Virginia Department of Human Services.

EVALUATOR: Manpower Demonstration Research Corporation. Key personnel: Joseph Ball (deceased) and Daniel Friedlander.

ENABLING LEGISLATION: Omnibus Budget Reconciliation Act of 1981. See introduction to "State Welfare-to-Work Initiatives."

POLICY EFFECTS: See introduction to "State Welfare-to-Work Initiatives."

INFORMATION SOURCES: Daniel Friedlander, Marjorie Erickson, Gayle Hamilton, and Virginia Knox, West Virginia: Final Report on the Community Work Experience Demonstrations, Manpower Demonstration Research Corporation, September 1986; Joseph Ball (deceased) with Gayle Hamilton, Gregory Hoerz, Barbara S. Goldman, and Judith M. Gueron, West Virginia: Interim Findings on the Community Work Experience Demonstrations, Manpower Demonstration Research Corporation, November 1984.

PUBLIC-USE ACCESS TO DATA: Public-use access does not exist.

FLORIDA TRADE WELFARE FOR WORK

SUMMARY: This demonstration, conducted from 1984 to 1986, tested the effects of subsidized work experience and on-the-job training on a large sample of AFDC recipients. Subjects were followed for one year.

COST: $734,363; research only, $163,191.

TIME FRAME: Demonstration period, July 1984–July 1986; data collected through September 1986; final report, February 1987.

TREATMENTS TESTED: The WIN regime in Florida consisted of a two-week job search in which clients looked for jobs on their own and were expected to complete at least six job applications (clients would be subject to sanctioning if they failed to do so). Those who did not find employment within two weeks were required to attend job clubs. Those who did not find employment within the Job Club time limits were randomly assigned to one of three groups:

1. WIN controls were placed in "extended job search," during which they were expected to fill out six employment applications a month and to address deficiencies in their employability. (In practice, sanctions for all three groups appear to have been rare.) The usual expenditure subsidies for travel, work clothes, and child care were available. Subsidies could continue for up to three months after employment.

2. JTPA controls were referred to the local Job Training Partnership Act agency. If found "appropriate" for on-the-job training (OJT), they could be placed with a private employer, who would receive a 50 percent subsidy on their wages (always the legal minimum) for a period not to exceed six months. If not found suitable, they were referred back to WIN.

3. TRADE experimentals were also referred to JTPA. If found "appropriate" for OJT, they could be placed with a private employer who received both the 50 percent JTPA subsidy and an additional $1.10 an hour subsidy from diversion of AFDC grants. Thus, an hour's work, at the minimum wage, would cost the employer 58 cents.

OUTCOMES OF INTEREST: (1) Unsubsidized employment; (2) Increase in JTPA placements of AFDC recipients; and (3) AFDC payments.

SAMPLE SIZE: TRADE experimentals, 2,617; JTPA controls, 1,024; WIN controls, 934.

TARGET POPULATION: WIN-mandatory and WIN-voluntary female clients. Usual exemptions for children under six, illness, or disability.

NUMBER OF TREATMENT GROUPS: Three (with two control groups).

NUMBER AND LOCATION OF SITES: 17 of the state's 24 JTPA agencies, covering most of the population of Florida.

RESEARCH COMPONENTS:

Process analysis: Conducted. Based on staff interviews and a survey questionnaire to subjects and employers.

Impact analysis: Conducted as a difference in means.
Benefit–cost analysis: Cost-effectiveness analysis.

MAJOR FINDINGS:

1. The evaluators found statistically significant differences between TRADE and JTPA subjects on the one hand, and WIN controls on the other, in months on AFDC, employment, and earnings. They found no differences between TRADE experimentals and JTPA controls. These findings are all based on extremely small samples (see "Design Issues").

2. Only 9 percent of the TRADE experimentals were actually placed in OJT, compared with 7.5 percent of the JTPAs and 5.8 percent of the WIN controls. One-third of the TRADE placements were without the special $1.10 subsidy. The program goal was OJT placement of one-half of all experimentals.

3. Cost-effectiveness analysis suggests savings from the program, but the analysts themselves say the data are not adequate to support any firm conclusions.

TIME TRENDS IN FINDINGS: Not applicable.

DESIGN ISSUES:

1. Twenty-seven percent of experimentals, 25 percent of JTPA controls, and 23 percent of WIN controls appeared in the Job Training Partnership Act (JTPA) Information system. The implication for the first two groups is that the majority of "clients were never referred to the SDAs [JTPA agencies], were referred but did not go, or were referred but were not registered. . . ." The WIN controls should not have appeared in the system. The implication of their appearance there is that "participants went to the SDAs on their own, or were inappropriately referred to them." Breakdown of WIN supervision and/or the random assignment system appears very likely, especially since some WIN personnel with TRADE responsibilities reported that they had received no training or direction in the program.

2. The DHRS information system on the subjects of the experiment could not be utilized "due to the lack of accurate and available data in the system on key indicators."

3. For some reason, which the report does not explain, the evaluators obtained the unemployment insurance and AFDC payment records of only a random sample of subjects, not the entire research sample. "Sufficient information was available for only 125 TRADE group participants, 99 JTPA group participants, and 126 WIN group par-

ticipants." The data used came from the routine quality control audit performed on a random sample of the welfare population.

4. The report is quite vague on what difference was supposed to exist between the treatment of JTPA controls by the SDAs and the treatment of TRADE experimentals. The SDA staffs refused to attempt to place people in OJT who were "inappropriate" because they lacked skills, training, or education. But the lack of these attributes was presumably the rationale for the deep wage subsidy. The leading cause for the lack of placements, however, was that the experimentals never showed up at the SDA offices.

5. The report seems to have been hastily assembled.

REPLICABILITY: Not replicable because of the lack of clarity cited in "Design Issues," number 4.

GENERALIZABILITY: Interagency coordination failure severely limits the generalizability of the findings. Other wage subsidy experiments, however, also have found very low employer responsiveness.

FUNDING SOURCE: U.S. Department of Health and Human Services, Office of Family Assistance.

TREATMENT ADMINISTRATORS: Florida Department of Health and Rehabilitative Services and local JTPA agencies. Key personnel: Jim Clark.

EVALUATOR: The experiment was designed by Manpower Demonstration Research Corporation, which is not associated with the evaluation. The latter was performed by the Florida Department of Health and Rehabilitative Services, Office of the Inspector General, Office of Evaluation and Management Review. Key personnel: Dawn Case.

ENABLING LEGISLATION: Florida Public Assistance Productivity Act.

INFORMATION SOURCES: Florida Department of Health and Rehabilitative Services (DHRS), Office of the Inspector General, Office of Evaluation and Management Review, "Evaluation of the TRADE Welfare for Work Program," February 1987.

PUBLIC-USE ACCESS TO DATA: Public-use access does not exist.

NEW JERSEY GRANT DIVERSION PROJECT

SUMMARY: This demonstration, conducted from 1984 to 1987, tested the effects of subsidized on-the-job training on a large sample of AFDC recipients. Subjects were followed for one year.

COST: See introduction to "State Welfare-to-Work Initiatives." Administrative cost of $921 per experimental, or about $910,000 (1985).

TIME FRAME: Demonstration period, October 1984–June 1987; data collected through August 1987; final report, November 1988.

TREATMENT TESTED: Experimentals were allowed to volunteer for on-the-job training (OJT) with private-sector employers. Fity percent of wages were subsidized through diversion of the AFDC grant. Controls were not offered this opportunity, but remained eligible for other WIN services.

OUTCOMES OF INTEREST: (1) Employment; (2) Earnings; and (3) AFDC recipiency and payments.

SAMPLE SIZE: Experimentals, 988; controls, 955. Much of the analysis, however, is based on a subsample of 508 experimentals and 488 controls, the "early sample."

TARGET POPULATION: Job-ready, WIN-eligible AFDC recipients.

NUMBER OF TREATMENT GROUPS: Two (with one control group).

NUMBER AND LOCATION OF SITES: Nine counties in New Jersey (Atlantic, Burlington, Camden, Essex, Hudson, Mercer, Middlesex, Monmouth, and Passaic), which include all the major cities.

RESEARCH COMPONENTS:
   Process analysis: Conducted.
   Impact analysis: Conducted with OLS regressions.
   Benefit–cost analysis: Conducted.

MAJOR FINDINGS:
1. "Nearly 43 percent of all experimentals worked at some point in an OJT position." The low rate of placement (200 a year) was attributed to various factors, one of them being the high turnover rate among job developers. About half of the placements completed the prescribed subsidy period (averaging 10 weeks), and nearly all of those who completed the subsidy period were retained by the employer without subsidy.
2. The treatment led to substantial employment gains in the first two quarters for experimentals versus controls. The impact essentially vanished by the fourth quarter.
3. The treatment "produced a statistically significant earnings gain of $634 during the first year after random assignment. Average earnings for experimentals were 22 percent higher than average earnings for controls." In combination with the first finding, this suggests that "experimentals worked in jobs that either paid more

or provided more hours of employment than the jobs in which controls were employed."

4. "Experimentals spent fewer months on AFDC and received $265 less in welfare payments than controls during the first year after random assignment." The difference is statistically significant.

5. Benefit–cost Analysis: "Over a five-year period, enrollees . . . are likely to benefit by an estimated $971 to $1,554 per person. . . . From the perspective of government budgets, the program can be expected to pay for itself within about two and one-half years. Net savings of between $601 and $1,284 are likely over a five-year period" (Freedman et al. 1988).

TIME TRENDS IN FINDINGS: Experimental/control differences in employment were insignificant in the early sample. In quarters five through seven, however, experimentals averaged $468 more in earnings than did controls and $238 less in AFDC payments. This latter difference was declining.

DESIGN ISSUES: The early sample was less disadvantaged than the remaining cohorts, because of improvements in the overall unemployment picture in the state and because Hudson and Middlesex counties, which joined the experiment later than the other seven, had higher numbers of very disadvantaged recipients.

REPLICABILITY: Replicable in principle, but the treatment is complex.

GENERALIZABILITY: A well-run OJT program funded by grant diversion in a state with low unemployment could be an effective but very limited part of the overall welfare strategy in other states as well. WIN registration in the nine counties averaged about 80,000 per month. About 20 OJT placements per month were made.

FUNDING SOURCES: See introduction to "State Welfare-to-Work Initiatives."

TREATMENT ADMINISTRATORS: New Jersey Department of Human Services (DHS) and the New Jersey Department of Labor (DOL). Key personnel: Sybil Stokes, Rowena Bopp (DHS), and Sally Hall (state DOL).

EVALUATOR: Manpower Demonstration Research Corporation. Key personnel: Stephen Freedman.

ENABLING LEGISLATION: OBRA.

POLICY EFFECTS: See introduction to "State Welfare-to-Work Initiatives."

INFORMATION SOURCES: Stephen Freedman, Jan Bryant, and George Cave, New Jersey: Final Report of the Grant Diversion Project, Manpower Demonstration Research Corporation, November 1988.

PUBLIC-USE ACCESS TO DATA: Public-use access does not exist.

COOK COUNTY JOB SEARCH AND WORK EXPERIENCE

SUMMARY: This demonstration, conducted from 1985 to 1987, tested the effects of mandatory training and work experience on a large sample of AFDC recipients. Subjects were followed for two years.

COST: Estimated incremental cost per experimental: Group 1, $157; group 2, $127 (about $636,000 and $515,000 [1985], respectively).

TIME FRAME: Demonstration period, February 1985–September 1985; data collected, February 1985–March 1987; final report, November 1987.

TREATMENTS TESTED:
1. Experimental group 1 was assigned first to WIN orientation and Independent Job Search (IJS), under which they were expected to contact 20 potential employers a month on their own; progress was monitored in biweekly two-hour group meetings. If unsuccessful in finding work, members were assigned thereafter to any of the other program components: the IWEP (Illinois Work Experience Program, i.e., Workfare), Preemployment (educational- or vocational-skills training programs), or Modified Job Search (a holding status). However, the program staff did not emphasize alternatives other than the IWEP. Program staff were evaluated largely on the basis of the grant reductions they achieved, and tended to sanction recipients automatically for failure to satisfy program requirements.
2. Experimental group 2 was assigned in the same manner as group 1, except for exclusion from the IWEP.

   Controls were required to attend orientation (they could be sanctioned for failure to attend), but were eligible thereafter only for support services if they were independently involved in educational or training activities.

OUTCOMES OF INTEREST: (1) Employment; (2) Earnings; and (3) AFDC payments.

SAMPLE SIZE: Group 1, 4,050; group 2, 4,057; controls, 3,805.

TARGET POPULATION: WIN-eligible AFDC recipients (but not AFDC-U recipients).

NUMBER OF TREATMENT GROUPS: Three (with one control group).

NUMBER AND LOCATION OF SITES: Cook County, Illinois.

RESEARCH COMPONENTS:
Process analysis: Conducted.
Impact analysis: Comparison of means and ordinary least squares (OLS) regressions.
Benefit–cost analysis: Conducted.

MAJOR FINDINGS:
1. Experimental/control differences in employment and earnings were not statistically significant.
2. Average AFDC payments, six quarters: Group 1, $4,416; group 2, $4,346; controls, $4,486. Differences of $70 and $140, respectively, are statistically significant. According to the project report, "The welfare savings were achieved mainly through closing welfare grants, rather than from reductions in the dollar amounts of grants that remained open. There does not appear to be any clear additional effect from the IWEP component over and above the effect of IJS."
3. "The reduction in AFDC and Medicaid expenditures, combined with the very low cost of the program, led to a net savings for the government. However, the welfare recipients assigned to the program did not benefit financially . . . since the losses in AFDC and Medicaid equaled or exceeded any earnings gains that might have occurred."
4. Among controls, 7.6 percent were sanctioned for failing to attend the WIN orientation. Among experimentals, 11.7 percent had been sanctioned within nine months after intake, either for failing to attend the WIN orientation or for failing to satisfy subsequent program requirements.
5. The project report authors could only speculate about the source of the AFDC savings, since they occurred in the absence of any earnings increase. Staff were more familiar with experimentals' activities, and therefore initiated more grant reduction actions because they learned of new employment more quickly. Also, the IJS program required regular attendance at various tasks, and may have served as a deterrent to continued recipiency for experimen-

tals with unreported income. Controls with unreported income had no such deterrent.

TIME TRENDS IN FINDINGS: Group 1 (Workfare) experimentals had higher AFDC payments, a tendency that seemed to grow over time.

DESIGN ISSUES:

1. A sufficiently strong deterrent effect from the treatments might have sent experimentals across state lines, causing a possible attrition bias not addressed here.
2. The higher motivation of the administrative staff to generate AFDC payment savings in this experiment compared with the other experiments is worth noting. It might explain why this experiment detected such savings, whereas many of the others did not.

REPLICABILITY: Replicable.

GENERALIZABILITY: The demonstration took place in two-thirds of the WIN offices of Cook County, which includes Chicago. This represents a large urban population.

FUNDING SOURCES: Ford Foundation and Illinois Department of Public Aid. Key personnel: Gordon Berlin, the Ford Foundation.

TREATMENT ADMINISTRATOR: Illinois Department of Public Aid. Key personnel: Randale Valenti.

EVALUATOR: Manpower Demonstration Research Corporation. Key personnel: Daniel Friedlander.

ENABLING LEGISLATION: OBRA.

POLICY EFFECTS: See introduction to "State Welfare-to-Work Initiatives." Illinois subsequently changed the focus of its WIN program from the techniques employed in this experiment to a greater encouragement of education and training and less frequent application of sanctions.

INFORMATION SOURCES: Daniel Friedlander, Stephen Freedman, Gayle Hamilton, and Janet Quint, "Illinois: Final Report on Job Search and Work Experience in Cook County," Manpower Development Research Corp., November 1987.

PUBLIC-USE ACCESS TO DATA: Public-use access does not exist.

SATURATION WORK INITIATIVE MODEL (SWIM)

SUMMARY: This demonstration, conducted from 1983 to 1988, tested the effects of mandatory job search assistance and work experience on a large sample of AFDC recipients. Subjects were followed for two years.

COST: See introduction to "State Welfare-to-Work Initiatives."

TIME FRAME: July 1985–September 1987; data collected, July 1985–March 1988; final report, November 1989.

TREATMENTS TESTED:

1. Experimentals received a fixed program sequence. They were initially assigned to a two-week job search workshop. Those who had not found jobs at the end of two weeks were assigned to three months of unpaid work experience and biweekly Job Club sessions. Those still unemployed after completing the work experience assignment were assessed and possibly referred to community education and training programs, which were not part of the experiment proper.
2. Controls received no services from the experiment.

OUTCOMES OF INTEREST: (1) Employment; (2) Earnings; and (3) Welfare receipt.

SAMPLE SIZE: Experimentals, 1,604; controls, 1,607.

TARGET POPULATION: WIN eligibles (single heads of AFDC households with children aged six or older, principal earners of two-parent AFDC-U households), both registrants and new applicants.

NUMBER OF TREATMENT GROUPS: Two (with one control group).

NUMBER AND LOCATION OF SITES: One—San Diego, California.

RESEARCH COMPONENTS:
   Process analysis: Conducted.
   Impact analysis: Conducted with ordinary least squares (OLS) regressions.
   Benefit–cost analysis: Conducted.

MAJOR FINDINGS:

1. "For AFDC (regular) registrants, SWIM led to sustained gains in employment and earnings and sustained reductions in welfare receipt and payments. During the 2 years following random assignment, experimentals had average earnings of $4,932 and controls had average earnings of $3,923, for a program effect of $1,009, a 26 percent increase over the control group mean. Over these 2 years, 63 percent of experimentals were employed at some point compared to 51 percent of controls, a 12 percentage point improvement. The data suggest that most of the earnings gains resulted from increased employment among experimentals rather than greater earnings during employment. For AFDC recipients—the more disadvantaged part of the sample—the employment and earnings impacts were strong and sustained; for AFDC applicants, ini-

tial employment and earnings gains declined substantially by the end of the follow-up period."

2. "During the follow-up period, experimentals received $8,590 in welfare payments, $1,097 less than the control group mean payments of $9,687, a savings of 11 percent. By the end of the follow-up period, 48 percent of experimentals were receiving welfare payments compared to 55 percent of controls, a 7 percentage point reduction in welfare use. Both applicants and recipients experienced sustained welfare grant reductions."

3. The experimental treatment appeared to raise earnings and lower welfare payments for AFDC-U recipients. However, sample sizes were small.

4. "Net program costs were $919 per AFDC experimental and $817 per AFDC-U experimental. . . . Over the five-year period (which includes projections) SWIM produced substantial net savings for governmental budgets, amounting to more than $1,500 per experimental among both AFDC and AFDC-U registrants (Hamilton and Friedlander 1989)."

5. From the perspective of all subjects, the treatment had little effect on net income over the five-year period, suggesting that earnings increases and welfare reductions were roughly offsetting. However, some subgroups had net gains and others net losses.

TIME TRENDS IN FINDINGS: Experimental/control differences among recipients did not seem to diminish over time, although these differences did diminish over time among applicants.

DESIGN ISSUES:
1. San Diego County volunteered to perform this program. It was a natural outgrowth of existing rigorous welfare employment programs, which enjoy widespread political support. Possible site self-selection bias.

2. Program operated in a tight labor market.

REPLICABILITY: Replicable.

GENERALIZABILITY: See "Design Issues."

FUNDING SOURCES: See introduction to "State Welfare-to-Work Initiatives." Key personnel: For California, Steve Munro.

TREATMENT ADMINISTRATOR: Welfare Department of San Diego County. Key personnel: John Robbins.

EVALUATOR: Manpower Demonstration Research Corporation. Key personnel: Gayle Hamilton.

ENABLING LEGISLATION: See introduction to "State Welfare-to-Work Initiatives."

POLICY EFFECTS: See introduction to "State Welfare-to-Work Initiatives."

INFORMATION SOURCES: Gayle Hamilton, *Interim Report on the Saturation Work Initiative Model in San Diego*, Manpower Demonstration Research Corporation, August 1988; Gayle Hamilton and Daniel Friedlander, *Final Report on the Saturation Work Initiative Model*, Manpower Demonstration Research Corporation, November 1989.

PUBLIC-USE ACCESS TO DATA: Public-use file exists; contact MDRC about *Welfare Employment Studies* 1 through 4.

References

Baum, Erica B. 1991. "When the Witch Doctors Agree: The Family Support Act and Social Science Research." *JPAM* 10 (4, Fall): 603–615.

Szanton, Peter L. 1991. " 'The Remarkable Quango': Knowledge, Politics and Welfare Reform." *JPAM* 10 (4, Fall): 590–602.

AFDC JOB COUNSELORS

SUMMARY: This demonstration, conducted from 1976 to 1979, tested the effects of employment counseling and placement resistance on a large sample of "inactive" WIN clients. Subjects were followed for 90 days.

COST: Research only, $164,400 (1977).

TIME FRAME: Demonstration Period, September 1976–January 1979; data collected, September 1976–January 1979; final report, December 1979.

TREATMENT TESTED:

1. Controls received certain minimal services (counseling without job referral in Oakland County, no counseling in Wayne County) from WIN.
2. Experimentals received an orientation in the Private Employment Agency (PEA) placement program, and, in general, one PEA received information on each subject's education, skills, and interests. The PEA would ask the subject to come for an interview, and if the PEA felt it could match the subject with appropriate jobs, would refer her to employers. PEA fees were paid by the state for successful placements, based on starting salaries, with lower fees where the job duration was less than 90 days.

OUTCOMES OF INTEREST: (1) Employment; (2) Duration of employment; (3) Wages; and (4) AFDC payment reductions.

SAMPLE SIZE: Experimentals, 2,593; controls, 1,691.

TARGET POPULATION: "Inactive" WIN clients: clients not actively receiving employment services from WIN because they were regarded as relatively less employable.

NUMBER OF TREATMENT GROUPS: Two (with one control group).

NUMBER AND LOCATION OF SITES: Wayne County (including Detroit) and Oakland County (including Pontiac), Michigan. Inner-city Detroit had a high unemployment rate and a predominantly black AFDC population. Oakland County is suburban with a predominantly white AFDC population.

RESEARCH COMPONENTS:

Process analysis: Conducted with an emphasis on explaining the low placement rate.

Impact analysis: Conducted with probit.

Benefit–cost analysis: Cost-effectiveness only.

MAJOR FINDINGS:

1. Placement rates for experimentals were very low, in part because most experimentals never came to the PEA for an interview. In fact, over half never came to the initial orientation.

Employment outcomes (PEA placement rates in parentheses):

	Oakland County (%)			Wayne County (%)		
	Experimentals		Controls	Experimentals		Controls
Full-time jobs	19.4	(3.5)	19.0	5.3	(2.0)	3.2
Part-time jobs	8.9	(0.2)	9.5	3.5	(0.0)	2.3
All jobs	27.4	(3.7)	27.4	8.6	(2.0)	5.5

2. The finding of no significant treatment impact in Oakland County is confirmed by a probit analysis. In Wayne County, the probability of employment, adjusted for personal characteristics, increases by a statistically significant 2.8 percent.

3. Costs per placement were $1,222 in Oakland County and $2,310 in Wayne County, but the PEA fees were only $341 and $385, respectively. The remainder of the costs were associated with the public administration side, and would have been lower per placement if the placement rate had been higher. In Oakland County, there was no significant difference in cost-effectiveness between the experimental and control treatments. In Wayne County, the experimental treatment was significantly less cost-effective because of its high costs.

TIME TRENDS IN FINDINGS: None reported.

REPLICABILITY: Replicable.

GENERALIZABILITY: The experiment is tested on a large urban population, characteristic of much of the national AFDC population. The findings could not be generalized to a similar program where there were sanctions for nonparticipation.

FUNDING SOURCE: U.S. Department of Health and Human Services, Family Support Administration. Key personnel: Ken Manihan.

TREATMENT ADMINISTRATOR: Michigan Department of Social Services. Key personnel: Robert Cecil.

EVALUATOR: Mathematica Policy Research. Key personnel: George J. Carcagno and James C. Ohls.

ENABLING LEGISLATION: None.

POLICY EFFECTS: According to Robert Cecil, the use of private employment agencies has been incorporated as an option, subject to local administrative discretion, for appropriate AFDC clients in Michigan, but is seldom chosen.

INFORMATION SOURCES: George J. Carcagno, Robert Cecil, and James C. Ohls, "Using Private Employment Agencies to Place Welfare Clients in Jobs," *Journal of Human Resources*, Winter 1982: 132–143.

PUBLIC-USE ACCESS TO DATA: We have no information about a public-use file for this demonstration.

COLORADO MONTHLY REPORTING EXPERIMENT AND PRETEST

SUMMARY: This demonstration, conducted from 1976 to 1979, tested the effects of monthly income reporting on a large sample of AFDC recipients. Subjects were followed for two years.

COST: $3.5 million (1977); $1.5 million for research.

TIME FRAME: Demonstration period, 1976–79; data collected, same years; final report, 1980.

TREATMENTS TESTED:
1. For controls subject to the existing AFDC system, there was a six-month eligibility determination and the expectation that they would inform caseworkers of changes in their circumstances, but there was no systematic device to report and monitor such changes.
2. Experimentals were required to submit monthly reports on income and household composition, and monthly grants were adjusted on

the basis of the report for the prior month. Failure to meet reporting deadlines or incomplete/inconsistent reporting would lead to delays in payment or, ultimately, to discontinuation.

OUTCOMES OF INTEREST: (1) Reductions in overall payments; (2) Impact of reporting on recipients; (3) Increases in administrative costs; and (4) Responsiveness of grants to changes in family circumstances.

SAMPLE SIZE: Experimentals, 1,825; controls, 1,841.

TARGET POPULATION: AFDC-regular (AFDC-R) and AFDC-unemployed-parent (AFDC-U) recipients.

NUMBER OF TREATMENT GROUPS: Two.

NUMBER AND LOCATION OF SITES: One—Denver, Colorado.

RESEARCH COMPONENTS:
    Process analysis: Conducted. Concerns centered on the ability of recipients to complete forms and on the effects on caseworkers. The difference between the findings of the early and the later reports is partly attributable to a change in the treatment of controls by the agency, which moved to regular in-person redeterminations for the whole nonexperimental caseload four months after the experiment began. The policy change coincided with an increase in discontinuance rates among controls and a decline in savings from monthly reporting. Other changes at that time (increasing automation of paperwork for the nonexperimental caseload, reductions in caseload per worker for controls but not experimentals) probably had a similar direction of impact on the experiment.
    Impact analysis: Conducted. Comparison of means. Subsequent regression study of characteristics of discontinued households.
    Benefit–cost analysis: Budgetary analysis only.

MAJOR FINDINGS:
1. Early findings were a 4.3 percent reduction in AFDC-R payments and a 5.6 percent reduction in AFDC-U payments. The primary cause was a higher rate of discontinuation, somewhat offset by higher rates of reapproval. Ninety-six percent of report forms were returned, but 44 percent of all treatment recipients had to wait at least an additional seven days for payment at least once during the first year owing to reporting errors, mainly of income. Grant changes other than discontinuations happened much more frequently in the treatment groups: increases were five times more frequent, and decreases were 2.2 times more frequent. An approximate 4% increase in administrative costs was found (from a nonexperimental demonstration in Boulder), or about one-twelfth the

calculated savings in payments. Eligibility staff believed the experimental process was fairer than the prior one, and, overall, improved their work and working conditions.

2. Later findings contradicted the earlier ones. Payment reductions over two years were about 1.8 percent, and in the second year were -0.7 percent. Investigators attributed the difference between the first and second-year results to improved administration of the control group by the Denver office during the second period, using regular in-person reviews of case circumstances. Monthly savings of 15 percent were reported for the one-quarter of AFDC-R households who ever reported earnings and were zero for the three-quarters of the caseload who never did. Changes in the administration of controls made administrative costs difficult to estimate.

TIME TRENDS IN FINDINGS: In the 1979 project report, the effects of the system were markedly higher for new AFDC applicants than for prior recipients. This was confirmed in the 1982 report: two-year estimates overstated the long-run impact on payments because the major impact was on new recipients, not on longer-run cases.

DESIGN ISSUES: Problems in the administration of the experiment occurred:

1. Some households received payments as experimentals in the first assistance spell, as controls in a subsequent spell, and vice versa.
2. Several assigned experimental cases were channeled into the control group because agency workers believed they were short-term cases.
3. Payment dates differed between the two systems, so that a pay-date difference could account for some of any observed impact.
4. Experimental cases were supposed to receive transition payments to cover the three weeks between their initial prospective payment and their first retrospective payment, but these checks were not always issued. An evident potential problem in the experiment was the self-selection of the Denver social services agency.

REPLICABILITY: Dependent on sophisticated computer hardware and software.

GENERALIZABILITY: Impact would probably vary inversely with the degree of aggressiveness already present in caseload management techniques used in the different states and counties.

FUNDING SOURCE: U.S. Department of Health and Human Services, Assistant Secretary for Planning and Evaluation. Key personnel: John Bayne.

TREATMENT ADMINISTRATOR: Colorado Department of Social Services. Key personnel: Jacob Shockley and Joseph Thompson.

EVALUATOR: Mathematica Policy Research. Key personnel: Robert G. Williams, Alan M. Hershey, and John A. Burghardt.

ENABLING LEGISLATION: Waivers of Colorado State Plan.

POLICY EFFECTS: Alan Hershey has stated that monthly reporting was incorporated into all AFDC and Food Stamp programs in the country, based on the early findings.

INFORMATION SOURCES: Robert G. Williams, David L. Horner, Alan M. Hershey, and Nancy L. Graham, First Year Research Results, Colorado Monthly Reporting Experiment and Pretest, Mathematica Policy Research, 1979; and John A. Burghardt, Impact of a Monthly Retrospective Reporting Requirement on AFDC-Benefit Payments: Evidence from the Second Year of the Colorado Monthly Reporting Experiment, Mathematica Policy Research, 1982.

PUBLIC-USE ACCESS TO DATA: We have no information about a public-use file for this demonstration.

WIN JOB-FINDING CLUBS

SUMMARY: This demonstration, conducted from 1976 to 1978, tested the effects of mandatory supervised group job search training and assistance on a medium-sized sample of Work Incentive Program registrants. Subjects were followed for one year.

COST: Administrative costs of the program at the three sites where a counselor was assigned full-time to the Job Club treatment were $167 per placement, excluding office rent and furniture. Multiplying by the number of placements (300) at all five sites yields $50,100 (1977), excluding counselor-training and research costs. However, the participants would have received some treatment in any case, and Elise Bruml, in an internal DOL memorandum, estimated $87 per experimental, which would mean $42,369 (1977). The cost of research only was roughly $300,000 (1977).

TIME FRAME: Demonstration period, September 1976–March 1978; data collected, essentially the same period; final report, 1978.

TREATMENTS TESTED:
1. Controls received whatever regular WIN (Work Incentive) program Intensive Manpower Service regime was in use at that site, such as counseling, training, subsidized job placement, and referrals to agency listings. The Wichita regime included group counseling and role-playing. Because the control regime was not standardized across sites, it is safest to assume five different control groups. The more conservative assumption does not materially affect the findings.
2. Experimentals received daily group job search training and supervised job search until a job was obtained. Further detail is given in the "Carbondale Job Club" summary later in this *Digest* (p. 303). Both controls and experimentals received $1.50 plus carfare per session attended.

OUTCOMES OF INTEREST: Employment.

SAMPLE SIZE: Experimentals, 487; controls, 490.

TARGET POPULATION: Registrants for the WIN (Work Incentive) program. Exclusions from this population varied by site. Wichita, Tacoma, and New Brunswick only enrolled "job-ready clients"; New York excluded "non-English speakers, illiterates, and clients already designated to receive training or counseling"; Milwaukee made no exclusions.

NUMBER OF TREATMENT GROUPS: Ten (one experimental and one control group at each site).

NUMBER AND LOCATION OF SITES: Five—New York City (Harlem); New Brunswick, New Jersey; Milwaukee, Wisconsin; Wichita, Kansas; and Tacoma, Washington.

RESEARCH COMPONENTS:
Process analysis: After training, the counselors were observed by the experimenters for the first few sessions of their initial Job Club groups to ensure general adherence to the experimental program. Experimentals also received all services from a single counselor; controls might receive them from several.
Impact analysis: Conducted as a difference in means.
Benefit–cost analysis: Not conducted.

MAJOR FINDINGS:
1. Employment (over 20 hours/week) after three months:

City	Experimentals	Controls
New York	56%	35%
New Brunswick	63%	30%
Tacoma	72%	39%
Wichita	60%	39%
Milwaukee	54%	12%
Mean starting wage (per week)	$137	$137

2. Effects were statistically significant for all groupings (by sex, age, education, ethnic group) except Hispanics.
3. Job Club effects were much stronger for mandatory participants (participation was a condition of continued receipt of AFDC) than for voluntary participants (83 percent of the sample were mandatories). This might have to do with the mandatory aspect or to the fact that volunteers generally had children less than six years old, whereas mandatories had older children.
4. Twenty-one percent of all jobs obtained by controls were temporary, compared with 16 percent of experimentals' jobs; 25 percent of controls' jobs were subsidized, compared with 16 percent of experimentals'.
5. AFDC payments to experimentals six months after enrollment were reduced by 48 percent; payments to controls were down by 15 percent.

TIME TRENDS IN FINDINGS: Follow-up questionnaires had a fairly poor response rate. Six-month differences from those who did respond do not show a drop-off in the experimental effect.

DESIGN ISSUES:
1. Job Club counselors were selected for training by their local WIN agency, probably not randomly. Their performance, at least initially, was more closely observed than that of their peers; thus a differential Hawthorne effect is a possibility.
2. At the same time, this observation was clearly necessary to standardize the treatment. Implementing the "Job Club model" on a larger scale would require extensive training and supervision.

REPLICABILITY: Replicable.

GENERALIZABILITY: This study would seem to generalize the earlier experiments for an important and relatively homogeneous group.

FUNDING SOURCE: U.S. Department of Labor, Employment and Training Administration. Key personnel: Unknown.

TREATMENT ADMINISTRATOR: WIN agencies of five states, all of whom are receiving training from the Anna Mental Health Center. Key personnel: Personnel at different agencies.

EVALUATOR: Anna Mental Health Center. Key personnel: Nathan H. Azrin.

ENABLING LEGISLATION: None.

POLICY EFFECTS: Nathan Azrin has stated that the Job Club became a requirement of the WIN program.

INFORMATION SOURCES: Nathan H. Azrin, Robert A. Philip, P. Thienes-Hontos, and V. A. Besalel, "Comparative Evaluation of the Job Club Program with Welfare Recipients," *Journal of Vocational Behavior,* 1980: 133–145; ibid., "Follow-up on Welfare Benefits Received by Job Club Clients," *Journal of Vocational Behavior,* 1981: 253–54.

PUBLIC-USE ACCESS TO DATA: We have no information about a public-use file for this demonstration.

DAYTON WAGE-SUBSIDY VOUCHER EXPERIMENT

SUMMARY: This demonstration, conducted from 1980 to 1981, tested the effects of a tax credit voucher for employers or a direct cash subsidy to employers on a medium-sized sample of welfare recipients. Subjects were followed for one year.

COST: It is not possible to separate the cost of the experiment from the cost of the Employment Opportunities Pilot Project (EOPP), a large-scale demonstration of employment and training initiatives under the Carter administration that was aborted by the Reagan administration in May 1981. Burtless has stated that his best guess as to the incremental cost of the experiment, beyond that of the EOPP, would be well under $500,000 (1980), largely for the research design. A second experiment also planned under the EOPP was never started, again because the new administration canceled it.

TIME FRAME: December 1980–May 1981; data collected, same period; no final report exists. A Brookings Institution working version of the cited article is dated August 31, 1984.

TREATMENTS TESTED:
1. Tax credit voucher. These experimentals received a Job-Club-type treatment. They were also given both vouchers, which employers could use to obtain credits on their tax returns, and training and written materials on using this subsidy to good advantage in their job search. The credit was good for 50 percent of wages paid in the first year of employment, with the total credit not to exceed $3,000, and 25 percent of wages in the second year of employment, with total credit not to exceed $1,500.
2. Direct cash subsidy. These experimentals received the same treatment as the first group, except that the subsidy was to be paid quarterly directly by the program operator, without regard to the employer's tax liability.
3. Controls. Controls received the Job Club treatment, but no voucher. They received instead a one-day course in using Job Bank listings at the local employment service (a placebo treatment). They were not told that they were eligible for wage subsidies (although by law they were).

OUTCOMES OF INTEREST: (1) Placement in an unsubsidized job; and (2) Initial wage.

SAMPLE SIZE: Tax credit group, 247; direct cash group, 299; controls, 262.

TARGET POPULATION: There were two: (1) Recipients of general assistance, typically single, or if a member of a couple, childless ("many were only temporarily destitute"); and (2) AFDC recipients, whose participation was not mandatory. However, many of those referred were WIN mandatories who had been unsuccessful in other WIN activities.

NUMBER OF TREATMENT GROUPS: Three (with one control group).

NUMBER AND LOCATION OF SITES: Montgomery County, Ohio, which includes Dayton.

RESEARCH COMPONENTS:
Process analysis: Not conducted because the experiment was canceled. Data are available only on those who had completed an eight-week cycle (two weeks of Job Club and six weeks of job search, for experimentals) as of that date.
Impact analysis: Conducted as a difference in means.
Benefit–cost analysis: Not conducted.

MAJOR FINDINGS:
1. Job placement rates. Controls, 20.6 percent; tax credit group, 13.0 percent; direct cash group, 12.7 percent. The advantage of the controls over the experimentals is statistically significant.
2. Use of the vouchers. Of 70 voucher-holders who found employment, only 19 worked for firms that requested certification for wage subsidies.
3. Initial wage rate. Average initial wages in all three groups were nearly identical.
4. Job-finding rates of AFDC and general assistance groups were almost equal. "When economically disadvantaged workers are clearly identified to potential employers as disadvantaged (by a subsidy offer), their chances of employment are harmed."

TIME TRENDS IN FINDINGS: No data available beyond eight weeks.

DESIGN ISSUES:
1. The experiment was conducted during a period of high and growing unemployment in the local area.
2. It is likely that marginally employable welfare recipients are not in a good position to explain and market their own wage subsidies. It is possible that job developers could improve on the results found here, but it is not clear that this improvement would be sufficient to justify the subsidy itself.
3. The absence of process analysis means that no documentation exists on any extraneous influences that might contaminate the findings.

REPLICABILITY: Replicable.

GENERALIZABILITY: The experiment took place in a depressed region, and its abrupt termination leaves open some questions about its administration. However, other experiments with wage subsidies (for example, the "Wage-Subsidy Variation Experiment," and the "Florida TRADE Welfare for Work" experiment) have results that are not inconsistent with those reported here.

FUNDING SOURCE: U.S. Department of Labor, Office of the Assistant Secretary for Policy, Evaluation and Research (ASPER). Key personnel: Gary Burtless, Larry L. Orr, and John Cheston.

TREATMENT ADMINISTRATOR: The CETA agency in Montgomery County, Ohio. Key personnel: Not available.

EVALUATOR: Mathematica Policy Research; U.S. Department of Labor, ASPER. Key personnel: The experiment was designed by John A. Burghardt, Gary Burtless, John Cheston, Larry Orr, and Harold Watts.

It was canceled by the Reagan administration at an early stage; Gary Burtless analyzed the limited data available, which had been collected by John Cheston.

ENABLING LEGISLATION: CETA (Comprehensive Employment and Training Act) Reauthorization Act of 1978.

INFORMATION SOURCES: Gary Burtless, "Are Targeted Wage Subsidies Harmful? Evidence from a Wage Voucher Experiment," *Industrial and Labor Relations Review*, October 1985: 105–14.

PUBLIC-USE ACCESS TO DATA: We have no information about a public-use file for this demonstration.

MONTHLY REPORTING IN THE AFDC PROGRAM

SUMMARY: This demonstration, conducted from 1981 to 1982, tested the effects of required monthly reporting of household information on a large sample of AFDC recipients. Subjects were followed for one year.

COST: Operations, $5.5 million; research, $3 million (1982).

TIME FRAME: Illinois, October 1981–September 1982; Massachusetts, August 1981–July 1982; data collected; same period; final report, September 1985.

TREATMENTS TESTED: Experimentals had to return a monthly report as a condition of continued receipt of AFDC. The report covered income received in the previous month and household composition. Payments for the following month (e.g., March) were determined by the report for the previous month (January). Thus, the accounting principle was retrospective. (Prospective accounting attempts to match grants to anticipated household needs.) Face-to-face redetermination of eligibility with a caseworker was conducted annually in Massachusetts; Illinois had no redetermination requirement.

Controls: Illinois conventionals faced retrospective accounting for income, prospective accounting for other factors, and semiannual face-to-face redeterminations. Monthly reports were required only for households with earnings.

Massachusetts had two controls. The conventionals faced retrospective accounting, semiannual redeterminations, and no regular reporting requirement. The voluntaries received a form each month that they had to return only if income or household composition had changed; accounting was prospective, and redeterminations were semiannual.

OUTCOMES OF INTEREST: (1) AFDC payments; (2) Caseloads; (3) Error rate; and (4) Administrative costs.

SAMPLE SIZE: Illinois: 7,000 experimentals, 3,600 controls; Massachusetts: 2,500 experimentals, 2,300 voluntary controls, 5,100 conventional controls.

TARGET POPULATION: AFDC-recipient households.

NUMBER OF TREATMENT GROUPS: A uniform experimental treatment was tested against controls that varied by state. Illinois had one control group; Massachusetts had two.

NUMBER AND LOCATION OF SITES: Two—Chicago, Illinois; Boston, Massachusetts.

RESEARCH COMPONENTS:

Process analysis: Conducted in both states, but more intensively in Illinois. Illinois encountered substantial problems with the automated data processing system that had been developed to support monthly reporting. These problems led to erroneous payments, inappropriate case closings, and a suspension of the policy of closing cases for failure to file reports. The fairness of the experimental treatment was studied with regard to terminations and the reporting burden. The investigators concluded that terminations for noncooperation occurred with roughly equal frequency in Illinois under both the experimental and control systems; the burden of reporting was minor for most experimentals in Illinois (seven minutes once they were used to it).

Impact analysis: Conducted as a difference in means.

Benefit–cost analysis: Effects on government budgets discussed.

MAJOR FINDINGS:

1. Effect on total payments over 12 months, experimentals versus conventionals: Illinois, + 4.3 percent; Massachusetts, − 1.9 percent. The Illinois figure is statistically significant; but for the second six months, when computer problems had been resolved, the measured impact was 0.6 percent, which was not statistically significant. The Massachusetts figure is not statistically significant.

2. Effect on caseload size over 12 months, experimentals versus conventionals: Illinois, + 3.0 percent, Massachusetts, − 2.7 percent. Both figures are statistically significant, but neither is important.

The Illinois figure for the second six months is +0.5 percent (not statistically significant). The Massachusetts reduction is concentrated around the fourth month of the experiment; "the policy of termination for failure to file was not implemented in Massachusetts until the fourth month of the demonstration. . . . A few months later, the caseloads under monthly reporting and the conventional system were approximately equal."

3. Effect on average AFDC payment size over 12 months, experimentals versus conventionals: Illinois +1.2 percent (statistically significant, but 1.0 percent and not significant the second six months); Massachusetts +0.8 percent (statistically significant). Monthly reporting led to more frequent grant adjustments; total increases exceeded total reductions.

4. Effects of voluntary change reporting in Massachusetts over 12 months, voluntary controls versus conventionals: No effects were statistically significant.

5. Effects on error rate in Illinois over 12 months, experimentals versus conventionals: Effects are not statistically significant.

6. Effects on administrative cost, experimentals versus conventionals: Net savings in Illinois of about $1 per case per month; net increase in Massachusetts of about $4.80 per case per month.

7. Net government expenditure effects, experimentals versus conventionals: Not statistically significant in either state.

8. Net government expenditure effects, voluntary controls versus conventional controls: Net increase of about $4.15 per case per month.

TIME TRENDS IN FINDINGS: Noted in "Major Findings."

DESIGN ISSUES: Illinois effects affected by computer problems noted above.

REPLICABILITY: Replicable.

GENERALIZABILITY: Sample sizes are very large. The substantial experimental effects in the Denver, Colorado, experiment were shown to be the consequence of the particular control treatment in that state at the time the experiment began. The effects of monthly reporting in large, urban, AFDC populations were shown in these experiments to be minor when compared with more-active welfare regimes. Although the effects on rural or medium-city populations are not tested, there is no obvious reason why they should be different.

FUNDING SOURCE: U.S. Department of Health and Human Services, Office of the Assistant Secretary for Planning and Evaluation. Key personnel: John Baine.

TREATMENT ADMINISTRATOR: Welfare Departments in Illinois and Massachusetts. Key personnel: Massachusetts officials no longer with the department; in Illinois, Stephen Spence.

EVALUATOR: Abt Associates. Key personnel: William L. Hamilton and Nancy R. Burstein.

ENABLING LEGISLATION: None.

POLICY EFFECTS: This study's finding that monthly reporting makes little difference was revealed after Congress had passed changes in the law making reporting mandatory. Since that time, the law has been revised in the direction of flexibility for the states. According to William Hamilton, state officials pressing for greater discretion probably cited the study's findings.

INFORMATION SOURCES: William L. Hamilton, "Monthly Reporting in the AFDC Program: Executive Summary of Demonstration Results," Abt Associates, September 1985.

PUBLIC-USE ACCESS TO DATA: No public-use file exists.

WASHINGTON STATE INTENSIVE APPLICANT EMPLOYMENT SERVICES EVALUATION

SUMMARY: This quasi-experimental demonstration, conducted from 1982 to 1983, tested the effects of offering immediate services to AFDC applicants and extending work search requirements on a large sample of AFDC applicants. Subjects were followed for up to 10 months.

COST: Cost figures not available.

TIME FRAME: Demonstration period, April 1982–April 1983; data collected, the same period; final report, June 1983.

TREATMENTS TESTED: The program provided counseling, job search assistance, day care, and transportation services to applicants for public assistance. At the same time, work search requirements were extended to include applicants as well as current AFDC recipients. Further, applicants with children ages 3–5 were required to participate in work search activities. The comparison group did not receive any services until they were actually recipients of public assistance. They were exempt from work search requirements until that time, and they were exempt if they had children under 6 years of age.

OUTCOMES OF INTEREST: (1) Application for, and participation in, AFDC; (2) Employment; (3) Earnings; and (4) Program costs.

SAMPLE SIZE: Total, 3,423; treatment, 1,802; comparison, 1,621.

TARGET POPULATION: AFDC applicants with children ages 3 or older.

NUMBER OF TREATMENT GROUPS: Two: treatment and matched-comparison.

NUMBER AND LOCATION OF SITES: Each of the Washington State Department of Social and Health Services' Community Service Offices (CSOs) was paired with another that was as similar as possible in terms of a number of variables (population, size, cost of living). A table of random numbers was used to determine which member of each pair became a treatment CSO and which became a comparison CSO. There were 20 treatment CSOs, 18 of which had a matched-comparison CSO.

RESEARCH COMPONENTS:
Process: Analysis of population data was used to examine project operations and applicant participation.
Impact: Comparison of means.
Benefit–cost analysis: A cost-effectiveness analysis was conducted.

MAJOR FINDINGS:
1. The program appeared to serve as a disincentive to applying for AFDC. The rate of growth in AFDC applications was three times lower in project areas than in comparison areas. The program also reduced the proportion of applicants who received AFDC grants. The difference was most pronounced in the first months after application, but persisted until at least the 10th month.
2. Average grants for nonexempt applicants were reduced by $142.10 per application annually. As a result, annual AFDC grant expenditures were $2.6 million lower than without the program.
3. Rates of employment and average earnings per applicant, as measured from unemployment compensation accounts, were not affected by the program.
4. After subtracting program costs, net annual program savings were $1.7 million. This is a return of $2.77 for each dollar spent.

TIME TRENDS IN FINDINGS: The program's effect on the proportion of applicants who received AFDC was greatest in the 1st month following application and was dissipating by the 10th month.

DESIGN ISSUES: The project report presented no information regarding the statistical significance of the findings or the use of statistical techniques that might have compensated for any initial differences between matched sites. This makes interpretation of the findings difficult.

REPLICABILITY: Replicable.

GENERALIZABILITY: Designed to generalize to the entire state of Washington. There are no obvious limitations on generalizability to this population.

FUNDING SOURCE: Washington State Department of Social and Health Services (DSHS), Division of Administration and Personnel, Office of Research and Data Analysis.

TREATMENT ADMINISTRATOR: Washington State DSHS.

EVALUATOR: Fred P. Fiedler, DSHS, Office of Research and Data Analysis.

ENABLING LEGISLATION: None.

INFORMATION SOURCES: Fred P. Fiedler, *Intensive Applicant Employment Services Evaluation*, Washington State Department of Social and Health Services, Division of Administration and Personnel, Olympia, July 1983.

PUBLIC-USE ACCESS TO DATA: Not available.

PENNSYLVANIA SATURATION WORK PROGRAM (PSWP)

SUMMARY: This demonstration, conducted from 1985 to 1987, tested the effects of intensive employment services on a large sample of welfare recipients. Subjects were followed for two years.

COST: Evaluation costs, $2.1 million.

TIME FRAME: Demonstration period, July 1985–September 1987. Final report, October 1989.

TREATMENTS TESTED: The PSWP was a mandatory program with sanctions for noncompliance. Services included individual case management, workshops, training and education, community work experience (CWEP), job clubs, and assistance with work plan development. The control group continued to receive existing County Assistance Office (CAO) services.

OUTCOMES OF INTEREST: (1) Employment; (2) Earnings; and (3) Welfare receipt.

SAMPLE SIZE: Total, 7,342; treatment, 4,024; control, 3,318.

TARGET POPULATION: Work-mandatory AFDC and AFDC-U claimants.

NUMBER OF TREATMENT GROUPS: Two (including control).

NUMBER AND LOCATION OF SITES: There were six district CAO offices in Philadelphia, Pennsylvania, that served as experimental sites.

RESEARCH COMPONENTS:
   Process analysis: Conducted. Frequent on-site visits and data examination were used to ensure that services were constant across sites and throughout the study. A three-month pilot program was conducted in one of the sites prior to beginning services at all sites.
   Impact analysis: Conducted using comparison of means.
   Benefit–cost analysis: Not conducted.

MAJOR FINDINGS:
1. AFDC treatment participants had significantly higher average earnings than control group participants in the first four quarters following random assignment. "Over the full two-year follow-up period, the treatment group had $340 more in average earnings, which is also a significant difference."
2. AFDC "not-job-ready" treatment participants (the priority caseload for this project) showed the most significant gains over the control group in employment and earnings.
3. No significant differences in welfare receipt between AFDC-U treatment and control group participants were produced. For the AFDC-R (i.e., AFDC-regular) participants, significantly fewer treatment group participants received welfare assistance for all quarters of follow-up. This was true for both job-ready and not-job-ready participants.

TIME TRENDS IN FINDINGS: The rate of employment and average earnings increased steadily over the evaluation period for both treatment and control participants (for both AFDC-R and AFDC-U).
   For AFDC-R participants, treatment group employment and earnings were significantly higher than those of the control group for the first year following random assignment, but differences dissipated in the second year.

For both treatment and control groups, there was a steady decline in the percentage of persons receiving welfare benefits over the two year period, though there were no significant differences between treatment and control group members.

DESIGN ISSUES:

1. During the early part of the project, more emphasis was given to education and training than was intended. Later, these services were made concurrent with job search activities.

2. Job-ready participants were to move immediately into an independent job search for 90 days, but it was discovered that many were receiving intensive services prior to the end of their 90-day independent search. A memorandum was sent to case workers to bring the implementation of these services in line with original plans. The evaluators felt that more monitoring was needed, but caseloads were too large.

3. A longer follow-up period was considered but did not materialize owing to loss of staff and a lack of funding.

4. The evaluators suspected that some case managers were "creaming" their caseloads; that is, they were putting more effort into helping those clients who they felt had the best chances of success. It is unclear whether this may have biased impacts or affected generalizability.

REPLICABILITY: Replicable.

GENERALIZABILITY: Designed to generalize to the city of Philadelphia. Site selection was based on the physical plant of the various districts, district performance, and demographic characteristics (6 of Philadelphia's 19 districts were chosen). Researchers felt the 6 sites "generally reflected the city's welfare population." There were significant differences among the districts selected, however (e.g., 1 district was 99 percent black, whereas another was 21 percent black). Unemployment rates for Philadelphia at this time were comparable to the state and national averages.

FUNDING SOURCE: U.S. Department of Health and Human Services, Office of Family Assistance. Key personnel: Liza Barnes.

TREATMENT ADMINISTRATOR: Pennsylvania Department of Public Welfare, Office of Policy, Evaluation, and Development; Sam McClea, director; Bureau of Policy, Evaluation, and Research; Frederick Richmond, director. Project director: Kathleen Nazar.

EVALUATOR: Pennsylvania Department of Public Welfare. Principal Investigators: Suzanne Hogarth and Roger Martin.

ENABLING LEGISLATION: State of Pennsylvania Act 1982–75.

POLICY EFFECTS: The evaluators noted that the state administration (Department of Public Welfare, Division of Income Maintenance) used the study results in implementing statewide changes in service delivery.

INFORMATION SOURCES: Suzanne Hogarth and Roger Martin, *Pennsylvania Saturation Work Program: Process Evaluation*, 1988. Suzanne Hogarth, Roger Martin, and Kathleen Nazar, *Pennsylvania Saturation Work Program: Impact Evaluation*, 1989. Both publications available through Pennsylvania Department of Public Welfare.

PUBLIC USE ACCESS TO DATA: Available at Pennsylvania Department of Public Welfare.

ILLINOIS ON-LINE CROSS-MATCH DEMONSTRATION

SUMMARY: This demonstration, conducted in 1986, tested the effects of immediate access to client information by caseworkers on a large sample of AFDC recipients and applicants. Subjects were followed for six months.

COST: Administrative cost, $148,000 (1986); research only, $69,290 (1986).

TIME FRAME: Demonstration period, May 1986–October 1986; data collected through December 1986; final report, September 1987.

TREATMENTS TESTED: At the initial determination of eligibility for AFDC and at subsequent face-to-face redetermination meetings, a caseworker could immediately call up on a computer screen certain information on experimentals: marriage and death information, state payroll and retirement pension data, and, in some cases, school records. Caseworkers were required to perform these cross-match inquiries for experimentals (odd last-digit identification numbers), and the system would not accept inquiries for controls (even last-digit identifications). School district information was available for Chicago and Rockford. The tested treatment was an incremental increase in the information already immediately accessible to the caseworker, the most important of which was wage records from the Illinois Department of Employment Security. Under the existing system (the control treatment), the additional information on marriages, deaths, and so forth would be periodically updated and circulated to caseworkers in hard copy.

OUTCOMES OF INTEREST: (1) AFDC applications denied and (2) Savings in payments.

SAMPLE SIZE: New applicants—experimentals, 5,305; controls, 5,489. Ongoing cases—experimentals, 20,429; controls, 20,323.

TARGET POPULATION: AFDC applicants and recipients.

NUMBER OF TREATMENT GROUPS: Two (with one control group).

NUMBER AND LOCATION OF SITES: Seven Illinois welfare offices (four in Cook County and three in other counties).

RESEARCH COMPONENTS:

Process analysis: Conducted through interviews and computer records to determine whether caseworkers actually used the system and whether they perceived it as useful. Workers who were using a fully automated system and who had access to school district records found it useful, and some of them succeeded in evading the system block on even numbers to use it on controls (thereby contaminating the control sample). Computer records showed that this happened in one office only; project report authors noted that although this produced a downward bias in the measured effect of the treatment in that office, it is itself evidence of perceived treatment effectiveness. Many workers did not understand the data format for state payments, marriages, and deaths.

Impact analysis: Comparison of means, ordinary least squares (OLS) regression.

Benefit–cost analysis: Cost-effectiveness analysis.

MAJOR FINDINGS:

	Experimentals	Controls
New applications denied	39.5%	40.5%
For applicants:		
Mean AFDC payments	$625.08	$609.34
Mean food stamps paid	238.24	231.49
For ongoing cases:		
Mean AFDC payments	1,571.02	1,574.22
Mean food stamps paid	774.63*	782.20

*Difference that is statistically significant at 90 percent confidence level.

Three Cook County offices had access to school records and had a fully automated information system. In these offices, denials of new applications increased from 23.9 percent to 26.4 percent (statistically significant at the 90 percent level). The difference in benefits paid was not statistically significant.

Although some downward bias was present, owing to the contamination discussed above under "Process analysis" (in "Research Components"), the project report authors did not believe it was large enough to change the analysis significantly.

Under most reasonable assumptions about benefits and costs, benefits of the system exceeded costs when school records were available, but the authors did not claim that the benefits were very precisely measured.

TIME TRENDS IN FINDINGS: There were no time trends, but there were curious discrepancies in treatment impacts across offices, which the authors discussed but cannot explain.

DESIGN ISSUES:
1. The inclusion of offices that were not fully automated (and where, accordingly, use of the additional data was more difficult) added little to the value of the experiment. Apparently it was not anticipated before the experiment that only the school records would be of much use to caseworkers.
2. The contamination of the control sample, previously noted, was not the only result of a vulnerable computer system. In particular, the authors had trouble designating the new applicant sample, for reasons discussed in the report.

REPLICABILITY: Replicable.

GENERALIZABILITY: The sample size is very large, but most results were not statistically significant. That would seem to imply that the savings are very small; on the other hand, the system costs seem to be small as well.

FUNDING SOURCE: U.S. Department of Health and Human Services, Office of Family Assistance. Key personnel: Penny Pendell.

TREATMENT ADMINISTRATOR: Illinois Department of Public Aid. Key personnel: Alan Whitaker.

EVALUATOR: Mathematica Policy Research. Key personnel: John A. Burghardt.

ENABLING LEGISLATION: None.

POLICY EFFECTS: Alan Whitaker has stated that the disappointing findings on the effects of the on-line cross-match treatment led the state not to extend further the scope of data collection for on-line use by caseworkers.

INFORMATION SOURCES: Nancy Holden, John A. Burghardt, and James C. Ohls, "Final Report for the Evaluation of the Illinois On-Line Cross-Match Demonstration," Mathematica Policy Research, September 11, 1987.

PUBLIC-USE ACCESS TO DATA: We have no information about a public-use file for this demonstration.

NEW YORK STATE COMPREHENSIVE EMPLOYMENT OPPORTUNITY SUPPORT CENTERS PROGRAM (CEOSC)

SUMMARY: This demonstration, conducted from 1987 to 1993, tested the effects of training, job-search assistance and supportive services on a medium-sized sample of single AFDC parents of preschool children. Subjects were followed for up to four years. This program was also tested in New York City, using a comparison group design.

COST: Evaluation costs—approximately $500,000.

TIME FRAME: Demonstration period, 1987–93; data collected, same period; final report, 1994.

TREATMENTS TESTED: This voluntary program tested assessment, education, skills training, job search assistance, child care, counseling, case management, and other supportive services. The control group received nothing from the demonstration.

OUTCOMES OF INTEREST: (1) Employment; (2) Earnings; (3) Welfare dependency; and (4) Welfare payments.

SAMPLE SIZE: Treatment, 261; control, 268.

TARGET POPULATION: Single AFDC parents of preschool children. This population is overwhelmingly female (98.7 percent).

NUMBER OF TREATMENT GROUPS: Two (including control).

NUMBER AND LOCATION OF SITES: Only one site, Albany, New York, used an experimental design. The program was also tested in New York City, using a comparison group design. There were also nine pilot sites throughout New York State.

RESEARCH COMPONENTS:
Process analysis: An implementation study was conducted over the first year of program operations in the nine pilot sites.

Impact analysis: Conducted only in the two program sites. Comparison of means and regression analysis were used in Albany. Only regression analysis was used in New York City.

Benefit–cost analysis: Not conducted.

MAJOR FINDINGS:

1. The treatment group recipiency of public assistance was significantly lower than that of the control group, though only in the final (14th) quarter of follow-up (control group rate, 69.3 percent; treatment group rate, 58.1 percent). In no quarter was there a significant impact on the monthly amount of public assistance received.
2. No significant impacts were found on the receipt, nor the benefit amount, of food stamps.
3. Employment rates were significantly lower for the treatment group in the 5th and 6th quarters, compared to the control group, but were somewhat higher than those of the control group after quarter 12. Employment earnings were significantly higher for the treatment group from the 12th quarter on (72.7 percent–173 percent effect).
4. Impacts were greater for an "early cohort" who had entered the sample earlier in the life of the program. This includes significant impacts on receipt of food stamps and public assistance.

TIME TRENDS IN FINDINGS: Impacts on earnings for the Albany site took longer to appear than in other welfare-to-work programs. Participants in the treatment group tended to remain outside the labor force during training, and participation in the program was sporadic. Once this group did enter the labor market, they appeared to find more stable, higher-paying employment on average than did control group members.

DESIGN ISSUES: Program enrollment during the period of intake for the research sample was lower than expected. Further, only a small percentage (approximately 29 percent) of the treatment group ever received training through the program beyond a two-week pre-employment workshop.

REPLICABILITY: Replicable. The report contains various sample forms, surveys, and guidelines for implementation.

GENERALIZABILITY: Participation rates were quite low. The program was voluntary, with random assignment after volunteering. Findings on welfare dependency are similar to those found in other welfare-to-work demonstrations. Findings on income developed over a longer period of time than in other programs, though direction of impacts was the same.

FUNDING SOURCE: New York State Department of Social Services. Key personnel: George Falco, director of research.

TREATMENT ADMINISTRATOR: New York State Department of Social Services oversaw both sites. The Albany program was administered by the Albany County Department of Social Services. The New York City site was administered by Federation Employment and Guidance Service, a private nonprofit organization.

EVALUATOR: Abt Associates. Principal investigator: Alan Werner.

ENABLING LEGISLATION: None.

INFORMATION SOURCES: Alan Werner, Gregory Mills, Michael Walker, and Nandinee Kutty, *The Evaluation of New York State Comprehensive Employment Opportunity Support Centers Program: Impact Study*, Abt Associates, January 1994.

PUBLIC-USE ACCESS TO DATA: Not available.

TEENAGE PARENT DEMONSTRATION

SUMMARY: This demonstration, conducted from 1987 to 1991, tested the effects of case management and employment and training services on a large sample of teenage mothers receiving welfare. Subjects are being followed for up to seven years, though only 30-month follow-up results are currently available.

COST: Evaluation costs were approximately $6.3 million.

TIME FRAME: Demonstration period, mid-1987–mid-1991; data for first phase collected over same period and for 30-month follow-up period. Additional follow-up of 5–7 years is being conducted and a report will be completed in early 1997.

TREATMENTS TESTED: Individual case management. All participants attended initial personal skills workshops. Individual plans included education, job training, and/or employment. Nonparticipation in these activities was subject to sanctions. Child care and transportation assistance were offered. The control group received no demonstration services.

OUTCOMES OF INTEREST: (1) Employment; (2) Earnings; (3) Welfare receipt; (4) School Attendance; and (5) Subsequent childbearing. Child development and parenting outcomes were also measured in the second follow-up.

SAMPLE SIZE: Total, 5,297; treatment, 2,647; control, 2,650. Total samples at each site: Chicago, Illinois, 2,889; Camden, New Jersey, 1,218; and Newark, New Jersey, 1,190.

TARGET POPULATION: Teenage mothers with only one child, receiving AFDC for self and/or the child.

NUMBER OF TREATMENT GROUPS: Two (including control) at each site.

NUMBER AND LOCATION OF SITES: Three—Project Advance in Chicago; and Teen Progress in Newark and Camden.

RESEARCH COMPONENTS:

Process analysis: Focus on participation rates and service delivery at the three sites. Forty to fifty percent of the New Jersey participants and 30 percent of those in Chicago were sanctioned (benefits were reduced until they complied with program requirements).

Impact analysis: Conducted predominantly with multivariate models.

Benefit—cost analysis: Will be conducted.

MAJOR FINDINGS:

1. Participation in employment and, especially, education activities was significantly higher for the treatment group (79 percent) than for the control group (66 percent). By the end of the two-year follow-up period, a significantly higher percentage of treatment group members, compared with control group members, had spent some time in school. These differences were largest in Camden (46 percent versus 26 percent). In Chicago and Camden, significantly more treatment group members obtained a diploma or equivalent.

2. The demonstration produced consistent but modest impacts on employment outcomes. For both Chicago and Camden, there were positive significant treatment—control differences in the percentage ever employed (Camden, 6.5 percent, Chicago, 7 percent) and in the percentage of total demonstration period employed (Camden, 2.4 percent, Chicago, 3.5 percent). There were no significant differences for the Newark site on employment outcomes.

3. Average monthly earnings were significantly higher for the treatment group at the Chicago site only ($24.40 higher than controls). In the New Jersey sites, the treatment groups had average monthly

earnings of roughly $21 over the control groups, but this was not statistically significant.
4. Welfare receipt was reduced by 7–8 percent in all three sites. Particularly in New Jersey, these reductions resulted from a combination of higher earnings and higher sanctions for noncompliance. Only the Chicago program produced a sustained significant reduction in the probability of receiving AFDC.

TIME TRENDS IN FINDINGS: Only short-term impacts are currently available. A five- to seven-year follow-up is currently being conducted.

DESIGN ISSUES:
1. Sample sizes for outcomes based on resurvey and retest data are substantially smaller than those based on records data. This was purposeful and *not* due to attrition and nonresponse (response to the surveys was roughly 85 percent). Evaluators attempted to survey and retest only 75 percent of the Chicago sample.
2. The evaluator reported that this project was very well designed and was implemented with few difficulties. The problems that existed related to how quickly the three sites implemented the project and to how faithfully they monitored it. One site was fairly slow and another site was inconsistent in monitoring the project.

REPLICABILITY: Replicable.

GENERALIZABILITY: Designed to generalize to urban populations nationwide. All three sites have high rates of unemployment, poverty, and crime. The program was mandatory and sanctioned. Only one-third of the demonstration sample would have been required to participate in employment, education, and training under federal law. Another one-third were at high risk for becoming JOBS mandatory. The sample is fairly representative of the population of first-time welfare-dependent teenage parents in the demonstration sites, because the project identified virtually all newly eligible teenage parents during the demonstration.

FUNDING SOURCE: U.S. Department of Health and Human Services (DHHS), Administration for Children and Families. Key personnel: Reuben Snipper, Nancye Campell, and Judith Reich.

TREATMENT ADMINISTRATORS: Chicago—Project Advance; key personnel: Melba McCarty. Newark—Teen Progress; key personnel: Yvonne Johnson. Camden—Teen Progress; key personnel: Frank Ambrose.

EVALUATOR: Mathematica Policy Research. Project director: Rebecca Maynard; deputy project director: Alan M. Hershey; co-investigator: Denise Polit. Ellen Kisker is currently working on the seven-year follow-up.

ENABLING LEGISLATION: None.

POLICY EFFECTS: The evaluator reported that the results of this demonstration figured prominently in state welfare reform debates. Briefings were held in many states, including California, Illinois, Wisconsin, Rhode Island, New Jersey, and Vermont, and testimony relating to the demonstration was heard in the U.S. Congress. The findings were also reportedly influential in the congressional debates over child care and welfare.

INFORMATION SOURCES: Rebecca Maynard, Walter Nicholson, and Anu Rangarajan, *Breaking the Cycle of Poverty: The Effectiveness of Mandatory Services for Welfare-Dependent Teenage Parents.* Mathematica Policy Research, December, 1993.

PUBLIC-USE ACCESS TO DATA: Will be available through DHHS when the follow-up is completed.

WISCONSIN WELFARE EMPLOYMENT EXPERIMENT— ROCK COUNTY

SUMMARY: This demonstration, conducted from 1987 to 1990, tested the effects of Wisconsin's new welfare program on a medium-sized sample of AFDC recipients. Subjects were followed for three years. The Rock County experiment was part of a statewide demonstration, but was the only site to use random assignment in its design. Twenty-nine other counties tested the new program using a matched-comparison design.

COST: Evaluation costs, approximately $20,000–$30,000 for Rock County alone; approximately $200,000 for all counties. Funding was terminated prior to completion of the final report.

TIME FRAME: Demonstration period, 1987–90; data collected, same period; final report, September 1993.

TREATMENTS TESTED: The Work Experience and Job Training Program (WEJT) featured an extensive array of services including remedial education, job search, subsidized employment, job training, and day care. Those clients not finding work after completing their training were required to participate in a mandatory Community Work Experience Program (CWEP), a "workfare" program. The control group received existing services (mainly job search activities).

OUTCOMES OF INTEREST: (1) Employment; (2) Earnings; and (3) Welfare receipt.

SAMPLE SIZE: Rock County only, 1,025. Treatment, 538; control, 487.

TARGET POPULATION: Recipients of AFDC benefits.

NUMBER OF TREATMENT GROUPS: Two (including control).

NUMBER AND LOCATION OF SITES: One—Rock County, Wisconsin. Twenty-nine other Wisconsin counties also tested this program, but did not use an experimental design.

RESEARCH COMPONENTS:
Process analysis: Several chapters of the final report are dedicated to the process of implementing the WEJT/CWEP program. Descriptions of the programs, participation patterns, and the roles of service providers are included.
Impact analysis: Comparison of means.
Benefit–cost analysis: Not conducted.

MAJOR FINDINGS:
1. By the fourth quarter of 1990 (three years after program implementation), 59 percent of the treatment group and 69 percent of the control group were off AFDC. Although this finding was not statistically significant, it reflects a lack of success of the experimental treatment.
2. Likewise, treatment group participants did not show improved earnings as compared to the control group. For two-parent families, experimentals had average fourth-quarter earnings of $2,126, compared to $2,354 for the control group. For single-parent families, the treatment group showed average quarterly earnings of $1,288, compared to $1,364 for the controls.

TIME TRENDS IN FINDINGS: None reported.

DESIGN ISSUES: According to the evaluator, the greatest difficulties were political rather than design-related. There was an "adversarial relationship" between the evaluators and the Wisconsin State Department of Health and Social Services. Considerable time and money were spent trying to get data from "recalcitrant bureaucrats" who did not want to supply it. The legislature, which had mandated the study, was used to enforce cooperation. The administrators did not agree with the findings and halted the evaluation. The evaluators then completed the data analysis and final report on their own.

REPLICABILITY: Replicable, with cautions regarding the politically charged nature of this evaluation.

GENERALIZABILITY: With the nonexperimental sites, designed to generalize to the entire state. The findings in Rock County are consistent with data collected by the Wisconsin Department of Health and Social Services evaluation staff in 1988.

FUNDING SOURCES: Wisconsin Department of Health and Social Services; U.S. Department of Health and Human Services.

TREATMENT ADMINISTRATOR: Wisconsin Department of Health and Social Services. Key personnel: Richard Larang.

EVALUATOR: Employment and Training Institute, University of Wisconsin-Milwaukee. Key personnel: John Pawasarat and Lois M. Quinn. The evaluator's contract was canceled in 1992, but the university was committed to completing the final stages of analysis and publication.

ENABLING LEGISLATION: Wisconsin Act 413.

INFORMATION SOURCES: John Pawasarat and Lois M. Quinn, *Wisconsin Welfare Employment Experiments: An Evaluation of the WEJT and CWEP Programs*, Employment and Training Institute, University of Wisconsin-Milwaukee, September 1993.

PUBLIC-USE ACCESS TO DATA: Not available.

CHILD ASSISTANCE PROGRAM (CAP)

SUMMARY: This demonstration, conducted from 1988 to 1995, tested the effects of financial incentives and intensive case management on a large sample of AFDC recipients. Subjects were followed for five years.

COST: Evaluation costs, approximately $1.9 million for initial evaluation and $1.2 million for the extension.

TIME FRAME: Demonstration period, October 1988–March 1994; experimental data collected for the first five years after enrollment (through 1995).

TREATMENTS TESTED: The Child Assistance Program (CAP) is a voluntary alternative to AFDC. Participation is limited to single-parent AFDC cases in which at least one child is covered by a child support order. The treatment consists of economic incentives (including an earned income disregard of 90 percent up to the poverty level and 33 percent beyond that; no $50 pass-through for child support; no resource limit; and cashed-out Food Stamp benefits) and intensive case management.

OUTCOMES OF INTEREST: (1) Establishment of child support orders; (2) Employment; and (3) Earnings.

SAMPLE SIZE: Total, 4,287. Roughly half assigned to each of two groups.

TARGET POPULATION: AFDC recipients.

NUMBER OF TREATMENT GROUPS: Two (including control).

NUMBER AND LOCATION OF SITES: Only three sites used random assignment and are included in this analysis—Monroe, Niagara, and Suffolk Counties, New York. There were also four saturation sites.

RESEARCH COMPONENTS:
Process analysis: Identified operational, organizational, and environmental factors associated with the implementation. These included participation rates, random assignment procedures, recruitment, and agency coordination.

Impact analysis: Three experimental sites only were estimated using regression analysis.

Benefit–cost analysis: Conducted.

MAJOR FINDINGS:
1. At the two-year follow-up, there were significant increases in the earnings of the treatment group. Average earnings over the two years were 27 percent higher for the treatment group (including those who did not participate) than for the control group. An earnings impact of roughly this magnitude or greater is also estimated for the full five-year follow-up.
2. There was a significant increase in the establishment of child support orders. Most recipients began the experiment lacking orders

for at least one child. On average, over the five years, clients were 21 percent more likely to gain new orders if they were in the treatment group. There was also an indication of increased child support payments, but this effect was not statistically significant.
3. At the two-year follow-up, there were no significant program impacts on the receipt of public assistance. At the five-year follow-up, there was a significant reduction in combined Food Stamp/AFDC payments (approximately 4 percent) and in Medicaid, but the reduction of cash assistance, by itself, was not statistically significant.
4. After combining benefit payments and administrative costs for the five years as a whole, there was a sizable savings in government outlays. Increased administrative costs resulting from CAP were more than offset by reductions in Food Stamp and cash assistance benefits and an increase in child support collections.

TIME TRENDS IN FINDINGS: Program impacts were sustained or increased over the full five-year period.

DESIGN ISSUES:
1. Client (self-report) surveys at one and two years were used to obtain employment and earnings data, because the New York system made access to employer data difficult. This could introduce error owing to faulty memory or other biases. Regulations were changed during the project, and employer data were available for the three-, four-, and five-year follow-ups.
2. Program enrollment relied heavily on recruitment efforts of staff. Staff needed to convince clients of the program's advantages. Program enrollment over the five-year period was roughly 16 percent of the AFDC caseload, although it varied by county. CAP had a clear priority in the Departments of Social Services of Monroe and Niagara Counties. Enrollments were higher in these counties than in Suffolk.

REPLICABILITY: Replicable.

GENERALIZABILITY: Designed to generalize to the entire state. The project was voluntary, and AFDC clients needed to meet certain requirements (obtain child support orders, earn $350 per month) before being deemed eligible. Because of this feature, most AFDC recipients would never enroll in the program, though evaluators predicted that more than the 16 percent enrollment that occurred in this demonstration would enroll in a nonexperimental program.

The full experimental sample was reasonably representative of the single-parent AFDC caseload nationwide. They were actually more comparable to the U.S. caseload than that of upstate New York. The full sample contained higher percentages of black and Hispanic clients, never-married clients, and clients with a child under age three than the upstate New York average.

FUNDING SOURCE: New York State Department of Social Services. Key personnel: Mike Warner and Susan Mitchell-Herzfeld.

TREATMENT ADMINISTRATOR: New York State Department of Social Services and the corresponding county departments in the experimental sites. Key personnel: Mike Warner and Susan Mitchell-Herzfeld.

EVALUATOR: Abt Associates. Key personnel: William Hamilton and Nancy Burstein.

ENABLING LEGISLATION: Omnibus Budget Reconciliation Act of 1987, section 9122, and provisions of section 1115 of the Social Security Act and section 17(b)(1) of the Food Stamp Act.

POLICY EFFECTS: On June 6, 1994, the U.S. Department of Health and Human Services authorized continued operation and expansion (to additional sites) of the Child Assistance Program from April 1, 1994, through March 31, 1999. The program continues to operate in the seven original counties and in seven additional counties. Although 10 percent of the new caseload will be assigned to a control group, there are no immediate plans to continue gathering experimental data. The five-year follow-up, which ended in March 1995, marks the completion of the experimental evaluation.

INFORMATION SOURCES: William L. Hamilton, Nancy R. Burstein, Margaret Hargreaves, David A. Moss, and Michael Walker, *The New York State Child Assistance Program: Program Impacts, Costs, and Benefits*, Abt Associates, July 1993; William L. Hamilton, Nancy R. Burstein, August J. Baker, Alison Earle, Stefanie Gluckman, Laura Peck, and Alan White, *The New York State Child Assistance Program: Five-Year Impacts, Costs, and Benefits*, Abt Associates, October 1996.

PUBLIC-USE ACCESS TO DATA: Upon completion of the analysis, Abt Associates will turn over the data set to the State of New York, Department of Social Services.

GREATER AVENUES FOR INDEPENDENCE (GAIN)

SUMMARY: This demonstration, conducted from 1988 to 1990, tested the effects of basic education, job search, and skills training on a large sample of AFDC recipients. Subjects were followed for up to four and one-half years.

COST: Manpower Demonstration Research Corporation's (MDRC's) multiyear contract with California encompassed much more than the six-county demonstration, and evaluators were thus unable to separate the costs. Average net program cost per experimental was $3,422 and per control, $1,472.

TIME FRAME: Demonstration period, March 1988–June 1990; final Report, September 1994.

TREATMENTS TESTED: Experimentals were subject to the Greater Avenues for Independence (GAIN) participation mandate, which combined basic education, job search activities, assessments, skills training, and work experience. The control group was precluded from receiving those services from the program, but could seek other services in the community on their own.

OUTCOMES OF INTEREST: (1) Participation in employment-related activities; (2) Earnings; (3) Welfare receipts; and (4) Employment.

SAMPLE SIZE: Total, 32,751; treatment, 24,528; control, 8,223.

TARGET POPULATION: AFDC recipients. Four of the six counties had resources to include all mandatory registrants; two focused on long-term recipients.

NUMBER OF TREATMENT GROUPS: Two (including control) in each county.

NUMBER AND LOCATION OF SITES: Six counties in California: Alameda, Butte, Los Angeles, Riverside, San Diego, and Tulare.

RESEARCH COMPONENTS:
Process analysis: Implementation among the six counties was analyzed, with special attention paid to communication, participation, use of sanctions, and services delivered.
Impact analysis: Impact estimates were regression adjusted.
Benefit–cost analysis: Conducted.

MAJOR FINDINGS: Effects varied by county.
1. Over the full four and one-half years, GAIN significantly increased the earnings for AFDC-FG (single parents) as compared to those of

the control group. There was a total difference of $2,527 per participant (24 percent). This is an all-county average, with each county weighted equally.

2. AFDC total benefit payments were, on average, $1,365 (7 percent) lower for the AFDC-FG treatment group than for the controls.
3. Earnings gains and AFDC-FG benefit reductions were greatest for Riverside County (+ 44 percent and − 15 percent, respectively). Earnings gains and AFDC-U reductions for Riverside County were + 15 percent and − 14.3 percent, respectively. Riverside's staff placed much more emphasis on moving registrants into the labor market quickly than did staff in any other county. Riverside staff attempted to communicate a strong message to all registrants that employment was the central goal of the program. In addition, the county's management established job placement standards as one means of assessing staff performance.
4. Employment and welfare savings impacts for the AFDC-U (two-parent families) group were less striking than for the AFDC-FG group, though they were statistically significant. Earnings for treatment groups members averaged 12 percent higher than those of their control group counterparts.

TIME TRENDS IN FINDINGS: The earnings impacts grew progressively stronger over time, whereas the impacts on AFDC receipt tended to level off over time.

DESIGN ISSUES:

1. In order for group assignment to occur, registrants were required to appear for orientation and appraisal. One-third of mandatory registrants did not appear and thus were not part of the research sample. By the six-month follow-up, two-thirds of these no-shows had either left welfare or were officially excused.
2. Four of the six counties were able to enroll the full mandatory caseload. Funding levels did not permit this in Alameda and Los Angeles, where they chose to focus exclusively on long-term recipients. Different intake policies and differences in the general makeup of each county's local population yielded research samples that varied markedly in demographic composition.

REPLICABILITY: Replicable. A random assignment replication study was recently launched in Los Angeles county. This study utilized many of Riverside County's strategies.

GENERALIZABILITY: Designed to generalize to the entire state of California. The program was mandatory under pre-JOBS rules. Thus, single parents with children under the age of six were exempted. The six counties represent diverse geographical regions of the state, vary widely in local economic conditions and population characteristics, and constitute a mix of urban and rural areas. GAIN, as California's version of the JOBS program, existed statewide. Although participants in the six experimental counties were not strictly representative of the statewide population, over one-half of the entire state AFDC caseload lived in those counties.

FUNDING SOURCE: California State Department of Social Services (SDSS).

TREATMENT ADMINISTRATOR: SDSS. Key personnel: Eloise Anderson, Michael Genest, and Bruce Wagstaff, as well as the county welfare directors in the six experimental counties.

EVALUATOR: Manpower Demonstration Research Corporation (MDRC). Principal investigator: James Riccio; other key personnel: Daniel Friedlander and Stephen Freedman.

ENABLING LEGISLATION: None.

INFORMATION SOURCES: James Riccio, Daniel Friedlander, and Stephen Freedman, GAIN: Benefits, Costs and Three Year Impacts of a Welfare to Work Program, Manpower Demonstration Research Corporation, 1994.

PUBLIC-USE ACCESS TO DATA: Available through MDRC.

WASHINGTON STATE FAMILY INDEPENDENCE PROGRAM (FIP)

SUMMARY: This quasi-experimental demonstration, conducted between 1988 and 1993, tested the effects of financial incentives (bonuses) that were intended to encourage training and work on a large sample of AFDC recipients. Subjects were followed for three years.

COST: $4.75 million over five years.

TIME FRAME: Demonstration period, July 1988–June 1993; data collected, same period.

TREATMENTS TESTED: The Family Independence Program (FIP) provided financial incentives to AFDC recipients to encourage education, training, and work; changed the structure of the income support system (e.g., "cashed-out" food stamps); expanded the availability of child care and supportive services; and provided transitional child care and Medicaid for one year. The comparison counties received traditional AFDC benefits, which were initially provided under the Washington Employment Opportunity Program (WEOP) and subsequently under JOBS in 1990. JOBS services were similar to those of FIP.

OUTCOMES OF INTEREST: (1) Participation in education and training; (2) Employment; and (3) Welfare receipt.

SAMPLE SIZE: Total, 33,304; treatment sites, 17,495; comparison sites, 15,809.

TARGET POPULATION: New and recertifying AFDC recipients.

NUMBER OF TREATMENT GROUPS: Two—FIP (treatment) and AFDC (comparison).

NUMBER AND LOCATION OF SITES: There were five treatment sites and five comparison sites throughout the state of Washington. Site selection involved first obtaining five matched pairs of sites. A coin toss was then used to assign one site in each matched pair to treatment status and the other site to comparison status. Treatment sites were located in: Everett/Skyhomish Valley; Spokane North; Burien/West Seattle; Columbia River Gorge; and Moses Lake/Othello.

RESEARCH COMPONENTS:

Process analysis: Addressed how the FIP offices and the comparison offices differed in their treatment of recipients, how FIP components differed from AFDC, how both programs changed over time, and how service delivery differed among local programs.

Impact analysis: Regression analysis using a differences-in-differences approach.

Benefit–cost analysis: Conducted.

MAJOR FINDINGS:
1. Relative to the AFDC program (the comparison group), FIP had little or no impact on the level of participation in education and training activities for adults in one-parent cases and men in two-parent cases. FIP women in two-parent cases were significantly less likely to participate in these activities than their AFDC counterparts in four of the eight follow-up quarters.
2. Relative to the AFDC program, FIP had little or no impact on the probability of employment or average earnings for adults in one-parent cases or women in two-parent cases. It significantly reduced both the probability of employment and average earnings for men in two-parent cases in all follow-up quarters.

3. The net FIP impacts on participation in welfare were relatively large and highly significant for both the one- and two-parent caseloads. Participants tended to stay on welfare longer under FIP, and those who did leave returned to welfare more quickly than those who exited under AFDC. Average welfare grants were also higher under FIP than under AFDC. Participation in welfare was up to 12 percentage points higher for adults in one-parent cases and 18 percentage points higher for adults in two-parent cases over the entire follow-up period.

TIME TRENDS IN FINDINGS: None reported.

DESIGN ISSUES:

1. Cost-neutrality issues and rapidly growing caseloads interfered with the implementation of some of the FIP components. Individualized case management and increased availability of training services were only minimally implemented, and some components (e.g. wage subsidies, emphasis on child support enforcement) were not implemented at all.
2. Client surveys indicated that a "substantial minority" of FIP participants did not fully understand the program or its benefits. Consequently, they could not be expected to change their behavior in response to those benefits.
3. Some of the inducements that FIP provided to encourage welfare recipients to move toward self-sufficiency, in the absence of strong staff involvement or any requirements, may have encouraged welfare participation under FIP.
4. In October 1990, the state implemented JOBS to replace the Work Incentive program. This change progressively reduced the FIP-AFDC program differences over time.
5. For a time, the standards for two-parent families for qualifying for AFDC were greatly liberalized at FIP sites. This caused the two-parent analysis sample at FIP sites to systematically differ from the two-parent analysis sample at comparison sites, and may have distorted comparisons between the two samples. A similar problem does *not* exist for comparisons between one-parent families.

REPLICABILITY: Replicable.

GENERALIZABILITY: Designed to generalize to the entire state of Washington. Welfare offices were stratified by urban/rural and east/west to ensure geographic representativeness within Washington State. Treatment and comparison site cohorts were very similar.

FUNDING SOURCE: Washington State Legislative Budget Committee. Key personnel: Denise Gaither and Kristen West.

TREATMENT ADMINISTRATOR: Employment Security Department and Department of Social and Health Services of the state of Washington.

EVALUATOR: The Urban Institute. Project director: D. Lee Bawden (deceased).

ENABLING LEGISLATION: This demonstration was federally mandated as part of the waiver of section 1115 of the Social Security Act.

INFORMATION SOURCES: Sharon K. Long, Demetra Smith Nightingale, and Douglas A. Wissoker, *The Evaluation of the Washington State Family Independence Program: Final Report*, The Urban Institute, December 1993.

PUBLIC-USE ACCESS TO DATA: Available through The Urban Institute; contact Sharon Long.

CHILD DAY CARE RECYCLING FUND EXPERIMENT—
NORTH CAROLINA

SUMMARY: This demonstration, conducted from 1989 to 1990, tested the effects of immediate, guaranteed, subsidized day care on a medium-sized sample of AFDC recipients. Subjects were followed for one year.

COST: Approximately $126,000 for planning and evaluation.

TIME FRAME: Demonstration period, February 1989–March 1990; data collected, same period.

TREATMENTS TESTED: Relatively immediate (within two weeks of a request being made), subsidized, employment-contingent child care. The control group was subject to the usual terms and conditions for receiving child care, which often meant a six- to 10-month waiting period after employment.

OUTCOMES OF INTEREST: (1) Welfare expenditures and (2) Welfare dependence.

SAMPLE SIZE: Total, 602; treatment, 300; control, 302.

TARGET POPULATION: Eligible AFDC families with the youngest child between the ages of one and five. In addition, target families were not already receiving state-supported child care and had an adult (18 or older) case head who was not a full-time student.

NUMBER OF TREATMENT GROUPS: Two (including control).

NUMBER AND LOCATION OF SITES: One, Mecklenberg County, North Carolina.

RESEARCH COMPONENTS:

Process analysis: Looked at participant characteristics and patterns of behavior, as well as service delivery by the treatment administrator.

Impact analysis: The evaluation design included the experimental component presented here, as well as a time-series analysis and a pre-/postintervention survey. Impact assessments for the experimental component consisted of a comparison of means and logistic regression analysis.

Benefit–cost analysis: Not conducted.

MAJOR FINDINGS:

1. The simple support offer of guaranteed subsidized child care assistance to support full-time employment, in isolation, had no statistically significant effect on employment outcomes or welfare expenditures (AFDC, Food Stamp, and Medicaid). The mean expenditure for the treatment group was $6,205 per participant compared to $6,260 for the control group.

2. Roughly one-half of the participants in the treatment group made some response to the offer of child care. However, this was significantly higher than the number of control group members who made a request for child care during the project period. Only 16.67 percent actually received state subsidized child care under the auspices of the special offer.

TIME TRENDS IN FINDINGS: None reported.

DESIGN ISSUES:

1. The project's short duration of one year makes it difficult to detect changes in the primary outcome of aggregate savings for AFDC, Food Stamp Program, and Medicaid expenditures. It is likely that study participants who accepted employment during this period would tend to take lower-paying jobs. In many cases, Food Stamp and Medicaid benefits would continue.

2. The passive offer of child care, by mail, may have been a poor mechanism to reach members of this population effectively. Many treatment group members may not have been fully aware of the offer or its intent.

REPLICABILITY: Replicable.

GENERALIZABILITY: The experimental sample had characteristics, and barriers to employment, that were similar to those of AFDC recipients in general. The type of jobs available in Mecklenberg County (largely low-paying and without health insurance) may differ across North Carolina and other states, thus affecting employment and employability.

FUNDING SOURCE: State of North Carolina Department of Human Resources. Key personnel: Quentin Uppercue. There was a federal matching grant from the U.S. Department of Health and Human Services. Key personnel: M.I. (Penny) Pendell. Additional support came from the University of North Carolina at Chapel Hill Office of Research Services.

TREATMENT ADMINISTRATOR: State of North Carolina Department of Human Resources and the county administered Department of Social Services in collaboration with Child Care Resources. Key personnel: Marjorie Warlick.

EVALUATOR: University of North Carolina at Chapel Hill School of Social Work. Key personnel: Gary Bowen, principal investigator; Peter Neenan, project director.

ENABLING LEGISLATION: Pursuant to section 1115 of the Social Security Act.

INFORMATION SOURCES: Gary L. Bowen and Peter A. Neenan, *Child Day Care Recycling Fund Experiment*, University of North Carolina at Chapel Hill School of Social Work, October 1990. Gary L. Bowen and Peter A. Neenan, "Does Subsidized Child-Care Availability Promote Welfare Independence of Mothers on AFDC? An Experimental Analysis," *Research on Social Work* 3(1993): 363–84.

PUBLIC-USE ACCESS TO DATA: Available through University of North Carolina, School of Social Work.

COMMUNITY GROUP PARTICIPATION AND HOUSING SUPPLEMENTATION DEMONSTRATION (BETHEL SELF-SUFFICIENCY PROGRAM)

SUMMARY: This demonstration, conducted from 1989 to 1994, tested the effects of providing education, employment, and training (E&T) services through a community-based organization. The subjects were followed for up to five years.

COST: Evaluation costs, $515,000 over six years.

TIME FRAME: Demonstration period, July 1989–June 1994; data collected, same period.

TREATMENTS TESTED: A community-based organization, Bethel New Life (BNL), was used to provide education, employment, and training (E&T) services under the Bethel Self-Sufficiency Program (BSSP). A small group of employed BSSP participants also had the opportunity to buy a new home using "sweat equity" as a down payment. The control group received E&T services through the local Illinois Department of Public Aid (IDPA) office. Both groups continued to receive AFDC, Food Stamp, and Medicaid services through IDPA.

OUTCOMES OF INTEREST: (1) Earnings; (2) Employment; and (3) Welfare receipt.

SAMPLE SIZE: Total, 994; treatment, 497; control, 497.

TARGET POPULATION: AFDC recipients.

NUMBER OF TREATMENT GROUPS: Two (including control).

NUMBER AND LOCATION OF SITES: One—West Garfield Park neighborhood of Chicago, Illinois.

RESEARCH COMPONENTS:

Process analysis: Service delivery and participant characteristics were monitored.

Impact analysis: Conducted using comparison of regression-adjusted means.

Benefit–cost analysis: Conducted.

MAJOR FINDINGS:

1. Rates of E&T assignments were higher for the treatment group clients. Eighty-one percent were assigned to at least one E&T activity sometime during the observation period as compared with fifty-nine percent of the control group clients. More treatment group clients (fifty-three percent) were assigned to literacy, basic education, and high-school-level programs than the control group (23 percent). Rates of assignment to other activities were similar for both groups.
2. The evaluation found no significant differences between treatment and control groups with regard to earnings or welfare receipt.
3. One impact that showed statistical significance was that of quarterly employment rates—the percentage of clients with any quarterly earnings. The average rate was 22 percent for the treatment group and 26 percent for the control group. However, there was no significant difference between average quarterly amounts earned.

4. The cost–benefit analysis indicated that the treatment yielded slightly higher net costs from a government and private provider perspective and slightly lower net benefits from a participant perspective.

TIME TRENDS IN FINDINGS: None reported.

DESIGN ISSUES:
1. Services provided by Bethel New Life, the organization working with the treatment group, were inconsistent. In the early stages, BNL was understaffed and focused primarily on providing intake and orientation services to new participants. During fall 1991, the program was fully staffed and offered a broad range of services to clients. In January 1992, they lost their director and also experienced funding problems, thus limiting services again. In addition, high staff turnover interfered with case management services.
2. The IDPA program, Project Chance, underwent staffing and fiscal crises. Therefore, control group participants also received inconsistent services.
3. The housing component of the demonstration was not implemented as planned. There was high turnover in the housing division of Bethel New Life and conflicts with the U.S. Department of Housing and Urban Development over mortgage assistance grants. By the end of the study period, only nine participants had enrolled in the program and none had yet received a house.

REPLICABILITY: Replicable.

GENERALIZABILITY: Designed to generalize to West Garfield Park and similar neighborhoods in Chicago. Demonstration participant characteristics closely matched the AFDC profile found in West Garfield Park. The sample comprised almost entirely (99 percent) African-American women. On average, they were in their 20s and 30s, with one or two children. More than two-thirds had never married, one-third reported no previous employment experience, and almost half had not finished high school.

FUNDING SOURCE: Illinois Department of Public Aid. Key personnel: Linda Brumleve and David Gruenenfelder.

TREATMENT ADMINISTRATOR: Illinois Department of Public Aid in conjunction with Bethel New Life. Key personnel: Mary Nelson.

EVALUATOR: Abt Associates. Key personnel: Gregory Mills, Bonnie Randall, Margaret Hargreaves, and Robert Kornfeld.

ENABLING LEGISLATION: None.

INFORMATION SOURCES: Margaret Hargreaves, Robert Kornfeld, and Gregory Mills, *Community Group Participation and Housing Supplementation Demonstration: Final Report*, Abt Associates, June 1995.

PUBLIC-USE ACCESS TO DATA: Not available.

ILLINOIS CAREER ADVANCEMENT PROJECT

SUMMARY: This demonstration, part of the Self-Sufficiency Demonstration, was conducted between 1989 and 1993. It tested the effects of financial assistance for educational programs on a large sample of former AFDC recipients. It was not successfully implemented as planned, ending one year early due to minimal participation. Subjects were followed for up to three years.

COST: Evaluation costs, $195,000.

TIME FRAME: Demonstration period, July 1989–October 1993; data collected, same period.

TREATMENTS TESTED: Financial assistance in the form of child care and transportation expenses and reimbursement for books and class fees for educational programs. Tuition was not provided.

OUTCOMES OF INTEREST: (1) Earnings; (2) Returns to cash welfare; and (3) Job status.

SAMPLE SIZE: Full sample, 2,841; treatment, 1,445; control, 1,396. Sample used in the analysis, 1,771 total (869 treatment and 902 control).

TARGET POPULATION: Former recipients of AFDC who left cash assistance rolls because of employment.

NUMBER OF TREATMENT GROUPS: Two (including control).

NUMBER AND LOCATION OF SITES: Throughout the state of Illinois.

RESEARCH COMPONENTS:

Process analysis: Project implementation, participant characteristics, and participation were analyzed through surveys of program leaders and participants.

Impact analysis: Comparison of means.

Benefit–cost analysis: Conducted.

Major Findings: Analysis was limited to those who were assigned during the first nine quarters.

1. No significant differences were found between the treatment and control groups regarding earnings, the rate at which they returned to welfare, job status, or time on cash assistance.
2. When the treatment group was split into those who did and those who did not participate in Career Advancement, the average earnings of those who did participate were found to be consistently lower by several hundred dollars.
3. The benefit–cost analysis revealed negative net present values from each of three perspectives (participant, nonparticipant, and society as a whole). Net *costs* were $188 for both participants and nonparticipants, and were $375 per person from the societal perspective.

Time Trends in Findings: None.

Design Issues:

1. Very low participation (less than 9 percent of treatment group) by those who were eligible. Little was done by the program to enhance participation beyond informing subjects of their eligibility by letter. Tuition costs and issues surrounding child care (time and emotional demands) also contributed to the low rate of participation.
2. The project was to run for five years, but was terminated early, mostly owing to insufficient participation.
3. The treatment was indirect, with a tenuous link to the ultimate effects. At best, positive impacts on employment would be produced only after schooling was completed. A longer follow-up would be necessary to capture these effects.
4. The evaluators felt the time frame was too restrictive for people to make use of the program. Applicants had a time limit within which to respond to the offer and another time limit within which to use the program.

Replicability: Any replication would need to include additional effort to ensure higher participation rates.

Generalizability: Participation rates were too low for any meaningful generalization.

Funding Source: Illinois Department of Public Aid (IDPA) and the White House Interagency Low-Income Opportunity Advisory Board. Key personnel: Linda Brandt-Levy.

Treatment Administrator: Illinois Department of Public Aid.

Evaluator: Institute of Applied Research, St. Louis, Missouri. Principal investigators: L. Anthony Loman and Gary Siegel.

ENABLING LEGISLATION: None.

INFORMATION SOURCES: Institute of Applied Research, *Career Advancement: Year Four Evaluation*, June 1994.

PUBLIC-USE ACCESS TO DATA: Not currently available. The data could be available in the future from the Institute of Applied Research; contact L. Anthony Loman or Gary Siegel.

CASH INCENTIVES IN A SELF-SUFFICIENCY PROGRAM— MONTGOMERY COUNTY, MARYLAND

SUMMARY: This demonstration, conducted from 1989 to 1991, tested the effects of cash incentive payments on a medium-sized sample of AFDC recipients. Subjects were followed for up to two and one-half years.

COST: Evaluation costs, approximately $25,000.

TIME FRAME: Demonstration period, July 1989–June 1991; data collected through end of 1991; final report, November 1992.

TREATMENTS TESTED: Maryland's Project Independence, the state's welfare reform initiative, was a program of educational and training activities. The experimental treatment in Montgomery County was cash incentive payments for participation in the program's activities. The control group did not receive these cash incentive payments.

OUTCOMES: (1) Program completion; (2) Employment; (3) Earnings; and (4) Welfare receipt.

SAMPLE SIZE: Total, 772; treatment, 379; control, 393.

TARGET POPULATION: Recipients of AFDC who participate (mandatorily or voluntarily) in education and training activities.

NUMBER OF TREATMENT GROUPS: Two (including control).

NUMBER AND LOCATION OF SITES: One—Montgomery County, Maryland.

RESEARCH COMPONENTS:
    Process: Special attention was paid to service delivery components and procedures.
    Impact: Conducted with comparison of means.
    Benefit–cost analysis: Not conducted.

MAJOR FINDINGS:

1. The program performance of the clients in the treatment group in completing education and skills training courses was slightly higher than the performance of those in the control group, but the difference was not statistically significant.
2. Differences in employment rates, average wages, and receipt of welfare benefits between the two groups were not statistically significant, although they tended to favor the treatment group (higher rates of employment and wages; lower receipt of welfare benefits).
3. The treatment group had a significantly higher overall completion rate of the job-readiness training component (the first phase of the program) than did the control group. There was no difference between groups per enrollment attempt, but the treatment group was more likely to make multiple attempts at completion.
4. Forty percent of the subjects (both groups) did not receive any education and training services beyond the initial job-readiness training.

TIME TRENDS IN THE FINDINGS: None.

DESIGN ISSUES:

1. The project was designed to last for three years, but was discontinued after two years owing to lack of significant effects of the treatment.
2. Over the first year of the project, orientation procedures changed several times. First, clients were enrolled individually, then in mixed groups (treatment and control), and finally in separate orientation groups. This last change necessitated altering the random assignment procedure. Groups of clients (rather than individuals) who were scheduled for eligibility determination and redetermination in a given month were assigned to the experimental or control group. The change in procedure was associated with shifts in the relative prior earnings between groups, but actually served to make them more comparable rather than more disparate.
3. The procedure for administering the cash incentives also changed mid-project. In the first nine months, individual counselors determined awards beyond the initial job-readiness training. As of May 1990, the system for incentive awards was standardized.

REPLICABILITY: Replicable.

GENERALIZABILITY: Designed to generalize to the entire state of Maryland. For roughly 75 percent of the sample, participation in employment and training activities was mandatory. Also, roughly 75 percent of the sample were members of Maryland's Project Independence target groups (young custodial parents who were without a diploma or work experience and were long-term AFDC recipients).

FUNDING SOURCE: Maryland Department of Social Services.

TREATMENT ADMINISTRATOR: Montgomery County Department of Social Services. Key personnel, Carol Pearson.

EVALUATOR: Principal investigator: Jeffrey J. Koshel (independent consultant).

ENABLING LEGISLATION: None.

INFORMATION SOURCE(S):   Jeffrey J. Koshel, Brian Sumerwell, and Carol Bazell, *Final Evaluation Report: Cash Incentives in a Self-Sufficiency Program*, Montgomery County, Maryland Department of Social Services, November 1992.

PUBLIC-USE ACCESS TO DATA: Not available.

NEW CHANCE

SUMMARY: This demonstration, conducted from 1989 to 1992, tested the effects of a comprehensive program emphasizing both human capital and personal development services on a large sample of young mothers on welfare who were high school dropouts and on their children. Subjects were followed for three and one-half years.

COST: Evaluation costs were approximately $6.5 million.

TIME FRAME: Demonstration period, 1989–92; data collected, same perid; final report, January 1997.

TREATMENTS TESTED: New Chance is a voluntary program that includes an orientation; adult education (basic education and GED preparation); personal and child development (Life Skills and Opportunities curricula, health education and health care services, family planning, parenting education, and pediatric health services); employment preparation (occupational skills training, internships, and job placement assistance); case management; and child care. Control group members were denied access to New Chance, but could participate in other services in the community.

OUTCOME(S) OF INTEREST: (1) Education; (2) Employment; (3) Earnings; (4) Welfare receipt; (5) Fertility; (6) Psychological well-being; and (7) Child development.

SAMPLE SIZE: Total, 2,079; treatment, 1,401; control, 678.

TARGET POPULATION: Families headed by young mothers aged 16–22 who had first given birth as teenagers, who were receiving AFDC, and were high school dropouts.

NUMBER OF TREATMENT GROUPS: Two (including control).

NUMBER AND LOCATION OF SITES: There were 16 sites in 10 states: Chula Vista, Inglewood, and San Jose, California; Denver, Colorado; Jacksonville, Florida; Chicago Heights, Illinois; Lexington, Kentucky; Detroit, Michigan; Minneapolis, Minnesota; Bronx and Harlem, New York; Portland and Salem, Oregon; Allentown, Philadelphia, and Pittsburgh, Pennsylvania.

RESEARCH COMPONENTS:

Process analysis: Describes the New Chance population, the treatment implementation, and patterns of program participation. Interviews were conducted with program coordinators and other key personnel.

Impact analysis: Regression adjustment of experimental–control differences.

Benefit–cost analysis: Not conducted.

MAJOR FINDINGS:
1. Because of absenteeism and early departures from the program, members of the experimental group received a much lower dose of services than had been anticipated. Also, the level of service receipt among control group members was much higher than anticipated. Thus, there was not a large differential between the quantity of services received by the treatment and control groups, especially with regard to education- and employment-related services.
2. Both experimentals and controls improved their status over time (e.g., they were more likely to be employed and less likely to be on welfare), but for the most part, experimentals did not improve more than controls.
3. Treatment group members were significantly more likely to have earned a high school diploma or GED than were control group members (53 percent versus 45 percent). They were also more likely to have earned college credits (15 percent versus 13 percent).

4. No significant differences were found between groups on measures of employment or earnings for the full 42-month follow-up period.
5. New Chance did not reduce the rates of pregnancies or childbearing or affect participants' health status.
6. The program had unexpected negative effects on participants' emotional well-being (the treatment group scored significantly higher on measures of depression and stress) and on their perceptions of their children's behavior (as measured by behavioral rating scores).

TIME TRENDS IN THE FINDINGS: None.

DESIGN ISSUES: Implementation of some program components (e.g., career exploration and pre-employment skills instruction) was hindered by sites' lack of experience with these kinds of services. Further, since later activities (skills training, internships, job placement) were mostly delivered off-site, they were difficult to implement and less uniform across sites.

REPLICABILITY: Replicable, although there was considerable variation by site in how the program services were administered.

GENERALIZABILITY: Designed to generalize to young mothers on welfare who are high school dropouts. New Chance was a voluntary program. Sample characteristics at random assignment include: average age, 18.8; 71 percent nonwhite; average age of youngest child, 1.2 years; 94 percent of sample did not have a high school diploma or equivalent; 3.1 percent were employed at baseline; and 95 percent received AFDC.

FUNDING SOURCE: The project was funded by the U.S. Department of Labor and a broad consortium of private foundations and corporations.

TREATMENT ADMINISTRATOR: Manpower Demonstration Research Corporation (MDRC) was responsible for the overall treatment. Direct administration was the responsibility of the individual sites.

EVALUATOR: Manpower Demonstration Research Corporation. Project director: Robert C. Granger.

ENABLING LEGISLATION: None.

INFORMATION SOURCE(S):   Janet C. Quint, Hans Bos, and Denise F. Polit, *New Chance: Final Findings on a Comprehensive Program for Disadvantaged Young Mothers and Their Children*, MDRC, New York, May 1997.

PUBLIC-USE ACCESS TO DATA: Available through Manpower Demonstration Research Corporation.

OHIO TRANSITIONS TO INDEPENDENCE
DEMONSTRATION—JOBS

SUMMARY: This demonstration, conducted from 1989 to 1992, tested the effects of employment and training participation on a large sample of welfare recipients. Subjects were followed for up to three years. The JOBS demonstration was one component of a larger evaluation, which also included the Work Choice demonstration.

COST: Evaluation costs, approximately $3 million (includes Work Choice).

TIME FRAME: Demonstration period, January 1989–December 1992; data collected, same period; final report, December 1994.

TREATMENT(S) TESTED: Mandatory employment and training services, which included basic and postsecondary education, community work experience, and job search assistance.

OUTCOMES OF INTEREST: (1) Employment; (2) Earnings; and (3) Welfare receipt.

SAMPLE SIZE: Total sample, 28,491; treatment, 24,120 (a random subsample was used for analysis); control, 4,371.

TARGET POPULATION: All recipients of ADC (Ohio's AFDC program).

NUMBER OF TREATMENT GROUPS: Two (including control).

NUMBER AND LOCATION OF SITES: 15 Ohio counties: Brown, Champaign, Clermont, Franklin, Lake, Lawrence, Montgomery, Perry, Pickaway, Richland, Seneca, Stark, Summit, Trumbull, and Wyandot.

RESEARCH COMPONENTS:
Process analysis: Implementation, participation rates, and assignment patterns analyzed.
Impact analysis: Conducted using regression-adjusted means.
Benefit–cost analysis: Conducted.

MAJOR FINDINGS:
1. JOBS produced significantly higher rates of employment for all treatment group cohorts compared to the control group (e.g., for third-year follow-up: treatment group, 45.5 percent; control group, 42.2 percent).
2. JOBS produced no significant differences between treatment and control groups for earnings or ADC receipt. However, subgroup analysis does indicate significant earnings impacts among clients with 12 or more years of education. This supports past research

suggesting that mandatory employment and training programs tend to boost earnings more for moderately disadvantaged clients than for the most or least disadvantaged.

TIME TRENDS IN FINDINGS: No trends were evident, though the report suggests that the nature of the program assignments implies that long-run impacts could take longer to emerge than the follow-up period covered in the evaluation.

DESIGN ISSUES:
1. The state found itself having to provide a wide new array of employment and training services to a broad clientele with extremely limited resources. Implementation of JOBS coincided with a recession. The resulting effects were lengthy waits for assessment and assignment, low rates of participation, and insufficient program staff to support key case management functions (e.g., monitoring and sanctioning).
2. A tradition of autonomous county governments contributed to the slow pace of JOBS implementation. Counties often had to develop their own approaches to many tasks.
3. Two different state systems made data file construction difficult. Further, the system was changed midway through the demonstration.

REPLICABILITY: Replicable.

GENERALIZABILITY: Designed to generalize to the entire state. The sample counties' populations resembled the state's as a whole and Ohio's ADC caseload characteristics and benefits closely resemble those of the nation as a whole. Random assignment at the point of eligibility determination provides an approximation of a fully implemented program. Impacts for the JOBS program are not as favorable as those found in other states (e.g., California and Florida).

FUNDING SOURCES: Ohio Department of Human Services. Key personnel: Jackie Martin, contract officer. The U.S. Department of Health and Human Services matched state funds.

TREATMENT ADMINISTRATOR: Ohio Department of Human Services. Key personnel: Ellen Seusy and Jackie Martin, contract officers. The County Departments of Human Services in the sample counties had substantial autonomy and responsibility for administering these programs.

EVALUATOR: Abt Associates. Principal evaluators: David Fein, Erik Beecroft, and John Blomquist.

ENABLING LEGISLATION: None.

INFORMATION SOURCES: David Fein, Erik Beecroft, and John Blomquist, *The Ohio Transitions to Independence Demonstration: Final Impacts for JOBS and Work Choice,* Abt Associates, December 1994.

PUBLIC-USE ACCESS TO DATA: A data tape from the demonstration is in the custody of the Ohio Department of Human Services. Jackie Martin, in a telephone communication (March 1997) stated that the Department had not made any decisions about public access.

OHIO TRANSITIONS TO INDEPENDENCE DEMONSTRATION—WORK CHOICE

SUMMARY: This demonstration, conducted from 1989 to 1990, tested the effects of voluntary employment and training services and extended transitional Medicaid and child care payments on a large sample of single-parent welfare recipients with children under age 6. These subjects were followed for up to 18 months. This was one component of a larger evaluation, which included the JOBS demonstration.

COST: Evaluation costs, approximately $3 million (for both Work Choice and JOBS demonstrations).

TIME FRAME: Demonstration period, January 1989–December 1990; data collected, same period; final report, December 1994.

TREATMENT(S) TESTED: Work Choice tested the same services as JOBS (employment and training services, basic and postsecondary education, community work experience, and job search assistance) plus extended transitional Medicaid and child care payments upon leaving ADC (Ohio's AFDC program) for work.

OUTCOMES OF INTEREST: (1) Employment; (2) Earnings; and (3) Welfare receipt.

SAMPLE SIZE: Total sample, 5,609; treatment, 4,265; control, 1,344.

TARGET POPULATION: Single-parent ADC clients with children aged 1 to 5.

NUMBER OF TREATMENT GROUPS: Two (including control).

NUMBER AND LOCATION OF SITES: Montgomery Country, Ohio (including city of Dayton).

RESEARCH COMPONENTS:
Process analysis: Implementation, participation rates, and assignment patterns analyzed.
Impact analysis: Conducted using regression-adjusted means.
Benefit–cost analysis: Conducted.

MAJOR FINDINGS:

1. The vast majority of Work Choice assignments were to education and training activities, mostly basic and postsecondary programs (34 percent of entrants volunteering for activities received basic education, 33 percent received postsecondary programs). By the end of follow-up, only 14 percent had volunteered for employment and training activities, half as many as in the JOBS program.
2. Work Choice had small, though significant, positive impacts on net employment and earnings. Employment rates were about 3 percentage points higher for members of the treatment group than for members of the control group, and their average earnings were about $177 higher over the 18-month period.
3. Only 4 percent of treatment group members and 3 percent of control-group members used extended Medicaid sometime during the 18-month follow-up period when they left ADC. Although this 1 percentage point difference is statistically significant, it is far from clear that the extended benefits were an incentive for welfare-to-work transitions.

TIME TRENDS IN FINDINGS: No trends were evident, though the report suggests that the nature of the program assignments implies that long-run impacts could take longer to emerge than the follow-up period covered in the evaluation.

DESIGN ISSUES:

1. The state found itself having to provide a wide new array of employment and training services to a broad clientele with extremely limited resources. Implementation coincided with a recession. The resulting effects were lengthy waits for assessment and assignment, low rates of participation, and insufficient program staff to support key case management functions (e.g., monitoring and sanctioning).
2. A tradition of autonomous county governments contributed to the slow pace of implementation. Counties often had to develop their own approaches to many tasks.
3. The Work Choice demonstration ended earlier than planned when, in April 1990, the state began offering eligibility for extended Medicaid and child-care benefits to members of the control group. This led to a maximum follow-up of only 18 months.

4. Two different state systems made data file construction difficult. Further, the system was changed midway through the demonstration.

REPLICABILITY: Replicable.

GENERALIZABILITY: Designed to generalize to the entire state. The sample county's population resembled the state's as a whole, and Ohio's ADC caseload characteristics and benefits closely resemble those of the nation as a whole. Random assignment at the point of eligibility determination provides an approximation of a fully implemented program.

FUNDING SOURCES: Ohio Department of Human Services. Key personnel: Jackie Martin, contract officer. The U.S. Department of Health and Human Services matched state funds.

TREATMENT ADMINISTRATOR: Ohio Department of Human Services. Key personnel: Ellen Seusy and Jackie Martin, contract officers. The County Departments of Human Services in the sample counties had substantial autonomy and responsibility for administering these programs.

EVALUATOR: Abt Associates. Principal evaluators: David Fein, Erik Beecroft, and John Blomquist.

ENABLING LEGISLATION: None.

INFORMATION SOURCES: David Fein, Erik Beecroft, and John Blomquist, *The Ohio Transitions to Independence Demonstration: Final Impacts for JOBS and Work Choice*, Abt Associates, December 1994.

PUBLIC-USE ACCESS TO DATA: A data tape from the demonstration is in the custody of the Ohio Department of Human Services. Jackie Martin, in a telephone communication (March 1997), stated that the Department had not made any decisions about public access.

OPPORTUNITY KNOCKS PROGRAM

SUMMARY: This demonstration, conducted from 1989 through 1992, tested the effects of intensive case management on a small sample of low-income single-parent families. Subjects were followed for two years.

COST: Evaluation costs, approximately $20,000–$22,000.

TIME FRAME: Demonstration period, July 1989–November 1991 with a one-year extension; data collected, same period; final report, April 1995.

TREATMENTS TESTED: Intensive case management, which included vocational assessment, education, training, and job search assistance. Funds were also made available for transportation, child care, and other employment-related expenses. The control group received minimal counseling and referral services, as well as job training and housing assistance.

OUTCOMES OF INTEREST: (1) Employment; (2) Earnings; and (3) Welfare receipt.

SAMPLE SIZE: Total, 163; treatment, 82; control, 81.

TARGET POPULATION: Single-parent families receiving AFDC, applying for or residing in section 8 housing, at or below 125 percent of the poverty level.

NUMBER OF TREATMENT GROUPS: Two (including control).

NUMBER AND LOCATION OF SITES: DuPage County, Illinois.

RESEARCH COMPONENTS:
   Process analysis: Conducted to describe the process of partnership development, service delivery, and program environment.
   Impact analysis: Conducted using comparison of means.
   Benefit–cost analysis: Not conducted.

MAJOR FINDINGS:
1. After a negative impact on employment during the first quarter after enrollment, the program produced steadily increasing employment effects for the treatment group. The difference between the treatment group and the control group became statistically significant in the sixth quarter and remained significant through the eighth quarter. The total impact of the program in the second year after enrollment was also significant, culminating in an almost 12 percent difference between the groups (employment rate: treatment group, 47 percent; control group, 35.2 percent).
2. The earning impacts closely resembled those found for employment. The earnings differential steadily increased to produce a significant impact of $415 per quarter per participant in the second year (treatment group, $1,251 per quarter; control group, $836).
3. It is estimated that the average treatment group family, despite significant earnings gains, remained below the poverty level.

TIME TRENDS IN FINDINGS: Employment and earnings impacts were negative (treatment group was employed at a lower rate and earned less) in the first and second quarters, respectively. Positive impacts became significant and increased over time and in the fifth and sixth quarters, respectively.

DESIGN ISSUES:

1. Because of problems recruiting sufficient AFDC families to the program, the target population needed to be expanded. As a result, nearly 25 percent of the sample was not receiving AFDC when they enrolled.
2. Due to difficulties surrounding the confidentiality of the public aid records and the technical complexity of conducting a database search, the use of a cash welfare benefit measure was not included in the analysis.
3. Lack of training and ambiguous or nonexistent definitions of data elements led to coding errors and to the omission of information.
4. After a brief intake, "no one was really involved" in the application procedure to contact participants and encourage their participation. Many participants were lost at this point. Nearly 45 percent of the treatment group never showed up, did not follow through, or were unable to participate. This group of nonparticipants was included in the analysis, which could have resulted in underestimation of the program impacts.

REPLICABILITY: Replicable. Documentation of the procedures is available to ensure consistency of service, though more training for case managers would be necessary to improve the correct implementation of these procedures.

GENERALIZABILITY: The small sample size and the design and implementation issues discourage attempts at generalizability. The sample characteristics do, however, generally reflect a nationwide population of low-income single-parent families.

FUNDING SOURCE: U.S. Department of Health and Human Services (DHHS), Administration for Children and Families, Office of Community Services; DuPage County.

TREATMENT ADMINISTRATOR: DuPage County Department of Human Resources, Division of Human Services. Key personnel: Jack Tenison, director; Betsey Eben, program manager.

EVALUATOR: Center for Governmental Studies, Northern Illinois University. Key personnel: Catherine Harned, senior research associate; Sean Fahey, research associate.

ENABLING LEGISLATION: Demonstration Partnership Program, under section 408 of the Human Services Reauthorization Act of 1986, as amended.

INFORMATION SOURCES: U.S. Department of Health and Human Services, *Summary of Final Evaluation Findings from FY 1991: Demonstration Partnership Program Projects. Monograph Series 100-91: Case Management/Family Development*, 1995.

PUBLIC-USE ACCESS TO DATA: Available through DHHS Office of Community Services.

WISCONSIN EARNED INCOME DISREGARD DEMONSTRATION

SUMMARY: This demonstration, conducted from 1989 to 1992, tested the effects of a more generous income disregard on a large sample of AFDC recipients. Subjects were followed for four years.

COST: The evaluations of both the Earned Income Disregard and the Medical Assistance Extension demonstrations were conducted together. Total evaluation costs were $368,953.

TIME FRAME;   Demonstration period, February 1989–March 1992; data collected, same period.

TREATMENTS TESTED: An increase in the earned income disregard to $30 and one-sixth of earned income for 12 months. The control group disregard was the existing $30 and one-third of earned income for four months and $30 for the remaining eight months. The disregard is used to calculate AFDC grant amounts.

OUTCOMES OF INTEREST: (1) Welfare participation and benefit receipt; (2) Employment; (3) Family Income; and (4) Program costs.

SAMPLE SIZE: Exact figures were unavailable, although the sample was the entire statewide caseload. Ninety percent of this caseload were in the treatment group; 10 percent were in the control group.

TARGET POPULATION: Recipients of AFDC.

NUMBER OF TREATMENT GROUPS: Two (including control).

NUMBER AND LOCATION OF SITES: Throughout the state of Wisconsin.

RESEARCH COMPONENTS:
    Process: The evaluators met regularly with the state team to discuss the demonstration's progress.

Impact: Comparison of means.

Benefit–cost analysis: Not conducted.

MAJOR FINDINGS: There was no significant difference between groups on welfare participation, AFDC grant level, overall program costs, or family income.

TIME TRENDS IN THE FINDINGS: None.

DESIGN ISSUES: Two separate evaluation teams worked on this project. Design and data collection were completed by one team. A second group of evaluators was brought in to conduct data analysis when, according to one evaluator of the second team, the state was not pleased with early results. There seems to have been little communication between the two teams. Process analysis was minimal and program goals were unclear to those involved in the analysis.

REPLICABILITY: Replicable.

GENERALIZABILITY: Designed to generalize to the entire state of Wisconsin.

FUNDING SOURCE: Wisconsin Department of Health and Social Services (DHSS). Key personnel: Richard Zynde.

TREATMENT ADMINISTRATOR: Wisconsin DHSS.

EVALUATOR: Deloitte and Touche LLP. Key personnel: Steve Blank.

ENABLING LEGISLATION: None.

INFORMATION SOURCE(S): Wisconsin Department of Health and Social Services, *Evaluation of Earned Income Disregard and MA Extension Waivers*, March 1995.

PUBLIC-USE ACCESS TO DATA: Available from Wisconsin DHSS.

WISCONSIN MEDICAL ASSISTANCE EXTENSION DEMONSTRATION

SUMMARY: This demonstration, conducted from 1989 to 1990, tested the effect of extending transitional Medical Assistance benefits on a large sample of ex-recipients of AFDC. Subjects were followed for 14 months.

COST: The evaluations of both the Earned Income Disregard and the Medical Assistance Extension demonstrations were conducted together. Total evaluation costs were $368,953.

TIME FRAME: Demonstration period, February 1989–April 1990. The demonstration period was designed to be longer, but was cut short when the state adopted the 12-month extension for all eligible individuals.

TREATMENTS TESTED: An extension of Medical Assistance (MA) for 12 months after termination of AFDC eligibility due to earned income or excess hours of employment. The control group received the existing 4/9 policy (cases were reviewed after 4 months and possibly approved for an additional 9 months).

OUTCOMES OF INTEREST: (1) Welfare participation and benefit receipt; (2) Employment; (3) Family Income; and (4) Program costs.

SAMPLE SIZE: Treatment, 135,334; control, 18,493.

TARGET POPULATION: Individuals leaving the AFDC rolls due to employment.

NUMBER OF TREATMENT GROUPS: Two (including control).

NUMBER AND LOCATION OF SITES: Wisconsin, statewide.

RESEARCH COMPONENTS:

Process: The evaluators met regularly with the state team to discuss the demonstration's progress.

Impact: Comparison of means.

Benefit–cost analysis: Not conducted.

MAJOR FINDINGS:

1. There was no significant difference between groups in welfare participation, overall costs, or family income. This indicates that the treatment did not result in an incentive for cases to leave the AFDC program.

2. There was a lower rate of recidivism (returning to the AFDC rolls after leaving) for the treatment group as compared to the control group. In the treatment group, 73.2 percent of cases that closed during the project period never reopened. For control group cases, this figure was 69.8 percent, for a difference of 3.4 percent.

TIME TRENDS IN THE FINDINGS: None.

DESIGN ISSUES:

1. Two separate evaluation teams worked on this project. Design and data collection were completed by one team. A second group of evaluators was brought in to conduct data analysis when, accord-

ing to one evaluator, the state was not pleased with early results. There seems to have been little communication between the two teams. Process analysis was minimal, and program goals were unclear to those involved in the analysis.

2. There was a limited comparison period because the 12-month MA extension was implemented as the standard program statewide in April 1990, thereby making the treatment available to the entire target population.

REPLICABILITY: Replicable.

GENERALIZABILITY: Designed to generalize to the entire state of Wisconsin.

FUNDING SOURCE: Wisconsin Department of Health and Social Services (DHHS). Key personnel: Richard Zynde.

TREATMENT ADMINISTRATOR: Wisconsin DHSS.

EVALUATOR: Deloitte and Touche LLP. Key personnel: Steve Blank.

ENABLING LEGISLATION: None.

INFORMATION SOURCE: Wisconsin Department of Health and Social Services, *Evaluation of Earned Income Disregard and MA Extension Waivers*, March 1995.

PUBLIC-USE ACCESS TO DATA: Available from Wisconsin DHSS.

AFDC JOBS PARTICIPANTS: PATHS TOWARD SELF-SUFFICIENCY

SUMMARY: This demonstration, conducted between 1990 and 1992, tested the effects of in-home case management on a medium-sized sample of AFDC recipients. Subjects were followed for one year.

COST: Cost figures are unavailable. The Demonstration Partnership Program grants were generally between $350,000 and $500,000, with roughly 10 percent going toward evaluation.

TIME FRAME: Demonstration period, October 1990–December 1992; data collected, same period; final report, December 1993.

TREATMENTS TESTED: In-home case management coupled with core support services. These included educational/job training assistance, basic living skills workshop, counseling, housing assistance, child care assistance, transportation, and health care assistance. Services were roughly the same for both the intensive and nonintensive groups, although the nature of the clients was different. The control group received existing AFDC services.

Outcomes of Interest:　(1) Earnings, AFDC receipt; (2) Educational or employment status; and (3) Other measures of self-sufficiency.

Sample Size:　Initial sample: intensive group, 121; nonintensive group, 92; comparison group, 123. Sample retained and used in analysis: intensive, 42; nonintensive, 70; comparison, 85.

Target Population:　AFDC recipients in the Lincoln, Nebraska, JOBS program, at or below 125 percent of the poverty level.

Number of Treatment Groups:　Three—intensive group (phase I, not randomly assigned); nonintensive group; and comparison group (phase II, random assignment).

Number and Location of Sites:　One—Lincoln, Nebraska.

Research Components:
Process analysis: Special attention was paid to program retention and service delivery.

Impact analysis: Pre/postproject comparison, comparison of means.

Benefit–cost analysis: SRI Gallup conducted a benefit–cost analysis in a separate report issued six months into the intervention. A benefit–cost analysis was not done as part of the final report.

Major Findings:　Note that random assignment occurred only in phase II. Direct comparisons should only be made between the nonintensive group and the comparison group. The project report does, however, combine the two project groups in the analysis for some outcome measures.

1. For all groups, salary increased significantly and AFDC payments decreased significantly from pretest to posttest. Project group numbers were larger than those of the comparison group though not statistically significant. (Average change in salary: intensive, $150.74; nonintensive, $200.01; comparison, $156.59. Average decrease in AFDC payments: intensive, $71.33; nonintensive, $76.47; comparison, $53.80.)
2. A significantly higher percentage of project (intensive and nonintensive) participants continued their education as compared to the comparison group.
3. Project groups had significantly greater gains on the Goal Attainment Scale (GAS), a measure of basic living skills, than did the comparison group.

TIME TRENDS IN FINDINGS: None mentioned.

DESIGN ISSUES:

1. Due to the referral process, initial participants faced severe barriers to self-sufficiency. This group was therefore not assigned randomly to treatment and control groups, but, rather, received intensive case management. They differed significantly from the other two groups on a number of variables.
2. The rate of attrition was higher than expected, especially for the intensive group. After mandatory referral from the Nebraska Department of Social Services, participants were allowed to voluntarily continue with case management. Many participants were lost at this point.
3. Lincoln Action Program sought the partnership of other community agencies as required by Demonstration Partnership Program guidelines (see Appendix I for an explanation of the DPP partnerships). However, partner involvement was often minimal owing to unforeseen problems such as high caseloads and lack of communication. This involvement increased toward the end of the project.
4. Staff turnover was problematic. A number of staff left the project when the agency received other longer-term grants. This may have reduced the project's effectiveness.

REPLICABILITY: The report states that replication of this project would be easy owing to the detailed explanation of the interventions used. The project's model has been replicated with other agency projects.

GENERALIZABILITY: Findings from the Phase I (intensive) group are not generalizable since no similar comparison group was used. Random assignment of the nonintensive group does allow for comparison and generalizations, although the sample was quite small. Both treatment groups tended to have greater barriers to self-sufficiency than the AFDC population in general.

FUNDING SOURCE: U.S. Department of Health and Human Services (DHHS), Administration for Children and Families, Office of Community Services. Key personnel: Anna Guidery.

TREATMENT ADMINISTRATOR: Lincoln Action Program. Key personnel: Beatty Brasch, director, and Anne Caruso.

EVALUATOR: Gary Hoeltke (deceased), SRI Gallup.

ENABLING LEGISLATION: Demonstration Partnership Program, under section 408 of the Human Services Reauthorization Act of 1986, as amended.

INFORMATION SOURCES: U.S. Department of Health and Human Services, *Demonstration Partnership Program Projects: Summary of Final Evaluation Findings from 1990. Case Management Family Intervention Models*, 1993.

PUBLIC-USE ACCESS TO DATA: Available through the DHHS Office of Community Services.

PROJECT INDEPENDENCE—FLORIDA

SUMMARY: This demonstration, conducted from 1990 to 1993, tested the effects of education, training, and enhanced support services on a large sample of AFDC recipients. Subjects were followed for three years.

COST: Evaluation costs, $3.6 million over five years.

TIME FRAME: Demonstration period, July 1990–September 1993; data collected, same period; final report, April 1995.

TREATMENTS TESTED: The treatment group was eligible to receive Project Independence services and was subject to a participation mandate. Services included independent job search, job club, assessment, basic education, and training. The control group was not eligible for these services and was not subject to a participation mandate. They were given a list of alternative employment and training services in the community.

OUTCOMES OF INTEREST: (1) Employment; (2) Earnings; and (3) AFDC receipts.

SAMPLE SIZE: Treatment group, 13,513; control group, 4,724.

TARGET POPULATION: Single-parent heads of household who were required to participate in the program (recipients of AFDC).

NUMBER OF TREATMENT GROUPS: Two (including control).

NUMBER OF LOCATION OF SITES: Nine randomly selected counties in Florida: Bay, Broward, Dade, Duval, Hillsborough, Lee, Orange, Pinellas, and Volusia.

RESEARCH COMPONENTS: Process analysis: The evaluators paid special attention to the changes in service delivery and resources that occurred over the evaluation period.

Impact analysis: Conducted using comparison of regression-adjusted means.

Benefit–cost analysis: Conducted.

MAJOR FINDINGS:

1. Project Independence resulted in a modest decrease in treatment group members' AFDC and food stamp receipts. Treatment group members received, on average, a total of $265 less than the control group members. This decrease persisted over the two-year follow-up period.
2. A modest earnings gain was achieved by the treatment group members in the first year, but declined greatly in the second year. Average two-year earnings increased by $227 per participant, or 4 percent.
3. Larger and more persistent program effects were found for the treatment group members who were referred to Project Independence before program resources were strained by growing caseloads. This group demonstrated average earnings gains of $439 over the control group.
4. Impacts were found mainly for individuals with no preschool-age children. Among those with preschool-age children, only those from the early group showed evidence of achieving short-term earnings gains.

TIME TRENDS IN FINDINGS: Treatment group members designated "not-job-ready" showed delayed earnings impacts in the second year of follow-up. "Job-ready" members showed greater first-year impacts.

DESIGN ISSUES:

1. Caseloads and unemployment rose during the experiment. Budget-induced hiring freezes prevented the project from increasing staffing capacity. Restrictions on the availability of child care also occurred during this time period. For these reasons, the researchers present data for two subgroups—the "early" group, who were exposed to Project Independence when its operations more closely matched the model originally intended, and the "late" group, who were exposed to the project during a period of restricted resources.
2. Randomization took place when people were applying for AFDC or were being assessed for eligibility for continued AFDC receipt. Most previous evaluations have randomized after orientation.
3. Eighty-eight percent of the research sample were first-time applicants or were reapplying after having been off the rolls. This suggests that they have been "somewhat less disadvantaged."

4. Some control group members were exposed to Project Independence by attending an orientation or participating in its employment-related activities. A 20 percent exposure was estimated.
5. The criteria for "job-readiness" was changed during the evaluation period to allow more participants to enter education and training services.

REPLICABILITY: Replicable.

GENERALIZABILITY: Designed to generalize to the entire state of Florida. The nine sample counties closely mirror Florida as a whole on a number of salient characteristics (e.g., poverty rates, unemployment rates). The nine counties had a smaller percentage of their population living in rural areas and a larger percentage of Hispanics than the state as a whole. Impacts, at least on the early cohort, are similar to those found in evaluations of similar projects nationwide.

FUNDING SOURCES: Florida Department of Health and Rehabilitative Services (HRS), the Ford Foundation, and the U.S. Department of Health and Human Services.

TREATMENT ADMINISTRATOR: HRS and its subcontractors (notably, the Department of Labor and Employment Security [LES]). Key Personnel at HRS: Don Winstead and Judy Moon.

EVALUATOR: Manpower Demonstration Research Corporation (MDRC). Key personnel: James Kemple, Daniel Friedlander, and Veronica Fellerath.

ENABLING LEGISLATION: Florida Employment Opportunity Act of 1987. Family Support Act of 1988.

POLICY EFFECTS: This study's findings were cited at a May 1994 hearing before the Subcommittee on Human Resources of the House of Representatives Committee on Ways and Means. The evaluator reported that the findings were also influential in the congressional welfare reform debates of 1996.

INFORMATION SOURCES: James J. Kemple, Daniel Friedlander, and Veronica Fellerath, *Florida's Project Independence: Benefits, Costs, and Two-Year Impacts of Florida's JOBS Program*, Manpower Demonstration Research Corporation, April 1995.

PUBLIC-USE ACCESS TO DATA: MDRC's contract with HRS did not include public-use files. They are not currently available, but should be available through MDRC at a later date.

MASSACHUSETTS WORK EXPERIENCE PROGRAM

SUMMARY: This demonstration, conducted from 1978 to 1979, tested the effects of a mandatory work experience program, assisted job search, and a lower tax rate on earnings on a medium-sized sample of unemployed fathers receiving Aid to Families with Dependent Children (AFDC). Subjects were followed for one year.

COST: $760,000 (if CETA-salaried staff not included, $570,000), 1978; research only, $300,000.

TIME FRAME: Demonstration period, January 1978–March 1979; data collected, same period; final report, October 1980.

TREATMENTS TESTED:
1. Controls received no treatment "other than any normal WIN actions."
2. Experimental group 1 received a waiver of the 100-hours-per-month-maximum-labor limitation for AFDC–Unemployed Fathers program recipients. Instead, they were subject to the "30 and 1/3" rule for six months. Under the latter, the first $30 earned does not count against the welfare benefit received, and earnings above $30 are subject to a 67 percent tax rate.
3. Experimental group 2 received the above treatment and, in addition, were assigned to unpaid work for public or nonprofit agencies three days a week. Failure to report to work could result in sanctions amounting to partial loss of AFDC benefits. The other two days a week were for participation in the agency-assisted job search. Unpaid workers received $30 per month incentive pay and lunch and travel reimbursement. If unable to find regular work within 13 weeks, they were assigned to a second work site.

OUTCOMES OF INTEREST: (1) Employment and (2) AFDC savings.

SAMPLE SIZE: Group 1, 150; group 2, 140; and group 3, 725.

TARGET POPULATION: Unemployed fathers receiving AFDC were screened for the following criteria: (1) not already in a special WIN treatment program, (2) unemployed for at least six months, (3) referred unsuccessfully to regular or CETA jobs, (4) "unsuitable for referral to another WIN component," and (5) found on interview to be physically and emotionally able to work.

NUMBER OF TREATMENT GROUPS: Three (with one control group).

NUMBER AND LOCATION OF SITES: Massachusetts, statewide.

RESEARCH COMPONENTS:
Process analysis: Extensive. Interviews conducted with WIN staff on selection and work-site assignment process, with work supervisors and experimental subjects.
Impact analysis: Conducted with logit regressions.
Benefit–cost analysis: Conducted.

MAJOR FINDINGS:
Percentage finding unsubsidized employment over the five quarters: controls, 28.7 percent; experimental 1, 30.7 percent; and experimental 2, 34.2 percent. These results were not statistically significant.
AFDC payments, average over five quarters: controls, $839; experimental 1, $864; and experimental 2, $925. (The authors pointed out that controls also received lower payments on average before the experiment began.)
Received no AFDC for at least one quarter: controls, 42.3 percent; experimental 1, 35.2 percent; and experimental 2, 38.3 percent.

TIME TRENDS IN FINDINGS: Nonattenders at work sites in experimental group 2 reported finding employment faster than attenders in early quarters; the reverse was true in later quarters. It is possible that for some nonattenders the program either was incompatible with employment not reported to Public Welfare workers or provided additional incentive to find work.

DESIGN ISSUES:
1. The Work Experience program was the subject of intense public controversy for months before its implementation. A court injunction was in force from March 14 to April 10, 1978, during which all work performed under it had to be voluntary. Also the ultimately unsuccessful court challenge made the intake process much more selective. Both unemployables and very employables were

screened out, and it would be difficult to compare the resulting sample with a population of interest.

2. The screening process was highly discretionary; persons assigned to the sample varied from 15 percent to 61 percent of the underlying pool, from one region of the state to another.

3. Cutbacks in CETA staff led to many potential subjects never being called in for an interview. This had different effects across the state, and introduced an additional regional bias.

4. Sanctions were weak and were seldom used. Two-thirds of experimental group 2 never went to assigned work sites, many of them because they were never told to. Some WIN teams in the state made no effort to enforce the sanctions, and the WIN staff in one region seems to have encouraged clients not to cooperate with the program.

5. Additional assistance in job search was minimal. The change in rules from 100 hours to 30⅓ hours was only effectively communicated to the WIN teams rather late in the experiment, which means it was never communicated to many of the subjects in experimental group 2.

REPLICABILITY: The treatment described in official documents is replicable.

GENERALIZABILITY: Workfare experiments in other states might have similar implementation problems, but the effects here are so severe that the findings probably cannot be generalized.

FUNDING SOURCE: U.S. Department of Labor, Manpower Administration. Key personnel: Howard Rosen.

TREATMENT ADMINISTRATORS: Massachusetts Department of Employment Security (MDES) and Massachusetts Department of Public Welfare (MDPW). Key personnel: MDES—Richard Sullivan and Richard Dill; MDPW—Richard McKinnon.

EVALUATOR: Brandeis University, Center for Employment and Income Studies. Key personnel: Barry Friedman.

ENABLING LEGISLATION: None.

INFORMATION SOURCES: Barry Friedman, Barbara Davenport, Robert Evans, Andrew Hahn, Leonard Hausman, and Cecile Papirno, "An Evaluation of the Massachusetts Work Experience Program," U.S. Department of Health and Human Services, Social Security Administration, SSA Publication No. 13-11730, October 1980.

PUBLIC-USE ACCESS TO DATA: We have no information about a public-use file for this demonstration.

WEST VIRGINIA COMMUNITY WORK EXPERIENCE
PROGRAM (CWEP)

SUMMARY: This quasi-experimental demonstration, conducted from 1983 through 1986, tested the effects of saturation Community Work Experience on a large sample of AFDC-U recipients (unemployed heads of two-parent families). Subjects were followed for two years.

COST: Cost figures not available.

TIME FRAME: Intake period, March 1983–April 1984; data collected, January 1986; final report, September 1986.

TREATMENTS TESTED: The effects of creating and filling as many Community Work Experience Program (CWEP) positions as possible (the saturation areas) versus limiting CWEP participation to 40 percent of the caseload (the comparison areas). The CWEP program consists of mandatory "workfare" in return for AFDC benefits.

OUTCOMES OF INTEREST: (1) Participation levels; (2) Employment; (3) Earnings; and (4) Welfare receipt.

SAMPLE SIZE: Total, 5,630 AFDC-U registrants; 2,798 in saturation areas; 2,832 in control areas.

TARGET POPULATION: All new and existing AFDC-U applicants; 93 percent of this sample was male.

NUMBER OF TREATMENT GROUPS: Two groups, those in saturation areas and those in comparison areas.

NUMBER AND LOCATION OF SITES: Four pairs of sites were matched, then randomly assigned to either the saturation condition or the comparison condition. The saturation sites were: Huntington; Martinsburg; Parkersburg; and Princeton. The comparison sites were: Clarksburg; Fairmont; Fayetteville; and Grafton.

RESEARCH COMPONENTS:

Process analysis: Researchers reviewed with caseworkers the situation of each nonparticipating AFDC-U recipient in the saturation areas to determine why these men were not participating.

Impact analysis: Conducted using OLS regressions, two-tailed.

Benefit–cost analysis: Conducted.

MAJOR FINDINGS:

1. AFDC-U caseload participation rates for the saturation areas as a whole peaked at 69 percent in June 1983. This is the percentage of registrants in the caseload each month who held CWEP jobs during

that month. As planned, participation rates for the comparison areas peaked at 40 percent in July 1983. The Parkersburg area achieved the highest caseload participation rate—81 percent in August 1983. In all study areas, rates began to decline in the fall of 1983 as the size of caseloads increased. During most months for which rates were calculated, the difference between rates for saturation and comparison sites was about 30 percentage points.

2. Employment rates for the saturation areas remained roughly the same throughout the follow-up, with no statistically significant differences in any quarter. Earnings decreased slightly for the saturation members, averaging $2,582 from quarters two through six, compared to $2,785 for the comparison area AFDC-Us. Whereas significant differences were found in two quarters, these total figures are not statistically significant.

3. AFDC-Us in the saturation areas received, on average, significantly less welfare benefits than did those in the comparison areas. In the saturation areas, 89.5 percent had received at least some payments in quarters two through seven versus 91 percent in the comparison areas. In dollar amounts, average total AFDC payments received in the saturation areas were $1,915.87 versus $2,144.76 in the comparison areas.

TIME TRENDS IN FINDINGS: Participation rates declined, as noted above.

DESIGN ISSUES:

1. Despite careful matching of the saturation and comparison sites, they differed on certain key factors. Although the analysis used techniques to statistically adjust for differences in the demographic and economic characteristics of the areas, the observed differences in outcomes may still partly reflect differences in the characteristics of the areas.

2. The quality of employment and earnings data probably differed in the saturation and comparison areas. For example, the UI earnings records that were relied upon in the evaluation do not contain information on individuals working out of state. All four saturation sites bordered on other states, whereas only two comparison sites were on borders.

REPLICABILITY: Replicable.

GENERALIZABILITY: Designed to generalize to the entire state. The West Virginia AFDC population likely faces greater barriers to employment than the population in most parts of the nation. For example, unemployment rates in the study areas were very high (up to 30 percent) during this demonstration.

FUNDING SOURCES: West Virginia Department of Human Services, the Ford Foundation, and the Claude Worthington Benedum Foundation.

TREATMENT ADMINISTRATOR: West Virginia Department of Human Services.

EVALUATOR: Manpower Demonstration Research Corporation (MDRC). Principal investigator: Joseph Ball (deceased). Other key personnel: Daniel Friedlander, Marjorie Erickson, Gayle Hamilton, and Virginia Knox.

ENABLING LEGISLATION: Omnibus Budget Reconciliation Act (OBRA) of 1981.

INFORMATION SOURCES: Daniel Friedlander, Marjorie Erickson, Gayle Hamilton, and Virginia Knox, *West Virginia: Final Report on the Community Work Experience Demonstration*, Manpower Demonstration Research Corporation, September 1986.

PUBLIC-USE ACCESS TO DATA: Not available.

LINK-UP

SUMMARY: This demonstration, conducted between 1992 and 1994, tested the effects of waiving the 100-hour rule for a large group of AFDC-U recipients. Subjects were followed for two years.

COST: Evaluation costs were approximately $300,000.

TIME FRAME: Demonstration period, January 1992–December 1994.

TREATMENTS TESTED: The treatment was a waiver of the 100-hour rule in the eligibility criteria for Aid to Families with Dependent Children with unemployed parents (AFDC-U). Primary wage earners in the experimental group maintained eligibility for AFDC-U benefits while working 100 hours or more per month. Members in the control group became ineligible for these benefits if the primary wage earner worked 100 hours or more per month, regardless of earnings.

OUTCOMES OF INTEREST: (1) Employment; (2) Earnings; and (3) Welfare receipt.

SAMPLE SIZE: The original sample (cases entering the experiment from 1992–94) was 11,310. The first-year cohort in the final analysis was 5,948: treatment group, 4,470; control group, 1,478.

TARGET POPULATION: Recipients of AFDC-U, that is, two-parent households where both parents are unemployed.

NUMBER OF TREATMENT GROUPS: Two (including a control).

NUMBER AND LOCATION OF SITES: Eight counties in the San Joaquin Valley, California: Fresno, Kern, Kings, Madera, Mariposa, Merced, Stanislaus, and Tulare.

RESEARCH COMPONENTS:
   Process Analysis: Focused on random assignment procedures and differences among experimental sites.
   Impact analysis: Conducted using regression adjusted means.
   Benefit-cost analysis: Conducted.

MAJOR FINDINGS: An earlier report analyzed data for the entire sample of 11,310. The findings presented below are for those cases that entered the experiment during the first year (1992). This allows for a longer and more uniform follow-up period of two years.
1. Waiving the 100-hour rule had no effect on employment and earnings of the primary or secondary wage earners in AFDC-U families.
2. Except for Fresno, the treatment had little effect on time-on-aid or AFDC-U payments. In all counties but Fresno, the percentage of experimentals receiving AFDC-U payments was significantly higher than the percentage of controls only in quarters seven and eight. There were no significant differences in average total amounts of benefits received.
3. In Fresno County, experimentals stayed on aid longer than controls (16.27 months versus 13.91 months, respectively) on average, and had higher average total AFDC-U payments ($12,061 versus $10,448).

TIME TRENDS IN THE FINDINGS: As mentioned above, for all counties except Fresno, there was a significant treatment–control difference in AFDC-U receipt only in the last two quarters.

DESIGN ISSUES:
1. In Fresno, the 100-hour rule had been waived for all AFDC-U recipients since 1987. To establish a control group, every other new and eligible applicant was assigned to the control group. Thus, there was an overrepresentation of new AFDC-U applicants in the control group. These cases differed in terms of aid history (and

perhaps in other salient ways). This is a potentially serious threat to validity and is why the Fresno results were analyzed separately.
2. The 100-hour rule might significantly reduce AFDC-U applications; this entry effect would not be measured by the experiment.

REPLICABILITY: Replicable.

GENERALIZABILITY: Designed to generalize to the entire state of California. The sample size was large, but all sample counties were within the San Joaquin Valley area of California.

FUNDING SOURCE: California State Department of Social Services.

TREATMENT ADMINISTRATOR: California State Department of Social Services.

EVALUATOR: University of California–Los Angeles (UCLA), Center for Child and Family Policy Research. Principal investigator: Yeheskel Hasenfeld.

ENABLING LEGISLATION: None.

INFORMATION SOURCES: Yeheskel Hasenfeld, Alisa Lewin, and Michael Mitchell, LINK-UP Evaluation of the 100-Hour Rule Waiver for AFDC-U: Impact Analysis Revisited, UCLA, Center for Child and Family Policy Research, School of Public Policy and Social Research, August 1996. Yeheskel Hasenfeld, Alisa Lewin, and Michael Mitchell, LINK-UP: Evaluation of the 100-Hour Rule Waiver for AFDC-U— Impact and Cost–Benefit Analysis, UCLA, Center for Child and Family Policy Studies, 1995.

PUBLIC-USE ACCESS TO DATA: Available through California State Department of Social Services.

Part Three

PUBLIC ASSISTANCE RECIPIENTS—
FOOD STAMPS

FOOD STAMP WORK REGISTRATION AND JOB SEARCH DEMONSTRATION

SUMMARY: This demonstration, conducted from 1981 to 1983, tested the effects of eight models of mandatory job search on a large sample of applicants for food stamps. Subjects were followed for two years.

COST: Research only, roughly $3–$4 million (1983).

TIME FRAME: Demonstration period, October 1981–December 1983; data collected through June 1984; final report, June 1986.

TREATMENTS TESTED: Although a total of eight treatments were tested, only one treatment was tested at each demonstration site. The first four treatments were tested during the Initial Demonstration period (October 1981–March 1983), a recessionary period. The remaining four treatments were tested during the Expanded Demonstration period (October 1982–June 1984), a recovery period. The eight kinds of treatments were:

1. In-person registration model (Cheyenne, Colorado Springs, Sarasota, and Washington). All members of a recipiency household who were not exempt from work were required to register for work in person at the State Employment Security Agency (SESA) and to report evidence of registration to the Food Stamp Agency (FSA). In three out of four cases, the SESA added a requirement for certain numbers of job contacts to be made within a specified period of time.

2. Job Club model (Tucson, Albuquerque, and Detroit). Work registration occurred at the Food Stamp Agency. Nonexempt household members were then called in for assessment by the SESA; job-ready registrants were assigned to a standard Job Club group job search model, which lasted two or three weeks.

3. In-person registration/Job Club model (Austin). Work registration occurred at the SESA, and nonexempt job-ready persons were assigned to the Job Club model. Findings for this treatment are combined with those of model 2, because only one site was found that implemented it.

4. Food Stamp Agency/Job Club model (Schenectady, Niagara County, and Toledo). All work registration and job search requirements were completed at the FSA. A special FSA Employment Unit (EU) performed registration, assessment, and supervision. Job-ready registrants were required to make up to 24 employer contacts in an eight-week period, reporting regularly to the EU.

[Note: The next four treatments were not initiated until after October 1982 and, consequently, involve the FSA only, because by 1982 SESAs had been removed from the work registration process by legislation.]

5. Applicant search model (Nassau and Fresno Counties). Before applicants were certified to receive food stamps, household members not exempt from work registration were required to complete a specified number of employer contacts. Following certification, the EU monitored continuing employer contacts.

6. Job Club model (Portland, Lewiston, Augusta, Pensacola, and Portsmouth). All job-ready work registrants were assigned to a two-, three-, or four-week Job Club. In Pensacola, subjects were also required to complete six employer contacts in a two-week period prior to assignment to the Job Club.

7. Group job search assistance model (Clark and Madison Counties). A two-day Employability Skills Training workshop was followed by an eight-week job search requirement with biweekly group monitoring meetings.

8. Job Club/Workfare model (San Diego County). After a three-week Job Club, job-ready registrants who did not find a job were assigned to Workfare, under which they were required to repay the household food stamp allotment with work at the minimum wage.

Controls were not subject to any work requirements.

OUTCOMES OF INTEREST: (1) Employment; (2) Earnings; and (3) Transfer payments.

SAMPLE SIZE: Sample sizes for the Initial Demonstration were not reported in the 1986 final report, but 31,000 persons are said to have been randomly assigned. Key findings (e.g., earnings, employment) are based on follow-up interviews with randomly selected subsamples of the experimental and control populations. Applicant search model (#5): experimentals, 4,396; controls, 4,116; Job Club model (#6): experimentals, 2,333; controls, 1,633; group job search (#7): experimentals, 870; controls, 586; Job Club with Workfare (#8): experimentals, 2,070; controls, 422.

TARGET POPULATION: All recipients of food stamps who were not exempt from work registration (i.e., able-bodied persons 18–65 years of age, not enrolled at least half-time in school or training programs, not working 30 or more hours per week, not otherwise incapacitated, and not caring for children under 12. In Nassau and Fresno counties, subjects applying for food stamps and meeting the above criteria had to meet job search requirements before they were certified.

NUMBER OF TREATMENT GROUPS: Sixteen: one experimental and one control group for each model.

NUMBER AND LOCATION OF SITES: Twenty-one: Tucson, Arizona; Fresno and San Diego Counties, California; Colorado Springs, Colorado; Washington, D.C.; Pensacola and Sarasota, Florida; Clark and Madison Counties, Kentucky; Portland, Lewiston, and Augusta, Maine; Detroit, Michigan; Albuquerque, New Mexico; Nassau and Niagara Counties, and Schenectady, New York; Toledo, Ohio; Austin, Texas; Portsmouth, Virginia; Cheyenne, Wyoming.

RESEARCH COMPONENTS:

Process analysis: Conducted. The analysis found that the treatments were implemented as planned, although treatments involving groups (models 2, 3, 4, 6, 7, and 8) sometimes had difficulty matching staff to clients. On average, FSA staff terminated benefits to 23 percent of experimentals for noncompliance, compared with 9 percent of controls. According to the project report, "Contrary to the conventional view of policy analysts, agency staff are indeed willing to conduct assessment interviews, provide job search assistance, and sanction those who fail to comply."

Impact analysis: Conducted by site with tobit, and the results were then pooled.

Benefit–cost analysis: Conducted from taxpayer, recipient, and social perspectives.

MAJOR FINDINGS:

Impacts are reported by quarter (Q) following random assignment. "Transfers" refers to all transfers.

Model	Earnings (1st Q)	Earnings (2nd Q)	Food Stamps (2nd Q)	Transfers (2nd Q)
1	−$8	+$113	−$53	−$62
2 and 3	+53	+59	−41	−93
4	+11	+6	−4	−17
5	+126	+117	−20	−111
6	+76	+29	−13	−31
7	−23	+54	−33	−60
8	+136	+208	−59	−117

Benefit–cost analysis showed positive social net benefits for all models except #4. Net social benefits per experimental ranged from −$55 for #4 to +$471 for #8. Taxpayers had a net benefit from all models except #4, with transfer savings greater than administrative costs. Recipients had a net loss of income in models 2 and 3, 4, and 7, but a net income gain in models 1, 5, 6, and 8. Since models 2 and

3 and 6 are identical in concept, implementation may matter. Implementation was also felt to be important with respect to model 8: "Given San Diego's extensive experience with Workfare, coupled with its high priority on rigorous implementation of job search and work requirements, the success of the Job Club/Workfare Model might be attributed to factors specific to San Diego as well as to the attributes of the model." Models 1 and 5, however, were effective in a wide range of sites.

TIME TRENDS IN FINDINGS: As shown.

DESIGN ISSUES:

1. Previous research had found that many registrants faced little or no actual treatment, owing to agency policy, administrative failure, insufficient resources, or other reasons, despite the legislative mandates for work registration and job search. This accounts for the decision that controls should face no work requirement. However, it might well be the case that the typical U.S. food stamp recipient did face some requirement, however small.

2. All the demonstration sites volunteered to participate in the experiment. Clearly, the findings of the experiment do not apply to agencies that would refuse to administer these treatments or that lacked the resources. In that sense, there is a site-selection bias. According to Kowal, managers at some sites were motivated by the prospect of savings in county payments to General Assistance, which is sometimes administered jointly with Food Stamps, and in others were simply strongly motivated to establish model programs. Thus, the results are best interpreted as predictions of the probable impact of an experimental treatment if local agency managers chose to implement it thoroughly, rather than enforce no requirement whatever.

3. The Food Stamp program interacts with other support programs (such as Unemployment Insurance and Aid to Families with Dependent Children [AFDC]). There is no discussion in the final report about what the consequences would be if the recipients of more than one income maintenance program were then subject to more than one work search requirement.

4. There is no discussion in the final report on the reasons for basing the employment and earnings findings on follow-up interviews rather than administrative records, such as are maintained for unemployment insurance. Follow-up interviews were only planned for about a sixth of the total sample, and the response rate was only 61 percent. The authors attempt to correct for potential non-

response bias, but no consistent technique exists for dealing with it.

REPLICABILITY: Replicable.

GENERALIZABILITY: Site self-selection bias is critical. Local agency managers will not always have the motivation or the ability to implement these programs as well as the agencies who ran them in this demonstration.

FUNDING SOURCE: U.S. Department of Agriculture, Food and Nutrition Service. Key personnel: Boyd Kowal.

TREATMENT ADMINISTRATORS: State employment security and social service agencies in 21 locations.

EVALUATORS: Center for Human Resources, Florence Heller Graduate School, Brandeis University; Abt Associates. Key personnel: Leonard Hausman, research design; Jane Kulik, project director; Robert Lerman and Barry Friedman, principal authors.

ENABLING LEGISLATION: None.

POLICY EFFECTS: Boyd Kowal has stated that the Agriculture Department had recommended that states be allowed flexibility in enforcing work registration and job search requirements. The act reauthorizing the Food Stamps Program in 1985 allowed for such flexibility, and the experimental findings might have influenced the congressional authors.

INFORMATION SOURCES: Robert Lerman and Barry Friedman, with Shari Ajemian, Charles K. Fairchild, JoAnn Jastrzab, Jane Kulik, Christopher Logan, Cecile Papirno, and Adam Seitchik, "Food Stamp Work Registration and Job Search Demonstration: Final Report," July 1986. The experiment was conducted in two independent phases; this report does not include significant information about the initial phase, which was discussed in a previous final report, dated June 1985.

PUBLIC-USE ACCESS TO DATA: We have no information about a public-use file for this demonstration.

ILLINOIS MONTHLY REPORTING FOOD STAMP DEMONSTRATION

SUMMARY: This demonstration, conducted from October 1981 to September 1982, tested the effects of monthly reporting of household circumstances on a large sample of joint Aid to Families with Dependent Children (AFDC)/food stamp recipients. Subjects were followed for one year.

COST: Evaluation costs, $1.2 million.

TIME FRAME: Demonstration period, October 1981–September 1982; final report, June 1985.

TREATMENTS TESTED: Recipients of AFDC/food stamps were required to submit monthly reports documenting their income and family composition. They were not required to appear at a welfare office for recertification. Both sets of benefits were determined on a retrospective basis by the content of their monthly reports. The control group households were recertified in the conventional manner, by appearing in-person after a specified period of time.

OUTCOME(S) OF INTEREST: (1) Food stamp caseloads and benefits; (2) Food stamp accuracy and error rates; (3) Administration costs; and (4) Experiences of food stamp recipients.

SAMPLE SIZE: Total, 10,600; treatment, 7,000; control, 3,600.

TARGET POPULATION: Joint AFDC/food stamp recipients.

NUMBER OF TREATMENT GROUPS: Three: a treatment group, a control group, and a variant group. The variant group was to be identical to the treatment group, but was scheduled to undergo in-person annual eligibility reviews. Since this rarely actually occurred, this group was usually combined with the treatment group for analysis.

NUMBER AND LOCATION OF SITES: One welfare office in Chicago, Illinois—the Southeast District Office. The demonstration also occurred in the Peoria office; however, data were not examined for this site.

RESEARCH COMPONENTS:
   Process analysis: Focused on the problems created by the computer system and the effects of monthly reporting on staff and recipients.
   Impact analysis: Effects on payments and caseload were studied, as well as the effect on food stamp payment accuracy. Conducted using comparison of means.
   Benefit–cost analysis: Conducted.

MAJOR FINDINGS:
1. Benefits paid to monthly reporting cases (the treatment group) were approximately 5.5 percent greater than those issued to cases under the conventional system (the control group). This effect was concentrated entirely in the first six months of the demonstration.

2. Comparisons of aggregate benefits for selected subgroups of the food stamp caseload showed that the treatment did not lead to significant payment savings within any of the identified subgroups. Positive, though not significant, effects were shown for large households, households in which the youngest child was between 16 and 18 years old, households with no adults, and households in which the head was at least 40 years old. All of these subgroups had consistent (but not statistically significant) payment savings throughout the demonstration, or had payment increases that were generally smaller than the average increase for the entire caseload.
3. The treatment did not lead to increased payment accuracy. Because of the computer problems, the incidence of errors increased by between 11 percent and 14 percent relative to the conventional system. Aside from the computer problems, error rates were largely unaffected.
4. The treatment did not affect recipients in any major way (e.g., changes in time and out-of-pocket expenses).

TIME TRENDS IN THE FINDINGS: As mentioned above, administration costs were significantly higher for the treatment group during the first six months owing to computer problems, but not during the last six months.

DESIGN ISSUES:
1. The new data processing system developed to handle the increased volume of information created by the program was difficult to implement. Problems existed throughout most of the project period, but mostly during the first six months. This led to incorrect benefits being issued and to inadvertent closings of some cases. Thus, caseworker activity and administrative costs were increased.
2. The group most often expected to show net benefits from monthly reporting, the earned income caseload, was not addressed by this evaluation. All earned income cases were subject to monthly reporting during the administration regardless of the treatment group to which they were assigned.

REPLICABILITY: Replicable, although it would be prudent to have a data processing system operational prior to program implementation.

GENERALIZABILITY: Designed to generalize to the entire state of Illinois. Results from this demonstration are generally supported by similar experiments in Massachusetts, Colorado, New York, and Michigan (the Colorado experiment showed significant AFDC payment reductions in the first year, but these effects dissipated in the second year).

FUNDING SOURCES: U.S. Department of Agriculture, Food and Nutrition Service, and U.S. Department of Health and Human Services.

TREATMENT ADMINISTRATOR: Illinois Department of Public Aid. Key personnel: Stephen Spence.

EVALUATOR: Abt Associates. Key personnel: Jean Wood, project director.

ENABLING LEGISLATION: None.

INFORMATION SOURCE: Jean C. Wood, Summary of Final Results of the Illinois Monthly Reporting Food Stamp Demonstration, Abt Associates, June 1985.

PUBLIC-USE ACCESS TO DATA: No public-use file exists.

FOOD STAMP EMPLOYMENT AND TRAINING PROGRAM

SUMMARY: This demonstration, which was conducted in 1988, tested the effects of the Food Stamp Employment and Training (E&T) program on a large sample of food stamp recipients. Subjects were followed for one year.

COST: Expenditures on participants, fiscal year 1988, $1.76 million. Total costs, including evaluation, approximately $3.5 million.

TIME FRAME: Demonstration period, 1988; final report, June 1990.

TREATMENTS TESTED: The E&T program included: job search; job search training; Workfare and work experience; and education and vocational skills training.

OUTCOMES OF INTEREST: (1) Employment; (2) Earnings; and (3) Receipt of public assistance.

SAMPLE SIZE: Total sample, 13,086; treatment, 6,376; control, 6,710.

TARGET POPULATION: All eligible food stamp recipients between the ages of 17 and 59, not exempted by the Food Stamp Administration (FSA).

NUMBER OF TREATMENT GROUPS: Two (including control) at each site.

NUMBER AND LOCATION OF SITES: Fifty-three sites in 23 states. Sites were local FSA offices, usually counties (Puma et al. 1990:4–11 list the sites).

RESEARCH COMPONENTS:

Process analysis: Conducted. Participant monitoring was used to ensure the accuracy of assignment, as well as the accuracy and timeliness of information flow; and to identify instances of noncompliance.

Impact analysis: Conducted, using multivariate regression models.

Benefit–cost analysis: Conducted.

MAJOR FINDINGS:

1. Although substantial gains in employment were observed over the 12-month period in both treatment and control group members, E&T had no discernible effect on aggregate earnings, probability of finding work, amount of time worked, or average wages. That is, there were no significant treatment–control group differences.
2. There were treatment–control group differences in the receipt of Food Stamp benefits, with a reduction in the treatment group of $65 per household. Some of this difference, however, was accounted for by the termination of benefits for noncompliance with E&T requirements. No differences in cash assistance were produced.
3. Despite being a low-cost program, the program was not found to be cost-effective, owing to its limited impact on employment and welfare receipt.
4. Some sites had heavy caseloads and/or limited staffing, which led to large percentages (up to 75 percent) of registrants who never received their initial appointment letters. In general, there were participation rates of approximately 50 percent. Males living alone, the largest group of participants, were the least likely to comply with program requirements.
5. Many control group members were able to find services on their own. 43 percent of treatment group members received services, whereas 31 percent of control group members received comparable services.
6. Because the evaluation was of an actual program as it operated in response to legislative and regulatory guidelines, treatment was dictated by local operating agencies rather than by the researchers. The flexibility afforded states, and their decentralized administrative arrangements, complicated the evaluation.

TIME TRENDS IN FINDINGS: Reduction in the receipt of food stamps came mostly in the second and third quarters after random assignment.

DESIGN ISSUES:
1. Because multiple service models do not normally exist in the same site, it was not possible to compare effects of different service models.
2. Potential effects on application behavior were missed because random assignment occurred at the point of certification.
3. The period studied was the first year of the program. Start-up effects may confound the observed results.
4. Due to extreme mobility on the part of the sample, difficulty obtaining addresses from the local Food Stamp office, and a large homeless contingent, full 12-month follow-up data were obtained for only 50 percent of the sample. Although statistical adjustments were developed to account for survey nonresponse, this could raise questions about reliability.

REPLICABILITY: There were wide variations in service delivery across sites. Many states dropped or added components (usually the training component) during the study.

GENERALIZABILITY: Designed to generalize to the entire nation. This was close to a nationally representative sample of sites. Sites were selected as a probability sample of the national population of Food Stamp offices. Characteristics of the sample closely matched the population of food stamp recipients as a whole.

FUNDING SOURCE: U.S. Department of Agriculture, Food and Nutrition Service. Key personnel: Boyd Kowal, Office of Analysis and Evaluation, project officer.

TREATMENT ADMINISTRATOR: Local FSAs acting under the U.S. Department of Agriculture, Food and Nutrition Service.

EVALUATOR: Abt Associates. Principal investigators: Jean Wood and Michael Puma.

ENABLING LEGISLATION: Food Security Act of 1985.

INFORMATION SOURCES: Michael J. Puma, Nancy R. Burstein, Katie Merrell, and Gary Silverstein, *Evaluation of the Food Stamp Employment and Training Program: Final Report*, June 1990.

PUBLIC-USE ACCESS TO DATA: Available at U.S. Department of Agriculture.

SAN DIEGO FOOD STAMP CASH-OUT DEMONSTRATION

SUMMARY: This demonstration, conducted in 1989 and 1990, tested the effects of issuing food stamp benefits by check rather than coupon on a large sample of Food Stamp Program (FSP) participants.

COST: Evaluation cost, $1,507,114.

TIME FRAME: Phase I, experimental: July 1989–August 1990; data collected, May–August 1990. Phase II, a saturation program, was begun in September 1990 and is currently in operation.

TREATMENTS TESTED: The treatment group received Food Stamp Program benefits in check form, rather than by coupon. The control group continued to receive the coupon form.

OUTCOMES OF INTEREST: (1) Food purchasing and food use patterns and (2) Administrative costs.

SAMPLE SIZE: Total sample, 1,226; treatment, 613; control, 613. The final sample used for analysis was reduced to 1,078; treatment, 542; control, 536.

TARGET POPULATION: Recipients of food stamps.

NUMBER OF TREATMENT GROUPS: Two (including control).

NUMBER AND LOCATION OF SITES: One, San Diego County, California.

RESEARCH COMPONENTS:
   Process analysis: Planning process for design and implementation. Detailed analysis of work activities that were changed in the implementation of cash-out. Analysis of data on lost or stolen benefits.
   Impact analysis: Comparison of means. Analysis of regression-adjusted means was also conducted, but did not prove to be substantially more precise than the simple difference-in-means estimates.
   Benefit–cost analysis: Not highly formalized, though integrated into administrative cost outcomes.

MAJOR FINDINGS:
1. Cash-out had a relatively small, but statistically significant, downward impact on household food use. The money value of food used at home was 4 percent to 7 percent lower (depending on the specific measure of food use) for check recipients than for coupon recipients. This finding suggests that cash-out reduced the effectiveness of the FSP in stimulating food use.

2. The reductions in the money value of food used at home resulting from cash-out were accompanied by decreases in the amounts of food energy and protein contained in the food that was used. These reductions, although relatively small (roughly 5 percent each) are statistically significant.
3. There was no significant impact on households running out of food during the month, nor was the impact on the purchase of food used away from home significant.
4. There was statistically significant increases for cash-out households in three expenditure categories: housing, medical costs, and education.
5. Cash-out led to clear reductions in administrative costs incurred at the state and county levels associated with the issuing of food stamp benefits. Savings of $2.21 per issuance were realized for recipients who also received AFDC (one check was issued for both). Savings of $1.19 per issuance were realized for cases not on AFDC.

TIME TRENDS IN FINDINGS: No long-term follow-up has been conducted.

DESIGN ISSUES:
1. The evaluators reported no significant problems with design or implementation. They stated that the administration in San Diego has been very active in trying innovative programs and that department personnel are "old hands" at these types of evaluations.
2. The data source is an after-the-fact questionnaire administered to the head of household. This could be subject to recall error or other problems.

REPLICABILITY: Replicable. Procedures are well documented in the report.

GENERALIZABILITY: San Diego county is highly urban. A high proportion of the Food Stamp caseload also receives AFDC relative to the nation as a whole. Because AFDC income is relatively high, food stamp benefit levels, relative to household income, are lower in San Diego than the national average (12 percent versus 23 percent, respectively).

For a more complete picture of the impacts of cash-out, these findings should be considered along with those from similar demonstrations. The Alabama Food Stamp Cash-Out Demonstration is a comparably "pure" cash-out. Those findings showed few significant impacts on recipients. Alabama's Avenues to Self-Sufficiency through Employment and Training Services (ASSETS) and Washington's Family Independence Program (FIP) are "mixed" programs, with cash-out being only one component.

FUNDING SOURCE: U.S. Department of Agriculture (USDA), Food and Nutrition Service. Key personnel: Boyd Kowal, project officer.

TREATMENT ADMINISTRATOR: San Diego County Department of Social Services. Key personnel: Jerry Hughs and Susan Gardner.

EVALUATOR: Mathematica Policy Research. Key personnel: James C. Ohls, project director. Also: Thomas Fraker, Alberto Martini, Michael Ponza, and Anne Ciemnecki.

ENABLING LEGISLATION: Food Stamp Act of 1977, as amended.

POLICY EFFECTS: These findings were presented by the USDA to Congress. Robert Greenstein, of the Center on Budget and Policy Priorities, predicted that the finding of a negative impact on food purchases would kill congressional cash-out proposals. The USDA has, in fact, moved in a different direction—toward electronic benefit transfers.

INFORMATION SOURCES: James C. Ohls, Thomas M. Fraker, Alberto P. Martini, and Michael Ponza, The Effects of Cash-Out on Food Use by Food Stamp Program Participants in San Diego, Mathematica Policy Research, 1992.

PUBLIC-USE ACCESS TO DATA: Available through Mathematica Policy Research.

ALABAMA FOOD STAMP CASH-OUT DEMONSTRATION

SUMMARY: This demonstration, conducted in 1990, tested the effects of paying food stamp benefits by check on a large sample of food stamp recipients. Subjects were followed for six months.

COST: Evaluation cost, $1,835,415.

TIME FRAME: Demonstration period, May 1990–December 1990; data collected, same period; final report, September 1992.

TREATMENTS TESTED: For the treatment group, food stamp benefits were paid in the form of checks, rather than coupons. The control group continued to receive food stamps in coupon form.

OUTCOMES OF INTEREST: (1) Food purchasing and food use patterns and (2) Administrative costs.

SAMPLE SIZE: Total sample, 4,486; treatment, 2,253; control, 2,233. Sample used for analysis: treatment, 1,255; control, 1,131.

TARGET POPULATION: Recipients of food stamp benefits.

NUMBER OF TREATMENT GROUPS: Two (including control).

NUMBER AND LOCATION OF SITES: Twelve Alabama counties: 2 urban and 10 rural.

RESEARCH COMPONENTS:

Process analysis: Planning and implementation outcomes were an integral part of the overall evaluation.

Impact analysis: Comparison of means.

Benefit–cost analysis: Conducted as an integral part of the evaluation.

MAJOR FINDINGS:

1. For almost all outcome measures, the difference in mean values between check and coupon recipients was small and not statistically significant. There were no significant differences in the money value of food used at home, nutrient availability, running out of food, or the purchase of food used away from home.

2. Check recipients did report a significantly larger (1.1 percent) expenditure share than coupon recipients on utilities. It is not clear whether this difference was caused by cash-out.

3. In Alabama, most Food Stamp Program coupons are issued in person. The cash-out checks were primarily mailed to recipients. Issuance-system vulnerabilities increased with cash-out because of the issuance of checks by mail. This is considered less a cost of cash-out than of the change in mode of delivering benefits. In general, costs were lower under check issuance. Overall check issuance cost $1.03 per case-month compared to $2.05 per case-month for coupons. Three-quarters of these savings accrued to the federal government and one-quarter accrued to the state government.

TIME TRENDS IN FINDINGS: No long-term follow-up was conducted.

DESIGN ISSUES:

1. Development of the computer software for the check-issuance system absorbed considerable resources and required more labor hours than expected. This is one reason that implementation was delayed for four months.

2. It is important to note some of the differences between this demonstration and the other cash-out programs. The San Diego cash-out was the only other "pure" cash-out (no other programmatic changes were being measured) and was also an experimental design. Alabama ASSETS and Washington FIP were quasi-

experimental designs.

In Alabama, joint Food Stamp Program and AFDC households received two checks; they received only one check in San Diego. San Diego normally issued coupons by mail, so there was less difference in issuance procedures compared to Alabama. The San Diego program ran longer than in Alabama. The evaluators feel that the Alabama program may have been too short to capture impacts.

3. The data source is an after-the-fact questionnaire administered to the head of household. This could be subject to recall error or to other problems.

REPLICABILITY: Replicable. The final report and its appendixes provide great detail regarding procedures and implementation.

GENERALIZABILITY: Designed to generalize to the entire state of Alabama. Alabama is more rural than the United States as a whole, and residents are more likely to be unemployed or to have low income (20 percent lower than in the United States as a whole). Only six states and Washington, D.C., have a higher percentage of food stamp users, and average food stamp benefits are 10 percent higher than the U.S. average. Alabama has lower levels of cash assistance (e.g., AFDC) than the nation as a whole. Food stamp recipients are more likely to be elderly.

The findings from the San Diego Food Stamp Cash-Out Demonstration showed a small but significant negative impact on food expenditures, on the nutritional value of food, and on other outcome variables. This suggests that cash-out impacts may depend on context and implementation.

FUNDING SOURCE: U.S. Department of Agriculture (USDA), Food and Nutrition Service. Key personnel: Pat McKinney, project officer.

TREATMENT ADMINISTRATOR: Alabama Department of Human Resources (DHR). Key personnel: Andrew Hornsby, commissioner; Gene Gandy and Bill Mintz, project facilitators. DHR county directors were also involved in administration.

EVALUATOR: Mathematica Policy Research. Thomas Fraker, project director. Other key personnel: Alberto Martini, James Ohls, Michael Ponza, Elizabeth Quinn, and Anne Ciemnecki.

ENABLING LEGISLATION: None.

POLICY EFFECTS: After findings of a negative impact on food purchases in San Diego were presented to Congress (see "San Diego Food Stamp Cash-Out Demonstration" summary), the USDA moved in another direction—toward electronic benefit transfers.

INFORMATION SOURCES: Thomas M. Fraker, Alberto P. Martini, James C. Ohls, Michael Ponza, and Elizabeth A. Quinn, *The Evaluation of the Alabama Food Stamp Cash-Out Demonstration: Volume I: Recipient Impacts* and *Volume II: Administrative Outcomes, Overall Conclusions, and Appendices*, Mathematica Policy Research, 1992.

PUBLIC-USE ACCESS TO DATA: Available through Mathematica Policy Research.

Part Four

PUBLIC ASSISTANCE RECIPIENTS— MEDICAID

SUMMARY: This demonstration, conducted from 1986 to 1992, tested the effects of incentives for using HMO plans on a large sample of Medicaid recipients. The evaluation of the demonstration was successfully implemented as planned at one site, but not the other. Subjects were followed for one year.

COST: Evaluation costs, approximately $2 million.

TIME FRAME: Demonstration period, 1986–92; data collected through 1997.

TREATMENTS TESTED: The treatment group received a guarantee of at least 6 months of Medicaid eligibility if they agreed to enter a capitated health plan. In New York, the treatment group also qualified for generous health care options (not otherwise covered by Medicaid) if they chose capitation. The control group remained in a fee-for-service (FFS) system.

OUTCOMES OF INTEREST: Health care costs and utilization were the primary economic outcomes. Health and satisfaction outcomes were also measured.

SAMPLE SIZE: Random assignment only. New York: assigned to treatment, 811; assigned to control, 1,077. Florida: assigned to treatment, 1,240; assigned to control, 1,061.

TARGET POPULATION: Medicaid recipients eligible through participation in the AFDC program. Samples were selected from Medicaid eligibility files.

NUMBER OF TREATMENT GROUPS: There were two experimental (randomly assigned) groups: Program for Prepaid Managed Health Care (PPMHC) and fee-for-service (FFS). There were also two self-selected groups at the experimental sites.

NUMBER AND LOCATION OF SITES: Two experimental sites: New York and Florida. A total of 10 sites were in the demonstration.

RESEARCH COMPONENTS:
   Process analysis: Focus groups were used to develop informed consent materials. A number of forms and interviews with participants were used at various stages of the evaluation to determine eligibility, language ability (primarily for Spanish-speaking participants), and health status.

Impact analysis: Conducted using logistic and OLS regression models. An intention to treat analysis is used.

Benefit–cost analysis: The cost to the state of allowing Medicaid beneficiaries to voluntarily enroll in capitated plans was calculated and contrasted with per-beneficiary costs in the FFS system.

MAJOR FINDINGS:
1. Participants in New York who were assigned to the PPHMC group but did not enroll had higher use and higher costs than either PPHMC enrollees or the control (FFS) group. Average per-person monthly expenditures were $61 for the randomly assigned PPHMC enrollees, $90 for the randomly assigned FFS group, and roughly $100 for those assigned to PPHMC but who did not enroll. The lower use of the PPHMC participants while they were in the plan appears to be entirely accounted for by selection effects because total costs for those assigned to the PPHMC (including nonenrollees) averaged more than total costs for people assigned to FFS.
2. In Florida, estimated monthly health care use was lower for the PPHMC groups (both randomly assigned and self-selected) than for their FFS counterparts. By assigned plan, average monthly per-person expenditures were: self-selected FFS, $37; randomly assigned FFS, $36; self-selected PPHMC, $27; and randomly assigned PPHMC, $31.

TIME TRENDS IN FINDINGS: None.

DESIGN ISSUES:
1. At the New York site, PPHMC enrollment was very difficult. Of the original 811 people assigned to this group, over half (427) refused to participate upon learning of their assignment or were refused by the PPHMC program. Of the remaining 384 who accepted, only 185 eventually enrolled. A total of 1,066 participants accepted the FFS assignment. The evaluators felt that the experimental portion of the design failed in New York. Those who refused study participation were significantly different from those who accepted (they were somewhat healthier, and younger, but had been on Medicaid longer). Enrollment was generally more successful in Florida.
2. Participation in the study was voluntary, so individuals did not necessarily agree to their assignment and others who agreed did not necessarily remain in their assigned groups. Therefore, some participants actually used both systems of care (PPHMC and FFS) during the study. For the major analyses, use was combined and

attributed to the "assigned" group. For other analysis, use patterns were considered by system of care actually used.

REPLICABILITY: Replicable.

GENERALIZABILITY: Designed to generalize to the AFDC Medicaid population.

FUNDING SOURCES: Robert Wood Johnson Foundation—Alan Cohen, project officer. Health Care Financing Administration, U.S. Department of Health and Human Services—Spike Duzor, Arne Anderson, and Sid Trieger, project officers. Technical assistance was provided by the National Governors Association.

TREATMENT ADMINISTRATOR: Technical oversight of the demonstration was contracted to a group at the New England Medical Center.

EVALUATOR: The New England Medical Center was responsible for health outcomes, physical outcomes, and satisfaction measures. The RAND Corporation was responsible for cost and utilization components as well as the case studies.

ENABLING LEGISLATION: None.

INFORMATION SOURCES: Joan L. Buchanan, Arleen Leibowitz, Joan Keesey, Joyce Mann, and Cheryl Damberg, *Cost and Use of Capitated Medical Services: Evaluation of the Program for Prepaid Managed Health Care*, RAND Corporation, 1992.

PUBLIC-USE ACCESS TO DATA: Available through the RAND Corporation.

Part Five

PUBLIC ASSISTANCE RECIPIENTS— CANADA

MANITOBA BASIC ANNUAL
INCOME EXPERIMENT—MINCOME

SUMMARY: This demonstration, conducted from 1975 to 1979, tested the effects of experimental tax rates and guaranteed income levels on a medium-sized sample of low-income households. Subjects were to be followed for three years.

COST: The original project grant for both the experimental and saturation sites was approximately $17 million. However, the government contribution in terms of services, and so forth, is not counted in this figure.

TIME FRAME: The Manitoba Basic Annual Income Experiment (Mincome) began in 1975 and officially ended in 1979. The original research design was not fully implemented. The data were archived and made available again in 1983. Some analysis of the data has occurred since 1983.

TREATMENTS TESTED: The eight experimental treatments were varying combinations of tax rates and guaranteed cash benefits, as follows:

Treatment	Maximum Annual Cash Benefit ($, based on family of four in 1975)	Tax Rate
1	3,800	0.35
2	4,800	0.35
3	3,800	0.50
4	4,800	0.50
5	5,800	0.50
6	3,800	0.75
7	4,800	0.75
8	5,800	0.75

The control group received existing Income Assistance (Canada's primary welfare program) benefits. Saturation site families (see below) received treatment 3.

OUTCOMES OF INTEREST: (1) Labor supply response for primary and secondary earners—hours worked, resources devoted to job search; (2) Family income; (3) Job satisfaction; and (4) Measures of family behavior—formation and disintegration.

SAMPLE SIZE: Experimental sample, 1,187; control, 612; Treatment, 575.

TARGET POPULATION: Low-income households—families with able-bodied heads under 58 years of age and with incomes below $13,000 (1975) for a family of four.

NUMBER OF TREATMENT GROUPS: Eight treatment; one control.

NUMBER AND LOCATION OF SITES: One experimental site—Winnipeg, Manitoba. In addition, there was a saturation site—Dauphin, Manitoba.

RESEARCH COMPONENTS:
  Process Analysis: Not conducted.
  Impact Analysis: Conducted using regression models.
  Benefit–cost analysis: Not conducted.

MAJOR FINDINGS:
1. In general, there is no conclusive evidence regarding treatment–control group differences vis-à-vis labor supply outcomes. The data show declining hours worked from the first (pre-experimental) year to the other three (experimental) years for most treatment groups, as well as for the control group.
2. However, for one of the regression models, there were some significant differences. For males, on average, the experimental groups worked significantly fewer annual hours than did the control group (– 92 hours). For female heads of household, the effect is also negative and significant. The experimental group, on average, worked 100 hours less than did controls.

TIME TRENDS IN THE FINDINGS: None reported.

DESIGN ISSUES:
1. The overarching problem may be that the funding and interest for this project waned prior to its completion. This limited the experiment's implementation and analysis.
2. The experiment limited payments to three years. This poses a problem for the prediction of effects of permanent programs because it implicitly assumes that the experimental families will make the same adjustment within three years that they would to an indefinite-length national program.
3. For some families, regular reporting and periodic interviews may influence behavior in addition to the effect of receiving payments. The reporting requirements alone may lead families to have more accurate views of their financial situation than they otherwise would. Only a portion of the control group had these requirements.

REPLICABILITY: Replicable.

GENERALIZABILITY: Designed to generalize to, at least, the entire province of Manitoba. The experiment's sample was narrower than the population that would be covered by a universal guaranteed income program. The aged, institutionalized, and disabled were excluded.

FUNDING SOURCES: Health and Welfare Canada and the Manitoba provincial government.

TREATMENT ADMINISTRATOR: Provincial level—Ministry for Health and Social Development.

EVALUATOR: Jointly conducted by the Department of National Health and Welfare Canada and Manitoba's provincial counterpart. Key personnel: Derek Hum, research director.

ENABLING LEGISLATION: None.

INFORMATION SOURCES: Derek Hum and Wayne Simpson, *Income Maintenance, Work Effort, and the Canadian Mincome Experiment*, Minister of Supply and Services Canada, 1991. Derek Hum and Wayne Simpson, "Economic Response to a Guaranteed Annual Income: Experience from Canada and the United States," *Journal of Labor Economics*, 11(1993): 5263–96. Derek P. Hum, "Social Security Reform during the 1970s," in *Canadian Social Welfare Policy: Federal and Provincial Dimensions*, edited by J. Ismael Institute for Public Administration in Canada–McGill–Queen's University Press, 1985.

PUBLIC-USE ACCESS TO DATA: Data are lodged with the Canadian and Manitoba governments. Derek Hum believes the Canadian government deposited its set of data in the National Archives. He is unsure about its accessibility.

Part Six

TAXPAYERS

MINNESOTA INCOME TAX COMPLIANCE EXPERIMENT

SUMMARY: This experiment, conducted in 1995, tested the effects of four separate strategies to increase tax compliance on a large sample of Minnesota taxpayers. Subjects were followed for one year.

COST: This was an in-house evaluation, and most costs were borne internally. There were other direct evaluation costs of approximately $50,000 to $80,000.

TIME FRAME: Project period, 1995; data were collected for previous and current tax years; final report, 1996.

TREATMENTS TESTED: There were four separate treatments: (1) an increased examination and audit rate of both state and federal tax returns with prior notice to taxpayers; (2) enhanced taxpayer services; (3) redesign of the standard Minnesota state tax form; and (4) letters to taxpayers with information messages on the importance of voluntary compliance.

OUTCOMES OF INTEREST: (1) Change in reported taxable federal income and (2) Change in state taxes paid from previous tax year.

SAMPLE SIZE: Approximately 47,000 taxpayers were assigned to the four treatments; control groups numbered approximately 23,500.

TARGET POPULATION: Minnesota taxpayers whose 1994 taxes were filed and processed by the Department of Revenue by the end of November 1995. Specific eligibility criteria were applied to individual treatments.

NUMBER OF TREATMENT GROUPS: Eight: four treatment and four control (one control group was shared by the audit and service treatments, one control group was used for the letter treatment, and two control groups were used for the test form treatment).

NUMBER AND LOCATION OF SITES: Throughout the state of Minnesota.

RESEARCH COMPONENTS:
   Process analysis: Implementation was carefully monitored and documented.
   Impact analysis: Conducted using analysis of variance and linear regression.
   Benefit–cost analysis: Not conducted.

MAJOR FINDINGS:
1. Low- and mid-income taxpayers facing an examination or audit reported significantly more income and paid more taxes relative to

the control group. As a whole, the treatment group reported $1,131 more income and paid $87 more in Minnesota state taxes than controls. Increases were generally larger among taxpayers who had business income and paid estimated taxes in 1993. Certain small groups of taxpayers who were especially responsive to the threat of an examination accounted for most of the group differences. High-income taxpayers had a mixed reaction to the examination threat—the net effect on them was slight.

2. The service offer, which was an incremental expansion of existing services, did not have a net effect on reported income or taxes paid. Only 14 percent of taxpayers who were offered the service telephoned the Department of Revenue—slightly below the normal rate.

3. One of the two information messages had a modest positive effect on reported income and taxes paid. This message refuted the idea that many taxpayers cheat on their taxes and reinforced social norms about tax compliance.

4. The experiment had little effect on timeliness of tax filings, on the rate of adjustments made to tax filings during the department's machine processing of returns, or on taxpayers' use of a tax practitioner.

TIME TRENDS IN THE FINDINGS: None, although the evaluator reported that subjects will continue to be followed for another two years.

DESIGN ISSUES:

1. The use of multiple control groups was overly complex. Some treatments shared the same control group, whereas other treatments had more than one control group. There was also a "quasi-control group" that received a simple letter advising them of available telephone numbers for assistance, which technically amounts to another treatment.

2. Although not part of the design or implementation, an important issue was the printing of a story in the St. Paul *Pioneer Press* (1995), reporting that many members of the treatment group were upset over the letters that hinted at an audit. The story was subsequently printed in several other newspapers. It is uncertain what effect this may have had on the results of the experiment.

REPLICABILITY: Replicable—all forms and letters are included in the report. Minnesota sent out another 20,000 information letters (treatment 4, above) in 1996 to check the findings reported here.

GENERALIZABILITY: Designed to generalize to the entire state. The strategy showing the greatest impact, the threat of examination or audit, may not be practical or cost effective on a large scale. In general, the findings point to greater effectiveness for small subgroups than for taxpayers as a whole.

FUNDING SOURCE: Minnesota Department of Revenue.

TREATMENT ADMINISTRATOR: Minnesota Department of Revenue.

EVALUATOR: Minnesota Department of Revenue. Stephen Coleman, project director.

ENABLING LEGISLATION: None.

INFORMATION SOURCE: Stephen Coleman, *The Minnesota Income Tax Compliance Experiment: State Tax Results*, Minnesota Department of Revenue, April 1996.

PUBLIC-USE ACCESS TO DATA: Not available.

Part Seven

ELECTRICITY USERS

INTRODUCTION

During the 1970s, the former Federal Energy Administration, which subsequently was absorbed by the U.S. Department of Energy, funded 16 residential electricity rate experiments in the following locations: Arizona, Arkansas, California, Connecticut, Los Angeles, Michigan, New Jersey, New York, North Carolina, Ohio, Oklahoma, Puerto Rico, Rhode Island, Vermont, Washington, and Wisconsin.[1] These experiments tested different combinations of pricing plans on residential users. All used declining block rates, with lower prices per kilowatt-hour for greater quantities of usage, as the control group treatment. Time-of-use rates, in which the prices are higher (lower) according to whether the electricity is consumed during peak (off-peak) hours, was the experimental treatment for all but the Michigan and Washington experiments. We were able to locate detailed information on only the Connecticut and Los Angeles experiments. Thus, only these two experiments are summarized here.

We traced the California and Connecticut reports through subsequent references in academic journals. We have not found any subsequent use of the other experiments. Some of the reports are available through the Electric Power Research Institute in Palo Alto, California; however, they are available only on microfiche and are quite expensive.

Comments from Hausman and Wise (1985)[2] have illustrated some of the limitations to the generalizability of these experiments. The utilities were given little guidance in their designs, a haphazard approach that led each project to define its universe differently. Coverage of the stated target population was often low, and the time-horizon was too short to allow households to adjust their stock of electricity-using equipment.

Also summarized in this section are two electricity rate experiments that focused on industrial, rather than residential, users.

Notes

1. For a brief summary of these experiments, see Jerry Hausman and David Wise, *Social Experimentation* (Chicago: University of Chicago Press), 1985:1401–3.

2. Ibid.

SOUTHERN CALIFORNIA EDISON
ELECTRICITY PRICING EXPERIMENT

SUMMARY: This experiment, conducted from 1980 to 1982, tested the effects of varying time-of-use electricity rates on a medium-sized sample of commercial and industrial customers. Subjects were followed for up to 21 months.

COST: Cost figures are unavailable.

TIME FRAME: October 1980–October 1982; data collected, same period.

TREATMENTS TESTED: There were a total of six experimental treatments. There were two experimental rate structures: time-varying energy rates and time-varying demand rates. "Energy" pricing varies by kilowatt-hours (kWh) of usage; "demand" pricing varies by reserved capacity or "maximum instantaneous load." For each of these rate structures, there were three *absolute* differences in rate levels: (1) a small difference between peak and off-peak rates ($0.01 per kWh for energy rates, $1 for demand rates); (2) a moderate difference between peak and off-peak rates ($0.03 and $3.50); and (3) an extreme difference between peak and off-peak rates ($0.06 and $6.00). The control group faced the conventional rates.

OUTCOMES OF INTEREST: (1) Energy usage (substitution between peak and off-peak consumption) and (2) Costs.

SAMPLE SIZE: Total, 733; treatment, 574; control, 159.

TARGET POPULATION: Commercial and industrial electricity customers with summer monthly demands between 20 kW and 500 kW.

NUMBER OF TREATMENT GROUPS: Seven: 6 treatment; one control.

NUMBER AND LOCATION OF SITES: Subjects were all customers of the Southern California Edison Company, Rosemead, California.

RESEARCH COMPONENTS:
Process analysis: Customer participation and compensation were monitored.
Impact analysis: Conducted using analysis of covariance and econometric analyses.
Benefit–cost analysis: Conducted.

MAJOR FINDINGS:
1. The time-of-use demand rate was more effective in eliciting substitution of peak and off-peak usage than was the time-of-use energy rate, especially in the summer season.
2. A small, but statistically significant, elasticity of substitution between peak and off-peak kWh consumption was estimated for the summer season in the overall sample for firms facing the time-of-use demand rate. A substantially larger response was estimated for the subgroup of "large" firms (200–500 kWh) in the experiment that faced the demand rate.
3. A small welfare gain of 1.1% was estimated when moving from the conventional, non-time-of-use (control) rate to a 2.5:1 effective energy:price ratio, which is suggestive of the time-of-use demand rate that might prevail were time-of-use pricing to be applied to this group of firms. For large customers, this more than offsets additional metering costs.

TIME TRENDS IN FINDINGS: Usage levels declined for all groups from 1981 to 1982. This likely reflects a response to the rising average price of electricity over the life of the experiment.

DESIGN ISSUES:
1. To attempt to nullify the divergence of impact on the customers in this heterogeneous sample, variable compensation payments were made to customers whose bills under time-of-use rates exceeded bills under normal rates by more than 10%. This offset some of the incentive to adjust usage patterns.
2. Since firms could elect to participate when initially contacted or could drop out during the course of the experiment, some self-selection bias was present. High-peak-usage customers tended not to participate.

REPLICABILITY: Replicable.

GENERALIZABILITY: Designed to generalize to the entire region (Southern California). However, the experiment was voluntary, and customers with high-peak usage were underrepresented.

FUNDING SOURCE: Southern California Edison Company. Key personnel: Leo Gargan, project manager.

TREATMENT ADMINISTRATOR: Same as funding source.

EVALUATORS: Dennis J. Aigner and Joseph G. Hirschberg, University of Southern California.

ENABLING LEGISLATION: None.

INFORMATION SOURCES: Dennis J. Aigner and Joseph G. Hirschberg, "Commercial/Industrial Customers' Response to Time-of-Use Electricity Prices: Some Experimental Results," *Rand Journal of Economics* 16(1985): 341–55.

PUBLIC-USE ACCESS TO DATA: Not available.

NIAGARA MOHAWK HOURLY INTEGRATED PRICING PROGRAM (HIPP)

SUMMARY: This demonstration, conducted from 1987 to 1989, tested the effects of real-time pricing (RTP), on a small sample of large industrial consumers of electricity.

COST: Cost figures were not available.

TIME FRAME: Project period, June 1987–1989. Baseline data extend back to July 1986.

TREATMENTS TESTED: The treatment group paid for electricity using real-time pricing, a "dynamic, fully time-differentiated marginal cost-based electricity rate" (Herriges et al. 1993). RTP bases the price of electricity on the production and transmission costs of electricity at various times. These costs are highest at peak times (e.g., 10 A.M.), less at shoulder periods (e.g., 6 P.M.), and least at off-peak times (e.g., midnight). The control group continued to use standard "time-of-use" tariffs, with on-peak, off-peak hourly rates.

OUTCOMES OF INTEREST: Electricity usage by time period.

SAMPLE SIZE: Total, 21 large industrial clients; only 9 treatment and 6 control clients were used for analysis.

TARGET POPULATION: Large, industrial customers of electric power.

NUMBER OF TREATMENT GROUPS: Two (including control).

NUMBER AND LOCATION OF SITES: Customers were located throughout western New York State. Niagara Mohawk Power Corporation is located in Syracuse.

RESEARCH COMPONENTS:
   Process analysis: Not formerly conducted.
   Impact analysis: Comparison of means, price index analysis, and econometric analysis.
   Benefit–cost analysis: Conducted.

MAJOR FINDINGS:
1. The hourly integrated pricing program (HIPP) resulted in a decrease in total energy consumed. The control group load growth was 5.1%, compared to that of the treatment group growth of -1.5%.
2. The treatment group's average price was over 6% lower under HIPP than under the standard rate. This difference suggests an ability to shift loads away from high-priced hours.
3. At the peak system hour, the treatment group reduced loads from their baseline level by 13.2%. The control group increased loads by 4.5%. At the HIPP price peak hour, the treatment group reduced loads by 36.2% compared to the control group reduction of only 4.4%.
4. The response to RTP was not uniform. That is, two customers were able to shift usage more than others and thus provided the bulk of the measured response.

TIME TRENDS IN FINDINGS: None.

DESIGN ISSUES: Because of unspecified data problems, only nine treatment and six control customers were available for the analysis. In other energy experiments, the sheer size of the data set—energy usage at every hour of the day for a considerable number of days—has forced analysts to be selective about how much data they use.

REPLICABILITY: Replicable, though the project report provides no details about operations, such as how customers were notified of the prices, and so forth.

GENERALIZABILITY: Participants were voluntary. The sample was very small, although the participating clients account for a large amount of electricity use. The large users in this study are more likely than smaller firms or individuals to generate benefits from RTP that exceed administration costs. Large users are also more likely to invest required resources to understand and evaluate the HIPP tariff.

FUNDING SOURCE: Niagara Mohawk Power Corporation. Key personnel: Mike Kalleher.

TREATMENT ADMINISTRATOR: Niagara Mohawk Power Corporation.

EVALUATORS: Joseph A. Herriges, Iowa State University; S. Mostafa Baladi and Douglas W. Caves, Laurits R. Christensen Associates; and Bernard F. Neenan, Niagara Mohawk Power Corporation.

ENABLING LEGISLATION: None.

INFORMATION SOURCES: Joseph A. Herriges, et al., "The Response of Industrial Customers to Electric Rates Based upon Dynamic Marginal Costs," *Review of Economics and Statistics* 75(1993): 446–54.

PUBLIC-USE ACCESS TO DATA: Not available.

CONNECTICUT PEAK LOAD PRICING EXPERIMENT

SUMMARY: This experiment, conducted from 1975 to 1976, tested the effects of peak load pricing (PLP) on a medium-sized sample of residential energy customers. Subjects were followed for two years.

COST: Cost figures were unavailable.

TIME FRAME: Experimental period, October 1975 to October 1976; data collected, October 1974–November 1976.

TREATMENTS TESTED: PLP is the adjustment of electricity rates to reflect the cost of supply at various times of the day. The experimental rates used in this experiment (per kilowatt-hour) were: $0.16 for peak periods; $0.03 for intermediate periods; and $0.01 for off-peak periods. The control group customers were billed using the existing rate structure (declining block rate, wherein rates are not affected by supply costs or seasonal variations).

OUTCOMES OF INTEREST: Changes in electricity use.

SAMPLE SIZE: A total of 250 residential customers were randomly selected for the treatment group; 199 of these agreed to participate in the experiment. For the control group, 195 customers were selected.

TARGET POPULATION: Residential energy customers.

NUMBER OF TREATMENT GROUPS: Two (including control).

NUMBER AND LOCATION OF SITES: Connecticut Light and Power (CLP) covers 60% of the state, serving 52% of the electric customers in Connecticut.

RESEARCH COMPONENTS:
   Process analysis: Customer interviews were designed to assess attitudes and demographic characteristics, and to provide information about energy consumption and its modification.

Impact analysis: Comparison of means.
Benefit–cost analysis: Not conducted.

MAJOR FINDINGS:

1. Peak hour consumption represented 13% of total electricity use by the test customers during the baseline year, but only 10% during the test year. During the test year, test customers consumed a smaller percentage of their electricity requirements during peak hours and a larger percentage during off-peak hours than they did during the prior year and than did the control group during the test year (see table below). Information regarding statistical significance of these findings was not provided.

	Test Group Prior Year kWh	Percent- age	Test Group Test Year kWh	Percent- age	Control Group Test Year kWh	Percent- age
Peak	1,058.1	12.8	822.0	10.0	1,120.4	13.0
Shoulder	4,021.1	48.8	3,890.5	47.6	4,270.8	49.6
Off-Peak	3,166.3	38.4	3,467.3	42.4	3,221.6	37.4
Total	8,245.6	100.0	8,180.0	100.0	8,612.9	100.0

2. Survey data indicated that the test participants preferred the time-of-day test rate to the current, declining-block rate. Further, more than 80 percent of the test customers made schedule and/or activity changes in their living patterns (e.g., cleanup, laundry, bathing). More changes were made by high-use customers than by low-use customers.

TIME TRENDS IN FINDINGS: None.

DESIGN ISSUES:

1. Significant selection bias is possible due to the nonparticipation of roughly 20 percent of those selected for the treatment group.
2. Savings by customers (and their enthusiastic response) were likely exaggerated by the high (16:1) ratio of peak to off-peak prices.
3. Since the rate was in effect for only one year, findings do not reflect long-term impacts such as changing appliance stocks.

REPLICABILITY: Replicable. The Connecticut project was one of seven funded by the former Federal Energy Administration.

GENERALIZABILITY: Designed to generalize to the entire state. The Connecticut Light and Power service area from which the sample was drawn includes a cross section of the urban, suburban, and rural areas of the state as well as examples of all types of residential uses of electricity. However, design issues may discourage attempts at generalization.

FUNDING SOURCE: Project was partially funded by the former Federal Energy Administration.

TREATMENT ADMINISTRATOR: Connecticut Light and Power Company, a subsidiary of Northeast Utilities.

EVALUATOR: Research Triangle Institute and Northeast Utilities. Key personnel: H. Donald Burbank.

ENABLING LEGISLATION: None.

INFORMATION SOURCES: H. Donald Burbank, "The Connecticut Peak-Load Pricing Experiment," in *Forecasting and Modeling Time-of-Day and Seasonal Electricity Demands*, edited by Anthony Lawrence, Special Report EA-578-SR, Electric Power Research Institute, December 1977 (1–3 to 1–31).

PUBLIC-USE ACCESS TO DATA: Not available.

LOS ANGELES PEAK LOAD PRICING EXPERIMENT FOR ELECTRICITY

SUMMARY: This demonstration, conducted from 1976 through 1980, tested the effects of alternative electricity pricing structures on a large sample of residential electric consumers. Subjects were followed for 30 months.

COST: The evaluators reported that the entire project cost approximately $4.3 million in 1976. More than half of that was for evaluation design and analysis.

TIME FRAME: Project period, summer 1976–1980; data collected, same period.

TREATMENT(S) TESTED: Treatment households were enrolled in one of 34 different experimental time-of-use (TOU) electricity tariffs. These rates are designed to reflect the cost of supplying electricity at different times of the day. TOU prices ranged from $0.05 to $0.13/ kilowatt hour (kWh) during peak hours and $0.01 or $0.02 during off-peak hours. Control groups had either seasonal and time invariant tariffs (flat rates of $0.02 to $0.08/kWh) or the standard declining-block rate structure available to all nonexperimental customers in the Los Angeles area.

OUTCOME(S) OF INTEREST: (1) Energy consumption in each period of the day; and (2) Total energy consumption.

SAMPLE SIZE: A total of 1,286 households were used for the analysis; 931 were assigned to one of 34 TOU rates; 337 faced seasonal, time-invariant or declining-block rates.

TARGET POPULATION: Residential electricity consumers.

NUMBER OF TREATMENT GROUPS: 40 groups—34 treatment groups and 6 control groups.

NUMBER AND LOCATION OF SITES: One—Los Angeles, California.

RESEARCH COMPONENTS:
    Process analysis: Demographic, economic, and attitudinal data were obtained through household interviews at several points in the study.
    Impact analysis: Conducted using analysis of covariance and econometric modeling.
    Benefit–cost analysis: Conducted.

MAJOR FINDINGS:
1. For all households, weather was the primary cause of variation in electricity consumption. This variation was largely independent of the price of electricity.
2. Relative to the control groups, the TOU rates reduced the share of electricity use during peak periods in all experimental groups. Most of the estimated effects differed significantly from the flat rates. In most cases, higher TOU rates resulted in greater reductions.
3. The higher experimental rates per kWh also reduced overall electricity use for 28 of the 34 treatment groups, although the difference was statistically significant for only 1 group.
4. Price responsiveness was markedly greater in households having certain types of appliances (e.g., those appliances associated with swimming pools).
5. The benefit–cost analysis suggested that, for all households, the average gain in welfare exceeded the metering costs only when consumption was above 1,100 kWh/month. This is the case for only 4% of residential users in the area. These users account for 17% of residential use.

TIME TRENDS IN THE FINDINGS: None.

DESIGN ISSUES:

1. A classical stratified random sample was not used. Instead, the stratification was purposive, with deliberate overrepresentation of high-usage customers. The effect was then accounted for in the statistical analysis. Whereas this is a widely accepted practice today, the evaluators say that it required extra explanation when they first proposed it.

REPLICABILITY: Replicable.

GENERALIZABILITY: Participation was voluntary. Eligible participants were offered the chance to join the study, and over 92% of eligible households accepted the experimental rate plans. Some households were offered compensation in the form of "participation payments" so that they would not be made worse off under the experimental treatment.

Considering the importance of weather, generalizability would be limited to Los Angeles or other urban areas with similar weather patterns and similar patterns of electricity use.

FUNDING SOURCES: Los Angeles Department of Water and Power and U.S. Department of Energy.

TREATMENT ADMINISTRATOR: Los Angeles Department of Water and Power. Michael T. Moore: project officer.

EVALUATOR: The RAND Corporation. Principal Investigators: Jan Paul Acton, Bridger Mitchell, and Willard G. Manning.

ENABLING LEGISLATION: None.

INFORMATION SOURCES: Bridger M. Mitchell and Jan Paul Acton, *Electricity Consumption by Time of Use in a Hybrid Demand System*, RAND Corporation, December 1980; Jan Paul Acton and Bridger Mitchell, *Evaluating Time-of-Day Electricity Rates for Residential Customers*, RAND Corporation, November 1979; Willard G. Manning, Jr., Bridger M. Mitchell, and Jan Paul Acton, *Design of the Los Angeles Peak-Load Pricing Experiment for Electricity*, RAND Corporation, November 1976.

PUBLIC-USE ACCESS TO DATA: There is no public-use file.

Part Eight

HEALTHCARE USERS

SUMMARY: This demonstration, conducted from 1974 to 1982, tested the effects of universal health insurance (at various deductibles and copayment rates) on a large sample of nonelderly, noninstitutionalized households. Subjects were followed for up to five years.

COST: $136 million (in 1984 dollars).

TIME FRAME: Demonstration period, November 1974–January 1982; data collected, same period.

TREATMENTS TESTED: Insurance benefits varied over two dimensions, the Maximum Dollar Expenditure (MDE) and the coinsurance rate (CR). The MDE was the upper limit on the annual out-of-pocket medical expenses for which the family was responsible. It was set at 5 percent, 10 percent, or 15 percent of income, up to a maximum of $1,000 (1973 money; this limit was held constant in real terms). The coinsurance rate was the percentage of expenditures below the MDE for which the family was responsible. It was set at 0 percent (free care), 25 percent, 50 percent, and 95 percent. An "individual deductible" (ID) plan had a coinsurance rate of 95 percent for outpatient care only, but the MDE was limited to $150 per person (fixed in nominal terms), or $450 per family. Inpatient care was free in the ID plan.

To obtain uniformity in the experiment, all participant families were induced to sign over the benefits from their existing insurance plan to the experiment. The inducement was the financial maintenance (where necessary) of the plan by the administrator and a guaranteed payment equal to the difference between the MDE assigned to the family and the maximum deductible of their previous coverage. Families therefore could not be financially worse off by participating and would in most cases have somewhat higher incomes.

Participant families were randomly assigned to three-year or five-year treatments. The experiment also randomly assigned Seattle participants between a health maintenance organization (HMO) and a fee-for-service (FFS) plan.

OUTCOMES OF INTEREST: (1) Total expenditures on health care; (2) Relative demand for services by poor and nonpoor; (3) Quantifiable health differences; and (4) Effect of HMO organizational structure on expenditures and care.

SAMPLE SIZE: Numbers are individuals. Free care: 1,893; 25 percent coinsurance: 1,137; 50 percent coinsurance: 383; 95 percent coinsurance: 1,120; ID plan: 1,276; total, 5,809.

TARGET POPULATION: Representative samples of the populations of the site areas with the following exclusions: (1) persons over 61 years; (2) persons with incomes in excess of $25,000 (1973 money); (3) those in jails or institutionalized; (4) those eligible for the Medicare disability program; (5) military personnel and their dependents; and (6) veterans with service-connected disabilities.

NUMBER OF TREATMENT GROUPS: Fourteen (for most analyses, however, these 14 groups are grouped into 5).

NUMBER AND LOCATION OF SITES: Six: Dayton, Ohio; Seattle, Washington; Fitchburg, Massachusetts; Franklin County, Massachusetts; Charleston, South Carolina; and Georgetown County, South Carolina.

RESEARCH COMPONENTS:

Process analysis: Careful analysis of characteristics of persons who refused to participate in the experiment. Although the rate of refusal rose with the coinsurance rate, the project report authors stated that the refusers do not appear statistically different from the participants. Attrition was very small. There was no analysis of the content of medical care received.

Impact analysis: Conducted with sample means and sophisticated analyses using regression and other methods.

Benefit–cost analysis: Not conducted, but see "Generalizability."

MAJOR FINDINGS:

1. Predicted annual per capita use of medical services, by plan (from a four-equation system designed to reduce the effects of individual catastrophic cases on the estimates; sample means generally show the same patterns; standard errors in parentheses):

Plan	Likelihood of Any Use (%)	One or More Admissions to Hospital (%)	Medical Expenses (1984 dollars)
Free care	86.7	10.37	777
	(0.67)	(0.42)	(32.8)
25 percent coinsurance rate (CR)	78.8	8.83	630
	(0.99)	(0.379)	(29.0)
50 percent CR	74.3	8.31	583
	(1.86)	(0.4)	(32.6)
95 percent CR	68.0	7.75	534
	(1.48)	(0.354)	(27.4)
Individual deductible (ID)	72.6	9.52	623
	(1.14)	(0.529)	(34.6)

"Our findings decisively reject the hypothesis that increased coverage of outpatient services, holding constant the coverage of inpatient services, will reduce expenditure" (Manning, Newhouse et al. 1987).

2. Predicted annual use of medical services, by income group:

Plan	Lowest Third (%)	Middle Third (%)	Highest Third (%)	Corrected t[a]
Likelihood of any use				
Free care	82.8	87.4	90.1	5.90
25 percent CR	71.8	80.1	84.8	6.28
50 percent CR	64.7	76.2	82.3	4.86
95 percent CR	61.7	68.9	73.8	4.64
ID	65.3	73.9	79.1	7.09
Likelihood of one or more hospital admissions				
Free care	10.6	10.1	10.4	− 0.35
25 percent CR	10.0	8.4	8.0	− 2.75
50 percent CR	9.1	8.1	7.8	− 1.66
95 percent CR	8.8	7.4	7.1	− 2.46
ID	9.3	9.4	9.9	0.68
Medical expenditures (in 1984 dollars)				
Free care	788	736	809	0.53
25 percent CR	680	588	623	− 1.47
50 percent CR	610	550	590	− 0.49
95 percent CR	581	494	527	− 1.41
ID	609	594	670	1.38

a. "Corrected t" is the t-test on the hypothesis that the population value for the upper third of households is the same as the population value for the lower third of households, corrected for intertemporal and intrafamily correlation. An absolute value of 1.96 or higher indicates that the probability of this hypothesis being true is 5 percent or less.

3. For the sample as a whole, the only statistically significant health gains from the free-care plan over the cost-sharing plans were for high blood pressure and the correction of nearsightedness. For the 25 percent of the sample judged to be in the poorest health, there was a 10 percent greater risk of dying, other things being equal, in the cost-sharing plans than in the free-care plan.

The project authors noted that gains in health were mostly due to improved control of blood pressure, and that a targeted program of free hypertension screening could accomplish the same result.

4. Valdez et al. (1985) reported: "For the typical child participant, we could not discern significant differences in health status between those who received free care and those insured by the cost-sharing plans. . . . Taking all the measures together, the direction of estimated effects favored neither the free plan nor the cost-sharing plans."

5. Ware et al. (1986) reported: "1,673 individuals aged 14 to 61 were randomly assigned to one HMO or FFS plan in Seattle. For non-

poor individuals assigned to the HMO who were initially in good health, there were no adverse effects. Health outcomes in the two systems of care differed for high and low income individuals who began the experiment with health problems. For the high income initially sick group, the HMO produced significant improvements in cholesterol levels and in general health ratings by comparison with free FFS care. The low income initially sick group assigned to the HMO reported significantly more bed-days per year due to poor health and more serious symptoms than those assigned free FFS care, and a greater risk of dying by comparison with pay FFS plans."

6. Annual use of medical services per capita, by HMO and FFS status:

Plan	Likelihood of Any Use (%)	One or More Admissions to Hospital (%)	Imputed Expenditures (1984 dollars)
HMO experimental	87.0	7.1	434
HMO control	91.1	6.4	432
Free FFS	85.3	11.2	640

HMO critics have long claimed that the apparent cost savings from the HMO organizational mode were partly due to self-selection; persons less likely to demand care are more likely to choose HMOs. To test this, HMO experimentals were randomly assigned to the HMO; HMO controls were assigned to it randomly but had already been enrolled in it anyway; the randomly assigned FFS group included people who had been HMO members before the experiment.

The project report stated: "Our results . . . show no evidence of selection in the single HMO that we studied; those previously enrolled at the HMO (the Controls) used services at approximately the same rate as those who were not previously enrolled (the Experimentals)."

TIME TRENDS IN FINDINGS: No differences between three-year and five-year groups were reported.

DESIGN ISSUES:
1. "There are no easy, quantitative measures of health in large populations" (Relman, in editorial accompanying Brook et al. 1983).
2. Poor families in this study reached their MDE quickly, since it was a function of income, and thereafter care was free. This will distort any projections from these findings to the effects of cost sharing on the poor when the deductible is set at a higher level and/or is not a function of income. These reservations do not apply to comparisons between the free-care plan and the ID plan, where the

limit was not a function of income; however, the ceiling in the ID plan was still fairly low.
3. "The fact that there was greater variation in the amount of care used by children between sites than between payment groups suggests that very different types of care were provided in different places. Unless one knows what care was delivered, it is difficult to come to conclusions about its relation to outcomes" (Haggerty, in editorial accompanying Valdez et al. 1985).
4. Although the refusal group was not statistically different from the participant group in observed characteristics, the rate of refusal rose with the coinsurance rate (25 percent of those offered the 95 percent plan refused), leaving open the question of differences in unobserved characteristics.
5. Published reports do not generally report the effects of differing levels of MDE on the variables of interest. Given the experimental design, this is a strange omission.
6. There could be a problem of underreporting of small claims, especially at the 95 percent coinsurance rate and in the high MDE plans. At 95 percent, filing a claim on a $50 office visit would have a reward of $2.50; healthy people might not bother.
7. The HMO study is clearly dependent on the characteristics of the HMO used, and perhaps on the characteristics of competing FFS physicians in Seattle as well.

REPLICABILITY: Would appear to be broadly replicable.

GENERALIZABILITY:
1. The key finding of the experiment is that the price elasticity of health care is substantial, even when price changes are compensated (in this case, overcompensated) by income supplements. Under standard economic theory, the provision of subsidized medical care will therefore result in an important loss in social welfare owing to the use of resources in medical care that have less value to the consumer than the money it costs to provide them. This has a clear bearing on the design of any national health insurance plan. Using strong assumptions, like competitive medical care prices and no externalities, Manning et al. (1987) calculated the "deadweight" loss in wasted resources in moving from a national 95 percent plan with $1,000 MDE to a national free-care plan. Their estimate is between $37 billion and $60 billion; expenditures on these services in 1984 by the under-65 population were around $200 billion.
2. In an early article (Newhouse et al., *New England Journal of Medicine* 305(25, December 17, 1981):1501–7) the authors noted some

limits to generalizability. An increase in subsidy to ambulatory care would result in increases in the quantity of services demanded sufficient to exceed the short-run capacity of the medical-care delivery system; this might well lead to a nonprice rationing of care, which would upset many of the conclusions in these articles. Large, long-run increases in capacity might not be allowed by the government for cost reasons, so this generalizability problem might be a long-run problem as well. On the other hand, a slackening in services demanded brought on by increased cost-sharing would in some theories cause physicians to "induce demand" by suggesting more costly therapies to their patients; this theory, however, is controversial.

FUNDING SOURCE: U.S. Department of Health and Human Services, Assistant Secretary for Planning and Evaluation. Key personnel: Larry L. Orr and James Schuttinga.

TREATMENT ADMINISTRATOR: RAND Corporation. Key personnel: Rae Archibald.

EVALUATOR: RAND Corporation. Key personnel: Joseph P. Newhouse.

ENABLING LEGISLATION: None.

INFORMATION SOURCES: Joseph P. Newhouse and The Insurance Experiment Group, *Free for All? Lessons from the RAND Health Insurance Experiment*, Harvard University Press, 1993; Willard G. Manning, Joseph P. Newhouse, Naihua Duan, et al., "Health Insurance and the Demand for Medical Care: Evidence from a Randomized Experiment," *American Economic Review*, 77(3, June 1987): 251–77. Robert H. Brook, John E. Ware, Jr., William H. Rogers, Emmett B. Keeler, et al., "Does Free Care Improve Adults' Health? Results from a Randomized Controlled Trial," *New England Journal of Medicine* 309:23 (December 8, 1983): 1426–34; John E. Ware, Jr., Robert H. Brook, William H. Rogers, Emmett B. Keeler, et al., "Comparison of Health Outcomes at a Health Maintenance Organization with Those of Fee-for-Service Care," *Lancet*, May 3, 1986: 1017–22; R. Burciaga Valdez, Robert H. Brook, William H. Rogers, John E. Ware, Jr., et al., "Consequences of Cost-Sharing for Children's Health," *Pediatrics* 75(5, May 1985), 952–61.

PUBLIC-USE ACCESS TO DATA: Public-use file available through RAND Corporation or National Technical Information Service, Springfield, Virginia.

UNITED HEALTHCARE GATEKEEPER PLAN EXPERIMENT

SUMMARY: This demonstration, conducted in 1979, tested the effects of a gatekeeper on health care usage and costs for a large sample of healthcare users. Subjects were followed for one year.

COST: Cost figures not available.

TIME FRAME: Data were collected on participants who enrolled in a health care plan in 1979.

TREATMENTS TESTED: The sample was randomly assigned to either a health care plan with a gatekeeper (physicians who control health care services and charges) or to a plan without a gatekeeper.

OUTCOMES OF INTEREST: Health care usage and costs.

SAMPLE SIZE: Treatment (gatekeeper plan), 555 subscribers and their dependents (1,419 enrollees); control (no gatekeeper), 558 subscribers and their dependents (1,408 enrollees).

TARGET POPULATION: Washington State employees in the Seattle metropolitan area enrolling for the first time in a health care plan with United Healthcare (UHC), excluding retirees.

NUMBER OF TREATMENT GROUPS: Two: gatekeeper and no gatekeeper.

NUMBER AND LOCATION OF SITES: One: Seattle metropolitan area.

RESEARCH COMPONENTS:
    Process analysis: None.
    Impact analysis: Comparison of means and analysis of covariance. (Since the adjusted and unadjusted results were essentially the same, unadjusted rates are presented in the report.)
    Benefit–cost analysis: Not conducted.

MAJOR FINDINGS:
1. People in the gatekeeper plan had 6 percent more visits to the primary care physician (PCP) and 9 percent fewer visits to a specialist.
2. There was no reported difference between plans in enrollees' use of other health insurance plans, in the proportion of claims submitted, or in out-of-pocket expenses.
3. On average, total charges were 6% less for the gatekeeper plan than for controls ($239 per person, per year versus $254.) The gatekeeper plan had lower ambulatory charges per enrollee, per year ($146 versus $167), primarily due to lower use of specialists. The gatekeeper plan had little impact on hospital use or charges. In

fact, the gatekeeper plan had slightly *higher* charges ($93 versus $87.)

TIME TRENDS IN FINDINGS: None reported.

DESIGN ISSUES:
1. The use of claims data precluded certain categories of examination. For example, the evaluators had no way of knowing who initiated a visit to the PCP, or whether a patient was seeing a particular provider as a PCP or as a specialist.
2. This 12-month study may not be representative of the plans' or enrollees' experiences over time.

REPLICABILITY: Replicable.

GENERALIZABILITY: The evaluation does not address this issue. This was a voluntary program, and subscribers who chose United Healthcare rather than another state health insurance plan had the opportunity to familiarize themselves with the standard UHC plan. They may have been oriented to use PCPs more than the general population.

FUNDING SOURCE: Health Care Financing Administration (HCFA).

TREATMENT ADMINISTRATOR: United Healthcare, operated by SAFECO Insurance Company.

EVALUATOR: Diane Martin, University of Washington-Seattle, School of Public Health and Community Medicine.

ENABLING LEGISLATION: None.

INFORMATION SOURCES: Martin, Diane P., et.al., "Effect of a Gatekeeper Plan on Health Service Use and Charges: A Randomized Trial," *American Journal of Public Health* 79(1989): 1628–32.

PUBLIC-USE ACCESS TO DATA: Not available.

Part Nine

CHARGED/CONVICTED

LIVING INSURANCE FOR EX-OFFENDERS (LIFE)

SUMMARY: This demonstration, conducted from 1972 to 1975, tested the effects of temporary financial assistance and job placement services on a medium-sized sample of male ex-offenders. Subjects were followed for one year.

COST: $230,000 (1973); research only, $30,000.

TIME FRAME: Fiscal years 1972–74; data collected, 1972–75; final report, 1978.

TREATMENTS TESTED:
1. Controls. No treatment.
2. Financial aid. Sixty dollars a week for 13 weeks, conditional on not being reimprisoned. If the subject had earnings above $40 a week, 50 percent of those earnings was subtracted from the weekly payment and deferred to a later week, thus slightly extending the 13-week period.
3. Job placement services. Staff members worked full-time finding job openings, chauffeuring experimentals to interviews and helping them fill out job applications, and advocating on experimentals' behalf with employers and bureaucrats.
4. Financial aid and job placement. Experimentals received both job services and financial aid.

OUTCOMES OF INTEREST: (1) Rearrest; (2) Employment; and (3) Earnings.

SAMPLE SIZE: Group 1, 108; group 2, 108; group 3, 108; group 4, 108.

TARGET POPULATION: Male ex-offenders returning to Baltimore from prison, nonaddicts, with records of multiple prior offenses, at least one of them for theft; under age 45; and having less than $400 in savings.

NUMBER OF TREATMENT GROUPS: Four (with one control group).

NUMBER AND LOCATION OF SITES: One—Baltimore, Maryland.

RESEARCH COMPONENTS:
Process analysis: Extensive interviews of experimentals.
Impact analysis: Conducted both as difference in means and by regression and probit.
Benefit–cost analysis: Conducted from several perspectives with upper and lower bounds on confidence.

MAJOR FINDINGS:
1. Job placement services had no statistically significant impacts. The remaining findings are reported for financial experimentals (groups 2 and 4) versus financial controls (groups 1 and 3).

2.

	Experimentals	Controls
New arrests, all theft crimes	48	66
Estimated new arrests, from regression with other factors	48.6	66
Estimated new arrests, from probit with other factors	45.5	66
New arrests, all crimes	107	123
In school or training, first quarter	3.7%	1.4%
second quarter	4.2%	2.0%
Employed full-time, fourth quarter	54.7%	49%

Note: All of the differences above are statistically significant; however, schooling differentials are not significant after the second quarter, and employment differentials are not significant in the first, second, and third quarters. There are no statistically significant differences in weekly earnings in any quarter.

3. Benefit–cost analysis from a social perspective: Lower bound— $108,565 benefits, $27,000 costs; 4.02 benefit–cost ratio. Upper bound—$870,431 benefits, $16,200 costs; 53.73 benefit–cost ratio. Benefit–cost ratio from other perspectives:

	Lower	Upper
Budgetary	0.49	2.67
Nonparticipant	0.77	3.99
Participant	1.93	3.76

TIME TRENDS IN FINDINGS: The difference in arrests was 16 in the second year, compared with 18 in the first year, indicating the effect did not disappear. However, the second-year data are lower in quality since they rely on Baltimore area court records, and some subjects had left the area.

DESIGN ISSUES: The primary grounds for uncertainty are the value of increased output and the size of the losses from theft. Benefit–cost ratios reflect various assumptions about the social discount rate, the rate of decline in the effect on recidivism, the costs of the judicial system, direct losses from theft, displacement effects, and the pattern of change in the dependence on welfare payments.

REPLICABILITY: Replicable.

GENERALIZABILITY: The sample selection criteria were deliberately chosen to assemble a group that was likely to show a strong response. Since a policy would necessarily embrace a larger group, the "Transitional Aid Research Project" (TARP) was funded to determine whether the experimental effects would be repeated in a wider population. Lenihan's (1978) report noted that Baltimore had fairly inexpensive inner-city housing at the time of the experiment, and thus the experimental response was obtainable there at a lower cost than in some other cities.

FUNDING SOURCE: U.S. Department of Labor, Employment and Training Administration. Key personnel: Howard Rosen.

TREATMENT ADMINISTRATOR: Bureau of Social Science Research. Key personnel: Kenneth J. Lenihan.

EVALUATORS: Bureau of Social Science Research (BSSR) and Mathematica Policy Research (MPR). Key personnel: Kenneth J. Lenihan, BSSR; Charles D. Mallar and Craig Thornton, MPR.

ENABLING LEGISLATION: None.

POLICY EFFECTS: Kenneth Lenihan has stated that a California legislator, citing LIFE results, eventually obtained financial assistance for released prisoners.

INFORMATION SOURCES: Charles D. Mallar and Craig Thornton, "Transitional Aid for Released Prisoners: Evidence from the LIFE Experiment," *Journal of Human Resources*, Spring 1978: 208–36. Kenneth J. Lenihan, *Unlocking the Second Gate: The Role of Financial Assistance in Reducing Recidivism among Ex-Prisoners*, R&D Monograph 45, U.S. Department of Labor, Employment and Training Administration, 1978.

PUBLIC-USE ACCESS TO DATA: We have no information about a public-use file for this demonstration.

TRANSITIONAL AID RESEARCH PROJECT (TARP)

SUMMARY: This demonstration, conducted from 1975 to 1977, tested the effects of a temporary negative income tax (at various levels of income guarantee and tax rate) on a large sample of released prisoners. Subjects were followed for up to two years.

COST: $3.4 million (1976) ($2.6 million federal; the rest is an estimate of the states' administrative expenses).

TIME FRAME: January–December 1976; data collected, December 1975–June 1977; final reports for each state were submitted in 1978.

TREATMENTS TESTED: Treatments varied in regard to whether or not there were guaranteed incomes to subjects for a time period following release. Payment treatments varied by the number of weeks of payments guaranteed and by the tax rate on earnings. Georgia and Texas unemployment insurance rules applied, accounting for differences in the size of payments and the maximum amount of untaxed, earned income permitted (weekly forgiveness amount). The Georgia and Texas unemployment rules are summarized as a 100 percent tax rate above the forgiveness amount; this is an oversimplification.

Treatment	State	Maximum Weekly Payment ($)	Maximum Number Weeks	Maximum Allowance ($)	Forgiveness	Tax Rate (%)
1.	Georgia	70	26	1,820	8	100
	Texas	63	26	1,638	15.75	100
2.	Georgia	70	13	910	8	100
	Texas	63	13	819	15.75	100
3.	Georgia	70	13	910	—	25
	Texas	63	13	819	—	25

4. Job placement services in both states, with grants up to $100 for tools, work clothes, and so forth. No eligibility for payment.
5. Interviewed controls in both states. Fifteen-dollar payment for each of the four interviews in Georgia; $10 average payment for each of the four interviews in Texas; no other payments.
6. Noninterviewed controls in both states, followed through arrest and FICA earnings records; no payments, did not know they were part of an experiment.

OUTCOMES OF INTEREST: (1) Recidivism and (2) Employment and earnings.

SAMPLE SIZE: Group 1—Georgia, 176; Texas, 175; group 2—Georgia, 199; Texas, 200; group 3—Georgia, 201; Texas, 200; group 4—Georgia, 200; Texas, 200; group 5—Georgia, 200; Texas, 200; group 6—Georgia, 1,031; Texas, 1,000.

TARGET POPULATION: All prisoners released from state prisons with the following exceptions: (1) those returning to a small number of remote rural counties; (2) those returning to some other state or country; (3) those for whom arrest warrants or detainers for other offenses were pending prior to release.

NUMBER OF TREATMENT GROUPS: Six (with two control groups).

NUMBER AND LOCATION OF SITES: Georgia and Texas, statewide, with limited exceptions.

RESEARCH COMPONENTS:

Process analysis: Wide-ranging interviews with members of the first five groups were conducted, in some cases with their family members. However, the researchers do not have any data about the content of the subjects' interactions with the employees of the employment security agencies. This is important for group 4, where virtually nothing is known except expenditures for tools and work clothes; it is also important for group 3, the low-tax group, because interviews showed no particular understanding of the tax system by that group or by the others. Tests were also performed on the possibility of underreporting of employment by the payment groups against unemployment insurance records; no such pattern was found.

Impact analysis: Conducted both as difference in means and with regression and other statistical techniques.

Benefit–cost analysis: Not conducted.

MAJOR FINDINGS:

1. No statistically significant differences in recidivism were found.
2. Employment and earnings, Georgia:

Variable	Group 1	Group 2	Group 3	Group 4	Group 5	Group 6
Mean weeks worked, first year after release	12.3	17.4	17.7	19.6	24.3	N/A
Mean weeks worked, first 14 weeks	2.4	2.8	3.1	4.9	5.9	N/A
Mean weeks worked, weeks 15–24	2.5	4.0	4.5	5.2	6.5	N/A
Percentage with some earnings	53.7	60.8	62.4	62.5	65.2	61.2
Mean earnings ($)	1,064	1,525	1,433	1,088	1,553	1,531

Note: In general, experimental groups have statistically significant differences from control group 5 in rows 1, 2, and 4.

3. Employment and earnings, Texas:

Variable	Group 1	Group 2	Group 3	Group 4	Group 5	Group 6
Mean weeks worked, first year after release	20.8	27.1	24.6	29.3	28.3	N/A
Mean weeks worked, first 14 weeks	4.0	4.9	5.2	7.0	7.1	N/A
Mean weeks worked, weeks 15–24	4.5	7.3	6.8	7.4	7.6	N/A
Percentage with some earnings	67.4	78.6	69.7	73.1	66.1	66.2
Earnings ($)	1,922	2,215	2,242	2,069	1,960	2,043

Note: In general, experimental-group differences from group 5 are statistically significant for all rows except the last one.

"The TARP payments, as administered, did not decrease arrests for property-related offenses in either state. . . . TARP payment eligibility exerted a clear and strong work-disincentive effect. . . ."

4. The project report authors set up and tested an elaborate multiple-equation system with the experimental data. Their conclusion is that the effect of the payments themselves was to reduce recidivism, but that the negative effects of the high tax rate led to low employment, which in turn led to higher recidivism.

TIME TRENDS IN FINDINGS: Data are for one year.

DESIGN ISSUES:

In Georgia, a "speeded-up" commutation procedure went into effect shortly before the experiment began. The effect of this change was to increase the number of prisoners in the Georgia sample who would be expected to exhibit an experimental effect if one existed; it tended to accelerate the release of older offenders with more than one prior theft conviction.

REPLICABILITY: As in many other experiments, "job placement services" is not replicable. The other portions of the experiment appear to be replicable.

GENERALIZABILITY: This experiment was planned to generalize the results of the "Living Insurance for Ex-offenders (LIFE)" experiment. It did not confirm those results.

FUNDING SOURCE: U.S. Department of Labor (DOL), Employment and Training Administration, and Department of Justice (DOJ), Law Enforcement Assistance Administration. Key personnel: Howard Rosen, DOL; Howard Rosen, DOJ.

TREATMENT ADMINISTRATORS: Texas Department of Corrections, Georgia Department of Corrections, and the Employment Security Agency. Key personnel: Coordination and experimental design were performed by Kenneth J. Lenihan. To identify persons at different agencies with Transitional Aid Research Project (TARP)-related responsibilities, contact Sheldon Olson for Texas and Lois Sanders for Georgia.

EVALUATORS: Social and Demographic Research Institute, University of Massachusetts at Amherst, and the Group for Research on Social Policy, University of California–Santa Barbara. Key personnel: Peter H. Rossi and Richard A. Berk.

ENABLING LEGISLATION: None.

INFORMATION SOURCE: Peter H. Rossi, Richard A. Berk, and Kenneth J. Lenihan, *Money, Work and Crime: Experimental Evidence*, Harcourt Brace Jovanovich, 1980.

PUBLIC-USE ACCESS TO DATA: We have no information about a public-use file for this demonstration.

COURT EMPLOYMENT PROJECT

SUMMARY: This demonstration, conducted from 1977 to 1979, tested the effects of case dismissal in exchange for acceptance of counseling and employment-related services on a medium-sized sample of individuals charged with felonies. Subjects were followed for one year.

COST: $750,000 (1977).

TIME FRAME: January 1977–March 1978; data collected through 1979; final report, June 1981.

TREATMENTS TESTED: Prosecutors would refer persons charged with felonies to the project, and an "approximately" random assignment, described below, would occur. Experimentals were offered a delay and eventually a dismissal of their cases if they agreed to attend counseling sessions over a four-month period and if they complied with the agreement. The counseling included job referral and placement services, needs assessment, and referral to services in experimentals' neighborhoods (for general equivalency diploma [GED] tutoring, substance abuse, etc.). This option was not open to controls. The approximately random process was adopted to make the experiment politically acceptable. The experimental period was randomly divided into time periods of varying length, and project staff did not know when the current subperiod would expire. Quotas were preset, proportional to the length of the subperiods: new participants who entered before the quota was reached were experimentals; the overflow were controls.

OUTCOMES OF INTEREST: (1) Disposition of case; (2) Employment; and (3) Education or training activity.

SAMPLE SIZE: Experimentals, 410; controls, 256.

TARGET POPULATION: Persons charged with felonies selected by prosecutors. Three-quarters of the felonies were property crimes.

NUMBER OF TREATMENT GROUPS: Two (with one control group).

NUMBER AND LOCATION OF SITES: Two—Brooklyn and Manhattan.

RESEARCH COMPONENTS:
   Process analysis: Conducted through interviews with prosecutors, implementation staff, and subjects. The key finding in the process analysis was that large numbers of controls either would not have been prosecuted; or, if prosecuted, would not have been convicted; or, if both prosecuted and convicted, would have faced minor penalties. Prosecutors used pretrial diversion to skim off a group who were not in serious trouble but "needed supervision." Defense attorneys cooperated with the tactic partly to economize on their own scarce resources. A second finding was that the Court Employment Project (CEP) staff felt they had not been successful in job development.
   Impact analysis: Conducted as a difference in means. OLS findings were not qualitatively different and were not reported.
   Benefit–cost analysis: Not conducted.

MAJOR FINDINGS: Charges were dropped against 72 percent of experimentals, as against 46 percent of controls. However, only 6.6 percent of controls were convicted of criminal charges, whereas 1.9 percent of experimentals were. Thus, the experimental treatment did not significantly conserve court resources. Effects on employment were negligible. At a six-month follow-up, the average experimental had been employed for 1.29 months, the average control for 1.41 months. Effects on education and training were negligible.

TIME TRENDS IN FINDINGS: A 12-month follow-up also found no effects of treatment.

DESIGN ISSUES: The assignment process was accepted as effectively random by a national panel of referees.

REPLICABILITY: Replicable.

GENERALIZABILITY: The final report emphasized that the "Court Employment Project," which was set up by the Vera Institute of Justice, was one of the earliest pretrial diversion programs; its policies conformed to standards set by a national professional organization. Thus, there is no obvious reason that the finding that pretrial diversion is ineffective and conceptually flawed should not have general validity.

FUNDING SOURCE: National Institute of Justice. Key personnel: Joel Garner.

TREATMENT ADMINISTRATOR: Court Employment Project. Key personnel: Ennis J. Olgiati (deceased), Bruce Eichner, and Rae Linefsky.

EVALUATOR: Vera Institute of Justice. Key personnel: Sally Hillsman Baker and Susan Sadd.

ENABLING LEGISLATION: None.

POLICY EFFECTS: Sally Hillsman Baker believes there have been three impacts. First, the project was the first successful implementation of random assignment in court settings for a long time. It supported the belief of the National Institute of Justice (NIJ) staff (notably that of Joel Garner) that random assignment was a feasible and necessary research tool, and it led to further experiments. Second, it fostered skepticism, especially among policymakers in New York, that the various "alternatives" to detention or custody were in fact alternatives, and subjected alternative projects to higher standards in proving their effectiveness. Third, it has caused pretrial diversion, as a strategy, to be largely abandoned in New York City. It has not had the same effect in the rest of the country, although Hillsman Baker feels the experiment has exposed pretrial diversion as conceptually flawed.

INFORMATION SOURCE: Sally Hillsman Baker and Susan Sadd, "Diversion of Felony Arrests. An Experiment in Pretrial Intervention: An Evaluation of the Court Employment Project," Summary Report, Department of Justice, National Institute of Justice, June 1981.

PUBLIC-USE ACCESS TO DATA: We have no information about a public-use file for this demonstration.

EX-OFFENDER RESEARCH PROJECT

SUMMARY: According to Lafayette Grisby of the Employment and Training Administration (ETA) this experiment was intended to determine the effects of guaranteed jobs on the behavior of ex-offenders on their release from prison. It was located in Baltimore, the contractor was Blackstone Associates, and $2.5 million (1981) was initially allocated to the project. The project was terminated within a few months of initiation because of a funding cutback, long before any results could have been observed.

FUNDING: U.S. Department of Labor, Employment and Training Administration.

INFORMATION SOURCE: None is known to exist.

PUBLIC-USE ACCESS TO DATA: No data.

Part Ten

LOW-INCOME CHILDREN AND THEIR FAMILIES

SUMMARY: This ongoing program, begun in 1962, is testing the effects of a structured preschool program on a small sample of low-income children and their families. Subjects have been followed for up to 27 years.

COST: Estimated program costs per child, $1,589 ($92,000 total). Evaluation costs have been approximately $2 million, over a considerable period of time, in nominal dollars.

TIME FRAME: The intervention began in 1962 and continued through five annual "waves" of children. Follow-up has been extensive and ongoing. The most recent results are for the 27-year follow-up, published in 1993.

TREATMENTS TESTED: The treatment was a "high-quality preschool program" offered for two and one-half hours daily for seven and one-half months. Four waves received two years of preschool, whereas wave 0 (the first wave) received only one year. Controls received no preschool.

OUTCOMES: (1) Cognitive development; (2) Academic achievement; (3) Delinquent behavior; (4) employment; and (5) Welfare receipt.

SAMPLE SIZE: Total, 123; treatment, 58; control, 65.

TARGET POPULATION: Low-income children and their families. All participants were African-American and from one neighborhood.

NUMBER OF TREATMENT GROUPS: Two (including control).

NUMBER AND LOCATION OF SITES: One—the Perry School in Ypsilanti, Michigan.

RESEARCH COMPONENTS:
   Process: Conducted. Much has been written on this program over the years, with different reports focusing on different aspects of implementation.
   Impact: In most cases, conducted with simple comparison of means.
   Benefit–cost analysis: Conducted.

MAJOR FINDINGS:
1. At age 19:

Category	Number Responding	Preschool Group	Control Group	Two-tailed p values
Employed	121	59%	32%	.032
High school graduate or equivalent	121	67%	49%	.034
College or vocational training	121	38%	21%	.029
Ever detained or arrested	121	31%	51%	.022
Total teen pregnancies, per 100 (females only)	49	64	117	.084
Functional competence (possible score 40)	109	24.6	21.8	.025
Percentage of years in special education	112	16%	28%	.039

In addition, the treatment group had significantly greater median earnings ($2,772 versus $1,070) per year, and received less welfare than controls. This last finding is statistically significant based on interviews, although not significant based on official social service records.

2. Major findings at age 27 (95 percent of original sample responding):

	Treatment (%)	Control (%)
Completed 12th grade	71	54
Had five or more arrests	7	35
Earned $2,000 + /month	29	7
Owned a home	36	13
Ever received welfare	59	80

Note: All of the above (age 27) findings shown here are statistically significant at the .05 level.

TIME TRENDS IN THE FINDINGS: IQ differences between treatment and control group members were found in the early follow-up, but diminished with time and were no longer significant by second grade. Similar trends were found for other measures of academic aptitude.

DESIGN ISSUES:
1. The initial design began as a local evaluation and then grew beyond the original intent. This has not caused major problems, although it required more funding and resources than originally planned.
2. The design was essentially random assignment, with some small compromises. Two children with employed mothers were reassigned rather than dropped. Also, children from the same families were assigned to the same treatment.

REPLICABILITY: Tracking the subjects over two decades has been difficult, although the evaluators have been very successful. They attribute this to having an excellent, dedicated interviewer who lived in the community and had the respect of the families involved. Further, the families tended to stay in the community, rather than move on to other cities or neighborhoods. This may be difficult to replicate.

GENERALIZABILITY: The sample size was very small and not representative of the state or the nation. All children were African-American and all were from one neighborhood. However, despite many constraints on generalizability, findings are quite persistent and supported by several similar studies.

FUNDING SOURCES: Core funding was provided by the Carnegie Foundation. Key personnel: Barbara Finberg. Additional funding was provided by the U.S. Office of Special Education and Rehabilitative Services, the Spencer Foundation, the Ford Foundation, the National Institute of Mental Health, the Rosenberg Foundation, the Levi-Strauss Foundation, and the State Department of Education of Michigan, supplemented by the Ypsilanti schools.

TREATMENT ADMINISTRATOR: David Weikart, director of special education for Ypsilanti Public Schools.

EVALUATOR: High/Scope Educational Research Foundation. Principal investigators: David Weikart and Larry Schweinhart. Ann Epstein, Steve Barnett, Ellen Barnes, and many others played a part in various stages of evaluation.

ENABLING LEGISLATION: None.

INFORMATION SOURCES: Six monographs have been published by High/Scope Press that cover the various follow-up periods. Numerous journal publications have also addressed this study, including, most recently: Lawrence J. Schweinhart and David P. Weikart, "Success by

Empowerment: The High/Scope Perry Preschool Study through Age 27," *Young Children*, November 1993.

PUBLIC-USE ACCESS TO DATA: Available through High/Scope Press.

WASHINGTON, D.C. MOBILE UNIT FOR CHILD HEALTH CARE

SUMMARY: This experiment, conducted between 1965 and 1972, tested the effects of mobile intensive prenatal and infant care on a small sample of low-income families. Subjects were followed for up to six years.

COST: The evaluators were not available to provide any cost figures.

TIME FRAME: Project period, 1965–72; data collected through 1976.

TREATMENTS TESTED: Intensive prenatal and infant care was provided by a pediatrician and a public health nurse. Care was provided by appointment in a mobile coach parked in front of the home. Prenatal care was begun at least by the seventh month of pregnancy and continued until the child's third birthday. Mothers also had telephone access to the nurse and pediatrician at any time. Care included routine medical examinations, immunizations, nutritional guidance, counseling, and a cognitive stimulation program. The control group was referred to area health clinics.

OUTCOMES OF INTEREST: (1) Child health, behavioral, and cognitive outcomes and (2) Parental behaviors, including parenting skills and employment stability.

SAMPLE SIZE: Treatment, 47 infants and their parents; control, 48 infants and their parents.

TARGET POPULATION: First-born African-American infants from low-income families. Mothers were unmarried school girls ages 15–18.

NUMBER OF TREATMENT GROUPS: Two (including one control).

NUMBER AND LOCATION OF SITES: One site—Washington, D.C. (neighborhoods surrounding Children's Hospital).

RESEARCH COMPONENTS:
   Process analysis: None.
   Impact analysis: Comparison of means.
   Benefit–cost analysis: Not conducted.

MAJOR FINDINGS:
1. A very large number of child outcome variables were measured (approximately 300). Statistically significant differences were found for 32 of these variables—all but 3 favored the treatment group. These 29 included: A more nutritious diet and healthier eating habits; fewer maladaptive behaviors such as thumb-sucking or extreme shyness; and higher levels of confidence and assurance.
2. Mothers in the experimental group, when compared to their control group counterparts, demonstrated significantly more instances of positive parenting skills such as: spending more time outdoors with the child; use of storybooks at home; and appropriate handling of child's misbehavior. They also were more likely to have taken some type of schooling during the first three years of the study, and significantly more were in some type of schooling at the four-year follow-up. Fathers in the experimental group were significantly less likely to have changed jobs during the three-year intervention period.
3. The children in the experimental group showed significantly higher cognitive development, compared to the control group children, on a standardized intelligence test at age three (IQ = 99.3 versus 91.2 for the control group children).

TIME TRENDS IN FINDINGS: The majority of findings persisted through the follow-up period.

DESIGN ISSUES:
1. Although attrition was low throughout the project intervention period (the first three years), by the end of the six-year follow-up, 9 treatment and 22 control group children were lost (had moved, broken contact with the evaluators, or had developed significant health problems). The excess loss of control subjects caused some bias in the results.
2. The staff of the project inadvertently provided the first group of mothers admitted to the program considerably more counseling and attention than was possible with the second half of the mothers. Outcomes were more favorable for this group.

REPLICABILITY: Replicable, though the evaluators cautioned that the medical professionals in this study were especially dedicated and talented counselors and that there was an enthusiasm for change among poor families in the 1960s.

GENERALIZABILITY: The sample was drawn from 16 census tracts in urban Washington, D.C., where crowded, rundown housing was the norm. Mothers were typically heads of households. Generalizability may be hindered, even to this population, for two reasons: (1) the sample size was quite small, especially for the outcomes regarding father's employment; and (2) the experiment was conducted 30 years ago, a time when attitudes may have differed from those of today.

FUNDING SOURCE: National Institute of Mental Health.

TREATMENT ADMINISTRATOR: Children's Hospital of Washington, D.C.

EVALUATORS: Department of Child Health and Development, George Washington University School of Medicine; and Research Foundation of Children's Hospital, Washington, D.C.

ENABLING LEGISLATION: None.

INFORMATION SOURCES: Margaret F. Gutelius, Arthur D. Kirsh, Sally MacDonald, Marion R. Brooks, and Toby McErlean, "Controlled Study of Child Health Supervision: Behavioral Results," *Pediatrics* 60(1977): 294–304.

PUBLIC-USE ACCESS TO DATA: Not available.

CAROLINA ABECEDARIAN PROJECT

SUMMARY: This demonstration, which began in 1972, is testing the effects of a developmental day-care program and a school-age intervention on a small sample of at-risk children and their families. Subjects were followed up to 15 years, and follow-up continues.

COST: Cost figures are not available. The National Institute for Child Health and Human Development (NICHHD), the primary funder, contributed approximately $6 million over the life of the project. Some of the evaluation costs were included in this figure. There were many other funding sources, however, and also considerable donated time.

TIME FRAME: Pilot work began in 1971; treatment period, 1972–85; data collection, continuing.

TREATMENTS TESTED:
1. Preschool intervention: A systematic, developmental day-care program and educational day-care services. The curriculum emphasized language development and appropriate and adaptive social behavior.

2. School-age intervention: Increased and enhanced parent involvement. Treatment group families were assigned a home/school resource teacher (HST) who provided home curriculum activities that reinforced concepts taught in school. The HST also helped families with non-school-related problems.

The control group children received no preschool intervention and received the existing school curriculum when they reached school age.

OUTCOMES OF INTEREST: (1) Children's cognitive development; (2) Maternal attitudes; and (3) Maternal employment.

SAMPLE SIZE: Total, 111; pre-school treatment, 57; pre-school control, 54. Roughly one-half of these initial groups were then randomly assigned to a school-age intervention as they entered school.

TARGET POPULATION: Infants and children believed to be at high risk for school failure. Criteria for selection included maternal IQ, family income, parent education, and intactness of family. All but one sample family were African-American.

NUMBER OF TREATMENT GROUPS: Four: preschool plus school age intervention; preschool only; school-age intervention only; and no intervention (control).

NUMBER AND LOCATION OF SITES: One site—Orange County, North Carolina.

RESEARCH COMPONENTS:

Process analysis: Service delivery was closely monitored, as was the admission of families to the sample.

Impact analysis: Comparison of means.

Benefit–cost analysis: Not conducted.

MAJOR FINDINGS: Findings have been summarized at various points in this experiment, highlighting wide variety of outcomes. Maternal outcomes were examined formally at the 54-month follow-up and informally at 12 years. The evaluators hope to look more closely at these outcomes in a future publication; they will also be studying the economic outcomes of the children themselves when data become available. Those interested in child development and academic outcomes are referred to the information sources below.

1. At the 54-month follow-up, mothers of day-care children (treatment group) had significantly more formal education (11.9 years) than the mothers of the control group children (10.3 years), although the groups were equivalent in the year of the children's births.

2. At 54 months, significantly more mothers with children in the treatment group held semiskilled or skilled jobs (55 percent) than did the control-group mothers (26 percent). Conversely, significantly more control-group mothers were unemployed or unskilled (65 percent) than were day-care mothers (36 percent). (Note: The remaining mothers not counted above were considered students.)
3. Whereas the parental data from the 12-year follow-up has not yet been analyzed, the evaluators reported that it appears that mothers of treatment group children still had more years of education, were less likely to be on welfare, and were more likely to own their own homes than mothers of control-group children.

TIME TRENDS IN FINDINGS: None reported for maternal outcomes. There was some fluctuation among cognitive development test scores.

DESIGN ISSUES:
1. At the 54-month follow-up (the point when maternal interviews were conducted), less than half of the sample was available for analysis. However, some subjects earlier lost to attrition were relocated and participated in the 12-year follow-up, increasing the follow-up rate to 81 percent of the original infants.
2. The subsample analysis is based on very small numbers because the original sample infants were further divided into four groups.

REPLICABILITY: Replicable. The information sources provide information regarding teacher training, curriculum, and so on.

GENERALIZABILITY: The sample, especially for maternal outcomes, was quite small, though other similar experiments tend to support these findings. On average, 72 percent of this sample had a female head of household, a mean income of $1,455 (1972 dollars), mother's education was roughly 10 years, and all but one family was black. In terms of academic achievement and cognitive ability, this experiment had comparable findings to other similar experiments (e.g., the Perry Preschool Project and the Milwaukee Project).

FUNDING SOURCES: National Institute for Child Health and Human Development; the Spencer Foundation; the Carnegie Foundation; the Office of Special Education, U.S. Department of Education; the Department of Human Resources of the State of North Carolina; and the Department of Social Services of Orange County, North Carolina.

TREATMENT ADMINISTRATOR: The curriculum developers and the day-care director were responsible for direct administration of the treatment. These positions have changed personnel many times over the life of the project.

EVALUATOR: Frank Porter Graham Child Development Center, University of North Carolina at Chapel Hill. Craig Ramey was the principal investigator for much of this experiment; Frances Campbell is the current principal investigator.

ENABLING LEGISLATION: None.

INFORMATION SOURCES: Craig T. Ramey, Keith Owen Yeates and Elizabeth J. Short, "The Plasticity of Intellectual Development: Insights from Preventive Intervention," *Child Development* 55(1984): 1913–25; Craig T. Ramey, David MacPhee, and Keith Owen Yeates, "Preventing Developmental Retardation: A General Systems Model," in *Facilitating Infant and Early Childhood Development*, edited by Lynne A. Bond and Justin M. Joffe, University Press of New England, 1982; Frances A. Campbell, and Craig T. Ramey, "Cognitive and School Outcomes for High-Risk African-American Students at Middle Adolescence: Positive Effects of Early Intervention," *American Educational Research Journal* 32(1995): 743–72; F.A. Campbell, and C.T. Ramey, "Effects of Early Intervention on Intellectual and Academic Achievement: A Follow-up Study of Children from Low-Income Families," *Child Development* 65(1994): 684–98.

PUBLIC-USE ACCESS TO DATA: The researchers are still collecting data, and it is not yet public information.

NEW YORK NURSE HOME VISITATION EXPERIMENT

SUMMARY: This demonstration, conducted from 1978 to 1980, tested the effects of nurse home visits on a medium-sized sample of pregnant women and their children. Subjects were followed for four years.

COST: The evaluators were unable to provide a figure for the costs of this experiment, although they did say that approximately 50 percent of the costs went toward program implementation and 50 percent toward evaluation.

TIME FRAME: Demonstration period, April 1978–September 1980; follow-up data collected through four years after birth of the child.

TREATMENTS TESTED: Treatment 1, sensory and developmental screening by an infant specialist at one and two years of age; treatment 2, same as treatment 1 plus free transportation for regular prenatal and well-child care at local clinics and physicians' offices; treatment 3, same as treatment 2 plus nurse home visitor during pregnancy twice a month; treatment 4, same as treatment 3 plus additional nurse visits through age two. Treatments 1 and 2 were combined for analysis and were considered the comparison group.

OUTCOMES OF INTEREST: (1) Maternal employment; (2) Aid to Families with Dependent Children (AFDC) receipt; and (3) Child development and other noneconomic outcomes.

SAMPLE SIZE: Total, 400; treatment group 1, 90; group 2, 94; group 3, 100; and group 4, 116.

TARGET POPULATION: Pregnant women with no prior live births meeting any of the following criteria: age less than 19 years; single-parent status; low socioeconomic status. Other women in their first pregnancy who were not high risk, but who asked permission to participate, were accepted.

NUMBER OF TREATMENT GROUPS: Four, condensed to three for analysis.

NUMBER AND LOCATION OF SITES: One—Chemung County (Elmira), New York.

RESEARCH COMPONENTS:
    Process analysis: The program was closely monitored and nurses used computerized forms to comment on program implementation, participation rates, attrition, and service delivery.
    Impact analysis: Generalized linear models and analysis of covariance were used.
    Benefit–cost analysis: Conducted.

MAJOR FINDINGS:
1. At the 6th-month postpartum follow up, among women who had not graduated from high school at registration, 59 percent of the nurse-visited groups (treatments 3 and 4) and 27 percent of the control group had either graduated or enrolled in an educational program. By the 10th month, the effects of the program held only for unmarried women, and no treatment effects were found at the 46th month follow-up.
2. Between birth and the 22nd month postpartum, nurse-visited poor unmarried older women had worked 2.5 times longer than their counterparts in the control group (9.27 months versus 3.61 months). By the 46th month, the nurse-visited poor unmarried teenagers also had begun to work more than their counterparts (14.9 months versus 10.03 months). There was an 83 percent increase in the number of months worked by the treatment group

mothers (older and teenagers) in contrast to poor unmarried women in the control group (average months of employment, 31.31 versus 17.17).

3. During the first two years after delivery, the nurse-visited poor unmarried older women were on public assistance 157 fewer days than their control counterparts (a 40 percent reduction). This effect did not extend into the two-year period following the end of the intervention.

4. The program produced significant savings (due to increased maternal employment, reductions in unintended pregnancies, and lower child health costs) for the sample families during the 24–48 month period after delivery, although not for the first 2 years. The savings for the whole 4-year period were not statistically significant (savings per family: 0–24 months, $325; 24–48 months, $1,448).

There were also a number of health and parenting outcomes, not reported here.

TIME TRENDS IN FINDINGS:
See above. There were time trends for most of the findings.

DESIGN ISSUES:
1. There were two deviations from random assignment. In six cases, women who lived in the same household as others who had already been assigned were assigned to the same treatment. Treatment group four was expanded (more people were randomly selected for this group) during the last six months of the enrollment period.

2. Of the sample (both treatment and control) 20–25 percent reported that they discussed pregnancy or child-care matters with nurse-visited women. In other words, people in groups 3 and 4 talked about the program with women in groups 1 and 2. This could be a source of horizontal diffusion.

REPLICABILITY: Replicable. Manuals were devised that describe methods used to screen, hire, and train the nurse home visitors.

GENERALIZABILITY: There are several factors that curtail generalizability of these findings: There were no urban participants; only white participants were used for the analysis (46 nonwhite participants were excluded from the analysis); nurses were hired and trained exclusively for this program and likely had more manageable caseloads than might be possible in an ongoing program.

FUNDING SOURCES: Bureau of Community Health Services (Gontran Lamberty); National Center for Nursing Research; the Robert Wood Johnson Foundation (Ruby Hearn); the William T. Grant Foundation (Robert Haggerty); and the Ford Foundation (Oscar Harkary).

TREATMENT ADMINISTRATOR: Oversight of the treatment was conducted by Comprehensive Interdisciplinary Development Service. Key personnel: John Shannon.

EVALUATORS: David Olds, University of Rochester; Robert Chamberlin, Dartmouth Hitchcock Medical Center; Charles Henderson, Cornell University; and Robert Tatelbaum, University of Rochester.

ENABLING LEGISLATION: None.

INFORMATION SOURCES: D.L. Olds, C.R. Henderson, R. Tatelbaum, and R. Chamberlin, "Preventing Child Abuse and Neglect: A Randomized Trial of Nurse Home Visitation," *Pediatrics* 77(1986): 16–28; D.L. Olds et al., "Improving the Life-Course Development of Socially Disadvantaged Mothers: A Randomized Trial of Nurse Home Visitation," *American Journal of Public Health* 78(1988): 1436–45.

PUBLIC-USE ACCESS TO DATA: Not available.

Note: The project evaluators are now conducting a 15-year follow up.

INCREASING THE IMMUNIZATION OF PRESCHOOL CHILDREN

SUMMARY: This experiment, conducted in 1981, tested the effects of various incentives to visit a clinic for immunization on a medium-sized sample of the parents of immunization-deficient preschool children. Subjects were followed for three months.

COST: This experiment was done as a master's thesis project. The coevaluator was unable to provide a figure for the evaluation costs.

TIME FRAME: The project was conducted over a three-month period in 1981; data collected, same period.

TREATMENTS TESTED: There were six treatments—four experimental incentives and two control groups: (1) a mailed general prompt to bring the child into the clinic for immunization; (2) a more client-specific prompt, which mentioned the target child by name and his or her specific immunization needs; (3) the same specific prompt plus increased clinic access ("off-hours" clinics); (4) the specific prompt plus a monetary incentive (a lottery ticket for a cash prize); (5) control—telephone contact with no prompt; and (6) control—no contact.

The control groups did receive prompts after the conclusion of the study.

OUTCOMES OF INTEREST: (1) Clinic attendance. Increased attendance is a desired outcome in itself. By getting families into the clinic, doctors not only complete the immunizations but also see other family members, make appointments, etc. (2) Inoculations.

SAMPLE SIZE: The parents of 1,133 children comprised the total sample. Some parents had more than one child who needed immunization. Numbers of children by treatment: treatment 1—195; treatment 2—190; treatment 3—185; treatment 4—183; treatment 5—189; treatment 6—191.

TARGET POPULATION: Parents of an identified group of immunization-deficient preschool children who were clients of the public health clinic. Children were five years of age or younger and in need of one or more inoculations.

NUMBER OF TREATMENT GROUPS: Six, including two control groups.

NUMBER AND LOCATION OF SITES: One public health clinic in Akron, Ohio.

RESEARCH COMPONENTS:

Process analysis: Efforts were made to ensure that target parents received prompts, that information (names, addresses, and inoculation records) was correct, and that the correct inoculations were actually given. Random samples were used to check the reliability.

Impact analysis: Comparison of means.

Benefit–cost analysis: A cost-effectiveness analysis was conducted.

MAJOR FINDINGS: Findings for attendance and inoculations are presented separately. Since some children needed more than one inoculation, one visit does not necessarily equal one inoculation. Further, some families brought in by the prompts made appointments and returned to the clinic for other services.

1. After two weeks, the specific prompt plus monetary incentive had significantly increased both clinic attendance (by 20.9 percent) and the number of inoculations (by 28.6 percent) as compared to the control group. The specific prompt plus access had produced significantly more inoculations (20.7 percent), but not attendance.

2. At two months, all treatment groups except the general prompt had produced significantly more inoculations. The prompt-plus treatments (treatments 3 and 4) also produced greater attendance.

3. As expected by the evaluators, the monetary incentive produced the greatest effects, followed by the increased access and the specific prompt without incentives. The general prompt produced slight (not significant) attendance and inoculation gains. This ranking persisted throughout the three-month period.
4. Secondary effects were produced, in that parents of target children also brought nontarget children to the clinic, some of whom received needed inoculations.

TIME TRENDS IN FINDINGS: The monetary incentive appeared to be the most cost-effective intervention in the short run (after two weeks) because of its immediate significant impact. In the long run, the specific prompt alone proved the most cost-effective intervention capable of demonstrating evidence of statistical significance.

DESIGN ISSUES:
1. Families, rather than children, were randomly assigned to prevent confounding due to different types of prompts being mailed to parents with two or more children.
2. The second follow-up measure was taken after three months. Data gathered after two months must be evaluated with caution because some inoculations are required again after two months. Experimental groups were compared on cost-effectiveness after the first follow-up period (two months).

REPLICABILITY: Replicable.

GENERALIZABILITY: The evaluation did not address this issue. No data were provided about the representativeness of the sample to Akron, Ohio, or to the nation as a whole. Children of the sample parents were 50 percent male, 64 percent white, averaged roughly three years old, and lacked an average of 5.2 inoculations. Findings from this study are consistent with some studies but at odds with others.

FUNDING SOURCES: Akron Department of Health—C. William Keck, director; B.F. Goodrich Company—key personnel: Thomas Duke; Kent State University, Department of Psychology—Roy Lilly, chairman.

TREATMENT ADMINISTRATOR: James Yokley, in conjunction with the Akron, Ohio, Department of Health.

EVALUATORS: James M. Yokley and David S. Glenwick, Kent State University, Department of Psychology.

ENABLING LEGISLATION: None.

INFORMATION SOURCES: James Yokley and David Glenwick, "Increasing the Immunization of Preschool Children: An Evaluation of Applied Community Interventions," *Journal of Applied Behavior Analysis* 17(1984): 313–25.

PUBLIC-USE ACCESS TO DATA: Not available.

INFANT HEALTH AND DEVELOPMENT PROGRAM

SUMMARY: This study, conducted from January 1985 to the present, tested the effects of early intervention services on a medium-sized sample of low-birthweight, premature children and their families. Subjects were followed for up to eight and one-half years.

COST: The evaluators are unable to separate evaluation and project costs. They estimate that approximately $15,000 per child was spent over the three years of the intervention ($5.7 million for the sample of 377 children).

TIME FRAME: Intervention, January 1985–89 (when last child reached the age of three years). Follow-up was done at five years and eight and one-half years. This last phase of the project is not yet published.

TREATMENTS TESTED: The treatment group received early intervention services including home visits, parent support and training groups, and a child development center program in addition to pediatric follow-up. The control group received pediatric follow-up only.

OUTCOMES OF INTEREST: (1) Child development outcomes included cognitive development, behavioral competence, and health; (2) Maternal outcomes included employment, education, and welfare receipt.

SAMPLE SIZE: Total, 985; treatment, 377; control, 608.

TARGET POPULATION: Low-birthweight (LBW), premature children and their families.

NUMBER OF TREATMENT GROUPS: Two (including control). The intervention group was subdivided into lighter LBW (< 2000 g) and heavier LBW (2001–2500g).

NUMBER AND LOCATION OF SITES: Eight sites: University of Arkansas, Albert Einstein College of Medicine, Harvard Medical School, University of Miami, University of Pennsylvania, University of Texas Health Science Center at Dallas, University of Washington, and Yale University.

RESEARCH COMPONENTS:

Process analysis: Conducted. Care was given to maintain both standardization across sites and the integrity of the experimental design.

Impact analysis: Conducted with multiple linear regression.

Benefit–cost analysis: Not conducted, though such an analysis may be done after the eight and one-half-year follow-up.

MAJOR FINDINGS:

1. Mothers in the intervention group were employed for a greater number of months than the control group mothers at the end of Phase I.
2. When controlling for employment and education, the treatment group was more likely to receive public assistance. That is, in the treatment group, mothers who had some college education and/or were employed received more months of welfare benefits than similar control group mothers.
3. Participation in the program had a positive effect on the children's cognitive development.

TIME TRENDS IN FINDINGS: At the five-year follow-up, significant cognitive differences were found only for the heavier LBW subgroup. No long-term follow-up was reported for the maternal measures (employment, welfare receipt).

DESIGN ISSUES: There were no significant problems with the design or implementation of this project.

REPLICABILITY: Replicable. The Centers for Disease Control is currently doing an effectiveness study based on this project.

GENERALIZABILITY: The sites were chosen for their ability to conduct good research, rather than based on a probability sample, but findings should otherwise be generalizable to the national population of low-birthweight children and their families.

FUNDING SOURCES: Primary funding came from the Robert Wood Johnson Foundation. Additional support came from the Pew Charitable Trusts; the Bureau of Maternal and Child Health and Resource Development, Health Resources Service Administration; the National

Institute of Child Health and Human Development; and the March of Dimes Foundation.

TREATMENT ADMINISTRATOR: Infant Health and Development Program, Program Development and Implementation Office, Frank Porter Graham Child Development Center, University of North Carolina at Chapel Hill. Key personnel: Craig Ramey, Director.

EVALUATOR: National Study Office, Stanford University. Key personnel: Ruth Gross, M.D. Other key personnel: Cecilia McCarton, Albert Einstein College of Medicine; James Tonascia, Johns Hopkins University.

ENABLING LEGISLATION: None.

INFORMATION SOURCES: Infant Health and Development Program Staff, "Enhancing the Outcomes of Low-Birthweight, Premature Infants: A Multisite Randomized Trial," Journal of the American Medical Association 263(1990):3035–42. J. Brooks-Gunn, C.M. McCarton, P.H. Casey, M.C. McCormick, C.R. Bauer, J.C. Bernbaum, J. Tyson, M. Swanson, F.C. Bennett, and D.T. Scott, "Early Intervention in Low Birth-Weight, Premature Infants: Results through Age 5 Years from the Infant Health and Development Program," Journal of the American Medical Association 272(1994):1257–64.

PUBLIC-USE ACCESS TO DATA: Available through Frank Porter Graham Child Development Center.

EVEN START FAMILY LITERACY PROGRAM

SUMMARY: This demonstration, conducted from 1991 to 1994, tested the effects of early childhood education, adult literacy or basic skills training, and parenting education on a medium-sized sample of low-income families. Subjects were followed for 18 months. The experimental portion of this evaluation, summarized below, was part of a larger nationwide evaluation involving more than 20,000 families.

COST: Evaluation costs, $2.9 million.

TIME FRAME: Demonstration period, Fall 1991 to Spring 1994; data collected, same period; final report, January 1995.

TREATMENTS TESTED: Even Start projects must provide families with an integrated program of early childhood education, adult literacy or basic skills training, and parenting education. However, there is flexibility in devising projects to meet local needs. Even Start both co-ordinates existing services and directly provides services when they are not locally available. Control group families did not receive Even Start services, but could find similar services elsewhere in the community.

OUTCOMES: (1) Child outcomes—school readiness and literacy; (2) Family outcomes—parental educational level, literacy, attainment of a general equivalency degree (GED), employment, and income.

SAMPLE SIZE: There were 565 families participating at all 10 sites that contributed data to the experimental component of the evaluation. Of these 10 sites, 5 implemented random assignment. At the five sites that implemented random assignment, there were 101 Even Start families (treatment) and 98 control group families.

TARGET POPULATION: Low-income families with at least one adult who is eligible for adult education programs under the Adult Education Act and who is a parent of a child less than eight years of age living in a Chapter 1 elementary school attendance area.

NUMBER OF GROUPS: Two (including control).

NUMBER AND LOCATION OF SITES: There were 10 sites in the experiment (asterisk indicates that random assignment was implemented): Birmingham, Alabama*; Phoenix, Arizona*; Golden, Colorado*; Indianapolis, Indiana; Waterville, Maine; Billings, Montana; Albuquerque, New Mexico*; Reading, Pennsylvania*; Estill, South Carolina; and Richmond, Virginia.

RESEARCH COMPONENTS:

Process analysis: Site visits were conducted in 1991 and again in 1993. Staff interviews and observation provided details about program activities and sample characteristics.

Impact analysis: Conducted using a comparison of unweighted means as well as regression models.

Benefit–cost analysis: Not conducted.

MAJOR FINDINGS:
1. From pretest to the second posttest, both treatment and control group children showed significant gains on a measure of school readiness. However, the gain for the treatment group children was not significantly greater than the gain for the control group children. Likewise, there was no significant program effect on a measure of child literacy.
2. Similarly, parents in both treatment and control groups showed significant pretest/posttest gains on a measure of adult literacy.

Again, there was not a significant difference between groups. There was a significant program effect on the attainment of a GED. Of treatment group adults, 22.4 percent attained a GED during the study period compared to 5.7 percent of control group adults.

3. There were no significant program effects on quantifiable measures of social support, adequacy of financial resources, income level, and employment status.

TIME TRENDS IN THE FINDINGS: Treatment group children gained significantly more than their control group counterparts on a measure of school readiness between the pretest and the first posttest (9 months), but the effect had dissipated at the second posttest (18 months).

DESIGN ISSUES:

1. Of the 10 selected sites, only 5 implemented random assignment. The remaining 5, with no comparison group, contributed information only to the descriptive and cost components of the study.

2. Sites varied considerably in their size, participant and staff characteristics, and program components. Because of small sample sizes at individual sites, participants were aggregated for the analysis.

REPLICABILITY: Replicable.

GENERALIZABILITY: Designed to generalize to all Even Start families in the selected projects, including those that drop out early. Even Start recruits and serves families that are willing to participate. The sample may be more motivated to succeed than the population served by less-demanding social programs such as Head Start. The 10 projects were selected purposively, based on geographic location, level of program implementation, and willingness to participate. They differ in a number of ways from the national Even Start sample used in the larger evaluation (e.g., a far greater number of Hispanics who speak Spanish as their primary language).

FUNDING SOURCE: U.S. Department of Education, Office of Planning and Evaluation Service. Key personnel: Nancy Rhett, project officer.

TREATMENT ADMINISTRATOR: The treatment was administered locally by the staff at each Even Start project site.

EVALUATOR: Abt Associates. Key personnel: Robert St. Pierre, Janet Swartz, and Beth Gamse.

ENABLING LEGISLATION: The Hawkins-Stafford Elementary and Secondary School Improvement Amendments of 1988, Part B of Chapter 1 of Title 1 (PL 100-297) and the National Literacy Act of 1991 (PL 102-73).

INFORMATION SOURCES: Robert St. Pierre, Janet Swartz, Beth Gamse, Stephen Murray, Dennis Deck, and Phil Nickel, *National Evaluation of the Even Start Family Literacy Program—Final Report*, U.S. Department of Education, Office of Planning and Evaluation Service, January 1995.

PUBLIC-USE ACCESS TO DATA: Available through RMC Research Corporation, Portland, Oregon. Contact Dennis Deck.

Part Eleven

YOUTH

PUBLIC- VERSUS PRIVATE-SECTOR JOBS
DEMONSTRATION PROJECT

SUMMARY: This demonstration, conducted from 1978 to 1980, tested the effects of subsidized work experience with either public or private employers on a large sample of low-income youths. Subjects were followed for one to eight months.

COST: About $600,000 (1979).

TIME FRAME: Demonstration period, summer 1978–spring 1979; data collected, spring 1980; final report, 1981.

TREATMENTS TESTED: Participating public- and private-sector employers were provided youths fully subsidized by the program at 100 percent of the minimum wage for 25 weeks. Employers were encouraged to place the young worker in an unsubsidized position at program's end, but where this was infeasible, program operators attempted to develop a different unsubsidized job with another employer. Young people from the same site were grouped according to age, race, sex, and a reading test score, and were randomly assigned to either a public- or private-sector job slot.

OUTCOME OF INTEREST: Employment.

SAMPLE SIZE: Public-sector workers, 1,366; private-sector workers, 1,470.

TARGET POPULATION: 16–21-year-old low-income youths who were not in school.

NUMBER OF TREATMENT GROUPS: Two (with no control group).

NUMBER AND LOCATION OF SITES: Five—Portland, Oregon; St. Louis, Missouri; Philadelphia, Pennsylvania; New York City; and rural Minnesota.

RESEARCH COMPONENTS:
Process analysis: Conducted. The analysis concluded that a much greater effort was needed to develop private-sector worksites for the demonstration.
Impact analysis: Conducted by comparison of means and ordinary least squares (OLS).
Benefit–cost analysis: Not conducted.

MAJOR FINDINGS: All findings are subject to some doubt because of heavy attrition in responses to follow-up surveys, and attrition may not have been random across treatments. Sixty percent of the sample could not be found at the first follow-up, which occurred 90 days after program termination. At the second follow-up, 240 days after termination, the nonresponse rate was 65 percent. In the comparison of means, Gilsinan's report (1984) does not state that any differences were statistically significant, although some of them appear to be.

1. Program flow data:

Stage	Public	Private
1. Random assignment	1,366	1,470
2. Starting program	1,034	1,092
3. Reporting to worksite	892	879
4. Early termination	530	675
(percentage of line 2)	51.1	61.8
5. Completing program	504	417
(percentage of line 2)	48.9	38.2

Thus, subjects assigned to the private sector were more likely to quit or be fired than their public counterparts.

2. Outcomes for those completing the program, at completion:

	Public (%)	Private (%)
Unsubsidized employment	39.2	52.5
Other positive (schooling, etc.)	12.6	5.1
"Nonpositive" outcomes	47.1	40.4

3. Outcomes for completers, 90 days after program completion:

	Public Responses (%)	Total (%)	Private Responses (%)	Total (%)
Unsubsidized full-time job	50.2	28.6	64.0	32.4
Unsubsidized part-time job	16.0	9.1	16.6	8.4
Education or training	25.6	14.7	17.5	8.9
"Nonpositive" outcomes	8.0	4.6	1.9	1.0
Unknown		43.1		49.4

Thus, private-sector experience was more likely to lead directly to employment than to public-sector experience for those who completed the program. This is confirmed in OLS regressions using discrete outcomes (employment, etc.) as the dependent variables. For example, private-sector assignment raised the probability of unsubsidized employment immediately after completion by 14 percent, an effect that is statistically significant at the 5 percent level.

TIME TRENDS IN FINDINGS: The 240-day follow-up results are similar to the 90-day results.

DESIGN ISSUES: According to the project report, "The high dropout rate clouds the issue of whether those who dropped out of the program and were never heard from again failed to gain meaningful employment." The failure to collect data on the subsequent experience of those terminated is a flaw in the experimental design; some of them may have dropped out in favor of better jobs, for example, and there is no information on whether the private-sector group of dropouts had a better career path than the public-sector group.

REPLICABILITY: Replicable.

GENERALIZABILITY: This project is unique; it is the only source of experimental information on the relative effects of job creation in government as opposed to business. The findings seem to indicate a trade-off between a higher attrition rate in business and lower prospects of a permanent job in government. However, the flawed design, discussed above in "Design Issues," limits the confidence that can be placed in the findings.

FUNDING SOURCE: U.S. Department of Labor, Office of Youth Programs. Key personnel: Robert Taggart and Joseph Seiler.

TREATMENT ADMINISTRATOR: Comprehensive Employment and Training Act (CETA), prime sponsors in five sites. Key personnel: None.

EVALUATOR: Center for Urban Programs, Saint Louis University. Key personnel: James F. Gilsinan and E. Allen Tomey.

ENABLING LEGISLATION: Youth Employment and Demonstration Projects Act (YEDPA) of 1977.

INFORMATION SOURCE: James F. Gilsinan, "Information and Knowledge Development Potential," *Evaluation Review*, June 1984: 371–88.

PUBLIC-USE ACCESS TO DATA: We have no information about a public-use file for this demonstration.

CAMBRIDGE JOB FACTORY

SUMMARY: This demonstration, conducted from 1979 to 1980, tested the effects of job clubs, supervised job search assistance, and a bonus for finding a job quickly on a medium-sized sample of unemployed youth. Subjects were followed for one year.

COST: $202,940 (1979).

TIME FRAME: Demonstration period, June 1979–July 1980; data collected through October 1980; final report, 1981.

TREATMENTS TESTED:

1. Experimentals. A four-week cycle in which participants were "hired and paid to get a job." The program components included minimum-wage payments for attendance (which could be docked or terminated); a one-week Job Club program with special group problem-solving exercises; three weeks of supervised job search; and a bonus (two days' pay) for finding a job within the first three weeks.

2. Controls were told that because of funding limitations, no slots were open for them.

OUTCOMES OF INTEREST: (1) Employment and (2) Earnings.

SAMPLE SIZE: Experimentals, 203; controls, 165.

TARGET POPULATION: Unemployed youth ages 15–21. Recent high-school graduates, dropouts, and graduating seniors (no in-school youth) from CETA-eligible (low-income) families.

NUMBER OF TREATMENT GROUPS: Two (with one control group).

NUMBER AND LOCATION OF SITES: One—Cambridge, Massachusetts.

RESEARCH COMPONENTS:

Process analysis: Conducted. It showed that enrollment targets for graduating seniors were difficult to meet (some of those enrolled were only temporarily unemployed), but that graduate and dropout participation targets were feasible. It also showed that without stipends paid to participants, it was not feasible to run the program. (However, this was shown only for a cycle of graduating seniors.)

Impact analysis: Comparison of means, logit, and ordinary least squares (OLS).

Benefit–cost analysis: Not conducted.

MAJOR FINDINGS:

(The data source used was follow-up surveys. The authors attempted to control for differential attrition bias by reporting both the results for all respondents and the results for respondents who completed all surveys. The pattern of response among the latter was much the same as among the former. Follow-ups were sent roughly once a quarter. The question being asked was essentially, "Have you found a job since intake?" The percentage answering yes can decrease as well as increase because of a less-than-complete response on each follow-up.)

Survey	Job-Finding Rates (%)	
	Experimentals	Controls
First	63.6	47.7
Second	77.1	73.2
Third	79.3	78.0
Fourth	79.2	81.8

(The question asked here was, "Are you now employed?")

Survey	Employment Rates (%)	
	Experimentals	Controls
First	63.1	47.7
Second	55.1	55.1
Third	56.4	51.4
Fourth	64.7	50.0

Logit and OLS confirmed that the experimental effect on job-finding was statistically significant in the first quarter.

Cost per experimental was $715. Cost per one net new job (where new jobs are the expected experimental/control differential at the close of the first quarter) was $4,468.

TIME TRENDS IN FINDINGS: Apparent above.

DESIGN ISSUES: The first graduating seniors cycle included many students who either planned to go on to other education or had (before the program started) signed up for CETA-subsidized employment commencing shortly after the treatment ended.

REPLICABILITY: Replicable.

GENERALIZABILITY: The sample is probably a representative low-income urban population, but the size is small and the targeting of graduating seniors problematic.

FUNDING SOURCE: U.S. Department of Labor, Office of Youth Programs. Key personnel: Robert Taggart, Joseph Seiler, and Gordon Berlin.

TREATMENT ADMINISTRATOR: Cambridge Job Factory Program. Key personnel: Joseph Fisher.

EVALUATOR: Center for Employment and Income Studies, Florence Heller Graduate School. Key personnel: Andrew Hahn and Barry Friedman.

ENABLING LEGISLATION: Youth Employment and Demonstration Projects Act of 1977.

POLICY EFFECTS: Andrew Hahn has stated that these findings have become part of a body of research relied on by youth assistance program operators. The gist of its message is that short-term programs have short-term benefits.

INFORMATION SOURCE: Andrew Hahn and Barry Friedman, "The Effectiveness of Two Job Search Assistance Programs for Disadvantaged Youth," with the assistance of Cecilia Rivera-Casale and Robert Evans, Center for Employment and Income Studies, Florence Heller Graduate School for Advanced Studies in Social Welfare, Brandeis University, Waltham, Massachusetts, 1981.

PUBLIC-USE ACCESS TO DATA: We have no information about a public-use file for this demonstration.

CAREER ADVANCEMENT VOUCHER
DEMONSTRATION PROJECT

SUMMARY: This demonstration, conducted from 1979 to 1980, tested the effects of financial support for postsecondary education on a medium-sized sample of low-income youth. Some subjects were followed for at least one college semester.

COST: $1.8 million (1980).

TIME FRAME: The period covered by the cited report is April 1, 1979–March 31, 1980; data collected, unknown; date of final report, unknown.

TREATMENTS TESTED: The experimental treatment was financial support for two years of a full-time college program (accredited, offering Associate of Arts, Bachelor of Arts, or both) plus counseling. In principle, the support was limited to schools charging $2,500 or less in tuition and located within commuting distance of the project site; but in practice, this was waived in Little Rock. Four variants of this treatment were randomly assigned in all five sites: (1) Voucher (no counselor approval for academic program required) plus assistance with involvement in college life; (2) Voucher without such assistance; (3) Nonvoucher (counselor approval required for academic program) plus assistance with involvement in college life; and (4) Nonvoucher, but no assistance with involvement in college life. The variants were to test the ability of the subjects to choose realistic programs without guidance (guidance would be more expensive and would reduce diversity) and the sociological finding that dropouts had little contact with the campus apart from attendance in class. The control treatment was designed to be regular CETA-subsidized employment.

OUTCOMES OF INTEREST: (1) College attendance; (2) Employment; (3) Earnings; and (4) Effectiveness of strategies to integrate subjects into ordinary college life.

SAMPLE SIZE: 490 experimentals (treatment 1: 125; treatment 2: 120; treatment 3: 125; treatment 4: 120); 205 controls.

TARGET POPULATION: CETA-eligible low-income youths, 16–21 years old, who (1) were out of school, (2) had obtained a high school diploma or general equivalency diploma (GED), (3) had had at most eight months of participation in other CETA programs, and (4) had a desire to attend college. (The last condition is emphasized because it critically affected the experiment.) In some sites there were additional screens. In Atlanta and Washington, subjects had to have a test score of 80 or better on an aptitude test (GATB). In El Paso, subjects needed proof of legal residency, letters of recommendation, and SAT or ACT scores. In Little Rock, they needed at least a C average in high school. In Pittsburgh, there were no additional requirements.

NUMBER OF TREATMENT GROUPS: Five (with one control group).

NUMBER AND LOCATION OF SITES: Five—Washington, D.C.; Pittsburgh, Pennsylvania; Atlanta, Georgia; Little Rock, Arkansas; and El Paso, Texas. The effectiveness of the experimental treatment was hypothesized to vary with the unemployment rate. El Paso and Pittsburgh had fairly high rates; the other three cities had fairly low rates.

RESEARCH COMPONENTS:

Process analysis: Control group youths failed to enroll in CETA programs. To be exact, only 20 out of 205 controls enrolled in CETA. The experiment, therefore, could not shed any light on whether college was more likely than subsidized employment to raise wages and employment among some representative group of low-income youths. The reasons for this failure were the recruitment sources and the identity of the program operators. Most subjects were recruited by high-school guidance counselors; many of them had no particular interest in subsidized employment or noncollege training. With the exception of Pittsburgh, the Career Advancement Voucher Demonstration (CAVD) projects were "semiautonomous" from the local CETA programs. The local projects did not have any CETA jobs to provide, and the coordination problem with the CETA prime sponsors was apparently not solved. According to the interim report we obtained, "The current manner in which the local sites relate to their respective regional offices does not particularly facilitate learning how to fit the CAVDP into the existing CETA system."

Impact analysis: None.

Benefit–cost analysis: None.

MAJOR FINDINGS: The major substantive finding that could be drawn from this experiment would be the effect of the scholarship offer on enrollment. This turned out to be significant, but was not a focus of the report.

The following figures are calculated from the interim report.

1. Attending college, October 1979:

	Experimentals	Controls
Atlanta	78 (89%)	22 (82%)
El Paso	109 (98%)	36 (77%)
Little Rock	103 (100%)	12 (50%)
Pittsburgh	77 (85%)	6 (32%)
Washington	94 (95%)	15 (56%)

The control percentages have been calculated as percentages of controls whose status was known. The project had no information on about 30 percent of the controls. About 5 percent of the experimentals were attending college without support from the project, usually because they had chosen colleges that they could not commute to from the project city.

2. First-semester dropout rates from college among experimentals were reported to be low, but were not compared with those of controls or of first-semester freshmen in general.

3. The effects of the voucher/nonvoucher experimental treatments on the diversity of colleges chosen were inconsistent.

TIME TRENDS IN FINDINGS: None.

DESIGN ISSUES: Like other YEDPA experiments, this one tested an interesting idea on a large population. It then dissipated much of its value with a needlessly complex experimental design, an inadequate data collection strategy, and a severely flawed implementation. The flawed implementation can be blamed on the severe haste with which the program was set up.

REPLICABILITY: Both the experimental treatment and the control treatment are replicable, but it is doubtful whether the two treatments can be simultaneously assigned to different members of the same population with reasonable results. It appears that low-income young people who are primarily interested in college and low-income young people who are primarily interested in subsidized employment are fundamentally different groups.

GENERALIZABILITY: This is the only experiment of its kind. The findings indicate that a substantial population of young poor people exists that would attend college if they received scholarships. The findings do not indicate whether they would finish their programs if they received such scholarships. It should be pointed out that the populations of the five cities differ by design, and that it is not possible to compute from these findings how large a national population would respond to such scholarships.

FUNDING SOURCE: U.S. Department of Labor, Office of Youth Programs. Key personnel: Robert Taggart.

TREATMENT ADMINISTRATOR: Negro Scholarship Service-Fund for Negro Students (Atlanta); CETA, prime sponsor (Pittsburgh); three "semiautonomous" projects in Little Rock, Arkansas; Washington, D.C.; and El Paso, Texas. Key personnel: Unknown.

EVALUATOR: Clark, Phipps, Clark, and Harris. Key personnel: Unknown.

ENABLING LEGISLATION: None.

INFORMATION SOURCES: Clark, Phipps, Clark, and Harris, "Advanced Education and Training—Interim Report on the Career Advancement Voucher Demonstration," U.S. Department of Labor (DOL), Employment and Training Administration, Youth Knowledge Development Report 5.3, May 1980. The names of the authors are not given in this report, which was obtained from William Showler of DOL. The only copy of the final report known to exist is in the files of Kenneth Clark and Associates (615 Broadway, Hastings-on-Hudson, NY 10706; 914-478-1010). The position of the firm is that its reports are proprietary to the client; on application to Dr. Clark, permission might be granted to inspect the report, but not to copy it. All copies sent to the funding agency, the Department of Labor's Office of Youth Programs, have apparently been lost. As of this writing, we have not been able to inspect this report.

PUBLIC-USE ACCESS TO DATA: We have no information about a public-use file for this demonstration.

WILKES-BARRE YES WORKSHOP PROGRAM

SUMMARY: This demonstration, conducted from 1979 to 1980, tested the effects of career counseling and job search assistance on a medium-sized sample of unemployed low-income youth. Subjects were followed for about one year.

COST: $164,162 (1980).

TIME FRAME: Demonstration period, May 1979–October 1980; data collected, same period; final report, 1981.

TREATMENTS TESTED:
1. Individual career counseling and job placement services (Job Bank only). The Job Bank included a job developer who would actively look for jobs for youths from employers in the community, and would try to locate specific kinds of jobs sought by youths if they were not already listed.
2. Career counseling, job placement services, and special job search skills workshops (Job Bank and workshop).
3. Career counseling and job search skills workshops (workshop only). No subjects were paid for participating.

OUTCOME OF INTEREST: Employment.

SAMPLE SIZE: Job Bank only, 138; Job Bank and workshop, 140; workshop only, 123.

TARGET POPULATION: Youths ages 16–21, unemployed, and from low-income families (CETA-eligible).

NUMBER OF TREATMENT GROUPS: Three (with no control group).

NUMBER AND LOCATION OF SITES: One—Wilkes-Barre, Pennsylvania.

RESEARCH COMPONENTS:
   Process analysis: Conducted. Focused on (1) low levels of enrollment, which were attributed to problems with outreach to targeted population, completion of income verification forms, and competition with CETA-subsidized jobs; (2) actual levels of participation, which were low in the group workshops, with typically only two or three young people present, apparently owing to lack of interest; and (3) effects of personnel turnover. The treatment organization was not fully in place prior to the commencement of the experiment, so difficulties in starting up may have affected the impact analysis.
   Impact analysis: Comparison of means, logit, and ordinary least squares (OLS).
   Benefit–cost analysis: Not conducted.

MAJOR FINDINGS:
(The data source used was follow-up surveys. The project report authors attempted to control for differential attrition bias by reporting both the results for all respondents and the results for respondents who completed all surveys. The pattern of response among the latter was much the same as among the former. Follow-ups were sent roughly once a quarter. The question being asked was essentially, "Have you found a job since intake?" The percentage answering yes could go down as well as up because of a less-than-complete response on each follow-up.)

| | Job-Finding Rates (%) | | |
Survey	Job Bank Only	Job Bank and Workshop	Workshop Only
1st	70.7	70.8	70.8
2nd	77.4	68.9	76.0
3rd	89.5	90.2	84.2
4th	92.3	83.3	89.5

Logit and OLS confirm that differences in outcome among the experimental groups were statistically insignificant.

Available data seem to indicate that individuals in the Job Bank and workshop group, despite their apparent lack of incremental success in finding jobs, were more likely to have first-time jobs that were full-time and unsubsidized, and that their median earnings were higher; but the data were too incomplete for statistical testing.

TIME TRENDS IN FINDINGS: Data too incomplete; response to surveys declines over time.

DESIGN ISSUES:
1. Treatment administrators believed that individual counseling was the most effective component of their program; however, all three groups received individual counseling and therefore this component is untested.

REPLICABILITY: It is not clear that there was a prescribed workshop format with a content different from the individual counseling available to all subjects. In this sense, the treatment is not replicable.

GENERALIZABILITY: Probably none.

FUNDING SOURCE: U.S. Department of Labor, Office of Youth Programs. Key personnel: Robert Taggart, Joseph Seiler, and Gordon Berlin.

TREATMENT ADMINISTRATOR: Youth Employment Service. Key personnel: Joey Kelly.

EVALUATOR: Center for Employment and Income Studies, Florence Heller Graduate School. Key personnel: Andrew Hahn and Barry Friedman.

ENABLING LEGISLATION: Youth Employment and Demonstration Projects Act of 1977.

INFORMATION SOURCE: Andrew Hahn and Barry Friedman, with the assistance of Cecilia Rivera-Casale and Robert Evans, "The Effectiveness of Two Job Search Assistance Programs for Disadvantaged Youth," Center for Employment and Income Studies, Florence Heller Graduate School for Advanced Studies in Social Welfare, Brandeis University, Waltham, Massachusetts, 1981.

PUBLIC-USE ACCESS TO DATA: We have no information about a public-use file for this demonstration.

ALTERNATIVE YOUTH EMPLOYMENT STRATEGIES PROJECT

SUMMARY: This demonstration, conducted from 1980 to 1982, tested the effects of various combinations of work experience, training, and placement assistance on a large sample of low-income unemployed youth. Subjects were followed for eight months.

COST: $4.8 million (1981) for implementation; research only, roughly $1.5 million (1981).

TIME FRAME: Demonstration period, July 1980–September 1981; data collected through May 1982; final report, August 1983.

TREATMENTS TESTED: All subjects receiving one of three experimental treatments could remain in the program for up to 26 weeks.

Model 1. Full-time work experience with counseling and placement services. The work was in entry-level jobs with, on the one hand, government or nonprofit agencies or, on the other hand, in a supported work environment in which crews of participants performed building rehabilitation, landscape, and clean-up work for community organizations. Jobs were 35 hours per week.

Model 2. Basic education or vocational education or prevocational training with counseling and placement services. Educational option selected by the subject, in consultation with counselors. Payment was based on 30 hours a week participation, equivalent to payment in model 1 because the stipend was not taxed.

Model 3. Balanced and complementary part-time work experience and part-time training, with counseling and placement services. Payment based on 30 hours a week participation.

Controls. Received no services from the project, but $10 for completing the intake interview. Both controls and experimentals received $10 per follow-up interview.

The assignment process was complex. Subjects were randomly assigned to be either controls or experimentals (where experimentals would be in any of the three models). The first 225 experimentals in each of the three sites chose which model they wanted for themselves, with guidance from a counselor. In every case, the client received either his first or second choice. The remaining experimentals in each site were randomly assigned.

OUTCOMES OF INTEREST: (1) Employment; (2) Earnings; and (3) Arrests.

SAMPLE SIZE: Controls, 1,137; experimentals, 1,082. Of the latter, 357 were in model 1; 355 were in model 2; and 370 in model 3. The experimentals assigned randomly were 186 in New York, 151 in Miami, and 70 in Albuquerque.

TARGET POPULATION: Persons 16–21 years old, unemployed, Youth Employment Training Program (YETP)-eligible (low-income), out of school, and "high-risk" (defined as having a prior involvement with the juvenile or criminal justice systems or "a substantial likelihood for such involvement in the future"). At least 50 percent of subjects, by design, were to be referred from the juvenile or criminal justice systems.

NUMBER OF TREATMENT GROUPS: Four (with one control group).

NUMBER AND LOCATION OF SITES: Three—Albuquerque, New Mexico; Miami, Florida; and New York City.

RESEARCH COMPONENTS:

Process analysis: Conducted. Probation officers in Albuquerque were uncooperative about referring clients to a random-assignment program where half of those referred received no services. Fifty-six percent of the New York subjects were justice-system referrals, as were 49 percent of the Miami subjects, but only 29 percent of the Albuquerque subjects. The Albuquerque sample is therefore unrepresentative of the target population: it was 41 percent female (compared with 26 percent in New York and 35 percent in Miami) and 43 percent had high-school diplomas or GEDs (11 percent in New York, 16 percent in Miami). Documentation of low-income status tended to screen out the high-risk target population. Criminal justice referrals were more likely than referrals from other sources to fail to bring documents with them and to fail to keep subsequent intake appointments. There was no starting-up period prior to intake; the initial cohort received lower-quality services as a consequence. Model 3 in most cases could not be implemented as designed, owing to insufficient preparation time; most participants received either mostly training or mostly work experience. The Labor Department's budget commitment to the experiment was uncertain throughout the life of the project; according to the project report, "no provision was made for assuring program staff of employment beyond the end of the data collection period," and "an atmosphere of imminent doom developed in the last few months," which probably affected the quality of service delivery, especially when important staff left the project early. (This would have been most serious in Albuquerque; funding from other sources continued for a while in New York and Miami.) Budget uncertainties caused job developer positions, vital to the placement service, to go unfilled for long periods in Miami, and they were never filled in Albuquerque or New York.

Impact analysis: Conducted as difference in means, and with ordinary least squares (OLS) and logit.

Benefit–cost analysis: Not conducted.

MAJOR FINDINGS:

1. Employment data from eight-month follow-up:

"Have you worked in the eight months since . . . [for experimentals, "exit from the program"; for controls, "intake"]?"

	Overall (%)	Albuquerque (%)	Miami (%)	New York City (%)
Experimentals	51	64.4	47.2	43.9
Controls	41	55.3	41.6	27.1

The overall difference was statistically significant, and was significant at all individual sites except Miami (the only site where job development was properly implemented).

2. Weekly earnings, most recent job (includes zeros for those who had no jobs):

	Overall ($)	Albuquerque ($)	Miami ($)	New York City ($)
Experimentals	63.16	68.39	62.37	59.12
Controls	47.67	52.82	56.12	32.78

The overall difference was statistically significant. The difference was due almost entirely to higher employment rates for experimentals, not to higher wages for those employed.

3. Percentage of the eight-month follow-up spent working: experimentals, 26.2 percent; controls, 19.2 percent. The difference was highly significant.

4. In a regression, the effects of the three different models were insignificantly different from each other, except that those model 1 subjects who were employed had higher earnings during the follow-up than both model 2 and model 3 subjects who were employed.

5. There was no effect on arrests. Three-quarters of both experimentals and controls stayed out of trouble during the data collection period.

TIME TRENDS IN FINDINGS: Only data from an eight-month follow-up were available for analysis.

DESIGN ISSUES:

1. One could argue that the selection of the treatment model by experimentals themselves almost necessarily prevented the evaluation from distinguishing true treatment effects from unobserved participant attributes; thus, the results of the experiment could not have substantially illuminated program design choices, even if the three different models had produced significantly different results. In designing the experiment, however, "the research staff came to believe that random assignment to model would substantially increase the rate at which participants failed to show up or dropped out of the program prematurely. . . . this would result in fewer people having a meaningful experience with the program. Moreover, since there was no reason to assume that the increased dropout rates would be uniform for the three models, there was no theoretical assurance of group equivalence at the start of the program."

2. The contradiction between the positive effects of model 1, as compared with controls, and the findings of the "National Supported Work Demonstration" (NSWD) project on the employment and earnings of young dropouts and ex-offenders in supported work is striking. The contradiction is even more striking because in New York City the same agency was administering both the NSWD and the Alternative Youth Employment Strategies (AYES) treatments. The project report did not address this discrepancy.

3. It is not possible to distinguish a site effect from an ethnic effect. For example, 79 percent of Albuquerque subjects were Mexican-

American. About three-quarters of subjects in New York and Miami were black (but some of the Miami subjects were Haitian).

4. The labor market in the country was steadily worsening throughout the course of the experiment, especially for young unskilled workers.

5. Using logit on the dichotomous variable "have you worked in the past 8 months?" models 2 and 3 did significantly better than model 1. According to the project report: "The different conclusions reflect the fact that the logistic regression was applied to the entire 8-month sample ($N > 1,300$) and is a more powerful statistical technique. Statistical significance is not hard to achieve with so large an N, but the size of the effect seems quite small." It might also reflect self-selection, given the assignment process. Some findings of the process analysis tend to support the proposition that this group needs education more than work experience. For example, the report stated that "it was the impression of job developers and senior staff that many, if not most, terminating participants in AYES were not job-ready"; this was mostly because they were functionally illiterate.

REPLICABILITY: Replicable.

GENERALIZABILITY: The AYES project was reviewed with other Youth Employment and Demonstration Projects Act (YEDPA) projects by a committee from the National Academy of Sciences (see Richard F. Elmore, 1985, "Knowledge Development under the Youth Employment and Demonstration Projects Act, 1977–1981," in Youth Employment and Training Programs, edited by Charles L. Betsey, Robinson B. Hollister, Jr., and Mary R. Papgeorgiou [Washington, D.C.: National Academy Press]). Their primary reaction was to the finding of no significant differences among the three experimental models. "In several other studies, similar null findings for alternative treatments were also found. Indeed, this is the one finding that was fairly robust throughout the studies of labor market preparation programs we reviewed." Comparing the results of the 26-week program with the 10–12-week program, they found evidence, subject to some caveats, that "the same marginal gains in employment can be achieved as well by a shorter program."

FUNDING SOURCE: U.S. Department of Labor, Office of Youth Programs. Key personnel: Robert Taggart.

TREATMENT ADMINISTRATORS: Three agencies—in Albuquerque, New Mexico (Office of Comprehensive Employment and Training Administration); in Miami, Florida (South Florida Employment and

Training Consortium); and in New York City (Court Employment Project). Key personnel: Claire Haaga of the Vera Institute of Justice was in charge of management and coordination among sites.

EVALUATOR: Vera Institute of Justice. Key personnel: Susan Sadd.

ENABLING LEGISLATION: Youth Employment and Demonstration Projects Act of 1977.

POLICY EFFECTS: Billions of dollars were appropriated by Congress throughout the Carter administration to deal with the emerging problem of minority youth unemployment. Congressional leaders were well aware that no treatment for this population was known to "work," and there was enormous pressure and funding to find alternatives that might. The experiment was completed under the Reagan administration, which cut back extensively on subsidized employment programs.

INFORMATION SOURCE: Susan Sadd, Mark Kotkin, and Samuel R. Friedman, "Alternative Youth Employment Strategies Project Final Report," Vera Institute of Justice, August 1983. This report is unpublished. A "Special Summary" is available free from the Vera Institute. The complete report may be purchased for $21.85.

PUBLIC-USE ACCESS TO DATA: We have no information about a public-use file for this demonstration.

CAMBRIDGE JOB SEARCH VOUCHER PROGRAM

SUMMARY: This demonstration, conducted from 1980 to 1982, tested the effects of job search assistance and a wage supplement on a medium-sized sample of low-income youth. Subjects were followed for up to 20 weeks.

COST: Administration, $272,625 (1981).

TIME FRAME: Demonstration period, November 1980–February 1982; data collected, April 1982; final report, September 1982.

TREATMENT TESTED: Full-treatment experimentals. This group received a Job Club model treatment over four weeks; the treatment combined a week-long workshop in job search skills with a supervised group job search organized around a telephone bank. For each hour spent in this Job Factory, subjects received the minimum wage. Those who obtained jobs were paid a supplemental bonus of $1.50 an hour (up to 48 hours a week) for the first 2 weeks on the job, and $1.00

an hour for the following 10 weeks. If the subject left one job for another during the 12 weeks, the subsidy would carry over to the new job.

Voucher-only experimentals received no help with job search, but were entitled to the same 12-week subsidy if they found a job.

Controls received neither job search assistance nor a subsidy.

Hours worked were verified by pay stubs or special employer records. There was generally a 4-week lag in voucher payments.

OUTCOME OF INTEREST: (1) Employment and (2) Earnings.

SAMPLE SIZE: Full-treatment experimentals, 161; voucher-only, 130; controls, 108.

TARGET POPULATION: CETA-eligible (low-income) Boston area youth, ages 16 to 22.

NUMBER OF TREATMENT GROUPS: Three (with one control group).

NUMBER AND LOCATION OF SITES: Cambridge, Massachusetts.

RESEARCH COMPONENTS:

Process analysis: Conducted. Later intake cycles were affected by turnover of top staff and office relocation. Payment of wages to subjects for attendance in the Job Factory treatment was believed to have brought in a number of "program hustlers" with no real interest in finding unsubsidized employment.

Impact analysis: Conducted with ordinary least squares (OLS) and logit.

Benefit–cost analysis: Cost per new job calculated.

MAJOR FINDINGS:

Data come from three follow-up surveys, taken at 4, 12, and 20 weeks after intake.

1. Difference in probability of having worked at all since the previous follow-up (or since intake), logit estimation:

	1st Follow-up	2nd Follow-up	3rd Follow-up
Experimentals (both groups) versus controls	.035	.123*	.190*
Full-treatment versus voucher-only	.142*	.008	−.150*
Actual control mean	.343	.446	.512

*Statistically significant at one-tail, five-percent-level test.

"A voucher paid to workers consistently raised employment of disadvantaged youth. . . . the voucher impacts rose over time. . . . the combined Job Factory plus voucher treatment produced employment gains in the initial period after program start-up, but the combined treatment did no better and sometimes worse than the voucher alone in later periods."

2. Effect on wage rates of those who worked, OLS estimate, in dollars:

	1st Follow-up	2nd Follow-up	3rd Follow-up
Experimentals dummy variable	−0.1183	−0.4620	−0.7830*
Full-treatment dummy	0.1997	0.5570*	0.5150*
Actual control mean	3.81	4.07	4.40

Notes: "Experimentals dummy" is a measure of the effect of the voucher alone. "Full-treatment dummy" is a measure of the additional effect of the Job Factory. The number of observations are 90, 72, and 89 among the three follow-ups, respectively. Asterisk (*) denotes statistically significant at one-tail 5-percent-level test.

The only data on job retention and hours worked come from voucher payments to experimentals. Differences between full-treatment and voucher-only groups are not significant.

3. Cost per new job (net over controls):

Full-treatment, 1st follow-up:	$6,739
Ever found job:	$8,611
Voucher-only, 1st follow-up:	$2,220
Ever found job:	$793

According to the project report, "the evidence from this experiment does not suggest any positive long-term benefits" from the Job Factory treatment, although short-term employment effects were noted.

TIME TRENDS IN FINDINGS: As noted above.

DESIGN ISSUES:

1. Findings about the Job Factory did not generalize to Job Club treatments where participants were not paid to attend.
2. No attention was paid to potential attrition bias, and sample attrition was considerable.

REPLICABILITY: Replicable.

GENERALIZABILITY: Findings are for one job market only.

FUNDING SOURCE: U.S. Department of Labor, Office of Youth Programs. Key personnel: Robert Taggart.

TREATMENT ADMINISTRATOR: Cambridge Office of Manpower Affairs (CETA, primary sponsor). Key personnel: Patricia Tankard and Timothy Reidy.

EVALUATOR: Center for Employment and Income Studies, Florence Heller Graduate School, Brandeis University. Key personnel: Cecilia Rivera-Casale, Barry Friedman, and Robert Lerman.

ENABLING LEGISLATION: Funded under the Youth Employment and Demonstration Projects Act of 1977.

INFORMATION SOURCE: Cecilia Rivera-Casale, Barry Friedman, and Robert Lerman, "Can Employer or Worker Subsidies Raise Youth Employment? An Evaluation of Two Financial Incentive Programs for Disadvantaged Youth," Center for Employment and Income Studies, Florence Heller Graduate School for Advanced Studies in Social Welfare, Brandeis University, September 1982. Only one copy of this report is known to exist. We have inspected it, courtesy of Barry Friedman and Andrew Hahn of the Florence Heller Graduate School.

PUBLIC-USE ACCESS TO DATA: We have no information about a public-use file for this demonstration.

SUMMER EXPERIMENTAL YOUTH TRANSITION PROJECT

SUMMARY: This demonstration, conducted in 1980, tested the effects of different forms of subsidized job search on a medium-sized sample of graduating low-income high school seniors. Subjects were followed for one month.

COST: Not available. Payments to participants must have been at least $130,000 (1980).

TIME FRAME: Demonstration period, July 1980–September 1980; data collected, same period; final report, May 1981.

TREATMENT TESTED: Model 1 received a standard Job Club treatment: one week of job search skills workshop followed by three weeks of supervised group job search using a telephone bank. Model 2 also received a one-week skills workshop, followed by three weeks of individual job search assisted by a professional job developer. Model 3 was the same as the last three weeks of model 2 (i.e., no workshop). Model 4 received three weeks of "standard . . . transition services," mostly counseling, if desired. Experimentals in models 1–3 received minimum-wage payments over the duration of the experiment.

OUTCOME OF INTEREST: Employment.

SAMPLE SIZE: Model 1, 65; model 2, 110; model 3, 110; model 4, 100.

TARGET POPULATION: Graduating low-income high-school seniors who had at least six months' experience in the Youth Incentive Entitlement Pilot Project (YIEPP). YIEPP was a major nonexperimental project guaranteeing full-time summer and part-time school-year jobs to disadvantaged youths, provided they remained in school.

NUMBER OF TREATMENT GROUPS: Four (with one control group).

NUMBER AND LOCATION OF SITES: Baltimore, Maryland.

RESEARCH COMPONENTS:

Process analysis: Conducted. The observers noted that the staff assigned to the workshop phase of the group 2 model did not adhere to the prescribed presentation. Thus, the intended pure test of the effectiveness of supervised group job search as compared with individual job search did not occur.

Impact analysis: Conducted as a difference in means.

Benefit–cost analysis: Unknown.

MAJOR FINDINGS:
1. For all subjects, the job-finding rate by the end of four weeks was:
   Model 1: 26 percent*
   Model 2: 12 percent
   Model 3: 10 percent
   Model 4: 7 percent
   *The difference from the combined job-finding rate of the three other groups is statistically significant at the 1 percent level.
2. Of those who were functionally illiterate, the job-finding rates were:
   Model 1: 50 percent
   Model 2: 26 percent
   Model 3: 17 percent
   Model 4: 0 percent
   Bruml (1981) did not provide the gross number of those who were functionally illiterate.

TIME TRENDS IN FINDINGS: Only four weeks of data collected.

DESIGN ISSUES: See "Process analysis" under "Research Components."

REPLICABILITY: This is a replication.

GENERALIZABILITY: Impossible to evaluate. Findings can be compared with those of the Cambridge Job Factory, a similar intervention with a similar population.

FUNDING SOURCE: U.S. Department of Labor, Office of Youth Programs. Key personnel: Unknown.

TREATMENT ADMINISTRATOR: City of Baltimore, Mayor's Office of Manpower Resources. Key personnel: Unknown.

EVALUATOR: City of Baltimore, Mayor's Office of Manpower Resources. Key personnel: Susan Radcliffe.

ENABLING LEGISLATION: None.

POLICY EFFECTS: This experiment tested different forms of subsidized job search among disadvantaged young people. Reagan administration cutbacks in the area of subsidized employment programs for disadvantaged youth were comprehensive.

INFORMATION SOURCE: The original report appears to have been lost. It is by Susan Radcliffe, "Summer Experimental Youth Transition Project Analysis and Evaluation Report," Mayor's Office of Manpower Resources, Research and Evaluation, Baltimore, May 1981. The data are discussed in an unpublished paper by Elise Bruml, "Self-Directed Group Job Search: The Results," July 13, 1981.

PUBLIC-USE ACCESS TO DATA: We have no information about a public-use file for this demonstration.

JOBSTART

SUMMARY: This demonstration, conducted between 1985 and 1992, tested the effects of education, training, and supportive services on a large sample of economically disadvantaged school dropouts. Subjects were followed for four years.

COST: The entire demonstration cost $6.2 million over 7½ years. Of this amount, $350,000 was paid to the sites and $800,000 was paid to operations staff who were providing assistance to the sites. The remainder was research cost.

TIME FRAME: Demonstration period, 1985–1988; data collected through 1992; final report, October 1993.

TREATMENTS TESTED: Education and vocational training, support services, and job placement assistance. Support services included assistance with transportation, child care, counseling, and incentive payments.

OUTCOMES OF INTEREST: (1) Educational attainment; (2) Employment; (3) Earnings; and (4) Welfare receipt.

SAMPLE SIZE: Total, 2,312 (1,941 used for analysis—see Design Issue #3). Treatment, 1,163; control, 1,149.

TARGET POPULATION: Economically disadvantaged school dropouts ages 17–21 who read below the eighth grade level and were eligible for Job Training Partnership Act (JTPA) Title IIA programs or the Job Corps. Some sites screened out youth with problems that the program was not equipped to handle. These problems included: emotional problems, drug and alcohol abuse, health problems, unstable living conditions, poor motivation, and those who were likely to prove dangerous or disruptive.

NUMBER OF TREATMENT GROUPS: Two (including a control).

NUMBER AND LOCATION OF SITES: 13—Buffalo and New York, New York; Atlanta, Georgia; Hartford, Connecticut; San Jose, Monterey Park, and Los Angeles, California; Chicago, Illinois; Pittsburgh, Pennsylvania; Dallas and Corpus Christi, Texas; Denver, Colorado; Phoenix, Arizona.

RESEARCH COMPONENTS:
   Process analysis: Conducted. Separate publications are available from Manpower Demonstration Research Corporation (MDRC) addressing implementation, site selection, and participation patterns.
   Impact analysis: Conducted using comparison of regression-adjusted means.
   Benefit–cost analysis: Conducted.

MAJOR FINDINGS:
1. Significantly more treatment group youths completed high school or equivalent as compared to the control group (42 percent versus 28.6 percent). This impact was fairly large for all subgroups studied.
2. Employment was significantly greater for the control group in the first year of follow-up. In the second year, significantly more treatment group youths were employed. There were no significant differences in the third and fourth years regarding this variable.
3. Similarly, control group members earned more in the first two years after follow-up whereas the treatment group earned more in the third and fourth years. This finding was statistically significant only for year one.
4. Few significant findings are found in subgroup analyses regarding employment. Trends are similar to those for the full sample.
5. For women who had no children when the program started, those in the treatment group were less likely to have children and to

receive AFDC payments at follow-up than were women in the control group. For custodial mothers (those with children at the start of the program), this finding was reversed; those in the treatment group were more likely to have more children at follow-up. However, this finding was not statistically significant.

6. There is some indication that JOBSTART led to a reduction in criminal activity (arrests and drug use), although impacts are generally not significant.

7. The San Jose site had higher earnings impacts than any other site. This finding was significant at the .01 level. The reasons for this are unclear. At the San Jose site, training and placement efforts were closely linked to the labor market, education and training efforts were coordinated, and the program had a clear organizational mission. Any or all of these factors may have affected program impacts.

TIME TRENDS IN FINDINGS: Treatment group payoffs did not usually occur until after year two.

DESIGN ISSUES:

1. The intake process was quite lengthy at some sites. Some youth who were eventually assigned to the treatment group had already found other opportunities or had lost interest.

2. At some sites, assessment was done after random assignment. This led to the inclusion of some participants with reading levels higher than the eighth grade.

3. Roughly 84 percent of the sample responded to the 48-month follow-up survey. These 1,941 youths were used for the analysis. There were significant differences between responders to the follow-up survey and nonresponders, although responders were not more likely to be experimentals than controls. Since nonresponse was randomly distributed, it does not alter the expected values of the adjusted mean outcomes, and thus does not bias impacts.

REPLICABILITY: Replicable. The U.S. Department of Labor is currently funding a large-scale replication of the San Jose program for youth. MDRC is conducting the evaluation.

GENERALIZABILITY: Designed to generalize to the entire nation. Site selection was not a probability sample. Sites were chosen for their ability to meet program guidelines, assemble operational funding, and yield sufficient sample members. At some sites, the assessment process screened out youths with significant problems. Despite this, the JOBSTART sample still appears to be slightly more disadvantaged than the majority of youth served nationwide by JTPA Title IIA programs, but had slightly fewer barriers to employment than those in Job Corps.

FUNDING SOURCES: Funding was through a consortium of the U.S. Department of Labor, the Rockefeller Foundation, the Ford Foundation, Charles Stewart Mott Foundation, the William and Flora Hewlett Foundation, National Commission for Employment Policy, the AT&T Foundation, Exxon Corporation, ARCO Foundation, Aetna Foundation, the Chase Manhattan Bank, and Stuart Foundations.

TREATMENT ADMINISTRATOR: Local Service Delivery Areas (SDAs) at the 13 sites. The final report (p. 20) lists all treatment administrators.

EVALUATOR: Manpower Demonstration Research Corporation. Principal investigators: George Cave, Fred Doolittle, Hans Bos, and Cyril Toussaint.

ENABLING LEGISLATION: Job Training Partnership Act of 1982.

INFORMATION SOURCES: George Cave, Hans Bos, Fred Doolittle, and Cyril Toussaint, *JOBSTART: Final Report on a Program for School Dropouts*. Manpower Demonstration Research Corporation, October 1993.

PUBLIC-USE ACCESS TO DATA: Contact MDRC.

SUMMER TRAINING AND EDUCATION PROGRAM (STEP)

SUMMARY: This demonstration, conducted from 1985 to 1988, tested the effects of a combined work and educational remediation program on a large sample of low-income youth. Subjects were followed for up to four and one-half years.

COST: Total program costs, approximately $12 million. Research costs, approximately $7 million over eight years.

TIME FRAME: Demonstration period, 1985–88; data collected, 1984–93.

TREATMENTS TESTED: The intervention took place over two consecutive summers, with approximately 200 hours of program involvement each summer. The treatment consisted of a half-day job and a half day of remedial reading and math. In addition, two sessions per week dealt with decision making and responsible social and sexual behavior. The control group was involved in the local Summer Youth Employment and Training Program (SYETP), which provided a job but no other services.

OUTCOMES OF INTEREST: (1) School dropout rates; (2) Academic achievement; (3) Employment and earnings; and (4) Parenting outcomes.

SAMPLE SIZE: The total original sample was 4,800, with 2,400 in both the treatment and control groups. Only cohorts 2 and 3 were used in the analysis. This total was 2,968.

TARGET POPULATION: Fourteen- and 15-year-olds from poor urban families who were seriously behind academically.

NUMBER OF TREATMENT GROUPS: Two (including a control).

NUMBER AND LOCATION OF SITES: Five—Boston, Massachusetts; Fresno and San Diego, California; Portland, Oregon; and Seattle, Washington.

RESEARCH COMPONENTS:

  Process analysis: Examined planning, coordination, and operations through structured observations, as well as data from application forms, questionnaires, and program records.

  Impact analysis: Comparison of means conducted using standardized test scores, school records, and participant interviews.

  Benefit–cost analysis: Not conducted, though some detail was provided about program costs.

MAJOR FINDINGS: The analysis was conducted only for the second and third cohorts. It compares STEP to SYETP, rather than to no program at all.
1. Over the first summer, STEP significantly boosted the treatment group's academic competence and knowledge of responsible sexual behavior. STEP had a net impact of .5 grade equivalents in reading, .6 equivalents in mathematics, and a 2-point increase on the 9-point contraceptive-knowledge scale.
2. The gains of the first summer did not translate into changes over the school year. No overall impacts on reading or mathematics, on credits earned, or on dropout behavior were found.
3. Second-summer impacts were again positive for academics and contraceptive knowledge, but were not as strong.
4. At follow-up (54 months after enrollment for cohort 2, 42 months for cohort 3), no significant impacts were found for any educational, employment, or parenting outcomes.

TIME TRENDS IN FINDINGS: As can be seen above, STEP produced immediate positive effects, yet had no measurable long-term impact.

DESIGN ISSUES:

1. Due to a fast start-up schedule, it was difficult to establish significant cooperation between employment and training agencies and local school districts. Thus, over 85 percent of the educational remediation costs were borne by the employment and training system.
2. During the second summer, the evaluators came to believe that the remedial component for the first cohort was of substantially lower quality. They revised the curriculum and added a third cohort, treating the first cohort as an extension of the pilot period.
3. Intensive outreach efforts were necessary at all sites to enroll the required number of STEP participants and ensure their return for the second summer (the return rate was 75%).
4. The program design called for a school-year component between summers. The students were to be contacted and assistance was to be provided as necessary. In practice, the school component had little substantive connection to the summer activities and low participation rates.

REPLICABILITY: The program is highly structured and detailed. This project was replicated in approximately 100 U.S. cities.

GENERALIZABILITY: Designed to generalize to the entire nation. However, only 15 of the potential 595 employment and training agencies applied to take part in STEP. The financial disincentive was cited as a reason for this lack of interest. Of the five cities selected, four were on the West Coast. The sample was similar to those youth eligible for JTPA programs: they all met JTPA low-income standards; approximately 86 percent were ethnic minorities; and they were split roughly evenly for gender.

FUNDING SOURCE: Primary funding came from the Ford Foundation. Additional funding was provided by the U.S. Department of Labor, the Robert Wood Johnson Foundation, the U.S. Department of Health and Human Services, William T. Grant Foundation, the Edna McConnell Clark Foundation, the Hewlett Foundation, Lilly Endowment, the Ahmanson Foundation, Aetna Life and Casualty Foundation, and James C. Penney Foundation.

TREATMENT ADMINISTRATOR: Local agencies at each site administered the programs. Lead agencies were: Boston—Mayor's Office of Jobs and Community Services; Fresno—Fresno Private Industry

278 The Digest of Social Experiments

Council; Portland—Portland Private Industry Council; San Diego—
San Diego Regional Employment and Training Consortium; Seattle—
Seattle Department of Human Resources. Key personnel changed over
the life of the project.

EVALUATOR: Public/Private Ventures. Principal investigators: Jean B.
Grossman and Cynthia Sipe.

ENABLING LEGISLATION: None.

POLICY EFFECTS: In large part due to the STEP program, and appear-
ances before the U.S. Congress by Public/Private Ventures staff,
amendments were made to the SYETP program (e.g., funding and a
requirement for remediation were added to SYETP).

INFORMATION SOURCES: Alvia Y. Branch, Julita Milliner, Susan Phil-
lipson Bloom, and Jon Bumbaugh, Summer Training and Education
Program: Report on the Pilot Experience, Public/Private Ventures,
March 1985; Alvia Y. Branch, Julita Milliner, and Jon Bumbaugh, Sum-
mer Training and Education Program (STEP): Report on the 1985
Summer Experience, Public/Private Ventures, April 1986; Cynthia L.
Sipe, Jean Baldwin Grossman, and Julita A. Milliner, Summer Train-
ing and Education Program (STEP): Report on the 1986 Experience,
Public/Private Ventures, April 1987; Cynthia L. Sipe, Jean Baldwin
Grossman, and Julita A. Milliner, Summer Training and Education
Program (STEP): Report on the 1987 Experience, Public/Private Ven-
tures, Summer 1988; Jean Baldwin Grossman and Cynthia L. Sipe,
Summer Training and Education Program (STEP): Report on Long-
Term Impacts, Public/Private Ventures, Winter 1992; Gary Walker and
Frances Vilella-Velez, The Summer Training and Education Program
(STEP): From Pilot through Replication and Post-Program Impacts,
Public/Private Ventures, 1992.

PUBLIC-USE ACCESS TO DATA: Available through Public/Private Ventures, Philadelphia, Pennsylvania.

NEW ORLEANS AND PHILADELPHIA NONRESIDENTIAL JOB CORPS CENTERS

INFORMATION SOURCE: Terry R. Johnson, Sally Leiderman, and Susan
Philipson Bloom, Review of Experiences and Outcomes of the New
Orleans and Philadelphia Non-residential Job Corps Centers: Final
Report. Bloom Associates, October 1991.

SUMMARY FROM ABOVE SOURCE: This demonstration, conducted from 1988 to 1990, was designed to test the effects of offering Job Corps services on a nonresidential basis to a large sample of economically and educationally disadvantaged youth.

Basic Job Corps services provided at both sites included an academic program of reading, mathematics, general equivalency diploma (GED) classes and a small Advanced Career Training program; vocational training classes; and other services such as counseling and health services.

Initially, the evaluators intended to evaluate this program using an experimental design. Subjects were randomly assigned to either a nonresidential Job Corps program (the treatment) or a traditional residential program (the control). Unfortunately, the subjects had strong feelings about the type of program in which they wanted to participate, and take-up rates for both treatment and control groups were unacceptable. Many of those assigned did not adhere to their assignments. The evaluators were left with very low sample sizes, and the experimental portion of the program was terminated before outcomes were measured.

The final report provides some qualitative and quantitative data concerning issues related to the types of youth served in the pilot centers, the services provided, and the outcomes achieved during the first few years of operations.

NUMBER AND LOCATION OF SITES: Two—New Orleans, Lousiana, and Philadelphia, Pennsylvania.

TREATMENT ADMINISTRATORS: New Orleans Job Corps Center—Maryetta Cunningham, project manager. Philadelphia Satellite Job Corps Center—Jim Kennedy, project manager.

EVALUATORS: A joint research effort involving Bloom Associates, Battelle Human Affairs Research Centers, and Abt Associates.

PUBLIC-USE ACCESS TO DATA: We have no information about a public-use file for this demonstration.

HIGH-RISK YOUTH DEMONSTRATION PROJECT— YOLO COUNTY, CALIFORNIA

SUMMARY: This demonstration, conducted between 1989 and 1991, tested the effects of a self-esteem-building/motivational curriculum on a small sample of high-risk youth. Subjects were followed for two years.

COST: Exact costs are not available, though the average evaluation cost for Demonstration Partnership Program (DPP) projects is between $35,000 and $50,000.

TIME FRAME: Demonstration period, July 1989–August 1991; final report, 1992.

TREATMENTS TESTED: The treatment was a 190-hour curriculum implemented in a classroom setting in a public school. The curriculum focused on social and emotional goals, rather than academic ones. Additional services included counseling and preemployment skills training. The control group continued with the traditional class structure offered at Yolo High School.

OUTCOMES OF INTEREST: (1) Self-esteem; (2) Academic Achievement; and (3) Employment.

SAMPLE SIZE: Total initial sample, 113; treatment, 30; control, 83. A considerably smaller sample was used for analysis.

TARGET POPULATION: High-risk youth between ages 16 to 18.

NUMBER OF TREATMENT GROUPS: Two (including a control).

NUMBER AND LOCATION OF SITES: One—Yolo High School in West Sacramento, California.

RESEARCH COMPONENTS:
   Process analysis: Attention was paid to attrition rates and the maintenance of the design integrity.
   Impact analysis: Comparison of means.
   Benefit–cost analysis: Not conducted.

MAJOR FINDINGS:
1. No significant differences were found between the treatment and control groups nor between pre- and posttest scores for either group on self-esteem or school attitude.
2. Grade-point average and academic unit completion rate were significantly greater for the treatment group at the end of the project compared to the control group. Attendance was also better for the treatment group, though the difference was not significant.
3. The dropout rate was lower for the treatment group. A greater percentage of the treatment group had either graduated or was still enrolled in an educational program.
4. Treatment group students were more likely than controls to be employed, more likely to be employed full-time, and more likely to have a history of work experience.

TIME TRENDS IN FINDINGS: None reported.

DESIGN ISSUES:
1. Attrition rates were high, with only 16 youth from the treatment group and 8 from the control group completing posttest measures of self-esteem and school attitude. Slightly larger numbers were available for analysis on educational and employment measures (80 and 59, respectively). High attrition also led to additional students being drawn (randomly) from the control group to receive the intervention.
2. Data collection was difficult due to a lack of computerization, as well as budgetary and staff shortages.
3. Since intervention was offered in a school environment, it was necessary to structure the curriculum to meet state and school district guidelines and graduation requirements. This required a change in teacher for the second year of the project. It also caused considerable inconvenience for the counseling component of the program.

REPLICABILITY: Replicable.

GENERALIZABILITY: Generalizing from this small sample would be speculative. Further, the experimental and control groups differed significantly on several demographic variables at the start of the program. This is likely owing to the small sample size, for there is no indication that the randomization procedure was contaminated. Finally, some students were excluded due to "hard-core drug use and/or violent behavior." Thus, this program may not generalize to some at-risk students.

FUNDING SOURCE: Demonstration Partnership Program, Office of Community Services, U.S. Department of Health and Human Services.

TREATMENT ADMINISTRATOR: Yolo County (California) Community Partnership Agency. Key personnel: Alexander M. Laiewski, agency director.

EVALUATOR: Gerald C. Shelton and Bill Kirby, University of Sacramento, Department of Economics.

ENABLING LEGISLATION: Demonstration Partnership Program under section 408 of the Human Services Reauthorization Act of 1986, as amended.

INFORMATION SOURCE: Department of Health and Human Services, Office of Community Services, *Summary of Final Evaluation Findings from FY 1989: Demonstration Partnership Program Projects* Monograph Series 400-89, 1992.

PUBLIC-USE ACCESS TO DATA: Available through U.S. Department of Health and Human Services, Office of Community Services.

QUANTUM OPPORTUNITIES PROGRAM (QOP)—PILOT

SUMMARY: This demonstration, conducted from 1989 to 1993, tested the effects of a comprehensive package of educational services, case management, and financial incentives on a medium-sized group of low-income high school students. Subjects were followed for four years.

COST: Total program costs (including evaluation) were $1,180,000 over four years.

TIME FRAME: Demonstration period, summer 1989–fall 1993; data collected, same period; final report, 1994.

TREATMENTS TESTED: The Quantum Opportunities Program (QOP) is a comprehensive program that can last up to four years. Program components include: basic education; LifeSkills and cultural enrichment curricula; community service; mentoring; summer activities (including a part-time job and summer school for those who need it); and financial incentives (a stipend for participation and a bonus for completion of major blocks of activities). There was also a financial incentive for staff to meet program participation rates. The control group received no demonstration services.

OUTCOMES OF INTEREST: Achievement of academic and social competencies such as high school graduation, postsecondary attendance, academic achievement (grades and test scores), involvement in community service, teen pregnancy, and employment.

SAMPLE SIZE: There were 50 students at each site: 25 in the treatment group and 25 in the control group. Therefore, after one site was discontinued, there was a total sample of 200.

TARGET POPULATION: High school students from low-income families (receiving public assistance).

NUMBER OF TREATMENT GROUPS: Two (including a control).

NUMBER AND LOCATION OF SITES: There were originally five sites—San Antonio, Texas; Philadelphia, Pennsylvania; Milwaukee, Wisconsin; Saginaw, Michigan; and Oklahoma City, Oklahoma. The Milwaukee site was discontinued.

RESEARCH COMPONENTS:
  Process analysis: Focused on participation rates and "team-building" (the ability to form a group identity) at each site.
  Impact analysis: Conducted using comparison of means.
  Benefit–cost analysis: Conducted.

MAJOR FINDINGS: Although the samples from four sites were pooled for analysis, the majority of the overall impacts were attributable to the Philadelphia site. The implementation at this site was superior, creating a group identity among QOP members. It offered a more reliable menu of program offerings, and provided stable, consistent relationships between youth and staff.
1. By the end of the fourth year, when most participants were leaving high school, average treatment group scores on all 11 academic and functional skills were much higher than control group scores, and all were statistically significant. Average academic skill levels had increased more than three grade levels for 27 percent of the treatment group compared to 14 percent of the control group.
2. Treatment group members were more likely to be high school graduates than were control group members (63 percent versus 42 percent), and they were more likely to enter postsecondary schools (42 percent versus 16 percent).

TIME TRENDS IN FINDINGS: Group differences did not appear until the second year of the program and continued to widen for the next two years.

DESIGN ISSUES:
1. The treatment varied considerably across sites and within sites over time. It is not clear what services were actually provided to participants and by whom. Implementation seemed to work best at the Philadelphia site, it failed at the Milwaukee site (which was dropped from the experiment), and it was somewhere in between for the remaining three sites.

2. Sample size was small, especially at individual sites. This makes it difficult to compare results across sites.

REPLICABILITY: Replicable, though clarification is needed regarding the exact services that are to be provided. This project was considered a pilot. The QOP demonstration is currently in progress (see appendix II, at end of this volume).

GENERALIZABILITY: Designed to generalize to the entire nation. However, the sample size was very small, especially at individual sites, and the majority of the impacts are based on the success of one site. An enhancement to generalizability is that the sample was randomly selected from lists of eighth-grade students rather than from a pre-screened group of volunteers.

FUNDING SOURCE: The Ford Foundation. Key personnel: Inca Mohamed, project officer.

TREATMENT ADMINISTRATOR: Opportunities Industrial Centers of America (OIC). Key personnel: Ben Lattimore and Ruben Mills.

EVALUATOR: Brandeis University, Center for Human Resources. Principal investigator: Andrew Hahn.

ENABLING LEGISLATION: None.

INFORMATION SOURCES: Andrew Hahn, *Evaluation of the Quantum Opportunities Program (QOP): Did the Program Work?* Brandeis University, Center for Human Resources, June 1994.

PUBLIC-USE ACCESS TO DATA: Not available.

BROTHERS

INFORMATION SOURCE: U.S. Department of Health and Human Services, *Summary of Final Evaluation Findings from FY 1991: Demonstration Partnership Program Projects—Monograph Series 500-91—Minority Male,* 1995.

SUMMARY FROM ABOVE SOURCE: This demonstration, which began in October 1991, sought to use volunteer mentors to help low-income, primarily African-American, males ages 14 to 16. The mentors were to meet with the youths at least two hours each week to increase their educational success and self-esteem, and improve their attitudes toward drug usage, sexual responsibility and work. Interested youth were randomly assigned to either be matched with a mentor or to be in the control group.

There were significant implementation problems, and far fewer mentor—youth matches were made than expected. Less than 15 percent of the referred mentors actually became mentors. At the six-month follow-up, there were only 23 participants in the treatment group with data available for analysis. At one-year, the sample had shrunk to below 10. The program director cited "systematic barriers in the community and political opposition" as reasons for the failed implementation. Also, a 25-member policy board responsible for planning, design, and oversight of the project had difficulty agreeing on program direction. Further, the evaluators had difficulty acquiring data from schools, mentors, and mentees.

Despite these significant problems, some positive correlations were found between length of time in the program and some of the outcome variables. This project has been replicated, and the program's director says there were far fewer problems in the newer version of Brothers. Results of this project were to be available at the end of 1996.

NUMBER AND LOCATION OF SITES: One—Lexington, Kentucky, serving Fayette County.

EVALUATION COSTS: Approximately $30,000 to $35,000.

TREATMENT ADMINISTRATOR: Community Action Council. Key personnel: Jack E. Burch, director; Mary Twitty, project director.

EVALUATOR: Bennie Robinson, Kentucky State University; and David Royse, University of Kentucky.

PUBLIC-USE ACCESS TO DATA: We have no information about a public-use file for this demonstration.

HOMELESS YOUTH SELF-SUFFICIENCY PROJECT

INFORMATION SOURCE: U.S. Department of Health and Human Services, Office of Community Services, *Homeless and Youth at Risk: Demonstration Partnership Program Projects: Summary of Final Evaluation Findings from 1990,* 1993.

SUMMARY FROM ABOVE SOURCE: This demonstration, conducted from 1991 through 1994, tested the effects of long-term transitional housing, case management, counseling, and a preemployment training and work experience program on a small sample of homeless youth. Subjects were to be followed for 6 months beyond the termination of services (the program period was to be at least 12 months).

There was a very high rate of attrition, the most program dropouts occurring in the treatment group. At the two-year follow-up, only 27 youths from both groups had completed the program and only 12 were available for interviews (the initial sample size was 76, with 53 in the treatment group and 23 in the control group—the program was considered completed after two years if the youth was living in a stable residence and was either working or attending school). Although there is some indication that the program led to more youth living off the street (i.e., in housing) and involved in educational programs or employment, there is insufficient data to make any meaningful claims regarding program effectiveness.

NUMBER AND LOCATION OF SITES: One—Multnomah County (Portland), Oregon.

EVALUATION COSTS: Unavailable, although the average Demonstration Partnership Program project evaluation costs are between $35,000 and $50,000.

TREATMENT ADMINISTRATOR: Multnomah County Community Action Program Office and the Outside In Agency. Key personnel: William B. Thomas, project director.

EVALUATOR: Robert Donough and Patricia Freeman, Tri-County Youth Services Consortium.

PUBLIC-USE ACCESS TO DATA: We have no information about a public-use file for this demonstration.

SUCCESS CONNECTION

SUMMARY: This demonstration, conducted from 1991 through 1993, tested the effects of adventure-based counseling and exposure to college on a small sample of at-risk rural youth. Subjects were followed for 18 months.

COST: Program costs, $350,000.

TIME FRAME: Demonstration period, October 1991–October 1993. Data collected, same period.

TREATMENTS TESTED: The treatment group received up to 377 hours of services over 18 months consisting of: (1) ongoing support groups with an "Adventure-based" curriculum (an "Outward Bound"-type of experience wherein participants learn trust, self-esteem, and teamwork by working together to overcome physical obstacles); (2) one-day leadership retreats; (3) two-week on-campus college experience; and (4) a goal-setting experience for their parents. The controls attended an initial orientation; thereafter, they received nothing from the program except $10 fees for cooperating with evaluation interviews.

OUTCOMES OF INTEREST: (1) Employment; (2) Wage rates; and (3) Welfare receipt.

SAMPLE SIZE: Total, 227; treatment, 107; control, 120.

TARGET POPULATION: At-risk youth, defined as persons aged 17–22 with at least two of the following characteristics: school dropout; unemployed and not enrolled in job training; employed but below minimum wage; ward of the court; AFDC-qualified or public assistance recipient; referred as "at-risk" by teachers, counselors, or agency personnel.

NUMBER OF TREATMENT GROUPS: Two (including a control).

NUMBER AND LOCATION OF SITES: One—Yakima Valley, Washington.

RESEARCH COMPONENTS:
  Process analysis: Contact forms, activity logs, assessment portfolio; implemented as designed, with 88 members of the treatment group completing the program.
  Impact analysis: Comparison of raw totals at conclusion of 18-month program.
  Benefit–cost analysis: Not conducted.

MAJOR FINDINGS: Evaluator compared the experience of control group members with the experience of 88 participating treatment group members. The participating treatment group members had significantly higher career aspirations than controls. Qualitatively, their jobs were more diverse and had greater potential for upward mobility; it is difficult to tell from the summary whether there was any difference in wages. Eleven controls received or applied for public assistance, whereas only one participant did, but the evaluator did not test for statistical significance because he did not feel the data were meaningful. Participating treatment group members also had a 94 percent high school graduation rate compared to 78 percent in the control group, but this was apparently not statistically significant.

TIME TRENDS IN FINDINGS: None.

DESIGN ISSUES: The evaluation was clearly compromised by the exclusion of nonparticipating treatment group members. The report attributed nonparticipation to "the transitory nature of migrancy in rural Washington" (many of the participants are the children of migrant farmworkers).

REPLICABILITY: Designed for replicability.

GENERALIZABILITY: Findings of modest impact might generalize to other migrant farmworker children, although the fairly small sample size and the design and implementation issues discourage attempts at generalization.

FUNDING SOURCE: Office of Community Services, Administration for Children and Families, U.S. Department of Health and Human Services.

TREATMENT ADMINISTRATOR: Yakima Valley Opportunities Industrialization Center. Key personnel: Raul Sital.

EVALUATOR: William Hansen, an independent consultant.

ENABLING LEGISLATION: Demonstration Partnership Program, under section 408 of the Human Services Reauthorization Act of 1986, as amended.

INFORMATION SOURCE: U.S. Department of Health and Human Services, *Summary of Final Evaluation Findings from FY 1991: Demonstration Partnership Program Projects, Monograph Series 400-91, Youth at Risk*, April 1995: 2-25 to 2-40.

PUBLIC-USE ACCESS TO DATA: Available through BHM International, contractor for the Office of Community Services.

Part Twelve

SINGLE/TEEN PARENT

MINORITY FEMALE SINGLE-PARENT DEMONSTRATION (MFSP)

SUMMARY: This demonstration, conducted from 1984 to 1987, tested the effects of education and training on a large sample of minority female single parents. Subjects were followed for up to five years.

COST: Evaluation costs, approximately $3 million.

TIME FRAME: Demonstration period, November 1984–December 1987. Data collected over same period, with follow-up of up to five years (San Jose only).

TREATMENTS TESTED: The four centers used different approaches, but all included assessment, education, job training, and support services such as counseling and child-care assistance. The control group was not eligible to receive services at the centers, but could seek them elsewhere.

OUTCOMES OF INTEREST: (1) Earnings; (2) Employment; and (3) Welfare receipt.

SAMPLE SIZE: Total applicants, 3,965. Total used in analysis, 3,175; treatment, 1,841; control, 1,334. By site (treatment; control): Atlanta, Georgia, 373; 299; San Jose, California, 440; 329; Providence, Rhode Island, 346; 163; and Washington, D.C., 682; 543.

TARGET POPULATION: Minority, single mothers.

NUMBER OF TREATMENT GROUPS: Two (including controls) at each site.

NUMBER AND LOCATION OF SITES: Four—Atlanta (Atlanta Urban League, AUL); San Jose (Center for Employment and Training, CET); Providence (Opportunities Industrialization Center, OIC); and Washington, D.C. (Wider Opportunities for Women, WOW).

RESEARCH COMPONENTS:
    Process analysis: Program operations, participant characteristics, and service delivery at the four sites was analyzed.
    Impact analysis: Comparison of regression-adjusted means.
    Benefit–cost analysis: Conducted.

MAJOR FINDINGS: The San Jose CET, unlike the three other sites, immediately provided job-specific skill training to all trainees and integrated basic literacy and mathematics skills into the job training curriculum. Participants at this site demonstrated the greatest employment and earnings gains. In contrast, the other sites provided more traditional remedial education and training.

1. The CET program generated the greatest gains in employment and earnings, and these lasted over the full 60-month period (only CET had a 5-year follow-up; the other three sites were followed for only 30 months). During the fifth year after program application, treatment group members earned an average of $95 per month more than did control group members, a statistically significant impact equal to 17 percent of control group mean earnings.
2. CET's impact on welfare receipt, at 30 and 60 months, was small and not statistically significant.
3. Over the 5-year period, CET produced a positive return from the perspectives both of society and of program participants (in 1986 dollars, $975 and $2,500 per participant, respectively). From a government-budget perspective, costs exceeded benefits by about $1,600 per participant.
4. WOW generated modest and significant gains in employment rates, but not in average earnings. Reductions in welfare receipts were small and not significant.
5. The investment in WOW did not produce a positive return from either the social or the government-budget perspective.
6. The projects at AUL and OIC had no significant impacts on any of the outcome variables.
7. None of the programs had significant long-term impacts on measures of psychological well-being, including depression and locus of control, or on fertility or marriage behavior.

TIME TRENDS IN FINDINGS: At the 30-month follow-up in the CET program, all treatment group members showed significant gains in employment and earnings. At five years, only sample members with 12 or more years of schooling showed significant gains. Impacts on general equivalency diploma (GED) attainment were significant for the treatment group at 30 months, but this effect had dissipated at 60 months.

DESIGN ISSUES: The Minority Female Single-Parent (MFSP) demonstration consisted of four projects in different locations. The impacts of each project may be due to the characteristics of each site. Differences in impacts across sites should be treated cautiously.

REPLICABILITY: Replicable.

GENERALIZABILITY: Designed to generalize to the entire nation. MFSP projects were operated by community-based organizations independent from the local welfare offices and reach a somewhat broader clientele than state-run JOBS programs. MFSP participation was entirely voluntary. In contrast, JOBS programs are closely linked to the local welfare office and serve only welfare recipients. Participation is mandatory for some AFDC recipients. MFSP participants were more disadvantaged than national samples of minority single mothers; on average, they were younger, had younger children, had less employment experience, and less education.

FUNDING SOURCE: The Rockefeller Foundation. Key personnel: Phoebe Cunningham (now at the Smith Richardson Foundation).

TREATMENT ADMINISTRATORS: Atlanta Urban League (AUL)—key personnel: Lyndon Wade and Edna Crenshaw; Center for Employment and Training (CET)—key personnel: Russ Tershey, Carmen Ponce, and Carmen Placido; Opportunities Industrialization Center of Rhode Island (OIC)—key personnel: Michael van Leesten and Kathy May; and Wider Opportunities for Women (WOW)—key personnel: Cindy Marano and Barbara Makris.

EVALUATOR: Mathematica Policy Research. John Burghardt: project director. Co-principal investigators: John Burghardt and Stuart Kerachsky. Other key personnel: Anne Gordon and Anu Rangarajan.

ENABLING LEGISLATION: None.

POLICY EFFECTS: The Rockefeller Foundation was active in disseminating the results of the CET findings and entering them into the policy debate. The U.S. Department of Labor has funded CET to replicate their model in other programs. There is also currently a Labor Department evaluation of CET replication projects. (See Appendix II, at the end of this volume, for a summary of this ongoing experiment.)

INFORMATION SOURCES: John Burghardt, Anu Rangarajan, Anne Gordon, and Ellen Kisker, *Evaluation of the Minority Female Single Parent Demonstration: Summary Report*, Mathematica Policy Research, October 1992; Amy Zambrowski and Anne Gordon, *Evaluation of the Minority Female Single Parent Demonstration: Fifth-Year Impacts at CET*, Mathematica Policy Research, December 1993.

PUBLIC-USE ACCESS TO DATA: Available through Mathematica Policy Research.

YOUNG FAMILIES CAN PROJECT

SUMMARY: This demonstration, conducted from 1987 through 1990, tested the effects of case-management and counseling on a medium-sized sample of teenage mothers. Subjects were followed for up to two years.

COST: Total evaluation costs over three years—approximately $50,000, plus sustantial in-kind services.

TIME FRAME: Demonstration period, September 1987–June 1990; final report, July 1991.

TREATMENTS TESTED: The program consisted of intensive case management and counseling. Case management included assessment, agency referrals, and cash resources for short-term resolution of individual issues. The control group received no demonstration services.

OUTCOMES OF INTEREST: The project measured 15 social, educational, family, and financial "client stressors," including high school graduation, employment, and money management.

SAMPLE SIZE: Total, 204; treatment, 104; control, 100.

TARGET POPULATION: Teenage mothers. Eligibility based on the following: 19 years old or younger; the custodial parent of at least one child; and a recipient of, or eligible for, AFDC benefits.

NUMBER OF TREATMENT GROUPS: Two (including control).

NUMBER AND LOCATION OF SITES: One—Phoenix, Arizona.

RESEARCH COMPONENTS:
   Process analysis: Some attention paid to implementation issues, the partnership process, and staff behaviors.
   Impact analysis: Comparison of means: experimental versus control, pretest versus posttest.
   Benefit–cost analysis: Not conducted.

MAJOR FINDINGS:
1. For the total sample, there were no significant differences between experimental and control groups on posttest measures on any outcomes. Further, there were no statistically significant improvements in any of the 15 stress areas in either group (in fact, there was some deterioration in the experimental group on measures of money management, parenting knowledge, and isolation that were statistically significant).
2. Progress was made in some areas for women who spent two years in the program. (There were two cohorts in the project; only those who enrolled at the beginning were in the program for two full years.) Education, family planning, career planning, housing, household maintenance, and self-esteem factors improved for these women. The treatment group had higher employment rates (mostly part-time) than the control group, though this finding was not

statistically significant. There was a significant difference, in favor of the treatment group, in rates of high school graduation (or its equivalent), as well as in junior college enrollment.

TIME TRENDS IN FINDINGS: Improvements were seen only for those women who had received the intervention for two years.

DESIGN ISSUES:

1. There was some friction between city and state workers during the first year. This caused some difficulties in accessing data and provision of uniform services. This problem was only resolved when the administrator re-assigned some key staff.
2. Higher than expected client needs in areas of education and housing led to some program changes.
3. There was high staff (caseworker) turnover due to high caseloads.
4. One battery of scales had to be thrown out when it was found that the largely Hispanic sample had difficulty reading the self-administered measure.

REPLICABILITY: Replicable, with cautions regarding the above issues.

GENERALIZABILITY: Designed to generalize to the city of Phoenix. The sample was largely Hispanic and the evaluator referred to the factor of a distinct Southwest culture. However, he stated that the program ideas are found in many similar programs, and he felt there is some generalizability.

FUNDING SOURCE: Demonstration Partnership Program, Office of Community Services, U.S. Department of Health and Human Services.

TREATMENT ADMINISTRATORS: City of Phoenix Human Resources Department (HRD)—key personnel; Nancy McLeod, agency director; Alnita McClure, project director. Arizona Department of Economic Security (DES)—key personnel: Karen Novachek.

EVALUATORS: Principal investigator: Robert Moroney; assistant investigators: Gwat Yong Lie and Peter Kettner, Arizona State University School of Social Work.

ENABLING LEGISLATION: Demonstration Partnership Program under section 408 of the Human Services Reauthorization Act of 1986, as amended.

POLICY EFFECTS: This program was modified and subsequently continued with Arizona state and local funding.

INFORMATION SOURCES: U.S. Department of Health and Human Services (DHHS), Office of Community Services, Demonstration Partnership Program: Summaries and Findings, FY 1988 and 1989, 1991.

PUBLIC-USE ACCESS TO DATA: Available through the Office of Community Services, DHHS.

SINGLE-PARENT ECONOMIC INDEPENDENCE
DEMONSTRATION (SPEID)

SUMMARY: This demonstration, conducted from 1988 to 1990, tested the effects of unpaid internships and mentoring on a medium-sized sample of single parents. Subjects were followed for up to one year. The random assignment design was not faithfully implemented, as program dropouts were removed from the treatment group in analysis.

COST: Evaluation costs, approximately $70,000.

TIME FRAME: Demonstration period, July 1988–November 1990; data collected, same period; final report, July 1991.

TREATMENTS TESTED: Unpaid internships with local businesses. Interns were also assigned a mentor at the business site. Control group participants were referred to other service agencies and received some supportive services.

OUTCOMES OF INTEREST: (1) Employment; (2) Earnings; (3) Welfare receipt; and (4) Other noneconomic indicators such as self-esteem and motivation.

SAMPLE SIZE: Total, 571; treatment (interns), randomly assigned, 197; not randomly assigned, 67; control, 182. An additional 125 interns entered the program after the initial evaluation phase.

TARGET POPULATION: Single parents. Participants were required to have a high school diploma or equivalent and a prior history of participation in pre-employment training.

NUMBER OF TREATMENT GROUPS: Three. Initially, all eligible applicants were placed in internships (non-RA interns). In a second phase, participants were randomly assigned to a treatment (RA interns) or a control group.

NUMBER AND LOCATION OF SITES: The program was implemented on a statewide basis at nine service delivery areas in the state of Utah.

RESEARCH COMPONENTS:

Process analysis: Included a review of measurement tools, organizational structure, and implementation.

Impact analysis: For economic outcomes, a comparison of means was conducted without employing tests of statistical significance. Analysis of variance was used in comparing pre- and posttest scores on measures of noneconomic outcomes.

Benefit–cost analysis: Not conducted.

MAJOR FINDINGS: In the analysis, treatment group dropouts are examined as a separate category. This seems to violate the random assignment design.

1. Interns (both RA and non-RA) had higher overall percentages of positive employment placements than did controls or dropouts. Over 50 percent of interns were employed full-time at the conclusion of the Single-Parent Economic Independence Demonstration (SPEID) compared to less than 30 percent of controls or dropouts.

2. Interns who were working were employed in jobs that brought them higher salaries and greater benefits than controls were receiving. For participants who had worked within Utah during the 12 months prior to intake and who were employed at posttreatment, general wage increases were seen. Non-RA interns' average salary increased by $.92 per hour; RA interns gained $1.50 per hour; controls gained $.54 per hour; and dropouts gained $.40 per hour.

3. Approximately 50 percent of employed interns were receiving medical benefits compared with 24 percent of employed controls.

4. There is some indication that involvement in SPEID had a positive influence on participant attitudes. Interns scored significantly higher on two of three posttreatment (compared to pretreatment) measures of self-esteem and assertiveness.

TIME TRENDS IN FINDINGS: Little or no long-term follow-up was done. Only 20 percent of the sample were contacted at 12 months.

DESIGN ISSUES:

1. There was a high attrition rate. There was difficulty obtaining posttreatment and follow-up information for controls and those not serving internships. Only 53 percent of the sample were contacted at the 6-month follow-up, and only 20 percent at the 12-month point.

2. The random assignment component created negative repercussions. Some staff were reluctant to refer clients to the program, and some applicants were also hesitant to enroll.

3. State SPEID directors and the evaluators agreed that serving four weeks or more with a sponsoring business constituted an internship experience. Outcome data were analyzed based on that criteria. Dropouts were not considered part of the treatment group.

Their employment and earnings were analyzed separately. This probably results in selectivity bias.

4. There were several salient differences between program dropouts and program completers. Dropouts were receiving higher salaries and had received less pre-employment training during the year prior to SPEID intake.

5. Since the program was not initially designed as a treatment-versus-no-treatment study and tests of statistical significance were not employed, it is difficult to discern the true import of the findings.

REPLICABILITY: This project was replicated in Boise, Idaho, and New York State.

GENERALIZABILITY: The project was designed to generalize to the entire state, and the sample did reflect the population of single parents in Utah. However, design and implementation issues discourage attempts at generalization. In addition, the evaluators feel that applicants to SPEID likely represented a segment of the population that was more difficult to place in employment than other low-income single parents.

FUNDING SOURCE: U.S. Department of Health and Human Services (DHHS), Office of Community Services, Administration on Children and Families. Key personnel: Marianne Mackenzie.

TREATMENT ADMINISTRATOR: Davis County Employment and Training. Richard Nelson, agency director; Susan Sheehan, project director.

EVALUATORS: Lenore Shisler and Garth Mangum, University of Utah.

ENABLING LEGISLATION: Demonstration Partnership Program under section 408 of the Human Services Reauthorization Act of 1986, as amended.

INFORMATION SOURCES: U.S. Department of Health and Human Services, Demonstration Partnership Program: Summaries and Findings, FY 1988 and 1989, 1991.

PUBLIC-USE ACCESS TO DATA: Available through the Office of Community Services, DHHS.

Part Thirteen

UNEMPLOYED

SUMMARY: This demonstration, conducted from 1964 to 1966, tested the effects of technical and general education in a medium-sized sample of unemployed males. Subjects were followed for one year.

COST: $1.75 million (1964); research only, roughly 25 percent.

TIME FRAME: January 1964–June 1965; data collected through June 1966; final report, 1966.

TREATMENTS TESTED:
1. Control. No treatment.
2. Placebo. "Simulated type of occupational information and guidance," received daily. No further description in report, and Brazziel does not remember.
3. Technical Education. One-half day of technical education, and one hour per day of supervised (but not guided) study. Classes were in auto mechanics, sheet metal, masonry, electronics, and maintenance technology (upkeep of buildings). Received $30/week stipend. Program placed graduates with employers.
4. General Education. Went to same courses as group 3 and, in addition, one-half day of systematic instruction in reading improvement, language arts, number skills, and occupational information. Received $30/week stipend. Program placed graduates with employers.

OUTCOMES OF INTEREST: (1) Employment; (2) Salary per week; and (3) Mobility.

SAMPLE SIZE: 45 in each of the four groups.

TARGET POPULATION: Male, unemployed for three months or more, laid off from previous work, typically for automation-related reasons.

NUMBER OF TREATMENT GROUPS: Four.

NUMBER AND LOCATION OF SITES: One—Norfolk, Virginia.

RESEARCH COMPONENTS:
   Process analysis: Considerable stress on making work in reading and mathematics both job-related and adult-oriented. Special materials prepared. Average gains of three years in reading and arithmetic for general education group. In follow-up surveys, some group-4 participants attributed their subsequent success to reading, language, and mathematics courses.

Impact analysis: Conducted. Comparison of means.
Benefit–cost analysis: Not conducted.

MAJOR FINDINGS:
From follow-up interviews, one year later:

Group	Employment Rate (%)	Average Weekly Salary ($)	Percentage Promoted
General education	95	83*	31
Technical education	74	71	25
Placebo	63	50	12
Control	59	46	12

*Statistically significant difference from technical education group, at 1 percent level.

TIME TRENDS IN FINDINGS: Only one follow-up reported; Brazziel does not know if any were conducted subsequently.

DESIGN ISSUES: (1) Self-selection of site. (2) An enthusiastic faculty who developed special instructional materials and therefore may not be replicable elsewhere.

REPLICABILITY: In principle, fully replicable. Principles are (1) use of job-related materials in general education, (2) an educational approach that recognizes the experience that adults bring to the classroom, and (3) adequate stipends.

GENERALIZABILITY: (1) Brazziel says having the program on a college campus seemed to make a positive difference in subject attitudes. (2) Jobs were available in Norfolk, but were mismatched to worker skills. The results may not generalize to the common inner-city situation in which transportation to jobs is costly.

FUNDING SOURCES: U.S. Department of Labor, Office of Automation; HEW, Office of Education; and an anonymous donor. Key personnel: David Kerrico, Office of Education.

TREATMENT ADMINISTRATOR: Norfolk Division, Virginia State College. Key personnel: William Cooper, Hampton University.

EVALUATOR: Norfolk Division, Virginia State College. Key personnel: William F. Brazziel.

ENABLING LEGISLATION: None.

POLICY EFFECTS: According to Brazziel, this experiment has long informed policy.

INFORMATION SOURCES: William F. Brazziel, "Effects of General Education in Manpower Programs," *Journal of Human Resources* 1 (1966):39–44; U.S. Department of Health, Education & Welfare

(HEW), Office of Education, "Reeducating Unemployed Workers," in *Cooperative Research.*

PUBLIC-USE ACCESS TO DATA: We have no information about a public-use file for this demonstration.

CARBONDALE JOB-FINDING CLUB

SUMMARY: This demonstration, conducted in 1973, tested the effects of supervised group job search assistance on a small sample of the unemployed. Subjects were followed for three months.

COST: Estimate of $200 per experimental cost increment (administration only), or $12,000 (1973); cost of research only, not available.

TIME FRAME: 1973; data collected, 1973; final report, 1975.

TREATMENTS TESTED:
1. Controls. No treatment.
2. Experimentals. Daily group meetings to teach job search methods and develop positive job search attitudes through group reinforcement. Subjects received supervision in job search until successful. Elements of the treatment included the buddy system, secretarial services for resumes and letters of recommendation, a telephone bank, and job leads from other clients.

Experimentals were matched one-for-one with controls by an overall criterion of probable employability based on age, sex, race, education, marital status, desired position and salary level, number of dependents, and current financial resources. Once matched, a coin flip determined which member of the pair would be a control and which an experimental.

OUTCOME OF INTEREST: Employment.

SAMPLE SIZE: Experimentals, 60; controls, 60.

TARGET POPULATION: Unemployed persons not receiving unemployment benefits.

NUMBER OF TREATMENT GROUPS: Two (with one control group).

NUMBER AND LOCATION OF SITES: One—Carbondale, Illinois.

RESEARCH COMPONENTS:

Process analysis: To eliminate attrition bias, those experimentals matched with nonresponding controls were dropped from the sample for reporting purposes.

Impact analysis: Conducted as difference in means or medians.

Benefit–cost analysis: Not conducted.

MAJOR FINDINGS:

	Experimentals	Controls
Employed (more than 20 hours/week) within two months of beginning treatment	90%	55%
Employed within three months of beginning treatment	92%	60%
Mean starting wage	$2.73	$2.01
Median time until job found (includes those who did not find jobs during the period)	14 days	53 days

Note: These figures exclude experimentals who attended less than five sessions and their matched controls. No data are available on those excluded. All differences shown are statistically significant.

TIME TRENDS IN FINDINGS: Results are only reported through three months of treatment.

DESIGN ISSUES:

1. Results may be biased by self-selection, since only data on those who chose to attend five or more sessions were presented. The matching process did not control for self-selection except to the degree that the observed variables captured it.
2. The sample was small and quite heterogeneous.
3. Displacement bias seems very likely.
4. Success of the Job Club method probably varies with the size of the informal (unadvertised) job market, and this may vary among communities.

REPLICABILITY: Treatment has been replicated in subsequent studies, and a training manual for counselors has been published.

GENERALIZABILITY: Findings are striking, since Carbondale was a high-unemployment community. The sample excluded persons receiving unemployment insurance benefits because the project report authors believed some individuals were likely to lack motivation to find employment until their benefits ran out. They suggested, however, that if participation were a condition of receiving benefits, it would motivate job search in this group too.

FUNDING SOURCE: Illinois Department of Mental Health. Key personnel: None.

TREATMENT ADMINISTRATOR: Anna Mental Health Center. Key personnel: Nathan H. Azrin.

EVALUATOR: Anna Mental Health Center. Key personnel: Nathan H. Azrin.

ENABLING LEGISLATION: None.

INFORMATION SOURCE: Nathan H. Azrin, T. Flores, and S. J. Kaplan, "Job-Finding Club: A Group-Assisted Program for Obtaining Employment," *Behavior Research and Therapy*, Vol. 13. 1975: 17–27.

PUBLIC-USE ACCESS TO DATA: We have no information about a public-use file for this demonstration.

CARBONDALE HANDICAPPED JOB-FINDING CLUB

SUMMARY: This demonstration, conducted from 1974 to 1975, tested the effects of supervised group job search assistance on a medium-sized sample of handicapped unemployed individuals. Subjects were followed for six months.

COST: Not available (experiment was one activity of an ongoing research laboratory); costs of research only, not available.

TIME FRAME: 1974–75; data collected, same period; final report, 1979.

TREATMENTS TESTED:
1. Controls received two days of group lectures, discussions, and role-playing in job search. The project report authors stated that this is the common format of the only other standardized method of job counseling.
2. Experimentals received daily group job search training and supervised job search until a job was obtained. A fuller description is in the preceding "Carbondale Job-Finding Club" summary.

OUTCOME OF INTEREST: Employment.

SAMPLE SIZE: Experimentals, 80; controls, 74.

TARGET POPULATION: Unemployed persons with "severe employability problems": persons with physical or mental handicaps, ex-prisoners or mental patients, welfare clients, substance abusers, and alcoholics; and other long-term job seekers.

NUMBER OF TREATMENT GROUPS: Two (with one control group).

NUMBER AND LOCATION OF SITES: One—Carbondale, Illinois.

RESEARCH COMPONENTS:
   Process analysis: The project report stated that "a principal difference between the two programs was that the comparison clients were
informed of the need for (certain) actions; the Job Club clients were
required to perform them under supervision."
   Impact analysis: Conducted as a difference in means or medians.
   Benefit–cost analysis: Not conducted.

MAJOR FINDINGS:

	Experimentals	Controls
Employed after two months at a job over 20 hours/week (based on survey with 100 percent response rate)	90%	20%
Employed after six months (based on survey with 32 percent response rate)	95%	28%
Mean starting wage	$3.01	$3.08
Median starting wage	$2.61	$2.20
Median time to find job (successful seekers only)	10 days	30 days
Percentage of days worked out of all available days over a three-month period	89%	23%

Notes: Table data exclude both experimentals and controls who attended less than two
sessions. Differences in employment are significant. The difference between mean and
median starting wages is due to a single high-wage control. All jobs found were
unsubsidized.

   According to the project report: "The program was found superior
to an alternative program, but the salaries were not extraordinary, and
some clients required weeks and months of continued diligent supervision and guidance."

TIME TRENDS IN FINDINGS: There was no tendency for differences to
narrow between two months and six months.

DESIGN ISSUES:
1. Experimental design eliminates any possibility of self-selection
   bias (because both experimentals and controls had to attend at
   least two sessions to be included in the sample), but the six-month
   follow-up is probably vulnerable to attrition bias.
2. The sample is small, and the clients' problems, although severe,
   are heterogeneous.

REPLICABILITY: See "Carbondale Job-Finding Club" summary.

GENERALIZABILITY: See "Carbondale Job-Finding Club" summary.

FUNDING SOURCE: Illinois Department of Mental Health. Key personnel: None.

TREATMENT ADMINISTRATOR: Anna Mental Health Center. Key personnel: Nathan H. Azrin.

EVALUATOR: Anna Mental Health Center. Key personnel: Nathan H. Azrin.

ENABLING LEGISLATION: None.

INFORMATION SOURCE: Nathan H. Azrin and Robert A. Philip, "The Job Club Method for the Job Handicapped: A Comparative Outcome Study," *Rehabilitation Counseling Bulletin*, 23 (December 1979), 144–155.

PUBLIC-USE ACCESS TO DATA: We have no information about a public-use file for this demonstration.

U.S. EMPLOYMENT SERVICE EFFECTIVENESS OF COUNSELING PILOT STUDY

SUMMARY: This demonstration, conducted from 1975 to 1976, tested the effects of employment counseling on a medium-sized sample of U.S. Employment Service (ES) clients. Subjects were followed for up to 10 months.

COST: Roughly $250,000 (1976).

TIME FRAME: November 1975–February 1976; data collected, August 1976; final report, August 1977.

TREATMENTS TESTED:
1.a. Persons determined by U.S. Employment Service interviewers to need counseling and who received it (ES experimentals).
1.b. Persons determined by ES interviewers to need counseling who did not receive it (ES controls).
2.a. Persons determined by Stanford Research Institute (SRI) interviewers (not ES interviewers) to need counseling and who then received it from the usual ES counselors (SRI experimentals).

2.b. Persons determined by SRI interviewers (not ES interviewers) to need counseling and who did not receive it (SRI controls).

Random assignment occurred after determination of need. The reason for the second set of experimentals/controls was the investigators' belief that ES interviewers tend to refer people to counseling not on the basis of need but on the basis of their low placement potential. People with a higher placement potential might need counseling to achieve that potential, whereas low-potential individuals might still not benefit from employment counseling.

OUTCOME OF INTEREST: Duration of unemployment.

SAMPLE SIZE: Experimentals (receiving counseling), 481; controls, 439.

TARGET POPULATION: Clients of the U.S. Employment Service determined by interviewers to need employment counseling.

NUMBER OF TREATMENT GROUPS: Four (with two control groups).

NUMBER AND LOCATION OF SITES: Three—Salt Lake City, Utah; Minneapolis, Minnesota; and West Palm Beach, Florida.

RESEARCH COMPONENTS:
Process analysis: Not conducted. This is a "black-box" experiment.
Impact analysis: Conducted with ordinary least squares (OLS) regressions. Other analytical methods were also used.
Benefit–cost analysis: Not conducted.

MAJOR FINDINGS:
1. Counseling had no significant impact on the duration of unemployment. This finding was the same for both ES and SRI subjects.
2. Counseling also had no significant impact on wages, job prestige, percentage of observation period employed, job satisfaction, or the number of job search methods used.

TIME TRENDS IN FINDINGS: Data series too short to find any.

DESIGN ISSUES:
1. Because this study was explicitly designed as a pilot for a more ambitious evaluation, the period for which the investigators had data was no more than 10 months for any subject, and as little as 6 months for some.

REPLICABILITY: None. The experiment was undertaken to demonstrate the feasibility of a larger study, which was never funded. The investigators did not inquire into the content of the counseling.

GENERALIZABILITY: The sites selected were not representative of the U.S. Employment Service nationally.

FUNDING SOURCE: U.S. Department of Labor, Employment and Training Administration. Key personnel: William Showler.

TREATMENT ADMINISTRATOR: U.S. Employment Service, three locations.

EVALUATOR: Stanford Research Institute (SRI). Key personnel: Jacob Benus.

ENABLING LEGISLATION: None.

INFORMATION SOURCES: Jacob Benus, Arden R. Hall, Patty Gwartney-Gibbs, Marilyn Coon, Caren Cole, Diane Leeds, and Doug Brent, "The Effectiveness of Counseling in the U.S. Employment Service: A Pilot Study; Analytic Results," Stanford Research Institute, August 1977. This study has never been published.

PUBLIC-USE ACCESS TO DATA: We have no information about a public-use file for this demonstration.

JOB CLUB BEHAVIORAL SUPERVISION TEST

SUMMARY: This demonstration, conducted from 1980 to 1981, tested the effects of supervised job search activities on a medium-sized sample of the unemployed. Subjects were followed for six months.

COST: Not possible to separate from other research.

TIME FRAME: Roughly 1980–81; data collected, roughly the same period; final report, March 1982.

TREATMENTS TESTED:
1. Controls were taught all skills and techniques used in the job search under the Job Club model. See "Carbondale Job-Finding Club" summary.
2. Experimentals received this information and were supervised in using it—for example, in telephoning employers and friends and writing résumés.

OUTCOME OF INTEREST: Employment.

SAMPLE SIZE: Experimentals, 186; controls, 133.

TARGET POPULATION: Unemployed persons of all sorts, especially (but not solely) referrals from the local employment service.

NUMBER OF TREATMENT GROUPS: Two (with one control group).

NUMBER AND LOCATION OF SITES: Carbondale, Illinois.

RESEARCH COMPONENTS:
Process analysis: This experiment is itself a form of process analysis.
Impact analysis: Conducted as a difference in means.
Benefit–cost analysis: Not conducted.

MAJOR FINDINGS:
Six months after enrollment:

	Controls	Experimentals
Obtained jobs of 20$^+$ hours/week	70.6%	87.6%*
Mean hours/week worked	33.6	36.9
Days required to find job	60.7	32.1*
Mean salary/hour	$3.93	$4.99

*Difference is statistically significant.

TIME TRENDS IN FINDINGS: Only six-month data are reported.

DESIGN ISSUES:
1. Attrition was higher in the controls than in the experimentals, and there was no analysis of it. (The initial sample included 196 experimentals and 150 controls.)
2. This study in particular would have benefited from a benefit–cost analysis, to show whether the experimental difference was worth the supervision cost.
3. As with all the Job Club experiments, the possibility of displacement exists. See also the comments on the other Job Club experiments.

REPLICABILITY: Replicable. See "Carbondale Job-Finding Club" summary.

GENERALIZABILITY: Apparently generalizable; there does not seem to be any community-specific effect here.

FUNDING SOURCE: Illinois Department of Mental Health. Key personnel: None.

TREATMENT ADMINISTRATOR: Anna Mental Health Center. Key personnel: Nathan H. Azrin.

EVALUATOR: Anna Mental Health Center. Key personnel: Nathan H. Azrin.

ENABLING LEGISLATION: None.

INFORMATION SOURCE: Nathan H. Azrin, V. A. Besalel, I. Wisotzek, M. McMorrow, and R. Bechtel, "Behavioral Supervision versus Informational Counseling of Job Seeking in the Job Club," *Rehabilitation Counseling Bulletin*, March 1982, 212–18, vol. 25.

PUBLIC-USE ACCESS TO DATA: We have no information about a public-use file for this demonstration.

BUFFALO DISLOCATED WORKER DEMONSTRATION PROGRAM

SUMMARY: This demonstration, conducted from 1982 to 1984, tested the effects of employment services (job search assistance, training, on-the-job training) on a medium-sized sample of laid-off workers. Subjects were followed for six months.

COST: The impact analysis was conducted as part of a six-site program evaluation, most of which was nonexperimental. It would be very difficult to disentangle the experimental and nonexperimental costs.

TIME FRAME: October 1982–September 1983; data collected through July 1984; final report, March 1985.

TREATMENTS TESTED: The "experiment" took place in the context of factory shutdowns and large-scale layoffs in the Buffalo area. Laid-off workers from six large "target plants" were recruited for reemployment-related services. Because resources were limited, treatment administrators rationed these services through a lottery system: at random, workers were either notified or not notified of the availability of program slots. The program offered testing and assessment, a four-day job search workshop, a job search resource center, classroom training for new careers, on-the-job training, job development services, relocation assistance, and Targeted Jobs Tax Credit eligibility determination. These component services were not assigned randomly.

OUTCOMES OF INTEREST: (1) Participation; (2) Employment; (3) Wages; and (4) Receipt of transfer payments.

SAMPLE SIZE: The analysis sample has 586 experimentals and 210 controls.

TARGET POPULATION: Laid-off workers from four steel plants, an automobile assembly plant, and a petroleum refinery. Workers over the age of 55 were excluded ex post from the analysis sample, because no such workers opted to receive the services offered.

NUMBER OF TREATMENT GROUPS: Two (with one control group).

NUMBER AND LOCATION OF SITES: Buffalo, New York.

RESEARCH COMPONENTS:
   Process analysis: Conducted. Some unexpected differences in background variables between experimentals and controls were noted, but were judged not to affect the results. The treatment was an expensive one, averaging $1,975 per participant. Participation was fairly low, with 27.7 percent of experimentals choosing to receive services.
   Impact analysis: Conducted with ordinary least squares and a Heckman selection term for participation. The inverse Mills ratio was set equal to zero for controls; a probit analysis was performed on the discrete choice to participate or not to participate among experimentals, and the inverse Mills ratio was derived for each experimental from that probit. The impact of the experimental treatment per participant was then calculated as the coefficient on a dummy variable (one if participant experimental, zero if nonparticipant experimental or control) in an equation that included among other variables the inverse Mills ratio. The project report authors presented alternative estimation models and argued that the one they used is the most efficient. Also, because of significant nonresponse rates, the observations were weighted so that the analysis sample of experimentals resembles the population of controls.
   Benefit–cost analysis: Not conducted.

MAJOR FINDINGS:
   Impacts on participant experimentals in the first six months after recruitment:

	Impact estimate	Mean for participants
Proportion of time employed	+0.33	0.57
Probability of ever being employed	+0.31	0.72
Average hours employed per week	+13.6	23.7
Average weekly earnings	$115	$174
All of these impacts are significant at the 95 percent level with a one-tail test.		
Weekly amount of food stamps	−$5.10	$3.60
Percentage of time receiving public assistance	−10.7	2.3
Weekly amount of public assistance	−$9.20	$1.10

All of these impacts are significant at the 90 percent level with a one-tail test. Public assistance includes Aid to Families with Dependent Children (AFDC), Supplement Security Income (SSI), and general assistance. Effects on unemployment insurance receipt and Supplemental Unemployment Benefit are not significant.

TIME TRENDS IN FINDINGS: Experimental/control employment differences narrow over time.

DESIGN ISSUES:
1. The most serious problem is the high nonresponse rate, nearly 46 percent among controls, over one-third of them refusals. The rate of refusals is higher among controls than among experimentals; nonresponse bias might well exist, and the weighting method will not eliminate it.
2. One of the great advantages of random-assignment experiments is that they do not require the use of econometric adjustments for self-selection like the Heckman procedure, which is not robust to deviations from the assumptions of the model concerning the distribution of the random disturbance. The use of the Heckman self-selection procedure here is driven by a desire to estimate impacts per participant, rather than per experimental, where the number of participants is small with respect to the number of experimentals. Average impact per experimental is the relevant focus for policy purposes, however, because a program would be made available to some population at some average cost, and would have some average benefit per individual in that population. Ex ante, the policymaker probably knows fairly well the number of persons who will be eligible, but can only guess the number who will participate in a voluntary program.
3. The Buffalo economy was quite depressed at the time of the experiment, with the unemployment rate rising from 9.7 percent to 12.6 percent over the course of 1982.

REPLICABILITY: Replicable.

GENERALIZABILITY: Limited by the small sample size, the possibility of nonresponse bias, and the particularly depressed condition of the local economy.

FUNDING SOURCE: U.S. Department of Labor, Employment and Training Administration. Key personnel: Beverly Bachemin and George Koch.

TREATMENT ADMINISTRATOR: Worker Re-employment Center. Key personnel: Harry Reeverts, Mark Cosgrove, and Edie Rifenburg.

EVALUATOR:　Mathematica Policy Research. Key personnel: Walter Corson, Sharon Long, and Rebecca A. Maynard.

ENABLING LEGISLATION:　None.

INFORMATION SOURCE:　Walter Corson, Sharon Long, and Rebecca A. Maynard, "An Impact Evaluation of the Buffalo Dislocated Worker Program," Mathematica Policy Research, March 12, 1985.

PUBLIC-USE ACCESS TO DATA:　Public-use file available; contact National Technical Information Service, Springfield, Virginia.

CLAIMANT PLACEMENT AND WORK TEST DEMONSTRATION

SUMMARY:　This demonstration, conducted in 1983, tested the effects of a deadline to register for work with the Employment Service, mandatory supervised job search, and job placement services on a large sample of Unemployment Insurance claimants. Subjects were followed for less than one year.

COST:　Administration, $25,000 (1983); research only, roughly $200,000 (1983).

TIME FRAME:　February–December 1983; data collected, same period; final report, July 31, 1984.

TREATMENTS TESTED:

Group A—Controls. The treatment of controls differed slightly from prior practice in that prior practice theoretically required Employment Service (ES) registration. Controls had no ES registration requirement and did not receive special job development efforts, although they could use the ES services voluntarily. They were required (as were experimentals) to come in periodically for eligibility reviews at the unemployment insurance (UI) office.

Group B. Improved work test, but regular Employment Service (ES) services. These experimentals were mailed notices coincidentally with their first week's UI check to come to the Employment Service office to register their availability for work. This practice differed from prior practice in that (1) the registration requirement was delayed so that those who never received a check did not come into ES offices, and (2) the registration was required as of some definite date. In general, failure to register would be taken as possible evidence of unavailability for work and, therefore, ineligibility for UI payments. New procedures were implemented to match ES and UI records so that this rule would be routinely enforced.

Group C. Improved work test and enhanced placement interviewer services. These experimentals received the same notice as group B. In addition, when the subject reported to the ES, an interviewer would attempt to develop a job for the subject unless he or she was a union member, was not job-ready, or was on layoff for some definite period. Group C subjects were also called in for a renewed job-placement attempt if still unemployed after nine weeks.

Group D. Improved work test, enhanced placement interviewer services, and job search workshops. In addition to group C experimentals, three-hour job search workshops were mandated for group D experimentals who were still receiving UI benefits four to five weeks after receiving enhanced placement interviewer services.

OUTCOMES OF INTEREST: (1) Employment and (2) UI payment reductions.

SAMPLE SIZE: Group A, 1,485; group B, 1,493; group C, 1,666; group D, 1,277.

TARGET POPULATION: New unemployment insurance (UI) claimants who had received an initial UI check, excluding those whose employers said they were on layoff for some definite period.

NUMBER OF TREATMENT GROUPS: Four (with one control group).

NUMBER AND LOCATION OF SITES: Charleston, South Carolina.

RESEARCH COMPONENTS:
Process analysis: Conducted. The process analysis indicates that the experiment was conducted essentially as planned. Roughly 25 percent of the experimentals failed to register on time with the ES the first time, and among experimentals subject to subsequent call-ins, about 9 percent of those eligible failed to respond. Nonresponse was more common among men than women, and varied inversely with age and education. Nonresponses by men and women were not homogeneous (i.e., could not be captured simply by an intercept term), and there was a cohort effect (the longer the call-in policy was in effect, the more likely subjects were to respond). Eight-five percent of experimentals received some ES service, compared with 35 percent of controls. Over 62 percent of group C and D members received some attempt at job development, compared with 33 percent of group B and 9 percent of group A members.

Impact analysis: Ordinary least squares (OLS), comparison of means. Probit conducted but not reported, since the results were similar to OLS.

Benefit–cost analysis: Cost-effectiveness analysis.

MAJOR FINDINGS:

	Group A	Group B	Group C	Group D
Percentage of subjects with nonmonetary determination (eligibility ruling)	5.8	13.4	16.7	18.4
Percentage of subjects with a denial (ruled ineligible)	4.2	7.4	9.2	8.7

1. OLS confirms that all experimental treatments had a statistically significant positive effect on the denial rate compared with the experience of controls. This effect was substantially higher in C and D than in B, but differences between C and D were negligible.
2. Treatment effects on employment and wages as recorded in the UI wage reporting system were weak, inconsistent, and usually not statistically significant.
3. Effects on weeks of UI payments (coefficients of OLS dummy variables for treatment group; this measures the treatment effect on experimentals by comparison with controls):

	Group B	Group C	Group D
Men	−0.83*	−1.15*	−1.14*
Women	−0.20	0.31	−0.15

*Statistical significance at 95 percent confidence level, on a two-tail test. OLS results control for cohort (week applying for UI).

Much of the difference between men and women results from the strong treatment effect on construction workers, who are mostly male. The experimental treatments reduced the weeks of UI received by male construction workers by about two weeks (the effects on female construction workers are about the same, but are not statistically significant because of small numbers). "A possible explanation for this result may relate to the casual, part-time nature of some construction employment (particularly during slack periods) and to the relatively low wage replacement rates that UI provides to construction workers."

All experimental treatments were inexpensive: $4.72, $13.17, and $17.58 per subject increments for treatments B, C, and D, respectively. The corresponding average reductions in UI payments were $52.93, $58.71, and $73.14. All experimental treatments are therefore cost-effective, with the most cost-effective being treatment D.

TIME TRENDS IN FINDINGS: The variable representing cohort has a negative and statistically significant effect on weeks of unemployment. However, it is not possible to distinguish between the effect of falling unemployment rates and the effect of learning about new registration requirements for UI. Since experimental treatments differ in the times at which interventions occur, treatment effects are also indistinguishable from time effects.

DESIGN ISSUES:

1. Unemployment in Charleston fell from 8.9 percent to 6.6 percent in 1983. The improving economy reduced UI claims and increased job orders at the ES office.
2. If a claimant stated that he or she had failed to report as required because of illness or lack of transportation, there would have been a denial of UI on the grounds that the claimant was unable to work or was unavailable for work. On the other hand, claims that the summons to register at the ES had been lost in the mail were always accepted, even when there had been no difficulty receiving the UI check sent under a separate cover. The summons was sent under a separate cover only because of the experimental character of the demonstration (controls were not supposed to receive a call-in, and it was apparently too complex to insert a call-in with some checks and not with others); experimental denial rates therefore slightly understate what could be expected upon implementation of the policy.
3. If the treatment effect is primarily centered on construction workers, it would not be surprising if no wage or employment effects were noted from UI data, because much of the industry is not covered or escapes reporting requirements.
4. In the cost-effectiveness analysis, instead of estimating the reduction in UI payments directly, the authors take the average UI weekly payment ($96.24) and multiply it by the experimental treatment effect on weeks of receipt. This procedure fails to take into account the possibility that the part of the population whose behavior is changed by the treatment will not have the same average weekly benefit as the overall population.

REPLICABILITY: Replicable.

GENERALIZABILITY: The project report authors were cautious about generalizability. They claimed that South Carolina Job Service/UI procedures are similar to those in most other states. The Charleston labor force has a higher percentage of blacks, however, than does the U.S. labor force. The importance of the construction industry, where much of the treatment impact was concentrated, varies across the country. State UI laws and regulations also vary; the maximum weekly payment in South Carolina, for example, was $118.

FUNDING SOURCE: U.S. Department of Labor, Employment and Training Administration. Key personnel: Norm Harvey and William Showler.

TREATMENT ADMINISTRATOR: South Carolina Employment Security Agency. Key personnel: Agency head, not named in report.

EVALUATOR: SRI International; Mathematica Policy Research; and Bloom Associates. Key personnel: Susan Philipson Bloom (Bloom Associates) and Terry R. Johnson (SRI) helped design the evaluation. Principal investigators: Walter Corson and Walter Nicholson both of MPR.

ENABLING LEGISLATION: None.

INFORMATION SOURCES: Terry R. Johnson, Jennifer M. Pfiester, Richard W. West, and Katherine P. Dickinson, "Design and Implementation of the Claimant Placement and Work Test Demonstration," SRI International, May 1984; Walter Corson, David A. Long, and Walter Nicholson, "Evaluation of the Charleston Claimant Placement and Work Test Demonstration," Mathematica Policy Research, July 31, 1984.

PUBLIC-USE ACCESS TO DATA: We have no information about a public-use file for this demonstration.

DELAWARE DISLOCATED WORKER PILOT PROGRAM

SUMMARY: This demonstration, conducted in 1983, tested the effects of job search assistance and employment counseling on a medium-sized sample of unemployment insurance (UI) claimants. Subjects were followed for up to six months.

COST: Research only, $10,000 (1983).

TIME FRAME: January 1983–July 1983; data collected through December 1983; final report, 1984.

TREATMENTS TESTED: Experimentals received four basic services in sequence: job search workshops, regular individual counseling sessions, services of job developers, and retraining. The retraining services were a last resource, and only 13 out of 65 experimentals received them.

OUTCOMES OF INTEREST: (1) UI benefit payments and (2) Earnings.

SAMPLE SIZE: Experimentals, 65; controls, 110.

TARGET POPULATION: Volunteers were taken from the population of all unemployment insurance (UI) claimants who had been receiving benefits for 7 to 12 weeks, attended an orientation, and applied for entry in the program. Those without at least 10 years of education or access to transportation were screened out, as were those who expected to be recalled by their most recent employer. Separate assignment lotteries were held in each of the state's three counties to even out the workload of program staff in the different locations.

NUMBER OF TREATMENT GROUPS: Two (with one control group).

NUMBER AND LOCATION OF SITES: All of the three counties in Delaware.

RESEARCH COMPONENTS:
    Process analysis: An analysis of participation was conducted; it generally found that nonparticipants had better-than-average employment prospects than participants, and that early dropouts had higher past earnings than did completers, but lower earnings after the program started. Program staff also commented unfavorably on one of the key concepts of the program, that of having high-school guidance counselors with very limited special training perform the counseling tasks. The program was also evaluated with no preliminary start-up period.
    Impact analysis: Conducted with OLS.
    Benefit–cost analysis: Not conducted.

MAJOR FINDINGS: The program had no statistically significant impact on UI payments or earnings. The impacts reported were in the wrong direction (higher UI payments, lower earnings).

TIME TRENDS IN FINDINGS: None.

DESIGN ISSUES: The sample size was extremely small. In this case, the underlying population also appeared to be extremely small—only 965 workers in the entire state had been unemployed for 7 to 12 weeks, and those who applied for program services were only about a third of the total. Statistically significant results could not have been expected from a sample this size unless the treatment impacts were quite large.

REPLICABILITY: Replicable.

GENERALIZABILITY: Probably none, because the sample is too small and the implementation, specifically the use of high-school guidance counselors, seems questionable.

FUNDING SOURCE: U.S. Department of Labor, Employment and Training Administration. Key personnel: None.

TREATMENT ADMINISTRATOR: Delaware Department of Labor. Key personnel: Dennis Carey, formerly state secretary of labor.

EVALUATOR: Bloom Associates. Key personnel: Howard S. Bloom and Susan Philipson Bloom.

ENABLING LEGISLATION: None.

INFORMATION SOURCE: Howard S. Bloom, "Lessons from the Delaware Dislocated Worker Pilot Program," *Evaluation Review*, April 1987: 157–77.

PUBLIC-USE ACCESS TO DATA: We have no information about a public-use file for this demonstration.

ILLINOIS UNEMPLOYMENT INSURANCE INCENTIVE EXPERIMENT

SUMMARY: This demonstration, conducted from 1984 to 1985, tested the effects of a reemployment bonus incentive on a large sample of unemployment insurance (UI) clients. Subjects were followed for up to one year.

COST: $800,000 (1985); research only, $200,000.

TIME FRAME: Mid-1984 to early 1985; data collected, mid-1984 to mid-1985; final report, February 1987.

TREATMENTS TESTED:
1. Claimant experiment. A $500 bonus was offered to an eligible claimant of unemployment insurance payments if he or she could find a job within 11 weeks and hold that job for four months.
2. Employer experiment. The same, except that the $500 bonus would be paid to the claimant's employer.
3. Controls. Standard unemployment insurance eligibility.

OUTCOMES OF INTEREST: (1) Reductions in unemployment spells and (2) Net program savings.

SAMPLE SIZE: 4,186 claimant experimentals; 3,963 employer experimentals; 3,963 controls.

TARGET POPULATION: Persons who are (1) eligible for 26 weeks of unemployment insurance (UI) benefits; (2) between 20 and 55 years of age; and (3) registrants with Job Service offices who were not on definite layoff, ineligible for a union hiring hall, or not recent veterans or federal employees.

NUMBER OF TREATMENT GROUPS: Three (with one control group).

NUMBER AND LOCATION OF SITES: 22 Job Service offices in northern and central Illinois.

RESEARCH COMPONENTS:
  Process analysis: Not conducted.
  Impact analysis: Conducted as difference in means.
  Benefit–cost analysis: Conducted from a budgetary perspective.

MAJOR FINDINGS:
1. A $194 reduction in 52-week benefit payments to the average claimant experimental was found, by comparison with the average control. The comparable $61 reduction for employer experimentals was not statistically significant.
2. A 1.15-week reduction in insured unemployment over 52 weeks was found for the average claimant experimental. The 0.36-week reduction for employer experimentals was not statistically significant.
3. The experimental treatments did not appear to curtail productive job search activity, because no statistically significant change in subsequent earnings was found between the control and experimental groups.
4. The employer experiment did result in a $164 reduction per claimant in benefit payments to white women, which was statistically significant. The effects of the employer experimental treatment among blacks (male and female) and white males were not significantly different from zero. The claimant experimental response was statistically significant for whites of both sexes, but not for blacks of either sex.
5. Of claimant experimentals, 13.6 percent received a bonus; 25 percent qualified for one. Of employer experimentals, 2.8 percent obtained a bonus for their employers; 22.8 percent of them could have obtained one for their employers.

6. The ratio of benefit payments reductions to bonus cost for the claimant experiment was 2.32, which is statistically significant. The ratio for the employer experiment was 4.29 (not significant). If 100 percent of those eligible for bonuses had claimed them, the benefit–cost ratio would have been 1.26 for claimant experimentals and 0.53 for employer experimentals.

TIME TRENDS IN FINDINGS: Reductions in the initial unemployment spell may be slightly offset by increases in subsequent unemployment, but this is not statistically significant.

DESIGN ISSUES:
1. A potential displacement effect among nonparticipants in the program clearly exists.
2. Long-term market bias effects are conceivable if workers adjusted to a permanent bonus program by undergoing frequent short unemployment spells with accompanying state bonuses instead of infrequent long spells.
3. The low rate at which the bonuses were claimed by those who qualified for them is puzzling.

REPLICABILITY: The treatments are clearly replicable.

GENERALIZABILITY: The 22 sites involved in the experiment represented very diverse labor markets, so locality effects should not be present. Spiegelman noted that roughly the first half of workers subject to the experiment would have been eligible for extended (38-week) federal unemployment payments if their unemployed status had lasted longer than 26 weeks, whereas subsequent claimants were ineligible for them. Experimental response seems to have been stronger in the first group, but this was not conclusively established.

FUNDING SOURCES: Illinois Department of Employment Security (DES, using Wagner-Peiser grants); and W. E. Upjohn Institute for Employment Research. Key personnel: Sally Ward, DES; and Robert G. Spiegelman, Upjohn.

TREATMENT ADMINISTRATOR: Illinois DES. Key personnel: Sally Ward.

EVALUATOR: W. E. Upjohn Institute for Employment Research. Key personnel: Robert G. Spiegelman and Stephen A. Woodbury.

ENABLING LEGISLATION: None.

INFORMATION SOURCES: Stephen A. Woodbury and Robert G. Spiegelman, "Bonuses to Workers and Employers to Reduce Unemployment: Randomized Trials in Illinois," American Economic Review,

September 1987: 513–30. Woodbury and Spiegelman, "The Illinois Unemployment Insurance Incentive Experiments," final report to Illinois Department of Employment Security, W.E. Upjohn Institute, February 1987.

PUBLIC-USE ACCESS TO DATA: We have no information about a public-use file for this demonstration.

TEXAS WORKER ADJUSTMENT DEMONSTRATION

SUMMARY: This demonstration, conducted from 1984 to 1985, tested the effects of assisted job search, job clubs, and training on a large sample of unemployed/displaced workers. Subjects were followed for one year.

COST: Total project costs, approximately $2 million; evaluation costs, under $500,000.

TIME FRAME: Demonstration period, April 1984–July 1985.

TREATMENTS TESTED: Two-tiered intervention. Tier I included assisted job search and job clubs. Tier II included classroom and on-the-job occupational training. Transportation services were available at all sites. Child care was provided only at the Houston site. Controls did not receive these services.

OUTCOMES OF INTEREST: (1) Earnings; (2) Employment; and (3) Unemployment insurance (UI) benefits.

SAMPLE SIZE: Total, 2,259. Tier I only (Houston site), 332; tiers I/II (all sites), 1,113; control (all sites), 814.

TARGET POPULATION: Unemployed/displaced workers. There were also site-specific guidelines targeting certain industries and/or specific occupations.

NUMBER OF TREATMENT GROUPS: Three in Houston (tier I only, tier I/II, control); two in both El Paso sites (tier I/II, control).

NUMBER AND LOCATION OF SITES: Three sites—Texas Employment Commission/Houston Community College (TEC/HCC); El Paso School for Educational Enrichment (SEE); and Greater El Paso SER Jobs for Progress (SER/JOBS).

RESEARCH COMPONENTS:

Process analysis: Focus on implementation, variation across sites, participation, and operations. Also, special care was taken to reduce control group crossovers and treatment group no-shows.

Impact analysis: Conducted using multiple regression models (ordinary least squares regression and maximum likelihood logit models).

Benefit–cost analysis: A formal benefit–cost analysis was not conducted, but a cost-effectiveness study was done.

MAJOR FINDINGS:

1. Program impacts for displaced female workers were substantial and sustained throughout the one-year follow-up. Female participants experienced a $1,148 (34 percent) average annual program-induced earnings gain. Correspondingly, these participants received 19 percent less in UI benefits during their first 30 weeks after entering the program.

2. Impacts for men were appreciable, but were much smaller and shorter-lived than for women. Male participants experienced an average annual program-induced earnings gain of $673 (8 percent), most of which occurred in the second quarter, when earnings gains averaged $329, or 16 percent. Impacts were statistically significant only in this quarter.

3. UI data suggested a statistically significant, though declining over time, increase in the likelihood of employment for women. No large or statistically significant effects on this outcome were suggested for men.

4. Average costs per participant varied considerably across sites, but were comparable to the Job Training Partnership Act (JTPA) Title III national average. Measured earnings impacts for women exceeded program costs.

5. Findings from the TEC/HCC site suggest that essentially no additional gains accrued from adding tier II services to job-search assistance. In fact, during the first year after random assignment, the tier I group had a significantly higher earnings gain than the tier I/II group ($403 versus $320).

TIME TRENDS IN FINDINGS: All program impacts declined over time.

DESIGN ISSUES:

1. Originally there were five sites, but two dropped out of the evaluation. One in Beaumont dropped out when alternate sources of reemployment assistance became available to control group mem-

bers. The Galveston site dropped out owing to insurmountable management problems and conflicts.
2. Initial recruitment at both El Paso sites was done through industry referrals and walk-ins. These strategies did not produce sufficient enrollment, and it was necessary to contract with the El Paso TEC office for UI claimant referrals.
3. Original demonstration plans specified that all sites identify target occupations, but SEE and SER/JOBS did not implement this feature.
4. TEC/HCC had a predominantly white-collar sample, yet offered mostly blue-collar-oriented classroom training. This could explain the weak impacts for the tier I/II group. Additional courses were added to help correct this mismatch.
5. Sites varied in their training focus. TEC/HCC focused overwhelmingly on classroom training; SER/JOBS focused overwhelmingly on on-the-job training; and SEE reflected an even mix of these activities.

REPLICABILITY: Replicable.

GENERALIZABILITY: The typical sample member was an experienced worker who recently lost a relatively good job and was using the UI system to help meet substantial family responsibilities. The TEC/HCC program targeted specific occupations that produced a mostly white-collar demonstration sample. This sample differed markedly from the local pool of unemployed workers and even more so from JTPA IIA (disadvantaged) counterparts. The El Paso sites reflected more the existing pool of the insured unemployed.

Population characteristics between Houston and El Paso also differed. Houston's population is more ethnically diverse and better educated. El Paso is predominantly Hispanic and less well educated. Houston wage rates are much higher than El Paso's. El Paso also had higher unemployment (10 percent versus 7 percent during the project period).

FUNDING SOURCE: Texas Department of Community Affairs (TDCA). Key personnel: Christopher King, Mary Jane Leahy, and Saundra Kirk.

TREATMENT ADMINISTRATOR: Under TDCA—TEC/HCC, Key personnel: Jean Wood; SEE, key personnel: Iris Burnham; SER/JOBS, key personnel: Ruben Villalobos.

EVALUATOR: Abt Associates. Key personnel: Howard Bloom, principal investigator; Jane Kulik, project director; and Linda Sharpe, on-site supervisor.

ENABLING LEGISLATION: None, although the project was linked to the JTPA Title III provisions for displaced workers.

INFORMATION SOURCES: Howard Bloom, *Back to Work: Testing Reemployment Services for Displaced Workers*, W.E. Upjohn Institute, 1990.

PUBLIC-USE ACCESS TO DATA: Not available.

NEW JERSEY UNEMPLOYMENT INSURANCE REEMPLOYMENT DEMONSTRATION

SUMMARY: This demonstration, conducted from 1986 to 1987, tested the effects of job search assistance, training, and a reemployment bonus payment on a large sample of dislocated (unemployed) workers. Subjects were followed for six years.

COST: Research only, $1.27 million (1987).

TIME FRAME: July 1986–fall 1987; data collected through July 1988; final report, April 1989. Six-year follow-up and summary report, January 1996.

TREATMENTS TESTED:
1. Job Search Assistance (JSA) only. Four weeks after subjects received their first weekly UI payment, they were directed to come to an orientation and testing session. The following week, subjects were (with certain exceptions) expected to attend a job search workshop lasting five days (half-day sessions). The week thereafter they were to attend individual sessions with counselors to assess their employment prospects. An employment resource center with job listings, telephones, and literature was set up in the UI office and subjects were expected to use it regularly. If they failed to do so, they would be recontacted every two weeks and reminded of this obligation. Failure to comply with these expectations would be grounds for termination of UI payments.
2. JSA plus Training and Relocation. The same treatment as JSA only, but in addition, at the individual counseling session subjects were informed of the availability of funds for vocational-training courses or expenses of relocation and job search in another area. (The option was training or relocation, but not both.) Counseling on training options was provided to those interested. As anticipated,

less than 1 percent of those offered the relocation option accepted assistance for that purpose; the incremental effect of this treatment over JSA only is essentially the training effect.

3. JSA plus Reemployment Bonus. The same treatment as JSA only, but, in addition, at the individual counseling session subjects were offered a reemployment bonus. The maximum bonus was equal to half of the remaining UI entitlement at the time of the interview (the average of the maximum bonus was $1,644). The bonus declined at the rate of 10 percent per week until UI was no longer available to the subject. The bonus was not available if the new job was with the subject's last employer or a relative, or if it was temporary, seasonal, or part-time. The subject received 60 percent of the bonus if employed 4 weeks, and the balance if employed 12 weeks.

4. Controls faced the usual obligation to look for work, but the use of existing job search services was voluntary.

OUTCOMES OF INTEREST: (1) UI payments; (2) Employment; and (3) Earnings.

SAMPLE SIZE: Controls, 2,385; JSA only, 2,416; JSA plus Training and Relocation, 3,810; JSA plus Reemployment Bonus, 2,449.

TARGET POPULATION: The treatments were intended for dislocated workers. The following types of UI claimants were therefore screened out of the sample: those who never received the first payment (they found work or were ineligible), those who had worked less than three years for their previous employer, those less than 25 years old, those who had definite recall dates from the last employer, those hired through a union hiring hall, and certain types of special claimants (e.g., ex-Armed Forces, ex-federal government, interstate movers).

NUMBER OF TREATMENT GROUPS: Four (with one control group).

NUMBER AND LOCATION OF SITES: Ten unemployment insurance (UI) offices in New Jersey. The sites were chosen to represent the New Jersey UI recipient population, and were located in Paterson, Hackensack, Jersey City, Butler, Bloomfield, Newark, Elizabeth, Perth Amboy, Burlington, and Deptford.

RESEARCH COMPONENTS:
   Process analysis: Conducted. Essentially the treatments were delivered as planned. Many subjects were excused from portions of the JSA treatments because they could not read, speak, or understand English well enough to benefit from them.

Impact analysis: Conducted with ordinary least squares (OLS), logit.

Benefit–cost analysis: Conducted from claimant, agency budget, government budget, and social perspectives.

MAJOR FINDINGS:

	JSA Only	JSA plus Training/Relocation	JSA plus Bonus
Change in UI benefits	−$87*	−$81*	−$170*
Change in weeks of UI payments, benefit year	−0.47*	−0.48*	−0.97*
Change in probability of exhausting benefits	−0.028*	−0.017	−0.037*
Change in weeks employed, benefit year:			
1st quarter	2.3*	1.9*	2.8*
2nd quarter	4.9*	2.8*	5.0*
3rd quarter	4.2*	2.2	2.3
4th quarter	2.8	1.7	0.6
Change in earnings ($)			
1st quarter	125*	82	160*
2nd quarter	263*	103*	278*
3rd quarter	171	83	131
4th quarter	49	77	22

*An effect significantly different from zero at a two-tailed 90 percent confidence level, and often at higher confidence levels.

1. Subgroup analysis indicates that "the treatments were less successful for individuals who faced hard-core, structural unemployment problems, such as blue-collar workers, workers from durable-goods manufacturing industries, and permanently separated workers."

2. The six-year follow-up found further significant reductions in regular UI receipt two years after the initial benefit year for the JSA-only group (−$94 and −0.53 weeks paid) and for the JSA plus Bonus group (−$78 and −0.44 weeks paid). The JSA plus Bonus group also received significantly fewer dollars in the third year (−$65). No statistically significant long-term effects on employment and earnings were found.

3. Claimants who received on-the-job training experienced high levels of employment and earnings throughout the period following the initial claim relative to the JSA-only claimants. Those who received classroom training initially experienced relatively lower earnings and less employment in the first three quarters, but higher employment and earnings in subsequent quarters.

4. Long-term findings suggest that all of the treatment components may have contributed to longer-term impacts. It is suggested that the treatments generated jobs that were more stable than those found by control group members.
5. When longer-term impacts from the six-year follow-up are included in the benefit-cost analysis, the results were more favorable than they were initially. The results suggest that all three treatments offered positive net benefits to claimants and to society as a whole, relative to existing services. The JSA-only treatment and the JSA plus Bonus treatment also led to net gains for the government. The JSA plus Training and Relocation treatment was expensive for the government sector, resulting in net losses.

TIME TRENDS IN FINDINGS: As shown above.

DESIGN ISSUES: The major issue is covered under "Generalizability," below. Subgroup analysis seems to consist mostly of the use of interaction terms (e.g., a dummy for industry multiplied by a dummy for treatment) in the regression. This type of analysis assumes that the slope coefficients on continuous variables, like prior earnings, are identical for all groups. Separate regressions for distinct groups might have been useful.

REPLICABILITY: Replicable.

GENERALIZABILITY: It is unlikely that a real social program would be set up using the particular eligibility criteria selected for this experiment. Only about one-fourth of the UI claimant population was eligible for the experiment. It is noteworthy that the treatments were less successful for the subgroups most typical of the population the experimental treatments were intended to assist (older workers, blue-collar workers).

FUNDING SOURCE: U.S. Department of Labor, Employment and Training Administration. Key personnel: Stephen Wandner and Wayne Zajac.

TREATMENT ADMINISTRATOR: New Jersey Department of Labor. Key personnel: Frederick Kniesler, Nancy Snyder, and Roger Emig.

EVALUATOR: Mathematica Policy Research (MPR). Key personnel: Walter Corson, Paul T. Decker, and Shari Miller Dunstan.

ENABLING LEGISLATION: None.

POLICY EFFECTS: Stephen Wander has stated that this experiment related to an ongoing debate in Congress over the appropriate government response to dislocated workers: a passive income maintenance approach or an active intervention approach. Elements of the New

Jersey model (early identification of dislocated workers, referrals to job search assistance) were adopted in the Economic Dislocation and Worker Adjustment Assistance Act. To encourage early intervention, needs-based stipends under that act are available to workers after the 13th week of an unemployment insurance (UI) claim only if they are in a training program. MPR found that the additional costs per claimant from adding the reemployment bonus as designed in New Jersey to the Job Search Assistance program were greater than the additional UI savings. Wander stated that this finding has led to other experiments with different bonus designs.

INFORMATION SOURCES: Walter Corson, Paul T. Decker, Shari Miller Dunstan, and Anne R. Gordon, with Patricia Anderson and John Homrighausen, "The New Jersey Unemployment Insurance Reemployment Demonstration Project: Final Evaluation Report," U.S. Department of Labor, Employment and Training Administration, Unemployment Insurance Occasional Paper 89-3, April 1989; Walter Corson and Joshua Hamilton, "The New Jersey Unemployment Insurance Reemployment Demonstration Project: Six-Year Follow-Up and Summary Report," rev. ed., U.S. Department of Labor, Employment and Training Administration, Unemployment Insurance Occasional Paper 96-2, January 1996.

PUBLIC-USE ACCESS TO DATA: Public-use file available; contact National Technical Information Service, Springfield, Virginia.

WASHINGTON STATE ALTERNATIVE WORK SEARCH EXPERIMENT

SUMMARY: This demonstration, conducted from 1986 through 1988, tested the effects of alternative work-search policies on a large sample of unemployment insurance claimants. Subjects were followed for one year.

COST: Battelle Human Affairs Research Centers reported that they received approximately $70,000 for the evaluation. Washington State Employment Security Department (ESD) reported program costs of approximately $100,000. Both sources acknowledge considerable donated services on this project.

TIME FRAME: Enrollment period: July 1986–August 1987; data collected for one year from enrollment; final report, January 1991.

TREATMENTS TESTED: Four variations of work-search policies:

Activity or Service	Group A	Group B (Control)	Group C	Group D
		Treatment Group		
Presentation of benefit rights	Special group interview	Regular group interview	Regular group interview	Regular group interview
Continued-claims process	By telephone, as necessary	Submit forms bi-weekly	Submit forms bi-weekly	Submit forms bi-weekly
Initial work search directive	Active search for work	Active search for work	Active search for work	Active search for work
Subsequent work search directive	None	Three contacts per week; later to report for eligibility review interview (ERI)	Directed to report for ERI 4 or 5 weeks into claim period	Directed to attend job search workshop after about 4 weeks; later to report for ERI
Eligibility review interview	None	13–15 weeks after filing claim; focus on UI eligibility	Individualized timing of ERI, with possible increase in work search requirements	13–15 weeks after filing claim; focus on employability development

OUTCOMES OF INTEREST: (1) UI benefit receipt; (2) Employment; and (3) Earnings.

SAMPLE SIZE: Total, 9,634. By treatment group: A, 2,246; B, 2,871; C, 1,964; D, 2,553.

TARGET POPULATION: Unemployed individuals filing new claims for unemployment insurance (UI) benefits. Claimants with employer or referral-union attachment were excluded.

NUMBER OF TREATMENT GROUPS: Four (including control—group B)

NUMBER AND LOCATION OF SITES: One—Tacoma, Washington.

RESEARCH COMPONENTS:

Process analysis: Looked at specific behaviors of local office staff related to ESD services.

Impact analysis: Comparison of means; regression; and probit models.

Benefit–cost analysis: Conducted, though not in-depth. All information and calculations are not presented in the cited report.

MAJOR FINDINGS:

1. Claimants in the exception-reporting group (group A) received significantly greater average UI benefits (+$265) than did control group members. They also received benefits for a significantly longer period (+3.3 weeks) than control group. Further, they were significantly more likely to exhaust their benefits.
2. The intensive work search group (group D) members received $68 less than controls in total UI benefits; however this is only significant at about the .11 level. They received payments for .5 fewer weeks than controls, significant at the .1 level.
3. Very small differences in UI payments and in period of receipt between group C and control group members were observed. None were statistically significant.
4. Few significant differences were noted among group members concerning employment and earnings. The more rapid reemployment of group D members did not result in lower earnings or hourly wage rates.

TIME TRENDS IN FINDINGS: There was a significant difference in the earnings for group A. Individuals in that group earned hourly wages that were 3 percent higher than controls, though they were less likely to be working during the first quarter following their claim. These results dissipate when examined over the complete year.

Overall impacts for groups A and D tend to be smaller for the full benefit year than for the first spell of UI receipt.

DESIGN ISSUE: As of May 1987, no additional claimants were assigned to group A, owing to preliminary findings suggesting that the costs of this treatment to the UI Trust Fund were substantial. For the remainder of the study, these claimants were assigned to group D. This required minor adjustments in the modeling.

REPLICABILITY: Replicable.

GENERALIZABILITY: The demonstration was conducted only in the Tacoma office, which serves Pierce County, the second most populated county in Washington. The county did have a diverse labor market and unemployment rates similar to the state average (8.6 in 1985 and declining during the period of study). Racial/ethnic composition was "reasonably representative" of the state as a whole, although African Americans are over-represented (Pierce County—86.5 percent white, 6.8 percent African American; Washington State—90.5 percent white, 2.9 percent African American).

Although difficult to generalize from one site, these findings fit well with those from similar demonstration projects.

FUNDING SOURCES: U.S. Department of Labor, Washington State Employment Security Department (ESD), and the W. E. Upjohn Institute. Key personnel: Gary Bodeutsch, Kathy Countryman, and Judy Johnson.

TREATMENT ADMINISTRATOR: Tacoma Job Service Center, operating under direction of ESD.

EVALUATOR: Battelle Human Affairs Research Centers. Terry Johnson and Daniel Klepinger, project directors.

ENABLING LEGISLATION: None reported.

POLICY EFFECTS: According to the project evaluator, these results were "definitely used" in the federal policy debate regarding alternative plans in the area of unemployment. Testimony regarding the project results was submitted in 1991 to a U.S. Senate subcommittee and was partly responsible for decisions not to implement exception reporting methods (treatment A in this project).

INFORMATION SOURCES: Terry R. Johnson and Daniel H. Klepinger, *Evaluation of the Impacts of the Washington Alternative Work Search Experiment: Final Report*, UI Occasional Paper 91-4, U.S. Department of Labor, 1991.

PUBLIC-USE ACCESS TO DATA: Available through U.S. Department of Labor.

NEVADA CONCENTRATED EMPLOYMENT PROGRAM (CEP)

SUMMARY: This demonstration, conducted from 1988 to 1989, tested the effects of enhanced employment services and training on a large sample of unemployed workers. Subjects were followed for one year.

COST: Total CEP project costs—$312,948. Evaluation costs were limited because automated administrative data systems were used.

TIME FRAME: Demonstration period, July 1988–June 1989; data collected, same period.

TREATMENT(S) TESTED: The Concentrated Employment Program (CEP) program included the development of an employment plan, job search assistance (workshops, referrals, and placements), and training, if necessary. The control group received normal Employment Service (ES) and unemployment insurance (UI) services.

OUTCOMES OF INTEREST: Unemployment Insurance benefits and duration of unemployment.

SAMPLE SIZE: Total, 2,962; treatment, 1,424; control, 1,538.

TARGET POPULATION: Unemployed workers.

NUMBER OF TREATMENT GROUPS: Two (including a control).

NUMBER AND LOCATION OF SITES: Two—Sparks and North Las Vegas, Nevada.

RESEARCH COMPONENTS:

Process analysis: Special attention was paid to sample characteristics, participation rates, and service delivery.

Impact analysis: Comparison of means.

Benefit–cost analysis: Conducted.

MAJOR FINDINGS:

1. The CEP program significantly reduced the average duration of UI benefits for all treatment subgroups. For the entire sample, excluding trainees, the program reduced average weekly duration by 2.1 weeks (11.9 weeks for the treatment group versus 14 weeks for controls). Including the trainees increased the average duration of the treatment group, though treatment–control differences remained statistically significant (treatment, 12.4 weeks; control, 14 weeks).
2. The CEP program had the greatest impact on females and claimants over 55 years of age.
3. For every dollar spent on providing enhanced services (excluding training), the program reduced UI payout by $2.39. Although more complicated to measure, estimated benefit–cost ratios when training was included ranged from 1.1 to 1.64, depending on the assumptions made.

TIME TRENDS IN FINDINGS: None.

DESIGN ISSUES:

1. Due to high CEP workloads, the "one-to-one" random assignment design was altered. Claimants remaining in the selection pool after assignments to treatment and control groups were made were all put into the control group. Although the larger number of control

participants does not present a problem, the alteration of random assignment led to some significant differences between the groups. A total of 120 older males were randomly removed from the control group to rectify the problem. The resulting groups were then not significantly different, but could have still differed on unobservable characteristics.

2. One hundred and thirty CEP claimants who received training were excluded from the test, which assessed the non-training impact on UI duration. Similar exclusions were not made with the control group owing to the difficulty in ascertaining training status. This probably introduces an upward bias on the CEP program impact.

3. The design did not incorporate a control group for CEP trainees, thus making it difficult to assess long-term training impacts. This does not cause problems in comparing *all* controls with *all* experimentals.

REPLICABILITY: Replicable.

GENERALIZABILITY: Designed to generalize to the entire state. Findings are supported by a prior Nevada study of the JTPA Title II program and the Nevada Claimant Placement Program. Although claimant characteristics were provided (claimants had an average age of 41 years, 17.4 percent were ethnic minorities, 38.2 percent were female, and they averaged 12.4 years of education), these characteristics were not compared with any larger population.

FUNDING SOURCE: UI Penalty and Interest fund of the Nevada Employment Security Department. Key personnel: Stan Jones, executive director.

TREATMENT ADMINISTRATOR: Nevada Employment Security Department. Local Job Training Partnership Act (JTPA) entities were responsible for the training component. Key personnel: Stan Jones.

EVALUATOR: Nevada Employment Security Department. Key personnel: Jim Hanna and Zina Turney.

ENABLING LEGISLATION: None.

POLICY EFFECTS: When these results were presented to the Nevada legislature, they decided to levy a .05 percent tax on state payrolls to fund the continuation of the program. The CEP remains a standard component of the UI program. The evaluators also testified before the U.S. Congress, and other states have adopted similar programs.

INFORMATION SOURCES: James Hanna and Zina Turney, "The Economic Impact of the Nevada Claimant Employment Program," in U.S. Dept. of Labor, Unemployment Insurance Service, *UI Research*

Exchange: *Information on Unemployment Research*, Unemployment Insurance Occasional Paper 90-4, Washington, D.C., 1990, 79–92; "Nevada Claimant Employment Program," in Esther R. Johnson, editor, *Reemployment Services to Unemployed Workers Having Difficulty Becoming Reemployed*, Unemp. Ins. Occasional Paper 90-2, U.S. Dept. of Labor, Unemployment Insurance Service, Washington, D.C., 1990, 150–163.

PUBLIC USE ACCESS TO DATA: Not available.

PENNSYLVANIA REEMPLOYMENT BONUS DEMONSTRATION

SUMMARY: This demonstration, which was conducted in 1988 and 1989, tested the effects of a reemployment bonus payment on a large sample of unemployment insurance (UI) recipients. Subjects were followed for one year.

COST: Design and evaluation costs, approximately $990,000. Per-claimant expenditures range from $70 per claimant for treatment 1 to $180 per claimant for treatment 4.

TIME FRAME: Demonstration period, July 1988–1989; data collected, same period. Final report, September 1991.

TREATMENTS TESTED: Five combinations of bonus amount and qualification period (time allotted to get a job and receive a bonus) were tested. A sixth group did not receive the job search assistance (JSA) component to test the effects of this component.

Group	Bonus Amount	Qualification Period	JSA Workshop Offered
0 (control)	0	0	No
1	3 × WBA*	6 weeks	Yes
2	3 × WBA	12 weeks	Yes
3	6 × WBA	6 weeks	Yes
4	6 × WBA	12 weeks	Yes
5	6 × WBA, declining	12 weeks	Yes
6	6 × WBA	12 weeks	No

*Weekly benefit amount.

OUTCOMES OF INTEREST: (1) UI receipt; (2) Employment; and (3) Earnings.

SAMPLE SIZE: Total selected, 15,005; analysis sample, 14,086; control, 3,392. Group 1, 1,395; group 2, 2,456; group 3, 1,910; groups 4 and 6 (combined for analysis), 3,073; group 5, 1,860.

TARGET POPULATION: Eligible UI claimants. Demonstration excluded those with a definite recall date, union attachment, filers of transitional claims, and filers separated from their jobs due to labor disputes.

NUMBER OF TREATMENT GROUPS: Seven (including control).

NUMBER AND LOCATION OF SITES: Twelve local UI/JS (Job Service) offices throughout Pennsylvania: Coatesville, Philadelphia North, Philadelphia Uptown, Reading, Lancaster, Lewistown, Butler, Connellsville, McKeesport, Erie, Pittston, and Scranton.

RESEARCH COMPONENTS:
Process analysis: Conducted—with special attention given to eligibility, JSA workshop, and verification of bonus amounts and claims.
Impact analysis: Conducted using comparison of means with regression.
Benefit–cost analysis: Conducted.

MAJOR FINDINGS:
1. Bonus offers significantly reduced UI receipt during the benefit year. Estimated impacts were generally larger for the more generous bonus offers.
2. Evidence suggests that the treatment increased employment and earnings. However, the significance of these findings differs for wage record data versus interview data. The latter provides stronger evidence of a positive effect.
3. Bonus offers yielded net benefits to claimants and to society as a whole. From the perspective of the UI system, bonus offers were not cost-effective, generating net losses for the UI trust fund. Some treatments generated positive net benefits for the government (treatments 2 and 3), and the government either broke even or incurred a modest loss for the other treatments.
4. Reemployment bonuses can be implemented successfully as part of the existing UI system. However, the job search component was ineffective due to very low participation rates.

TIME TRENDS IN FINDINGS: None.

DESIGN ISSUES: The low participation rate (less than 3 percent) for the job search workshop, due to lack of interest among claimants, led to the combining of two treatment groups for analysis. According to the final report, the bonus "may have provided a disincentive to participate in the workshop."

REPLICABILITY: Replicable.

GENERALIZABILITY: Designed to generalize to the entire state. UI/JS offices were selected randomly with a probability of selection proportional to caseload size. Site characteristics closely matched statewide characteristics in many salient respects. The local economy was quite strong during the demonstration and the unemployment rate was low (4.5%). Effects of bonus and the ability of participants to meet qualification requirements may differ under more adverse economic conditions. Examining the four similarly designed bonus experiments together suggests generalizability across states.

FUNDING SOURCE: U.S. Department of Labor (DOL). Key personnel: William Coyne, initial project officer; Wayne Zajac, project officer for operational and analysis phases.

TREATMENT ADMINISTRATOR: Pennsylvania Department of Labor and Industry. Key personnel: Frances Curtin and Robert Peebles, project coordinators.

EVALUATOR: Mathematica Policy Research. Principal investigators: Walter Corson and Stuart Kerachsky; other key personnel: Paul Decker and Shari Dunstan.

ENABLING LEGISLATION: None.

POLICY EFFECTS: The U.S. Department of Labor cited this study in 1994, proposing to allow states to change their UI laws, but the legislation was not enacted. The bonus concept continues to be examined at DOL.

INFORMATION SOURCE: Walter Corson, Paul Decker, Shari Dunstan, and Stuart Kerachsky, *Pennsylvania Reemployment Bonus Demonstration: Final Report*, Mathematica Policy Research, September 1991.

PUBLIC-USE ACCESS TO DATA: Available through the U.S. Department of Labor.

REEMPLOY MINNESOTA (REM)

SUMMARY: This demonstration, conducted from 1988 to 1990, tested the effects of intensive case management services on a large sample of unemployed workers. Subjects were followed for two years.

COST: Total program cost, $835,000. The evaluation was done in-house. Evaluation costs were not separated other than hiring a research analyst for three months at $10,000.

TIME FRAME: Demonstration period, July 1988–June 1990; data collected, same period.

TREATMENTS TESTED: More personalized and intensive unemployment insurance (UI) services, including case management, intensive job search assistance and job matching, claimant targeting for special assistance, and a job-seeking skills seminar. The control group received regular UI services.

OUTCOMES OF INTEREST: Duration and amount of UI benefits.

SAMPLE SIZE: Treatment, 4,212. The control group was roughly 10 times as large as the treatment group. Those randomly selected were in the treatment group, all claimants not chosen and not excluded were in the control group.

TARGET POPULATION: Unemployed workers. A number of claimants were screened out, including those on short-term layoff, union-attached workers, and claimants enrolled in training.

NUMBER OF TREATMENT GROUPS: Two (including controls).

NUMBER AND LOCATION OF SITES: Ten offices: 8 in the Minneapolis/St. Paul area and 1 in both Duluth and Mankato (outstate).

RESEARCH COMPONENTS:

Process analysis: Job Services database and a survey were used to examine client characteristics, satisfaction, and participation.

Impact analysis: Regression analysis.

Benefit–cost analysis: Not conducted, though cost savings are reported.

MAJOR FINDINGS:
1. During the first year of the program, the treatment group's average claim duration was 11.16 weeks, compared to 15.24 weeks for the control group. Multiplied by the average weekly benefit amount for the treatment group, the result was an estimated $1,476,000 cost savings for the UI Trust Fund.
2. Over the two-year period, the average claim reduction for the treatment group was 4.32 weeks. This translates to a gross savings of $3,285,554 and a net savings (subtracting administrative costs) of $1,570,554.
3. In the metro area, among clients who attributed their reemployment to area office services, the Reemploy Minnesota (REM) group

was reemployed at a significantly higher rate than were regular clients (35 percent versus 25 percent). In the outstate offices, there was no significant difference in the reemployment rate (both REM and regular client rates were approximately 35 percent).

TIME TRENDS IN FINDINGS: None.

DESIGN ISSUES:
1. There were problems with program coordination between the intake staff and the case managers. Without cooperation and vigilance of the intake staff, the case managers could not keep their caseloads (40 clients) full.
2. Because caseloads were at times full, there were occasional breaches of the random assignment design. There was no purposeful selection of clients based on any client characteristics, but not all individuals had an equal chance of being selected at all times of the year.
3. The REM case managers were all volunteers and were eager to do well with this program. They were the "best and brightest," because there was a push to make an impression on the administration. This group may well have been different from the staff that worked on the control cases.
4. People coming in with large severance packages were put into the control group rather than excluded. They differed from the treatment group participants in a number of ways. They did not begin receiving benefits right away and usually came from higher-paying jobs. Although it is not clear how many claimants were in this category, this could pose a threat to internal validity.

REPLICABILITY: Replicable. Forms and procedures are available from the Minnesota Department of Jobs and Training.

GENERALIZABILITY: Designed to generalize to the entire state. Approximately 50 percent of all new claims went into the sample (treatment and control). The remainder were excluded for reasons mentioned above. The REM sample differed from regular UI clients on gender (10 percent more women), salary (earned 10 percent less), and occupation. Also, several of the design and implementation issues mentioned above may affect generalizability.

FUNDING SOURCE: Unemployment Insurance Contingent Account of the Minnesota Department of Jobs and Training.

TREATMENT ADMINISTRATOR: Minnesota Department of Jobs and Training. Key personnel: Tom Romens.

EVALUATOR: Minnesota Department of Jobs and Training. Key personnel: Tom Romens and Steve Scholl.

ENABLING LEGISLATION: None.

INFORMATION SOURCES: Several in-house documents obtained from the Minnesota Department of Jobs and Training, including a copy of the original proposal as well as Steven R. Scholl's *Data Analysis: Reemploy Minnesota Evaluation*, Research and Statistics Office, Minnesota Department of Jobs and Training, October 1989. Also U.S. Department of Labor, Employment and Training Administration, *Reemployment Services to Unemployed Workers Having Difficulty Becoming Reemployed*, Unemployment Insurance Occasional Paper 90-2, 1990.

PUBLIC-USE ACCESS TO DATA: Not available.

WASHINGTON STATE REEMPLOYMENT BONUS EXPERIMENT

SUMMARY: This demonstration, conducted from 1988 through 1990, tested the effects of a reemployment bonus on a large sample of the unemployed who were applying for unemployment insurance (UI) benefits. Subjects were followed for one year.

COST: Approximately $450,000 for design and evaluation.

TIME FRAME: February 1988–January 1990; final report, 1992.

TREATMENTS TESTED: The reemployment bonus had two parts: the bonus amount and the qualification period (the time allotted for applicant to find a job in order to receive a bonus payment). This demonstration varied these two components in the following way:

	Qualification Period	
Bonus Amount	.2 × Duration + 1[a]	.4 × Duration + 1[b]
2 × WBA	Treatment 1	T4
4 × WBA	T2	T5
6 × WBA	T3	T6

Notes: Duration refers to the number of weeks that a claimant would be eligible for UI benefits. The control group received no bonus payment. WBA = Weekly Benefit Amount.
a. Longest period, 7 weeks.
b. Longest period, 13 weeks.

OUTCOMES OF INTEREST: (1) Weeks of insured unemployment and (2) UI receipt.

SAMPLE SIZE: Treatment group, 12,451 (T1—2,239, T2—2,343, T3—1,577, T4—2,380, T5—2,344, T6—1,530); control, 3,083.

TARGET POPULATION: Eligible UI claimants filing new claims. Contrary to previous studies, claimants awaiting recall to their previous employer and union hiring hall members were *not* excluded (though they were not paid a bonus if they accepted employment under these conditions). Filers of interstate claims were excluded.

NUMBER OF TREATMENT GROUPS: Seven (including control).

NUMBER AND LOCATION OF SITES: The experiment was conducted in 21 of Washington's 31 regional Job Service Centers (JSCs) located throughout the state. The project's final report (p. 26) provides a complete listing of sites.

RESEARCH COMPONENTS:

Process analysis: Operations were closely monitored through computer checks and personal visits.

Impact analysis: Conducted using regression.

Benefit–cost analysis: Conducted.

MAJOR FINDINGS:

1. High bonus-level treatments produced substantial and statistically significant reductions in UI compensation and weeks of insured unemployment.
2. Three of the four low- and middle-level bonus treatments (treatments 1, 2, and 5) failed to produce statistically significant effects.
3. There were few statistically significant differences in the subgroup analyses, although estimates suggest that males respond more than females to bonus incentives; that whites and Hispanics respond more than blacks, but less than other racial/ethnic groups; and that older claimants respond more than younger claimants.
4. No significant impacts on overall earnings were produced.
5. From a societal perspective, the bonus program has large net benefits. From the perspective of the UI system, net losses were incurred. For the government as a whole, the bonus program is roughly a break-even proposition.

TIME TRENDS IN FINDINGS: None are reported; the follow-up period is relatively short.

DESIGN ISSUES:

1. Despite the use of random assignment, few impacts were statistically significant prior to the introduction of control variables due

to differences among the treatment groups. The evaluators do not feel that random assignment was compromised.

2. There was always a question of adequate communication and understanding of the program by the subjects. Approximately 45 percent of those eligible for the bonus payment did not take advantage of the program (i.e., claim their bonus).

3. Entry and displacement effects, which would be likely to occur in a fully operational program, were not captured by the design in this demonstration. Also, to avoid a negative employment effect, some bonuses were paid to claimants who may not have been eligible for nonmonetary reasons (e.g., attachment to a previous employer or union hall).

REPLICABILITY: Replicable; the final report provides great detail regarding implementation and design.

GENERALIZABILITY: Designed to generalize to the entire state. The 21 JSCs handled 85 percent of the state's claimant population. Eligible claimants were included in the sample even if they did not receive any UI benefits. A large number of claimants (33 percent) assigned to the experiment did not participate. The cost of a fully implemented program could be substantially increased if widescale knowledge of the bonuses led to larger rates of participation.

The findings of this demonstration are consistent with the other reemployment bonus experiments that have been conducted. Therefore, results should be considered generalizable across states, as well.

FUNDING SOURCE: Core funding came from the Alfred P. Sloan Foundation (Albert Rees, president). Additional funding came from the U.S. Department of Labor, Employment and Training Administration. Key personnel: Stephen Wandner, deputy director of the Office of Legislation and Actuarial Services.

TREATMENT ADMINISTRATOR: State of Washington Employment Security Department. Key personnel: Jim Wolfe, UI assistant commissioner; Gary Bodeutsch and Kathy Countryman, project managers; Patricia Remy, project coordinator.

EVALUATOR: W. E. Upjohn Institute for Employment Research. Principal investigators: Robert Spiegelman and Christopher O'Leary.

ENABLING LEGISLATION: None.

INFORMATION SOURCES: Robert G. Spiegelman, Christopher J. O'Leary, and Kenneth J. Kline, *The Washington Reemployment Bonus Experiment: Final Report*, Unemployment Insurance Occasional Paper

92-6, U.S. Dept. of Labor, Unemployment Insurance Service, Washington, 1992.

PUBLIC-USE ACCESS TO DATA: Available through W. E. Upjohn Institute.

WASHINGTON AND MASSACHUSETTS UNEMPLOYMENT INSURANCE SELF-EMPLOYMENT WORK SEARCH DEMONSTRATIONS

SUMMARY: This demonstration, conducted from 1989 to 1991, tested the effects of business start-up services, including financial assistance, counseling, and workshop sessions, on a large sample of the recently unemployed. Subjects were followed for three years.

COST: Research component, approximately $2 million.

TIME FRAME: Demonstration period—Washington State: September 1989–March 1991; Massachusetts: May 1990–April 1993; data collected, same period; final report, December 1994.

TREATMENTS TESTED: Washington State: Subjects were offered four business training sessions; they continued to receive regular unemployment insurance (UI) payments and, in addition, were eligible for a lump-sum payment after achieving five program milestones (e.g., completion of training sessions and development of an acceptable business plan). Massachusetts: Subjects attended a one-day training session, an individual counseling session, and six workshop sessions on a variety of business topics. They continued to receive regular UI benefits and were exempted from UI work search requirements. Controls in both states remained eligible for regular UI benefits.

OUTCOMES OF INTEREST: (1) Self-employment; (2) Combined self- and wage and salary employment; and (3) Earnings.

SAMPLE SIZE: Washington: treatment, 755; control, 752. Massachusetts: treatment, 614; control, 608.

TARGET POPULATION: New UI claimants were targeted. Filers of interstate claims, filers who were employer-attached (i.e., on standby to return to their former employer), and those who were under 18 were excluded. Massachusetts also excluded new claimants with a low predicted probability of exhausting UI benefits.

NUMBER OF TREATMENT GROUPS: Two (including controls) in each state.

NUMBER AND LOCATION OF SITES: Six sites in Washington State: Vancouver, Olympia, King County, Snohomish County, Wenatchee, and Yakima; seven sites in Massachusetts: Gloucester, Greenfield, Lowell, New Bedford, Roxbury, Springfield, and Woburn.

RESEARCH COMPONENTS:
   Process analysis: Conducted. Focused on recruitment and intake procedures as well as the timing of service delivery.
   Impact analysis: Conducted. Comparison of means.
   Benefit–cost analysis: Conducted.

MAJOR FINDINGS: Results based on the longer of two observation periods (33 months in Washington, 31 months in Massachusetts).
1. Treatment group members in both states were much more likely than controls to have had a self-employment experience (+ 22 percent in Washington; + 12 percent in Massachusetts) and to have spent more time per year in self-employment (+ 2 months in Washington; + 0.8 months in Massachusetts). The Washington group was more likely to be still self-employed at the time of the second follow-up survey (the experimental–control difference was not statistically significant).
2. Annual self-employment earnings increased significantly in Washington (+ $1,675). These earnings also increased in Massachusetts, though not significantly.
3. In Washington, claimants' likelihood of working in wage and salary employment, and their earnings from that employment, were significantly reduced. Wage and salary earnings for the Massachusetts group increased significantly.
4. Combining self- and wage employment, the treatment groups in both states significantly increased their likelihood of employment and time employed when compared to control groups. Further, a significant increase in total annual earnings was seen in Massachusetts (+ $3,053).
5. The Washington treatment had a significant positive impact on the employment of nonparticipants (family and nonfamily employees).
6. The Washington demonstration significantly increased total program benefit payments. Taking into account both regular UI benefits and the lump-sum payment, total benefits were increased by approximately $1,000. In contrast, the Massachusetts demonstration significantly reduced receipt of total benefits by nearly $900.

7. The Massachusetts treatment generated large net gains from each of several benefit–cost perspectives (participant, nonparticipant, society, and government). The Washington treatment generated net gains from the perspective of participants and society, but resulted in net losses from nonparticipants and government perspectives.

TIME TRENDS IN FINDINGS: In Massachusetts, treatment group members were more likely than controls to have had a self-employment experience, but there was no difference in the percentage of self-employment after 33 months (at the time of the second follow-up survey). No time trends were reported for the Washington group.

DESIGN ISSUES:
1. In both states, only a small fraction (3.6 percent in Washington, 1.9 percent in Massachusetts) of targeted UI claimants met the initial requirements of attending an orientation meeting and submitting an application. Random assignment occurred at this point.
2. Massachusetts had legislative requirements to focus on UI claimants who were likely to exhaust their UI benefits. Sample selection was based on a statistical model that predicted claimants' likelihood of benefit exhaustion. Those with low predicted probability were eliminated from the target group. There were no comparable requirements in Washington.

REPLICABILITY: Replicable. Note design differences between the two states (e.g., lump-sum payment in Washington, not Massachusetts). Several locations, domestic and foreign, are currently replicating this study.

GENERALIZABILITY: Interest in self-employment is concentrated in a specific subgroup of the unemployed (males, ages 36–55, better educated, and with experience in professional, managerial, and technical occupations). Washington used a purposive site selection method based on an index of representativeness. Selected sites had the characteristics and diversity to enhance generalizability. Massachusetts' sites were self-selected, though they represented a wide geographic distribution and mix of salient characteristics.

FUNDING SOURCE: U.S. Department of Labor, Employment and Training Administration, Unemployment Insurance Service. Key personnel: Jon Messenger and Stephen Wandner, project officers.

TREATMENT ADMINISTRATORS: Massachusetts—Department of Employment and Training (DET); Bonnie Dallinger, project manager. Washington—State Employment Security Department (ESD); Judy Johnson, project manager.

EVALUATORS: Abt Associates. Key personnel: Jacob Benus. Battelle Memorial Institute. Key personnel: Terry Johnson.

ENABLING LEGISLATION: Section 9152 of the Omnibus Budget Reconciliation Act of 1987 (Massachusetts only).

POLICY EFFECTS: According to the researchers, this demonstration had a "great impact" on the policy debate. It was cited by Congress, as part of the North American Free Trade Agreement (NAFTA), in the decision to authorize states to implement self-employment programs.

INFORMATION SOURCE: Jacob M. Benus, Terry R. Johnson, Michelle Wood, Neelima Grover, and Theodore Shen, *Self-Employment Programs—A New Reemployment Strategy: Final Impact Analysis of the Washington and Massachusetts Self-Employment Demonstrations*, U.S. Department of Labor, Employment and Training Administration, Unemployment Insurance Occasional Paper 95-4, Washington, 1995.

PUBLIC-USE ACCESS TO DATA: Available through U.S. Department of Labor.

MINORITY MALE OPPORTUNITY AND RESPONSIBILITY PROGRAM

SUMMARY: This demonstration, conducted between 1991 and 1994, tested the effects of intensive case management on a small sample of unemployed minority males. Subjects were followed for up to 12 months. The design was not implemented as planned, owing to a number of difficulties.

COST: Evaluation funded at $12,500, although the evaluator felt the actual cost was greater owing to considerable donated services.

TIME FRAME: Demonstration period, November 1991–August 1994; final report, 1995.

TREATMENTS TESTED: Program services included intensive case management, educational skills development, job search and placement activities, and Job Club. Control participants received limited services and engaged in independent job search.

OUTCOMES OF INTEREST: (1) Employment and wages; (2) Educational levels; (3) Health; and (4) Family functioning.

SAMPLE SIZE: Analysis sample, 168; treatment, 79; control, 89.

TARGET POPULATION: Unemployed minority males ages 18–34. Additional selection criteria included: low income, at least one child, and low academic achievement.

NUMBER OF TREATMENT GROUPS: Two (including control).

NUMBER AND LOCATION OF SITES: One—Milwaukee, Wisconsin.

RESEARCH COMPONENTS:

Process analysis: A participant observer attended several sessions and interviewed program participants and staff members to check implementation of the program.

Impact analysis: Conducted with multivariate regression analysis.

Benefit–cost analysis: Not conducted.

MAJOR FINDINGS:
1. Treatment group was significantly more likely to be employed at closure (treatment group, 28 percent; control group, 10 percent) and at follow-up (treatment, 47 percent; control, 12 percent) than was the control group. There was little difference between the groups in the nature of the employment or the wages received.
2. No significant differences were found between groups on educational achievement or health status. Only one significant change was found (baseline to follow-up) on measures of family relationships. The treatment group reported an increase in family conflicts, a finding counter to program hypotheses. The project report offered no explanation for this finding.
3. Frequency of case manager contacts and past employment experience were significantly related to the probability of current employment. Educational achievement was also found to be predictive of employment.

TIME TRENDS IN FINDINGS: There was insufficient data to document any time trends.

DESIGN ISSUES:
1. Overall implementation of program and services was "far less intensive" than planned, owing to higher than expected caseloads and minimal compliance from some participants. Further, the follow-up return rate was low, with only 38 percent of participants returning for interviews and testing.
2. Data on approximately 100 participants entering the project prior to June 1992 were discarded owing to design contamination and inconsistent data collection and reporting. Thus, the first year of the project was treated as an unevaluated pilot effort, and results

are based on participation during the final year (summer 1992–June 1993).
3. Some problems arose due to evaluation issues. The number of clients needed for evaluation purposes exceeded the capacity of the program. The evaluator "concluded that attempting an experimental design was inappropriate given the level of funding," and the design was "resented and (possibly) sabotaged at first."
4. In general, the evaluator felt that the expectations of the funder were unrealistic given the level of funding.

Given the considerable difficulty encountered in the design implementation of this project, the findings should be interpreted cautiously.

REPLICABILITY: The evaluation was too rigorous given the limited resources available. The evaluator recommended against replicating such an evaluation unless sufficient staff, financial resources, and technical expertise are in place.

GENERALIZABILITY: The small sample size and the design and implementation issues discourage attempts at generalization.

FUNDING SOURCE: U.S. Department of Health and Human Services (DHHS), Administration for Children and Families, Office of Community Services. Key personnel: John Tabori.

TREATMENT ADMINISTRATOR: Social Development Commission of Milwaukee, Wisconsin. Key personnel: George Gerharz, acting director; Janice Wilberg, Office of Research and Planning.

EVALUATOR: D. Paul Moberg, director of the Center for Health Policy and Program Evaluation, University of Wisconsin–Madison.

ENABLING LEGISLATION: Demonstration Partnership Program under section 408 of the Human Services Reauthorization Act of 1986.

INFORMATION SOURCES: U.S. Department of Health and Human Services, Demonstration Partnership Program: Summary of Final Evaluation Findings From FY 1991, 1995.

PUBLIC-USE ACCESS TO DATA: Available at Office of Community Services, DHHS.

UNEMPLOYED—THE NETHERLANDS: COUNSELING AND MONITORING PROGRAM

SUMMARY: This demonstration, conducted between 1989 and 1990, tested the effects of intensive job search assistance on a medium-sized sample of the unemployed. Subjects were followed for one year.

COST: Total evaluation costs, approximately 200,000 Dutch guilders. At the January 1990 exchange rate, this equals $104,820 U.S. dollars. Total project costs (excluding evaluation), 1,200,000 to 1,400,000 Dutch guilders ($628,920 to $733,740 U.S. dollars).

TIME FRAME: Intake period, November 1989–January 1990. Data were collected and subjects were followed for up to one year after intake.

TREATMENTS TESTED: The treatment was an intensive job search assistance program provided by the staff at the Joint Administrations Office (JAO). More time was spent with each unemployed person to discuss job applications, direct the job search, offer suggestions, and provide information regarding vacancies that might be suitable. More time was also spent in checking information given by the unemployed in order to detect falsification and administer penalities. The control group received the traditional, less intensive, service.

OUTCOMES OF INTEREST: (1) Period of unemployment and (2) Cost savings.

SAMPLE SIZE: The original sample was 1,631, but fell to 722 used for analysis because a full "search history" was not available for all of the original sample members. Roughly half were assigned to each group.

TARGET POPULATION: Unemployed persons making application for benefits at a JAO in the Netherlands. To be eligible, applicants had to be younger than 57.5 years old and willing to apply for permanent employment.

NUMBER OF TREATMENT GROUPS: Two (including control).

NUMBER AND LOCATION OF SITES: Seven sites in the Netherlands: Haarlem, Maastricht, Arnhem, Vlaardingen, Apeldoorn, Venlo, and Rijswijk.

RESEARCH COMPONENTS:
   Process analysis: Conducted through interviews with subjects. Search activities and labor market events of the sample were recorded.
   Impact analysis: Effects were estimated by means of a job search model in which the job finding rate was analyzed as the product of application intensity and the conditional matching probability.

BENEFIT–COST ANALYSIS: Conducted.

MAJOR FINDINGS:
1. The treatment group participants made significantly more job applications than the control group participants. However, the matching (or success) probability was not significantly different for the two groups. In fact, the treatment group had a slightly lower match-

ing probability. Overall, the estimated program effects on the job-finding rate were not statistically significant, although they did favor the treatment group.

2. For the full sample, there was a weakly significant reduction of unemployment for the treatment group of 8–14 percent. This translates to a reduction in unemployment duration of two to four days. The associated cost savings to the JAO, based on this reduction in unemployment, were estimated at between 8 million and 9.6 million Dutch guilders (approximately $4.2 million to $5 million U.S. dollars.) This greatly exceeded the costs of the Counseling and Monitoring program.

TIME TRENDS IN FINDINGS: None.

DESIGN ISSUES:

1. It appears that cost savings reported in finding 2 above are based on nonsignificant group differences regarding the job finding rate. Gorter and Kalb (1996) did not provide the statistical significance of the unemployment duration reduction separately, although Gorter mentioned an unpublished JAO analysis that did find "(very) weakly significant values" for this finding.

2. It is noted that despite the large sample loss (from 1,631 to 722) due to the addition of other selection criteria, the random assignment remained valid. The randomness was confirmed by a test showing no difference between groups on labor market history variables.

REPLICABILITY: Replicable.

GENERALIZABILITY: Designed to generalize to the entire nation (the Netherlands.)

FUNDING SOURCE: Department of Statistics and Research, Joint Administration Office, the Netherlands.

TREATMENT ADMINISTRATOR: Joint Administration Office.

EVALUATOR: Guyonne R.J. Kalb, Department of Statistics and Research, JAO, Amsterdam; and Cees Gorter, Department of Regional Economics, Free University, Amsterdam.

ENABLING LEGISLATION: None.

INFORMATION SOURCES: Cees Gorter and Guyonne R.J. Kalb, "Estimating the Effect of Counseling and Monitoring the Unemployed Using a Job Search Model," Journal of Human Resources 31(1996):590–610.

PUBLIC-USE ACCESS TO DATA: Available through October 1999 from Cees Gorter, Department of Regional Economics, Free University, Amsterdam.

Part Fourteen

EMPLOYERS

WAGE-SUBSIDY VARIATION EXPERIMENT

SUMMARY: This demonstration, conducted in 1980, tested the effects of a wage subsidy paid to employers on a medium-sized sample of private-sector businesses. Subjects were followed for less than one year.

COST: Cannot be separated from Youth Incentive Entitlement Pilot Project (YIEPP), a large nonexperimental demonstration, of which this experiment was a small component.

TIME FRAME: Treatment administered January–May 1980; data collected, same period; final report, March 1981.

TREATMENTS TESTED:

1. A 100 percent wage subsidy was offered to businesses that would employ disadvantaged 16–19-year-olds who would be assigned by the project. Youths were guaranteed minimum wage employment if they stayed in school and maintained satisfactory school performance.
2. A 75 percent wage subsidy was offered.

A list of over 1,000 possible employers was compiled, and the firms were randomly assigned to one treatment or the other. Payroll was handled by the project administrator.

OUTCOMES OF INTEREST: Agreement to participate in youth employment.

SAMPLE SIZE: Group 1, 519 businesses; group 2, 569 businesses.

TARGET POPULATION: Private-sector businesses within commuting distance of the impact neighborhoods of the project.

NUMBER OF TREATMENT GROUPS: Two (including control).

NUMBER AND LOCATION OF SITES: Detroit, Michigan.

RESEARCH COMPONENTS:

Process analysis: Interviews with subjects on reasons for participating or not participating.

Impact analysis: Difference in means; also some logit.

Benefit–cost analysis: Not conducted.

MAJOR FINDINGS:

Treatment	Contacted	Agreed to Participate	Rate
75 percent subsidy	569	44	7.7 percent
100 percent subsidy	519	81	15.6 percent

The difference is statistically significant, but "wage considerations did not appear to be a first priority for most businesses."

Most important reasons for agreeing: "Chance to do something for disadvantaged youth; cheap or no-cost labor."

Most important reasons for not agreeing: "Not enough work for them to do; work inappropriate for teenagers."

TIME TRENDS IN FINDINGS: Not applicable.

DESIGN ISSUES:
1. The project could not offer wage subsidies beyond August 1980.
2. "Both local economic conditions and the diligence of the call-back effort (to employers) appeared to affect the yield (of participants)."
3. Current or former YIEPP employer participants were excluded from the sample. The bias could be in either direction (current participants are presumably positive responders, former participants presumably negative), but since current participants exceeded former participants, the probable direction of the bias was to reduce participation rates in both treatments.
4. The experiment occurred during a serious recession in Detroit.
5. Displacement bias is a virtual certainty, and the project authors concluded that the more real work a job involved, the more likely it was that a wage-subsidy placement would displace an unsubsidized worker.

REPLICABILITY: Replicable.

GENERALIZABILITY: Very limited, since only two levels of the subsidy were tested and, moreover, were tested in the context of a serious local recession. Diaz has argued, however, that the results point to a very limited efficacy for a subminimum wage.

FUNDING SOURCE: U.S. Department of Labor, Employment and Training Administration, Office of Youth Programs. Key personnel: Robert Taggart.

TREATMENT ADMINISTRATOR: Detroit Employment and Training Department. Key personnel: William Diaz does not recall.

EVALUATOR: Manpower Demonstration Research Corporation. Key personnel: Joseph Ball (deceased) and Carl Wolfhagen. Primary author of the project evaluation was William Diaz.

ENABLING LEGISLATION: The Youth Employment and Demonstration Projects Act of 1977 authorized YIEPP.

INFORMATION SOURCES: Joseph Ball (deceased) and Carl Wolfhagen, "The Participation of Private Businesses as Work Sponsors in the Youth Entitlement Demonstration," Manpower Demonstration Research Corporation, 1981.

PUBLIC-USE ACCESS TO DATA: Public-use file does not exist.

WILKES-BARRE JOB SEARCH VOUCHER PROJECT

SUMMARY: This demonstration, conducted in 1981, tested the effects of employer subsidies on a medium-sized sample of area employers. Subjects were followed for less than one year.

COST: Cost of operations, $181,044 (1981).

TIME FRAME: January–December 1981; data collected, same period; final report, September 1982.

TREATMENTS TESTED:

1. Voucher and Targeted Jobs Tax Credit (TJTC), a wage subsidy in the form of a reduction on personal or corporate federal income tax available for employers of low-income 18–24-year-olds). Job developers visited these employers, informed them about the TJTC and also made available to them a special subsidy (the voucher) for hiring 16- and 17-year-olds. The voucher subsidy was $1.80 per hour for the first three months a youth worked for the firm, and $1.00 per hour for the next five months. The intention was to stimulate the hiring of youths from the Wilkes-Barre YES program, although the TJTC could not be restricted to them.
2. TJTC only. Job developers visited these employers, informed them of the availability of the TJTC, and encouraged them to hire program youths.
3. Control employers were not contacted by job developers.

A sample of 375 employers was drawn and stratified according to size, location, and the intensity of youth employment in their industries. Random assignment was performed within strata. Program youths attended individual and group counseling sessions to develop career goals and job search skills.

OUTCOME OF INTEREST: Employment of low-income youths by employers who received wage subsidies.

SAMPLE SIZE: Group 1, 125; group 2, 125; group 3, 125. Total, 375.

TARGET POPULATION: Potential employers.

NUMBER OF TREATMENT GROUPS: Three (with one control group).

NUMBER AND LOCATION OF SITES: One—Wilkes-Barre, Pennsylvania.

RESEARCH COMPONENTS:

Process analysis: Conducted. The program was affected by high staff turnover. The turnover itself was increased by the near certainty that the Labor Department would terminate the program at the end of the period.

Impact analysis: Not conducted, for reasons obvious in "Major Findings," below.

Benefit–cost analysis: Not conducted.

MAJOR FINDINGS:
1. Impact of voucher. Of 125 firms contacted, three took advantage of the voucher. Another firm, outside the sample, asked to use the subsidy and was allowed to; the four firms hired five workers.
2. Impact of TJTC. Precisely one firm from each group used the TJTC. The voucher-group firm employed seven youths; the other two firms hired one each.

TIME TRENDS IN FINDINGS: None.

DESIGN ISSUES:
1. It is not clear why the Wilkes-Barre YES organization was selected to run this experiment. The previous Workshop experiment, run by YES and evaluated by the same team from Brandeis, was poorly implemented. The program was plagued by many of the same factors that are discussed in the process analysis of this experiment, and ceased operation when the Labor Department grant ended in December 1981.

REPLICABILITY: Replicable.

GENERALIZABILITY: The unemployment rate in Wilkes-Barre in December 1981 was 11.7 percent. High unemployment among all workers would in any case have resulted in poor job prospects for teenagers ("On the average employers report 11 applicants for each entry level opening . . . among all ages.") It could be argued that a wage subsidy would be most effective in the special case in which overall unemployment is very low but in which youth unemployment is much higher than overall unemployment. Wilkes-Barre in 1981 did not fit this special case.

FUNDING SOURCE: U.S. Department of Labor, Office of Youth Programs. Key personnel: Robert Taggart.

TREATMENT ADMINISTRATOR: Youth Employment Service. Key personnel: Frank Hines and Richard Borofsky.

EVALUATOR: Center for Employment and Income Studies, Brandeis University. Key personnel: Cecilia Rivera-Casale, Barry Friedman, and Robert Lerman.

ENABLING LEGISLATION: Funded under the Youth Employment and Demonstration Projects Act of 1977.

INFORMATION SOURCES: Cecilia Rivera-Casale, Barry Friedman, and Robert Lerman, "Can Employeror Worker Subsidies Raise Youth Employment? An Evaluation of Two Financial Incentive Programs for Disadvantaged Youth," Center for Employment and Income Studies, Florence Heller Graduate School for Advanced Studies in Social Welfare, Brandeis University, September 1982.

PUBLIC-USE ACCESS TO DATA: We have no information about a public-use file for this demonstration.

Part Fifteen

LOW-INCOME

NEW JERSEY INCOME MAINTENANCE EXPERIMENT

SUMMARY: This demonstration, conducted from 1968 to 1972, tested the effects of negative income tax (NIT) at various levels of income guarantee and tax rate, on a large sample of low-income households. Subjects were followed for three years.

COST: $7.8 million (1971); research and administrative costs only, $5.4 million.

TIME FRAME: August 1968–September 1972; data collected, same period; final report, December 1973 (to Department of Health, Education & Welfare).

TREATMENTS TESTED: The negative income tax consists of an income guarantee accompanied by a tax rate on other income. Eight combinations of guarantees and tax rates (partial reductions in payments as other income rises) were tested: (1) 50 percent (of poverty line) guarantee, 30 percent tax rate (on earnings); (2) 50 percent guarantee, 50 percent tax rate; (3) 75 percent guarantee, 30 percent tax rate; (4) 75 percent guarantee, 50 percent tax rate; (5) 75 percent guarantee, 70 percent tax rate; (6) 100 percent guarantee, 50 percent tax rate; (7) 100 percent guarantee, 70 percent tax rate; and (8) 125 percent guarantee, 50 percent tax rate. All families were paid for participating in interviews, and controls received a small monthly fee for mailing in a postcard with current address.

OUTCOMES OF INTEREST: (1) Reduction in work effort and (2) Lifestyle changes.

SAMPLE SIZE: By payment group: (1) 46; (2) 76; (3) 100; (4) 117; (5) 85; (6) 77; (7) 86; and (8) 138. Total experimentals, 725; controls, 632.

TARGET POPULATION: Households having one nondisabled male between 18 and 59 years old, at least one other member, and a total family income not exceeding 150 percent of the poverty line.

NUMBER OF TREATMENT GROUPS: Nine (with one control group).

NUMBER AND LOCATION OF SITES: Four—Trenton, Jersey City, and Paterson, New Jersey; and Scranton, Pennsylvania.

RESEARCH COMPONENTS:
    Process analysis: Two important questions considered in the project report (volume 2, chapter 11; and volume 3, chapter 12) were the extent to which experimentals understood program parameters and

the extent to which state welfare changes contaminated the results. In January 1969, New Jersey instituted an Aid to Families with Dependent Children (AFDC) plan allowing benefits to two-parent families (AFDC-UP), and until July 1971 these benefits were among the highest in the country. Thus, differences between controls and experimentals did not have the same meaning that they were expected to have; low-guarantee experimentals found that AFDC-UP offered higher payments.

Impact analysis: Conducted by regression.

Benefit–cost analysis: Not conducted.

MAJOR FINDINGS:

1. Average nominal payments rose 6.4 percent over three years, but real payments decreased because the cost of living rose between 11 percent and 17 percent. Unemployment also increased during this period, from 4.4 percent to 7.1 percent (weighted average).
2. The number of hours of employment reduction for male family heads was not statistically significant. However, a significant experimental elasticity was calculated; the experimental variable was defined as the ratio of the guarantee to the net wage. At the experimental mean, the regression results imply a reduction of 1 percent to 1.6 percent in hours worked between experimentals and controls.
3. Experimental wives worked 23 percent fewer hours per week than controls; differences in labor-force participation were highly significant. Differences were concentrated in white families. However, the reduction was from a fairly small base, since large families with nonworking wives dominated the sample.
4. Teenagers enrolled in the treatment were (for the medium-generosity plans) 25 percent to 50 percent more likely to complete high school than controls, other things being equal. Specifically, the higher the tax rate, the more likely was high-school completion; but the higher the guarantee rate, the less likely was high-school completion. Experiment participation was associated with lower teen earnings.
5. Observed life-style changes were mostly negligible. Some increase in the ownership of both homes and major appliances by experimentals over controls was noted.

TIME TRENDS IN FINDINGS: Findings reported are typically for the middle period of the experiment, because of the learning curve expected in the early quarters and the possibility of gaming behavior in the later quarters.

DESIGN ISSUES:

1. Although assignments to treatment were random, given pretreatment income, they were not independent of income. Sample designs resulted in experimentals with very low incomes being directed mainly into low-guarantee programs or into the control group. Families at 100 percent of the poverty line or less are overrepresented in the control group.
2. All of the project report authors admitted that the long-term labor-supply effects of a permanent national program might differ from the effects of a three-year experiment. The biases are believed to be the following: effects on adult males are underestimated, effects on adult females and young people, overestimated.
3. No attempt was made to verify the income reports, so a misreporting of earnings might have occurred. Simultaneous, inappropriate receipts of both experimental transfers and AFDC payments are known to have occurred in several cases.
4. Experimentals also reported income more frequently than controls, and are believed to have learned to report gross rather than net income more quickly; as a consequence, early months of data from all sites are contaminated for purposes of comparison.
5. The sample is truncated by total family income, rather than by the income of husbands, leading to a substantial underrepresentation of working wives.
6. A set of anomalous results for black households (essentially, male hours of labor) appears to be a product of unexpected labor-supply reductions in the black control group. Experimental labor hours changed little among experimentals, but fell sharply among controls.
7. Reported results are for intact families. Experimental families were slightly more likely to break up.

REPLICABILITY: Designed for replicability through the Internal Revenue Service.

GENERALIZABILITY:

1. Blacks were deliberately overrepresented in this study, to test the culture-of-poverty hypothesis.
2. Large numbers of Puerto Ricans in the sample do not correspond to their numbers in the United States as a whole.
3. The sample was drawn from areas of concentrated poverty; poor people (principally white) living in nonpoor areas were not represented.
4. The concentration of findings on two-parent families limits current applicability.

5. The more-generous treatment plans would have applied potentially to large numbers of nonpoor families, especially two-earner families, who were excluded from the sample design. Thus, potential negative income tax effects on the behavior of married women who work full-time cannot be estimated from this experiment.

FUNDING SOURCE: Office of Economic Opportunity. Key personnel: James Lyday and Robert Levine.

TREATMENT ADMINISTRATOR: Mathematica Policy Research. Key personnel: David N. Kershaw (deceased).

EVALUATORS: Institute for Research on Poverty, University of Wisconsin-Madison, and Mathematica Policy Research. Key personnel: Harold Watts.

ENABLING LEGISLATION: None. The experiment did require an Internal Revenue Service ruling that program payments were not taxable income.

POLICY EFFECTS: The Nixon administration's proposed Family Assistance Plan was related in concept to this experiment. The preliminary data report noted above, which showed the negative income tax as increasing work effort, was prepared for hearings on this proposal. Dennis Coyle and Aaron Wildavsky's "Social Experimentation in the Face of Formidable Fables," in *Lessons from the Income Maintenance Experiments*, edited by Alicia H. Munnell (Federal Reserve Bank of Boston and Brookings Institution, 1987), stated that this finding was cited by NIT supporters such as then-Senator Fred Harris and House Ways and Means Committee (former) Chairman Wilbur Mills.

INFORMATION SOURCES: David N. Kershaw (deceased) and Jerilyn Fair, *The New Jersey Income-Maintenance Experiment, Volume 1: Operations, Surveys and Administration*; Harold Watts and Albert W. Rees, ed., *Volume 2: Labor-Supply Responses*; Kershaw and Fair, *Volume 3: Expenditures, Health, and Social Behavior*; and Kershaw and Fair, *The Quality of the Evidence*, Academic Press, 1976, 1977.

PUBLIC-USE ACCESS TO DATA: We have no information about a public-use file for this demonstration.

RURAL INCOME MAINTENANCE EXPERIMENT

SUMMARY: This demonstration, conducted from 1970 to 1972, tested the effects of a negative income tax (at various levels of income guarantee and tax rate) on a medium-sized sample of rural low-income families. Subjects were followed for three years.

COST: $6.1 million (1971); research and administrative costs only, $3.7 million.

TIME FRAME: 1970–72; data collected, 1969–73; final report, 1976.

TREATMENTS TESTED: Five negative income tax plans were tested: (1) a 50 percent of poverty line income guarantee with a 50 percent tax rate; (2) a 75 percent guarantee with 30 percent tax rate; (3) a 75 percent guarantee with 50 percent tax rate; (4) a 75 percent guarantee with a 70 percent tax rate; and (5) a 100 percent guarantee with a 50 percent tax rate.

OUTCOMES OF INTEREST: (1) Work behavior; (2) Health, school, and other effects on poor children; and (3) Savings and consumption behavior.

SAMPLE SIZE: Although formally there were 809 families in the experiment, only 587 were families headed by working-age males whose behavior was of primary interest. (The others were female-headed families or those with an aged male head.) Of the 587, 318 were controls. Of the 269 experimentals, the allocation among the negative income tax (NIT) plans listed above was (1) 37, (2) 67, (3) 75, (4) 30, and (5) 60.

TARGET POPULATION: Rural, low-income families, in which the male head was 18–58 years of age and not disabled.

NUMBER OF TREATMENT GROUPS: Six (with one control group).

NUMBER AND LOCATION OF SITES: Duplin County, North Carolina; and Pocahontas and Calhoun Counties, Iowa.

RESEARCH COMPONENTS:
  Process analysis: Conducted. Fifty-four percent did not know their guarantee within 20 percent; 23 percent did not know earnings were taxed; 8 percent thought earnings tax was 100 percent. Attrition bias was studied and found not likely to affect results.
  Impact analysis: Conducted with sophisticated regression techniques.
  Benefit–cost analysis: Not conducted.

MAJOR FINDINGS:
1. For a weighted average of the sample, family income of experimentals compared to controls fell by 13 percent, family wage income by 13 percent, family wage hours by 13 percent. The employment rate of wives fell 28 percent and that of dependents by 46 percent; changes in male work efforts were small (a 1 percent reduction in hours).

2. "An income maintenance scheme which must administer a program to the self-employed will entail more cost from income reporting problems than cost from disincentives in labor supply" (Primus, in Palmer and Pechman 1978).
3. Among renters, the probability of buying a home was .06 percent higher among experimentals than among controls.

TIME TRENDS IN FINDINGS: Sharp drop in farm incomes in last year of experiment, possibly deferral of sales of storable commodities to an untaxed year.

DESIGN ISSUES:
1. "The sample size was probably too small to provide definitive answers to some of the relevant policy questions" (Bawden and Harrar, in Palmer and Pechman 1978).
2. More than one-fourth of the households in the sample had no relevance to the question under investigation, because they were female-headed or aged. This is one of the reasons that many effects of a large magnitude but no statistical significance were found.
3. The heterogeneity of responses was much larger than the planners expected. Investigators found it necessary to disaggregate the sample of 587 by state, race, farm, and nonfarm. After they had performed this disaggregation, most effects were statistically insignificant, though some were large in size. Effects that were significant were just as often anomalous (coefficient had the wrong sign) as not.
4. As a group, farmers substantially underreported their incomes, and probably manipulated loopholes in the payment rules.

REPLICABILITY: The application of the NIT to the self-employed would require some carryover-income concept such as that used in this experiment.

GENERALIZABILITY: Intended for generalization to rural poverty populations in the South and Midwest. Generalizations based on this experiment would be suspect, however, because of its small sample size and the internal heterogeneity of the sample groups.

FUNDING SOURCES: The Ford Foundation and the Office of Economic Opportunity; subsequently, Assistant Secretary for Planning and Evaluation, U.S. Department of Health, Education, & Welfare. Key personnel: Larry L. Orr, HEW.

TREATMENT ADMINISTRATOR: Institute for Research on Poverty, University of Wisconsin-Madison. Key personnel: D. Lee Bawden, Philip Salisbury, and William S. Harrar.

EVALUATOR: Institute for Research on Poverty. Key Personnel: D. Lee Bawden.

ENABLING LEGISLATION: None.

INFORMATION SOURCES: U.S. Department of Health, Education & Welfare (HEW), *Summary Report: Rural Income Maintenance Experiment*, November 1976. John L. Palmer and Joseph A. Pechman, ed., *Welfare in Rural Areas: the North Carolina-Iowa Income Maintenance Experiment*, Brookings Institution, 1978. A six-volume, unpublished final report is on file at the Institute for Research on Poverty, University of Wisconsin-Madison.

PUBLIC-USE ACCESS TO DATA: We have no information about a public-use file for this demonstration.

SEATTLE-DENVER INCOME MAINTENANCE EXPERIMENT

SUMMARY: This demonstration, conducted from 1970 to 1977, tested the effects of both a negative income tax (at various levels of income guarantee and tax rate) and subsidized vocational counseling and training on a large sample of low-income families. Subjects were followed for up to five years.

COST: $77.5 million (1975); research and administrative costs only, $57.1 million.

TIME FRAME: October 1970–August 1977 (93 families were assigned to a 20-year negative income tax (NIT) plan); data collected, October 1970–December 1978; final report, May 1983.

TREATMENTS TESTED: There were two types of treatment. One consisted of a negative income tax plan. In this plan, some treatments had a declining rate of benefit reductions (tax rate) as nonprogram income rose. The other treatment was a subsidy to vocational counseling and training.
1. Financial treatments (income guarantee as a percentage of poverty line, tax rate, and change in tax rate for each $1,000 of nonprogram income): (1) 95 percent, 50 percent, 0 percent; (2) 95 percent, 70 percent, 0 percent; (3) 95 percent, 70 percent, − 2.5 percent; (4) 95 percent, 80 percent, − 2.5 percent; (5) 120 percent, 50 percent, 0 percent; (6) 120 percent, 70 percent, 0 percent; (7) 120 percent, 70

percent, -2.5 percent; (8) 120 percent, 80 percent, -2.5 percent; (9) 140 percent, 50 percent, 0 percent; (10) 140 percent, 70 percent, 0 percent; and (11) 140 percent, 80 percent, -2.5 percent. Experimental subjects were randomly assigned to programs that were either three or five years in duration in order to test for effects owing solely to the temporary nature of the experiment. As noted above, 93 Denver families were switched without warning into a 20-year plan in the third year of their NIT participation for the same reason.

2. Counseling/training treatments: (1) Control, no treatment; (2) Free, nondirective, vocational counseling of a standardized form provided by staffs of the community colleges; (3) Free counseling plus a 50 percent tuition subsidy for either career-related training or enrollment at any institution the student wished to attend; (4) Free counseling plus a 100 percent tuition subsidy.

OUTCOMES OF INTEREST: (1) Effects on labor supply; (2) Marital stability; and (3) Other life-style changes.

SAMPLE SIZE: Two presentations of sample sizes are relevant. Numbers are households.
1. Financial/counseling
   Control/control: 1,041
   Control/experimental: 1,012
   Experimental/control: 946
   Experimental/experimental: 1,801
2. Second-year (after attrition) distribution of experimentals by the financial treatments listed above in "Treatments Tested":
   (1) 346, (2) 184, (3) 204, (4) 163, (5) 237, (6) 278, (7) 241, (8) 224, (9) 93, (10) 193, and (11) 251. There were 1,715 controls in the second year.

TARGET POPULATION: Families who met all of the following requirements: (1) Either married couples (with or without children) or single heads of households with at least one dependent child younger than 18; (2) either earning less than $9,000 per year (if just one worker in the family) or less than $11,000 per year (if two workers), in 1971 dollars; and (3) either includes a nondisabled husband, 18 to 58 years old, or a single, nondisabled, female head of household, 18 to 58.

NUMBER OF TREATMENT GROUPS: Forty-eight (with 1 pure control group).

NUMBER AND LOCATION OF SITES: Two—Seattle, Washington; and Denver, Colorado.

RESEARCH COMPONENTS:

Process analysis: Investigators extensively tested the verbally artic-
ulated degree of comprehension of the program among experimentals,
but did not find that the degree of comprehension was associated with
any labor-supply effects. They also tested for Hawthorne effects by
paying half of the Denver controls to report income on a monthly
basis, as all experimentals had to do, and did not find any significant
effects in interview data between reporting and nonreporting controls.
The investigators did not, however, expect the surprising results for
the counseling program, which are discussed below, and no interview
data with experimentals or counselors are available to explain them.

Impact analysis: Conducted with sophisticated regression techniques.

Benefit–cost analysis: Not conducted.

MAJOR FINDINGS:

1. According to the project report, "A universal NIT program without
   any work requirements in which the mean guarantee level [is]
   about 110 percent of the poverty level and the mean tax rate is
   about 50 percent would lead to significant reductions in virtually
   every major dimension of labor supply."
   Mean second-year experimental response across 11 NIT treatments
   compared with the control mean:

Variable	Husbands (%)	Wives (%)	Female Heads (%)
Annual hours of work	−9	−21	−14
Annual weeks worked	−7	−19	−14
Probability of working at all			
during the year	−7	−19	−11
Earnings	−8	−20	−16

   The major effect of the experiment was not a marginal reduction
   in hours worked per week but a lengthening of unemployment
   spells. Among youths, the experimental effect was a major reduction in hours worked. The project report stated: "There is no evidence that the work effort reduction is accompanied by any increase
   in school attendance."

2. The counseling-only program did not significantly increase years
   of schooling. The 50 percent subsidy only had significant effects
   on schooling among female heads. The 100 percent subsidy significantly affected the schooling of husbands, wives, and female
   heads: the average increase in schooling was .11 to .27 years.

3. The counseling/training programs had a negative impact, as anticipated, on hours and earnings in the first year. The unexpected

finding was that the impact on wages and earnings of the counseling/training programs, where significant, was negative in the subsequent years of the program and in the postexperimental data, for both husbands and wives. Single-female heads consistently showed a positive earnings and wage effect from the counseling-only program (not necessarily significant), but the same generally consistent (not necessarily significant) negative impact from the subsidy programs. The effects appear to be independent of participation in the NIT experiment.

Disaggregated regressions suggest that the negative effect of counseling was most serious for the following groups: (1) Husbands who were, before the experiment, unemployed or members of families with normal incomes below $5,000, and who were eligible for counseling only—they earned $1,600 to $1,700 less than their control counterparts in the year following the five-year experiment; (2) Wives who, before the experiment, were employed; they earned $500 to $650 less than their control counterparts under all three counseling/training plans in the year following the five-year experiment.

The investigators believed that nondirective counseling led some husbands and some wives to enter into unduly ambitious academic programs, which they either did not finish or could not use to good effect in the labor market.

4. According to the project report, "The negative income tax . . . plans tested in SIME/DIME dramatically increased the rates at which marriages dissolved among white and black couples, and decreased the rate at which Chicano women entered marriages." Twenty-eight percent of marriages among black experimentals broke up in the first three years, compared with 21 percent among black controls; 20 percent of marriages among white experimentals broke up, compared with 15 percent of marriages among white controls.

5. The project further reported: "SIME/DIME probably did not affect the health of participants"; "no experimental effect on psychological distress"; "SIME/DIME . . . does not appear to have had an effect on infant health status." For married women, the experiment seems to have raised fertility rates among Chicanos, to have had no effect on blacks, and to have had inconsistent effects on whites. Effects on the fertility rate of single women were insignificant.

Other reported findings: "SIME/DIME resulted in increased debt"; "white migrants receiving experimental treatments were more likely than controls to move to destinations with a better climate"; "SIME/DIME had little effect on intracity residential mobility and no effect on integration."

Time Trends in Findings:

1. Labor-supply effects tended to grow after the first year; to diminish as the program neared an end; and vanished in the year after NIT program-eligibility expired. An exception was single-female heads, who continued to work fewer hours after the program ends.
2. The marital-stability findings are controversial; one reason for this is that the experimental/control differential at an early point in the treatment was greater than the subsequent differential.

Design Issues:

1. A portion of the labor-supply difference between experimentals and controls comes from a systematic underreporting of earnings and hours by experimentals. This problem was known at the time of the final report and does not appear to substantively change the conclusion.
2. Marital-dissolution effects are strongest in the first two years of the experiment, and seem to be sensitive to the presence of the counseling experiment, the preexperimental income, and the guarantee level. The higher the guarantee level, the lower the experimental effect. Since assignment to guarantee levels was not independent of preexperimental income (low-income families were more likely to be assigned to low-guarantee plans), the marital-dissolution findings may be in part an artifact of the assignment system. The marital-dissolution findings remain controversial, partly because of the time trend noted above, because dissolution is a relatively rare event, and because attrition bias in the controls is difficult to evaluate. There is no evidence that the NIT increased the stability of marriages, which was the expected outcome.
3. Much of the benefit to be derived from the extremely large sample was dissipated by the excessive number of treatments. Cell sizes are then reduced further by race, marital status, previous employment history, and so on.

Replicability: NIT plans were designed for national replicability. The methodology of the counseling program is summarized in the final report, and does not appear very different from vocational-counseling programs in common use.

Generalizability:

1. Findings may have been affected by the serious recession in Seattle in the early 1970s. The experiment was extended to Denver, a city with low unemployment rates, for this reason.
2. All participants were, at least initially, residents of low-income communities. SIME/DIME does not address the effects of an NIT on dispersed poverty, as opposed to concentrated poverty.

3. Other studies in the 1970s reported very low rates of return to schooling in the labor market. The counseling/training findings may be specific to that era.

4. SIME/DIME is the best available source for income- and leisure-substitution parameters that can be applied to project the effects of national policy proposals affecting low-income people.

FUNDING SOURCES: U.S. Department of Health, Education & Welfare; and U.S. Department of Health and Human Services (DHHS), Assistant Secretary for Planning and Evaluation. Key personnel: Joseph Corbett.

TREATMENT ADMINISTRATORS: Mathematica Policy Research (MPR, for payments and data collection); Seattle Central Community College and Community College of Denver (for vocational counseling). Key personnel: MPR—David N. Kershaw (deceased) and Gary Christopherson; Seattle CCC—N. John Andersen.

EVALUATOR: SRI International. Key personnel: Robert G. Spiegelman.

ENABLING LEGISLATION: None.

POLICY EFFECTS: David Greenberg, formerly of the DHHS, stated that the experiment data were used to estimate labor-supply parameters that, in turn, were incorporated into microsimulation models. These models were used to cost out and predict the future effects of various welfare-reform proposals under consideration by policymakers. In addition, the marital-stability findings were widely circulated at a time when policy makers were seriously considering welfare reform.

INFORMATION SOURCES:
   SRI International, Final Report of the Seattle-Denver Income Experiment, Volume 1: Design and Results; Gary Christopherson, Volume 2: Administration, SRI International, May 1983; U.S. Department of Health and Human Services, Assistant Secretary for Planning and Evaluation, Office of Income Security Policy, Overview of the Seattle-Denver Income Maintenance Experiment Final Report, Summary Report, May 1983; Robert G. Spiegelman, K. E. Yaeger, Michael C. Keeley, Philip K. Robins, Richard W. West, Nancy Brandon Tuma, Arden R. Hall, Yoram Weiss, Fred Dong, and Lyle P. Groeneveld, articles in Journal of Human Resources, Fall 1980.

PUBLIC-USE ACCESS TO DATA: We have no information about a public-use file for this demonstration.

GARY INCOME MAINTENANCE EXPERIMENT

SUMMARY: This demonstration, conducted from 1971 to 1974, tested the effects of a negative income tax (at various levels of income guarantee and tax rate) on a large sample of low-income African-American families. Subjects were followed for three years.

COST: $20.3 million (1973); research and administrative costs only, $14.8 million.

TIME FRAME: 1971–74; data collected, 1971–74; final report, 1980

TREATMENTS TESTED: Four combinations of guarantee and tax rate were tested: (1) 75 percent of poverty line guarantee, 40 percent tax rate; (2) 75 percent and 60 percent; (3) 100 percent and 40 percent; and (4) 100 percent and 60 percent.

OUTCOMES OF INTEREST: (1) Employment; (2) Schooling; (3) Infant mortality and morbidity; (4) Educational achievement; and (5) Housing consumption.

SAMPLE SIZE: Controls, 771; experimentals by treatment plans listed above: (1) 313, (2) 314, (3) 203, and (4) 198; total experimentals, 1,028.

TARGET POPULATION: Black families with at least one child under the age of 18.

NUMBER OF TREATMENT GROUPS: Five (with one control group).

NUMBER AND LOCATION OF SITES: One—Gary, Indiana.

RESEARCH COMPONENTS:
   Process analysis: Conducted. Experimental treatments with social service access and day care terminated.
   Impact analysis: Conducted through sophisticated regression and other analytical models.
   Benefit–cost analysis: Not conducted.

MAJOR FINDINGS:
1. Statistically significant reductions in the employment rate of experimental husbands (2.7 percent to 4.9 percent) and female heads of households (25.8 percent to 26.8 percent), compared with controls. No significant effects on married women's labor-market participation.
2. No significant effects of the experimental tax rate were found.
3. Some experimental teenagers were significantly more likely to continue schooling and less likely to enter the labor market than controls. The effect was concentrated in lower-income experimentals.

4. Significantly fewer low-birth-weight infants were born to high-risk experimental mothers than to high-risk control mothers, in which the high-risk group consists of women who smoke and had previously given birth within 16 months or less. The experimental effect is consistently greater the higher the risk.
5. Experimental children in grades four through six had a significantly better reading achievement than the controls. The effect is limited to the third or fourth year after enrollment in the experiment. No effects were found for students grades 7 through 10.
6. Experimentals increased their rental payments about 4.3 percent above the rent levels paid by controls. Six percent of the net increase in income was spent on rent; an elasticity of rent payment with respect to income of about .3 was calculated. There was a small, statistically significant increase in the probability of an experimental buying a home compared with a control.

TIME TRENDS IN FINDINGS: As noted above.

DESIGN ISSUES:
1. The Gary experiment also intended to test two other treatments. One of these was a social service access worker (a personal ombudsman); the other was the expansion of day-care services in one neighborhood. Both services were undersubscribed, and subsequently were discontinued.
2. Gary findings are probably highly conditional on the specific Gary labor market. See "Generalizability."
3. The Gary sample was not selected on the basis of total family income, and therefore does not have the truncation bias found in the New Jersey and rural experiments against two-earner families.

REPLICABILITY: Treatment is intended for replication through the Internal Revenue Service.

GENERALIZABILITY: The Gary labor market at the time of the experiment was heavily dominated by the steel industry, which offered almost exclusively full-time jobs. Opportunities for part-time work and for other marginal adjustments in hours like overtime and moonlighting appear to have been rare. This probably explains (a) the absence of responses to the experimental tax rate, (b) the absence of experimental responses among wives, and (c) the relatively high experimental responses among married men and female heads of households. Instead of a marginal choice about how many hours to work, many in the sample probably faced a discrete choice about whether to be employed full-time or not to be employed at all.

FUNDING SOURCE: U.S. Department of Health, Education & Welfare (HEW), Assistant Secretary for Planning and Evaluation. Key personnel: Joseph Corbett.

TREATMENT ADMINISTRATOR: Indiana University (subcontractor through the Indiana Department of Public Welfare). Key personnel: Kenneth C. Kehrer and John Maiolo.

EVALUATOR: Indiana University, Mathematica Policy Research. Key personnel: Kenneth C. Kehrer and Andy Anderson.

ENABLING LEGISLATION: None.

POLICY EFFECTS: Kenneth Kehrer recalled the results of all four income maintenance experiments being discussed in the context of the Carter welfare reform proposal.

INFORMATION SOURCES: Kenneth C. Kehrer, Barbara H. Kehrer, Charles M. Wolin, Rebecca A. Maynard, Richard J. Murnane, Robert A. Moffitt, John F. McDonald, Stanley P. Stephenson, Jr., and Richard L. Kaluzny, 1979, five articles in *Journal of Human Resources*, 14 (4, Fall): 431–506; Kenneth C. Kehrer, John F. McDonald, and Robert A. Moffitt, "Final Report of the Gary Income Maintenance Experiment: Labor Supply," Mathematica Policy Research, 1980.

PUBLIC-USE ACCESS TO DATA: We have no information about a public-use file for this experiment.

HOUSING ALLOWANCE DEMAND EXPERIMENT

SUMMARY: This demonstration, conducted from 1973 to 1977, tested the effects of two forms of housing subsidy on a large sample of low-income renter households. Subjects were followed for two years.

COST: $31.2 million (1976); payments, $3.6 million; administration, $2 million; research and monitoring, $25.6 million.

TIME FRAME: April 1973–February 1977; data collected, April 1973–February 1976; final report, June 1980.

TREATMENTS TESTED: The principal treatments tested were payments to households based on a "Housing Gap" and payments based on a percentage of the rent.

For the Housing Gap treatment, a panel of experts at each site estimated the cost of housing meeting certain standards in modest neighborhoods in that city. This number was C^*. Payment (P) was based on the formula $P = dC^* - bY$, where Y was disposable income less $300 per year for each working member of the family, and d and b were experimental parameters (higher d and lower b imply a greater generosity). Treatments also varied in housing requirements: a minimum rent requirement, set at .7 or .9 of C^*, or a minimum standards requirement, under which occupied units would be inspected for conformity with standards for health and safety. Households living in units that did not meet the standard specified for the treatment to which they were assigned could not receive payments.

Treatment	d	b	Housing Requirement
1	1	.15	Minimum standards
2	1.2	.25	Minimum standards
3	1	.25	Minimum standards
4	0.8	.25	Minimum standards
5	1	.35	Minimum standards
6	1.2	.25	Minimum rent (.7)
7	1	.25	Minimum rent (.7)
8	0.8	.25	Minimum rent (.7)
9	1.2	.25	Minimum rent (.9)
10	1	.25	Minimum rent (.9)
11	0.8	.25	Minimum rent (.9)
12	1	.25	No requirements

In the percentage-of-rent treatments, payment (P) was determined by the formula $P = aR$, where R is rent and a is a program parameter. There were no housing requirements.

Treatment	a
13	.6
14	.5
15	.4
16	.3
17	.2

Controls were paid $10 a month for filling out a monthly form and $25 for periodic interviews. Experimentals were not paid for interviews. The payment system for experimentals lasted three years. Information was collected for two years.

OUTCOMES OF INTEREST: (1) Enrollment; (2) Rate of participation (actual receipt of payment); and (3) Effects on housing expenditures, quality, and residential segregation.

SAMPLE SIZE: The number of households invited to enroll either as experimentals or as controls was 3,600—1,800 in each city. The numbers actually enrolling (not necessarily receiving payments) were recorded for the initial enrollment offer and two years later. The difference between the second and third columns below is attrition, which in this case was of independent interest.

Treatment	Initial	Two Years
1	212	181
2	91	63
3	133	77
4	128	82
5	137	75
6	85	58
7	132	89
8	124	79
9	88	60
10	145	88
11	137	78
12	145	103
13	66	49
14	235	190
15	265	179
16	258	176
17	176	111
Controls	950	603

A different way of presenting the second-year numbers is as follows:

Treatment Type	Phoenix	Pittsburgh	Total
Housing gap (minimum standards)	174	204	378
Housing gap (minimum rent)	207	245	452
Housing gap (no requirements)	40	63	103
Percentage of rent	298	407	705
Controls	282	321	603
Total	1,001	1,240	2,241

TARGET POPULATION: Renter households, residing in the counties of the experiment, and meeting the following tests: (1) Disposable income (less than $300 per worker annually) less than one-quarter of the C^* figure for households of that size in that city; (2) assets of under $5,000 (under $10,000 if 62 or older); (3) either two or more related persons of any age or with household head who was handicapped, disabled, 62 or older, or displaced by an urban renewal project; (4) resident in unsubsidized housing—public housing tenants were only eligible if they moved.

NUMBER OF TREATMENT GROUPS: Nineteen (with 2 control groups).

NUMBER AND LOCATION OF SITES: Two—Pittsburgh, Pennsylvania, and Phoenix, Arizona.

RESEARCH COMPONENTS:

Process analysis: Obtained reasons for refusal to enroll, choice not to participate, and condition of initial housing units.

Impact analysis: By comparison of means and various response-surface estimation techniques.

Benefit–cost analysis: A relative cost-effectiveness study was conducted comparing costs of housing allowances and public subsidies to housing construction.

MAJOR FINDINGS:

1. Many families refused to enroll, a finding that is important in estimating the costs of a national program; refusal to enroll did not seem to be related to the variables in the experiment, but to a disinterest in receiving public assistance. Many of those who did enroll did not participate (receive a payment), and this nonparticipation was substantially affected by the stringency of the housing requirements, the household's race, and the relative availability of housing meeting the minimum requirements (which varied between the sites). Participation is stated as the percentage of those enrolling (all of whom were eligible for immediate payments on income grounds) who received one or more payments.

Treatment/Site	Enrollment (%)	Participation (%)
No housing requirements		
Percentage of rent		
Pittsburgh	82	100
Phoenix	87	100
Housing gap		
Pittsburgh	78	100
Phoenix	90	100
Minimum standards		
Pittsburgh	75	40
Phoenix	84	54
Minimum rent (.7)		
Pittsburgh	74	81
Phoenix	82	74
Minimum rent (.9)		
Pittsburgh	73	58
Phoenix	81	54

Higher payments increased participation. At an average monthly payment level of $43, one-fourth of all renters who had to meet housing requirements participated; at twice that level, twice as many participated.

2. Estimated Experimental Effect on Housing Expenditures and Services among Households Meeting Requirements Two Years after Enrollment (services measured with "hedonic index" based on characteristics of the housing unit).

Site/Treatment	Change in Expenditures (%)	Change in Expenditures as Share of Payment (%)	Change in Services (%)
Pittsburgh			
No restriction	2.6	5.7	3.4
Percentage of rent	8.0	14.0	3.0
Minimum rent (.7)	− 3.6	− 7.8	0
Minimum rent (.9)	8.5*	23.3	0.9
Minimum standards	4.3	8.6	3.1
Phoenix:			
No restriction	16.0*	19.0	12.6*
Percentage of rent	8.0	23.7	− 1.0
Minimum rent (.7)	15.7	25.5	11.0*
Minimum rent (.9)	28.4*	41.3	18.9*
Minimum standards	16.2*	27.4	10.2*

*Statistically significant difference from zero.

To date no satisfactory explanation for this divergence (in sites) has been found.

3. The impact on housing expenditures in the Housing Gap treatments differs according to whether the household initially occupied a unit satisfying the minimum standards at enrollment. Of those whose units did not, most who ended up participating satisfied the requirements by moving. The numbers of those who moved and the distances they moved were such that the impact on residential segregation would have been negligible.

Site/Treatment	Estimated Experimental Effects		Change in Services (%)
	Change in Expenditures (%)	As Share of Payment (%)	
Pittsburgh:			
Satisfactory			
Minimum rent (.7)	2.4	(5.7)	0.5
Minimum rent (.9)	4.6	(13.7)	− 0.7
Minimum standards	1.1	(2.3)	0.8

Site/Treatment	Estimated Experimental Effects		Change in Services (%)
	Change in Expenditures (%)	As Share of Payment (%)	
Unsatisfactory			
Minimum rent (.7)	8.7	(15.4)	−0.9
Minimum rent (.9)	15.8*	(38.8)	3.1
Minimum standards	7.5*	(14.2)	5.6
Phoenix:			
Satisfactory			
Minimum rent (.7)	−1.2	(−2.7)	2.5
Minimum rent (.9)	7.4	(15.4)	4.2
Minimum standards	−0.7	(−2.1)	8.2*
Unsatisfactory			
Minimum rent (.7)	42.0*	(41.7)	20.2*
Minimum rent (.9)	42.6*	(50.0)	26.0*
Minimum standards	23.6*	(32.8)	10.5*

*Statistically significant difference from zero.

4. Estimates of income elasticity ranged from .29 to .34 in Pittsburgh and from .26 to .44 in Phoenix. Estimates of price elasticity ranged from −.11 to −.18 in Pittsburgh and from −.23 to −.24 in Phoenix. Differences come in part from econometric specification, in part from differences in the definition of income.

TIME TRENDS IN FINDINGS: Only two years of data were collected.

DESIGN ISSUES:

1. Payments guaranteed over three years may not induce the same behavioral changes as a permanent program. For instance, a family that would need to move in order to receive payments might also realize that a second move would be necessary at the close of the experiment, because they could not afford the unit the experiment had subsidized.

2. The measure of housing services, a hedonic quality index, was developed for this experiment and is not completely satisfactory.

3. The least-generous plans were assigned only to very low-income members of the sample, because otherwise many enrolled persons would have been eligible only for very small payments or none at all, limiting their benefits from participating in the experiment. However, this tends to confound the treatment effect with the characteristics of households assigned to the treatment.

4. "The price elasticity per se is unlikely to be of much use in designing a housing-allowance program. A percent-of-rent formula offers such attractive opportunities for mutually beneficial fraud

on the part of landlords and renters that (it) is hard to imagine it ever being implemented" (Harvey Rosen, in Bradbury and Downs 1981).
5. Most households change their housing units infrequently, and the effect of the experiment will occur with some lag; however, the timing of the lag is not known with certainty and requires modeling assumptions.

REPLICABILITY: Replicable. Administrative policy manuals developed, and so forth.

GENERALIZABILITY:
1. The single most important finding of this experiment is the extremely low income elasticity of housing demand among low-income people. This result was confirmed in the "Supply" portion of the Experimental Housing Allowance Program. One implication of this finding is that housing allowances would not result in large inflation of rents. Another implication is that in the objectives of a housing-allowance program, there is a trade-off between assisting large numbers of people and improving the quality of the existing housing stock.
2. Results of this experiment and the other components of the EHAP were used by the Urban Institute to project total costs of housing-allowance programs using microsimulation techniques.

FUNDING SOURCE: HUD, Assistant Secretary for Policy Development and Research. Key personnel: Jerry Fitts and Terrence Connell.

TREATMENT ADMINISTRATOR: Abt Associates. Key personnel: Ellen Bakeman.

EVALUATOR: Abt Associates. Key personnel: Stephen D. Kennedy and James Wallace.

ENABLING LEGISLATION: Housing and Urban Development Act of 1970, title V; amended in 1974 for additional funding. The experiment was one component of an Experimental Housing Allowance Program (EHAP), which included a Supply Experiment and an Administrative Agency Experiment; these other components were not random-assignment treatment evaluations.

INFORMATION SOURCES: A large number of unpublished reports are available from Abt Associates. The following are published sources: Raymond J. Struyk and Mark Bendick, Jr., ed., Housing Vouchers for the Poor: Lessons from a National Experiment, Urban Institute, 1981; Katharine L. Bradbury and Anthony Downs, ed., Do Housing Allowances Work? Brookings Institution, 1981; U.S. Department of Housing and Urban Development (HUD), *Experimental Housing Allowance Program: A 1979 Report of Findings*, 1979; and HUD, *The Experimental Housing Allowance Program: Conclusions*, 1980.

PUBLIC-USE ACCESS TO DATA: No public-use file exists.

FREESTANDING HOUSING VOUCHER DEMONSTRATION

SUMMARY: This demonstration, conducted from 1985 to 1988, tested the effects of having vouchers with an experimental payment formula on a large sample of low-income families. Subjects were followed for one year.

COST: Roughly $3 million (1987).

TIME FRAME: April 1985–September 1988; data collected, same. Final report, May 1990.

TREATMENTS TESTED:
1. Certificate program (controls). The pre-existing Section 8 program. It pays a monthly stipend to the landlord on behalf of a tenant living in privately owned, existing housing. The amount of the payment is the difference between the rent (plus certain scheduled utility allowances, if they are not included in the rent) and the tenant's contribution, which is essentially 30 percent of income. Tenants must live in a unit meeting HUD's housing quality criteria, and the rent must be less than or equal to the local fair market rent (FMR) (set by HUD) and judged "reasonable" by the Public Housing Agency (PHA). From the time of enrollment into the program, tenants have two to four months to find acceptable housing under the program.
2. Housing Voucher program (experimentals). This treatment differs from the current program in the payment formula; the housing unit must still meet HUD quality criteria. The housing assistance payment is equal to $P - .3Y$, where P is the local rental payment standard, initially set equal to the fair market rent, or FMR, and Y is income. Thus, the Public Housing Agency no longer sets a ceiling on gross rent. The tenant has, on the one hand, an incentive to obtain housing at a lower cost than the FMR, if it can be found,

and, on the other hand, the option to secure housing that costs more than the PHA would allow under the Certificate program.

OUTCOMES OF INTEREST: (1) Success rate (percentage of those enrolled who find acceptable units and become recipients); (2) Rent payments; (3) Rent burdens; (4) Program payments; and (5) Administrative costs.

SAMPLE SIZE: 12,390, evenly divided. Many of the analyses, however, use subsamples of about 4,500.

TARGET POPULATION: Lower-income families certified as eligible for Section 8 who live in large urban areas.

NUMBER OF TREATMENT GROUPS: Two (with one control group).

NUMBER AND LOCATION OF SITES: Sixteen—Atlanta, Georgia; Boston, Massachusetts; Buffalo and New York City, New York; Cleveland and Dayton, Ohio; Minneapolis, Minnesota; Montgomery County, Maryland; New Haven, Connecticut; Oakland, California; Omaha, Nebraska; Pittsburgh, Pennsylvania; St. Petersburg, Florida; San Antonio, Texas; and Seattle, Washington.

RESEARCH COMPONENTS:
   Process analysis: Not conducted.
   Impact analysis: Comparison of means and ordinary least squares (OLS).
   Benefit–cost analysis: Not conducted.

MAJOR FINDINGS:

	Voucher	Certificate
Success rate, overall	64.6	61.0%*
Success rate when $P=$ FMR (PHAs had some discretion about changing P)	64.4	59.5*
Total rent paid by recipients	$463	$437*
Rent burden as percentage of income:		
At initial payment	34%	31%
At annual recertification	35	31*
Among recipients who:		
Did not move	28	31**
Moved	39	31
Monthly assistance payments, overall average	$310	$293**
Initial assistance payment	307	287**
Payment at recertification	304	298

	Voucher	Certificate
Administrative cost per slot:		
Initial eligibility	$579	$598
Annual ongoing	257	261

*Difference significant at .05 percent level.
**Difference significant at .01 percent level.

Regressions on housing quality appear to show that roughly half of the higher rent payments under the Voucher plan go to improved housing quality, with the other half going to higher landlord income.

TIME TRENDS IN FINDINGS: As noted above under "Rent burden" and "Monthly assistance payments" in "Major Findings."

DESIGN ISSUES: The most obvious problem is the absence of a process analysis. The voucher program changes the budget constraint of the Public Housing Agency as well as that of the subjects, and the absence of a process analysis means that we do not know how the PHAs responded or whether their responses affect experimental results.

REPLICABILITY: Replicable.

GENERALIZABILITY: Designed for generalizability to the population of large urban PHAs. Two special caveats are (1) the sample is drawn from applicants for the current Section 8 program; and (2) more important, many experimentals were renting from landlords with substantial Section 8 experience. If the entire program changed over to vouchers, landlord rent-setting behavior might change as well. PHAs may have effective monopsony power with respect to a group of Section 8 landlords that tenants shopping individually cannot match.

FUNDING SOURCE: HUD, Office of Policy Development and Research. Key personnel: David Einhorn.

TREATMENT ADMINISTRATORS: Nineteen Public Housing Agencies (PHAs). Key personnel: None.

EVALUATOR: Abt Associates. Key personnel: Mireille L. Leger and Stephen D. Kennedy.

ENABLING LEGISLATION: Housing and Urban/Rural Recovery Act of 1983, PL 98-181.

POLICY EFFECTS: The results of the experiment show that vouchers are both more flexible (serve more people) and more expensive (for recipients and the government alike) than certificates; there is no clearcut winner. Both sides of the argument can mine the results for evidence supporting their positions. While the experiment was being conducted, the Reagan and Bush administrations took various incremental actions to increase the number of vouchers through administrative action.

INFORMATION SOURCE: Mireille L. Leger and Stephen D. Kennedy, *Final Comprehensive Report of the Freestanding Housing Voucher Demonstration*, 2 vols., U.S. Department of Housing and Urban Development (HUD), Office of Policy Development and Research, May 1990.

PUBLIC-USE ACCESS TO DATA: HUD possesses the data, but has not created a public-use file.

NATIONAL JOB TRAINING PARTNERSHIP ACT (JTPA) STUDY

SUMMARY: This demonstration, conducted from 1987 to 1991, tested the effects of the Job Training Partnership Act (JTPA) Title II program's employment and training services on a large sample of economically disadvantaged adults and youths. Subjects were followed for 30 months.

COST: Total evaluation costs were approximately $23 million from 1986 to 1994.

TIME FRAME: Enrollment period, November 1987–September 1989; data collected through December 1991; final report, 1994.

TREATMENTS TESTED: Access to Title II-A services under the JTPA. Participants were divided into three groups by local staff according to which services were deemed appropriate. They were then randomly assigned to a treatment or control group for each service strategy. Specific services varied widely across sites, but could include the following:

Specific Program Service	Service Strategy		
	Classroom Training Group	On-the-Job Training (OJT)/Job Search Assistance Group	Other Activities Group
Classroom training in occupational skills	Yes	No	Yes
OJT	No	Yes	Yes
Job Search Assistance	Yes	Yes	Yes
Basic education	Yes	Yes	Yes
Work experience	Yes	Yes	Yes
Miscellaneous	Yes	Yes	Yes

The control group was not allowed to receive services for 18 months.

OUTCOMES OF INTEREST: (1) Earnings; (2) Employment; (3) Welfare receipt; and (4) Attainment of educational credentials and occupational competencies.

SAMPLE SIZE: Full experimental sample, 20,602. Classroom training group, 7,090; on-the-job training group, 7,412; and other activities group, 6,100. Sample size includes both treatment and control group members. On average, 68 percent of sample members were randomly assigned to treatment groups.

TARGET POPULATION: Eligible JTPA Title II adults and out-of-school youth. The study focused on four subgroups: adult women; adult men; female out-of-school youths; and male out-of-school youths.

NUMBER OF TREATMENT GROUPS: Two groups (including control) in each of the three service subgroups.

NUMBER AND LOCATION OF SITES: Sixteen sites throughout the United States: Fort Wayne, Indiana; Coosa Valley, Georgia; Corpus Christi, Texas; Jackson, Mississippi; Providence, Rhode Island; Springfield, Missouri; Jersey City, New Jersey; Marion, Ohio; Oakland, California; Omaha, Nebraska; Larimer County, Colorado; Heartland, Florida; Northwest, Minnessota; Butte, Montanta; Decatur, Illinois; and Cedar Rapids, Iowa.

RESEARCH COMPONENTS:
   Process analysis: Examined sample and participant characteristics, patterns of enrollment and participation, and the random assignment process.
   Impact analysis: Conducted using multiple regression.
   Benefit–cost analysis: Conducted.

MAJOR FINDINGS: Because the control group was able to receive employment and training services from non-JTPA providers, impacts reflect the incremental effect of JTPA services beyond what sample members could have accomplished without access to JTPA. Impacts were estimated separately by subgroups: adult men; adult women; female youth; male youth, nonarrestees; and male youth, arrestees.

ADULTS

1. The treatment group received significantly ($p = .01$) more employment and training services than did the control group; on average, men received 169 more hours of service and women received 136 more hours.
2. For adult women, average earnings over the 30-month period following random assignment were $1,176 (9.6 percent) greater for the treatment group than the control group. This is significant at the .01 level. For men, earnings were $978 (5.3 percent) greater for the treatment group. This is significant at the .10 level.
3. Earnings gains came more from an increase in hours worked (an employment effect), than from an increase in average hourly earnings (a wage effect). This was especially true for women.
4. JTPA resulted in a substantial and statistically significant impact on the attainment of a high school credential (diploma or equivalent) for adult female school dropouts. The findings for adult males were also positive, although not statistically significant.
5. The greatest earnings impact was estimated for women in the OJT/ JST and other activities subgroups.
6. For adult women, there was no significant program impact on Aid to Families with Dependent Children (AFDC) or food stamp receipt. For men, there was a small, but significant, *increase* in AFDC receipt for the treatment group.

YOUTH

1. JTPA resulted in a significant increase in the amount of employment and training services for all categories of youth. (Female youth in the treatment group received, on average, 182 more hours than their control group counterparts; male youth nonarrestees received 175 more hours; and male youth arrestees received 127 more hours.)
2. There were no significant treatment–control group differences for the quarterly earnings of female youths and male youth nonarrestees. For male youth arrestees, there was a great discrepancy between survey data and data using unemployment wage records. The former suggests significantly *less* earnings for the treatment

group. The wage record data suggest no significant treatment–control group difference.

3. JTPA had a significant positive effect on the attainment of a high school credential for female youths (7.7 percent more treatment group females, compared to their control group counterparts, had a high school diploma or GED 30 months after random assignment), but not for male youths.

4. No significant treatment–control group differences were found for welfare receipts for male or female youths.

TIME TRENDS IN FINDINGS: There was a gradual increase in the earnings of all adult participants—treatment and control group—over time.

DESIGN ISSUES:

1. Impacts are reported per assignee, but 34 percent of women and 38 percent of men in the treatment group did not participate in JTPA. Therefore, this reflects the impact of *offering* JTPA services, rather than receiving them. Impacts per participant were not estimated directly from the experimental data, but, rather, were inferred using an extension of the data. The estimates reported above are in terms of impact per assignee, rather than per participant.

2. Site selection was done on a voluntary basis. Service delivery areas (SDAs) were not mandated to participate. Many were reluctant because they feared political fallout from random assignment, they found the design too complex, or they could not obtain agreement among all local participants.

3. Because JTPA program staff often recommend more than one program service for an applicant, the study was designed to measure impacts of clusters of program services, not single services in isolation, such as classroom training, on-the-job training, or job search assistance.

4. Formal agreements with some of the SDAs excluded certain small groups of applicants from the study (and from random assignment) owing to logistical reasons, recruitment difficulties, and/or the nonvoluntary nature of certain applications.

5. A 2 to 1 ratio of treatment to control group members was used to minimize the number of persons that had to be turned away by local program staff.

REPLICABILITY: Replicable.

GENERALIZABILITY: Designed to generalize to the entire nation. However, site selection was not a probability sample, and the SDAs that volunteered to be part of the study may differ from the national population in unobservable ways. They differed in two observable ways: (1) No large, central cities were included owing to the decentralized nature of service in these locations; and (2) The study sites tended to emphasize classroom training and job search assistance *more*, and OJT and miscellaneous services *less*, than their counterparts nationally.

FUNDING SOURCE: U.S. Department of Labor. Key personnel: David Lah.

TREATMENT ADMINISTRATOR: Local service delivery areas (SDAs) in the 16 sites. See Orr et al. (1996: ix–x) for key personnel at each site.

EVALUATORS: There were two separate U.S. Department of Labor contracts. Part A went to Manpower Demonstration Research Corporation (MDRC) and its subcontractors, who were responsible for site recruiting and implementation of random assignment. Part B went to Abt Associates and its subcontractors to design the study, collect data, and conduct the analyses. Co-principal investigators: Larry Orr and Howard Bloom, Abt Associates; and Judith Gueron, MDRC.

ENABLING LEGISLATION: Job Training Partnership Act of 1982.

POLICY EFFECTS: Following the results and recommendations of the National JTPA study, the U.S. Department of Labor proposed a 47 percent reduction in funding for Title II-C (the program for out-of-school youth) and a modest increase for Title II-A (the adult program). Congress responded by applying a large reduction for Title II-C and allowing the 11 percent increase in funding for the adult program to remain intact. Thus, findings appear to have had an impact on national policy.

INFORMATION SOURCES: Larry L. Orr, Howard S. Bloom, Stephen H. Bell, Fred Doolittle, Winston Lin, and George Cave, *Does Training for the Disadvantaged Work? Evidence from the National JTPA Study*, Urban Institute Press, 1996; Larry L. Orr, Howard S. Bloom, Stephen H. Bell, Winston Lin, George Cave, and Fred Doolittle, *The National JTPA Study: Impacts, Benefits, and Costs of Title II-A*, Abt Associates, 1994; Fred Doolittle and Linda Traeger, *Implementing the National JTPA Study*, Manpower Demonstration Research Corporation, 1990.

PUBLIC-USE ACCESS TO DATA: Available through U.S. Department of Labor.

EMERGENCY FOOD AND HOMELESSNESS INTERVENTION PROJECT

SUMMARY: This demonstration, conducted between 1988 and 1990, tested the effects of in-home case management on a medium-sized sample of low-income families. Subjects were followed for six months.

COST: The evaluation cost approximately $5,000, but there was a considerable amount of donated services. Service cost per treatment family was estimated at $700.

TIME FRAME: October 1988–October 1990.

TREATMENTS TESTED: Home-based case management that included assessment, agency referrals (for counseling or health services), home visits, and transportation. The control group received food and referrals with no additional follow-up.

OUTCOMES OF INTEREST: (1) Employment; (2) Income; and (3) Welfare receipt.

SAMPLE SIZE: Total, 394; treatment, 199; control, 195.

TARGET POPULATION: Low-income families requesting emergency food.

NUMBER OF TREATMENT GROUPS: Two (including control).

NUMBER AND LOCATION OF SITES: One—Lincoln, Nebraska.

RESEARCH COMPONENTS:
    Process analysis: Conducted with attention given to intake and assignment procedures, attrition, and follow-up.
    Impact analysis: Conducted—comparison of means.
    Benefit-cost analysis: Conducted.

MAJOR FINDINGS:
1. The project group had significantly higher wages compared to the control group. Average wages for project group increased $192 per month; control group wages increased $124 per month.
2. Treatment group families had a significantly greater reduction (9.3 percent) in their level of poverty as compared to the control families.
3. Repeat requests for emergency food and the risk of homelessness were unaffected by the intervention.
4. Families with a male head of household and no evidence of alcohol or drug abuse showed the greatest gains.
5. Benefit–cost analysis suggests that the rate of return on investment of case management was excellent (intervention cost per family, per year, $696; income gain in wages by project families over control families, $812 per year).

TIME TRENDS IN FINDINGS: The report suggests that some clients were not ready (owing to personal problems and other obstacles) for further training and education until the short-term case management was completed. While no long-term follow-up was done, informal sources suggest that many clients did go on to receive these services after the six-month period of case management.

DESIGN ISSUES: The evaluators felt that the tool used to assess outcomes such as risk of homelessness and self-sufficiency was not as good as it could have been. It was very subjective and made some outcomes difficult to measure. A new tool was developed for later projects.

REPLICABILITY: Replicable. The Lincoln Action Program (LAP) has replicated this model in other agency projects.

GENERALIZABILITY: The project was voluntary and offered only to those families requesting emergency food. This may represent a distinct subgroup of low-income families. Few participant demographic characteristics are given to judge the representativeness of the sample (e.g., age, ethnicity, educational level are not given). However, Beatty Brasch of LAP contends the project is generalizable because the model has been well supported by other projects.

FUNDING SOURCE: Demonstration Partnership Program, Office of Community Services, Administration on Children and Families, U.S. Department of Health and Human Services (DHHS). Key personnel: Anne Guidery.

TREATMENT ADMINISTRATOR: Lincoln Action Program. Key personnel: Beatty Brasch, agency director; Mary Barry-Magsamen: project director.

EVALUATOR: SRI Gallup. Principal investigator: Gary Hoeltke.

ENABLING LEGISLATION: Demonstration Partnership Program under Section 408 of the Human Services Reauthorization Act of 1986, as amended.

INFORMATION SOURCES: U.S. Department of Health and Human Services, *Demonstration Partnership Programs: Summaries and Findings, FY 1988 and 1989,* 1991.

PUBLIC-USE ACCESS TO DATA: Available through Office of Community Services, DHHS.

PROJECT HOPE (HEAD START OPPORTUNITIES FOR PARENTS THROUGH EMPLOYMENT)

SUMMARY: This demonstration, conducted between 1989 and 1991, tested the effects of intensive case management, life-skills and job-readiness training on a small sample of parents with children enrolled in Head Start. Serious failures occurred in attempts to obtain follow-up information from the sample.

COST: $250,000, of which $25,000 was for evaluation.

TIME FRAME: October 1989–April 1991.

TREATMENTS TESTED: All treatment subjects received intensive case management, and were enrolled in a six-week program of life-skills and job-readiness training. In addition, they could receive child care, tuition assistance, entrepreneur training workshops, or bus fare, depending on their needs and goals. Controls were referred to other agencies.

OUTCOMES OF INTEREST: (1) Employment; (2) Enrollment in training.

SAMPLE SIZE: Total, 140; treatment, 73; control, 67.

TARGET POPULATION: Parents of children enrolled in Head Start (i.e., low-income—three-quarters received public assistance).

NUMBER OF TREATMENT GROUPS: Two (including control).

NUMBER AND LOCATION OF SITES: One—Columbus, Ohio.

RESEARCH COMPONENTS:

Process analysis: Mailed questionnaire with telephone follow-up on employment, sense of progress, participation, and helpfulness of staff.

Impact analysis: Telephone interview.

Benefit–cost analysis: Not conducted.

MAJOR FINDINGS:

1. Only 75 total subjects were reached (by telephone) for the evaluation instrument, and only 24 of them were willing to be interviewed. Among respondents, the 13 controls were more likely to be employed, and were less likely to be in training or educational programs, than the 11 experimentals.

TIME TRENDS IN FINDINGS: None.

DESIGN ISSUES:

1. The sample was too small at the outset. Furthermore, the evaluator only attempted to contact 116 of the 140 in the sample; of the 116, 55 telephone numbers were disconnected; of the 61 connections, only 24 responded.
2. The "formative analysis" (questionnaire followed up with a telephone call) shed less light on what actually happened in the program than the usual observation and record keeping of a process analysis would have.
3. The follow-up period for the evaluation was inadequate.

REPLICABILITY: There is always a question as to whether "intensive case management" is replicable. Presumably, there were written materials for the life-skills and job-readiness courses, but there was no treatment manual.

GENERALIZABILITY: There were no findings to generalize.

FUNDING SOURCE: Demonstration Partnership Program, Office of Community Services, Administration for Children and Families, U.S. Department of Health and Human Services.

TREATMENT ADMINISTRATOR: Columbus Metropolitan Area Community Action Organization, with four "partner" service providers. (See Appendix I for an explanation of the DPP project "partners.") Key personnel: Robert Day.

EVALUATOR: Robert Ransom, Ohio State University.

ENABLING LEGISLATION: Demonstration Partnership Program under Section 408 of the Human Services Reauthorization Act of 1986, as amended.

INFORMATION SOURCE: Office of Community Services, U.S. Department of Health and Human Services, *Demonstration Partnership Programs Projects: Summary of Final Evaluation Findings from FY 1989,* Monograph Series 100-89: Case Management Family Intervention Models, 1992.

PUBLIC-USE ACCESS TO DATA: Available through Office of Community Services, DHHS.

Part Sixteen

SUBSTANCE ABUSERS

SUMMARY: This demonstration, conducted from 1972 to 1978, tested the effects of supported work experience on a medium-sized sample of adult substance abusers. Subjects were followed for three years.

COST: $36.2 million (1975)—does not include research cost. Also includes the payments to treatment participants who were not in the initial sample; cost of research only, not available.

TIME FRAME: July 1972–June 1976; data collected, July 1972–June 1978; final report, 1978.

TREATMENTS TESTED: Experimentals were randomly selected for work from volunteers. They were placed in small work crews with persons of similar background, and were confronted with graduated demands for productivity, graduated rewards for performance, sympathetic but firm supervision, and consistent daily communication of management expectations. One crew member was the designated crew chief, and there were additional supportive services. Typical work: office/clerical, messenger, and building maintenance; usually the work was performed for the city government. Controls received no services from the demonstration.

OUTCOMES OF INTEREST: (1) Employment; (2) Earnings; (3) Rearrest; and (4) Drug and alcohol use.

SAMPLE SIZE: Experimentals, 194; controls, 207.

TARGET POPULATION: Substance abusers, at least 18 years old, enrolled in drug abuse treatment for at least three months, currently unemployed, receiving public assistance, unemployed at least 12 of the past 24 months, and not intoxicated at interview.

NUMBER OF TREATMENT GROUPS: Two (with one control group).

NUMBER AND LOCATION OF SITES: One—New York City.

RESEARCH COMPONENTS:
   Process analysis: Conducted with open-ended interviewing. Self-reported earnings, arrests, and drug use tested against data available from tax, police, and drug treatment clinic sources.
   Impact analysis: Conducted as a difference in means.
   Benefit–cost analysis: Conducted from a taxpayer perspective.

MAJOR FINDINGS:

1.	Experimentals	Controls
Weeks worked in three years	101	46
Earnings	$12,236	$4,968
Weekly earnings (if working) in unsubsidized jobs	$133	$108
Never received welfare payments over three years	46%	6%
Probability of arrest, first year	19%	31%
All of these differences are statistically significant.		

2. No significant impact was found on drug or alcohol use.
3. Experimentals were more likely to marry and to stay married.
4. Average taxpayer expenditures on experimentals: $13,127; average taxpayer benefits: $15,405; benefit-cost ratio: 1.12.

TIME TRENDS IN FINDINGS: All experimental effects diminished over time. For example, at the end of the first year, 74 percent of experimentals were working, compared with 30 percent of controls; at the end of three years, 49 percent of experimentals were working, compared with 36 percent of controls. Rearrest differences also vanish.

DESIGN ISSUES:
1. The benefit–cost evaluation is most sensitive to the valuation of the services provided, although conservative methods seem to have been used.
2. Displacement of outside contractors and of other workers is possible. Wildcat made a policy of not bidding for work performed by members of public service unions; on the other hand, it frequently offered services to city agencies at zero cost.

REPLICABILITY: Crew chiefs required special training. Project supervisors apparently had to possess entrepreneurial skills of a high order.

GENERALIZABILITY: The "National Supported Work Demonstration" (NSWD) was performed to determine whether the findings could be generalized. The "Wildcat" and NSWD participants were mostly addicted to heroin and were receiving methadone maintenance.

FUNDING SOURCES: New York City Addiction Services Agency, Department of Employment; U.S. Department of Health and Human Services, National Institute on Drug Abuse; U.S. Department of Justice, Law Enforcement Assistance Administration; and the U.S. Department of Labor, Labor, Employment, and Training Administration. Key personnel: Unknown.

TREATMENT ADMINISTRATOR: Vera Institute of Justice, which set up the Wildcat Service Corporation. Key personnel: Herbert Sturz and Kenneth Marion.

EVALUATOR: Vera Institute of Justice. Key personnel: Lucy N. Friedman.

ENABLING LEGISLATION: Waiver of regulations to permit diversion to wages of welfare funds otherwise payable to participants.

POLICY EFFECTS: The findings from this experiment, according to both the "Wildcat Experiment" and the "National Supported Work Demonstration" reports, led the Ford Foundation and the Department of Labor, with support from other sources, to initiate the creation of the Manpower Demonstration Research Corporation to oversee a national experimental evaluation of the supported work concept.

INFORMATION SOURCE: Lucy N. Friedman, "The Wildcat Experiment: An Early Test of Supported Work in Drug Abuse Rehabilitation," National Institute on Drug Abuse, 1978.

PUBLIC-USE ACCESS TO DATA: We have no information about a public-use file for this demonstration.

JOB SEEKERS' WORKSHOP

SUMMARY: This demonstration, conducted from 1976 to 1979, tested the effects of an employment-related workshop and modified job club on small samples of heroin abusers. Subjects were followed for three months.

COST: Roughly $120,000 (1979) for the latter two studies.

TIME FRAME: First study, 1976; second and third studies, 1978–1979; data collected, three-month follow-ups only; final report, 1981.

TREATMENTS TESTED: There were three experiments:
1. A (Hall et al. 1977). Random assignment was performed by use of the date of the workshop the subject chose, relying on the fact that experimental and control workshops alternated randomly according to a schedule not known at intake. Controls attended a three-hour meeting during which they learned about available employment resources (e.g., union halls); they discussed their job interests

with group leaders, and leaders made appropriate suggestions. Experimentals attended a similar meeting. They then attended a workshop lasting eight hours over three days, corresponding to the initial phases of the Job Club model but with much less supervised job search. Much more attention was placed on appropriate interview behavior than on obtaining interviews (probably because of the favorable local job market). Interviews in which participants role-played were set up two days after the workshop for both groups.

2. *B* (Hall, Loeb, Coyne, et al. 1981). Subjects were stratified according to sex, parole/probation status (yes or no), and past job history. Members of each stratum were randomly assigned to experimental or control treatments. These treatments were the same as in *A*, although the experimental treatment took 12 hours over four days.

3. *C* (Hall, Loeb, LeVois, et al. 1981). The pilot study had simple random assignment, with an experimental treatment that was a little longer than that in *A* or *B*, mostly because of two days at the end with no preset structure, where subjects could identify areas in which they wanted more work.

In all three experiments, self-reported employment was verified with other sources.

OUTCOMES OF INTEREST: (1) Employment and (2) Performance at simulated interview.

SAMPLE SIZE: Experiment *A*: 35 experimentals, 20 controls; experiment *B*: 30 experimentals, 30 controls; experiment *C*: 23 experimentals, 26 controls.

TARGET POPULATION: For experiment *A*, the target population were parolees or those on probation with documented histories of heroin abuse. Those who were psychotic, illiterate, or anticipated serving jail time in the next three months were screened out. For experiments *B* and *C*, the target populations were patients at methadone maintenance clinics, with the same exclusion criteria as in *A*. For experiment *C*, the target population was the same as for *B*.

NUMBER OF TREATMENT GROUPS: Two (with one control group).

NUMBER AND LOCATION OF SITES: One—San Francisco, California.

RESEARCH COMPONENTS:
Process analysis: Not conducted.
Impact analysis: Conducted as a difference in means.
Benefit–cost analysis: Not conducted.

MAJOR FINDINGS:

1. Experiment *A*. Eighty-six percent of experimentals found full- or part-time employment over the three-month follow-up, compared with 54 percent of controls. This difference is significant at the 1 percent level.
2. Experiment *B*. At the end of three months, 52 percent of experimentals had found jobs, compared with 30 percent of controls. The difference is not quite significant. "Regardless of [experimental or control] condition, subjects who reported no job history in the 5 years prior to the study start failed to find employment."
3. Experiment *C*. At three-month follow-up, 50 percent (9 of 18) of experimentals were employed, compared with 14 percent (3 of 23) of controls, a statistically significant difference. This difference may be partly biased by the dropping of 3 experimentals who failed to attend workshops from the sample.

TIME TRENDS IN FINDINGS: "Life Tables" are presented in Hall, Loeb, Coyne, et al. (1981) and Hall, Loeb, LeVois, et al. (1981), showing the differences in job-finding success over 12 weeks for each group. In *A*, the difference continues to increase up to 10 weeks; in *B*, the difference is stable after 3 weeks. There is no follow-up beyond three months.

DESIGN ISSUES: Differences in job-finding success were reported, but not relative wages or tenure on the job.

REPLICABILITY: Replicable.

GENERALIZABILITY: The samples were small, and the San Francisco job market is very favorable to job seekers.

FUNDING SOURCE: U.S. Department of Health and Human Services, National Institute on Drug Abuse, U.S. Public Health Service. Key personnel: None.

TREATMENT ADMINISTRATOR: University of California, Behavioral Treatment Research. Key personnel: Sharon Martinelli Hall.

EVALUATOR: University of California, Behavioral Treatment Research. Key personnel: Sharon Martinelli Hall.

ENABLING LEGISLATION: None.

INFORMATION SOURCES: Sharon Martinelli Hall, Peter Loeb, Joseph Norton, and Ray Yang, "Improving Vocational Placement in Drug Treatment Clients: a Pilot Study," *Addictive Behaviors*, vol. 2, 1977: 227–34; Sharon Martinelli Hall, Peter Loeb, Kristin Coyne, and James Cooper, "Increasing Employment in Ex-Heroin Addicts I: Criminal

Justice Sample," *Behavior Therapy*, vol. 12, 1981: 443–52; Sharon Martinelli Hall, Peter Loeb, Michel LeVois, and James Cooper, "Increasing Employment in Ex-Heroin Addicts II: Methadone Maintenance Sample," *Behavior Therapy*, volume 12, 1981: 453–60.

PUBLIC-USE ACCESS TO DATA: We have no information about a public-use file for this demonstration.

TRANSITION PROJECT

SUMMARY: This demonstration, conducted from 1980 to 1981, tested the effects of job orientation meetings on a medium-sized sample of substance abusers. Subjects were followed for up to one year.

COST: Research only: $187,000 (1980).

TIME FRAME: Demonstration period, 1980; data collected through 1981; final report, 1982.

TREATMENTS TESTED: Experimentals were able to attend two meetings a week over seven weeks, one at their own drug-treatment site, one at a corporation to which their group had been assigned. Company personnel would explain what types of jobs were available in that firm, the entry-level job requirements, what they looked for in job applications and interviews, how job performance was evaluated, and opportunities for advancement and benefits. Experimentals practiced interviewing people who made hiring decisions and observed employees at work. Lessons were reinforced at counseling sessions at the treatment site. Five corporations (a bank, a pharmaceutical, and three insurance companies) participated. There was no expectation that the corporation would hire the experimentals; the purpose was orientation to the rewards and demands of corporate life. Controls were not eligible for these services, although they were told about job-placement services offered by the administrator. All subjects were paid for their time in research interviews.

OUTCOMES OF INTEREST: (1) Employment; (2) Wages; (3) Education or training activity; (4) Drug or alcohol use; and (5) Criminal behavior.

SAMPLE SIZE: Experimentals, 146; controls, 78.

TARGET POPULATION: Substance abusers who (1) had been involved in drug treatment for at least six months, (2) were in good standing within treatment program guidelines (e.g., no evidence of recent substance abuse), (3) had no major time conflicts with participation (child care, criminal justice, medical), (4) could read at least on a sixth-grade level, (5) had no more than 6 months' work experience in the previous 12 months, (6) were considered nearing job readiness by counselors, but still having substantial barriers to employability, and (7) volunteered to participate.

NUMBER OF TREATMENT GROUPS: Two (with one control group).

NUMBER AND LOCATION OF SITES: One—New York City.

RESEARCH COMPONENTS:

Process analysis: Evaluations of the value of the program by participants, corporate staff, and treatment center staff. Attendance at sessions was on average about 50 percent of planned attendance.

Impact analysis: Used ordinary least squares, but reported only unadjusted means to facilitate exposition.

Benefit–cost analysis: Not conducted.

MAJOR FINDINGS:
1. Treatment effects on employment and wages were not significant.
2. Comparing only employed experimentals and employed controls, experimentals earned higher wages at their longest full-time job ($212 versus $193) and were more likely to work in a company with over 100 employees (36 percent versus 21 percent); but these results are not statistically significant, possibly because only 52 experimentals and 25 controls were reached during the follow-up who had held full-time jobs.
3. Differences in enrollment in academic or vocational training were insignificant, but experimentals were more likely to choose academic training, whereas controls were more likely to choose vocational training.
4. Subgroup analysis did not find statistically significant differences. The evaluators came to believe that the experimental/control differences were greatest in subgroups where controls had the poorest outcomes (i.e., were the most disadvantaged).
5. Controls were more likely than were experimentals to report that their principal activity in the previous year was illegal (10 percent versus 3 percent, a significant difference). The most common illegal activity was drug dealing.

6. There was no significant difference in alcohol or drug use. Most participants were in methadone maintenance, which only inhibits heroin use, but the majority in both groups had used cocaine since treatment. There was no significant difference in self-reported criminal activity.

TIME TRENDS IN FINDINGS: The patterns in 6-month and 12-month follow-ups are similar.

DESIGN ISSUES:

1. Small sample size does not permit finding statistical significance for subtle effects, if they are present.
2. Treatment counselors were usually not well trained in group counseling skills, which limited the usefulness of the clinic sessions.

REPLICABILITY: Replicable.

GENERALIZABILITY: See "Design Issues."

FUNDING SOURCE: U.S. Department of Labor, Employment and Training Administration. Key personnel: Unknown.

TREATMENT ADMINISTRATOR: National Association on Drug Abuse Problems (NADAP). Key personnel: Holly Robinson.

EVALUATOR: NADAP. Key personnel: Don Des Jarlais.

ENABLING LEGISLATION: None.

INFORMATION SOURCES: Ellen Rossman, Don Des Jarlais, Sherry Derren, and Holly Robinson, "An Evaluation of a Corporate-Based Job Preparation Training Program, the Transition Project," National Association on Drug Abuse Problems (NADAP), 1982; photocopy—copies available from the NADAP.

PUBLIC-USE ACCESS TO DATA: We have no information about a public-use file for this demonstration.

Part Seventeen

INDIVIDUALS WITH MENTAL IMPAIRMENT

SUMMARY: This demonstration, conducted from 1972 to 1976, tested the effects of on-call care and case management by trained staff members on a small sample of adults with mental disabilities. Subjects were followed for up to three years.

COST: Unknown.

TIME FRAME: Demonstration period, 1972–75; data collected, 1972–76; final report, April 1980.

TREATMENTS TESTED:
1. Controls treated in hospital as long as necessary, and referrals made on release to community agencies. Outpatient follow-up was available.
2. Experimentals were seldom hospitalized initially and received 24-hour, on-call care from specially trained staff members focusing on coping skills (laundry, shopping, grooming, finding work, problem solving on the job, constructive use of leisure) over a 14-month period. Staff assertively sought out patients when they missed appointments or failed to show up for work; monitored use of medication; and counseled family members and employers.

OUTCOMES OF INTEREST: (1) Reductions in institutionalization; (2) Reductions in unemployment; and (3) Increases in earnings.

SAMPLE SIZE: Experimentals, 62; controls, 60.

TARGET POPULATION: Residents of Dane County, Wisconsin, aged 18–62, voluntarily seeking admission to a mental hospital, with any diagnosis other than severe organic brain syndrome or primary alcoholism.

NUMBER OF TREATMENT GROUPS: Two (with one control group).

NUMBER AND LOCATION OF SITES: One—Madison, Wisconsin.

RESEARCH COMPONENTS:
   Process analysis: Not conducted. Researchers could not say to what extent the effects observed were primarily due to increased compliance with prescribed medications.
   Impact analysis: Comparison of means.
   Benefit–cost analysis: Formal social benefit–cost analysis conducted.

MAJOR FINDINGS:
1. Significant reduction in time spent in psychiatric institutions. Significant differences extending over the first 16 months.
2. No significant differences in time spent in penal or general medical institutions.
3. Significant increase (through 20 months) in time spent in unsupervised living situations.
4. Significant reduction (through 28 months) in time spent unemployed, mostly achieved through substantial increase in time spent in sheltered employment.
5. Significant increases (through end of observation period) in nonsheltered earned income.
6. Net social benefits of $399 per patient. (Valued costs exceeded valued benefits by $6,128 for controls, $5,729 for experimentals.) However, the reduction in transfer payments of $564 per patient is essentially treated as a social benefit, which is not customary.

TIME TRENDS IN FINDINGS: All differences except in nonsheltered earnings tended to erode after treatment ended.

DESIGN ISSUES: The main employment effect comes from increasing use of sheltered employment. Where sheltered employment opportunity is less available than in the treatment community, this result may not generalize. Also, the use of sheltered placements raises questions about (1) possible displacement of other persons who might have found work in the sheltering agencies and (2) whether increased subsidies were needed by these sheltering agencies, which are not included as costs. If they were, the analysis did not include them.

REPLICABILITY: Requires specially trained, "assertive," around-the-clock staff.

GENERALIZABILITY: Investigators could not extrapolate the findings to larger or smaller communities, or to different labor-market conditions. See also comments on sheltered employment in "Design Issues."

FUNDING SOURCE: National Institute of Mental Health. Key personnel: None.

TREATMENT ADMINISTRATOR: Mendota Mental Health Institute. Key personnel: Leonard Stein and Mary Ann Test.

EVALUATOR: Mendota Mental Health Institute, Institute for Research on Poverty. Key Personnel: Burton Weisbrod.

ENABLING LEGISLATION: None.

INFORMATION SOURCES: Leonard Stein, Mary Ann Test, and Burton Weisbrod, "Alternative to Mental Hospital Treatment," *Archives of General Psychiatry*, 37 (April 1980): 392–412; Burton Weisbrod, "Benefit-Cost Analysis of a Controlled Experiment: Treating the Mentally Ill," Institute for Research on Poverty Reprint 444, University of Wisconsin–Madison, 1981.

PUBLIC-USE ACCESS TO DATA: We have no information about a public-use file for this information.

JOB PATH

SUMMARY: This demonstration, conducted from 1978 to 1980, tested the effects of subsidized and supervised work assignments on a small sample of adults with mental retardation. Subjects were followed for 18 months.

COST: Not available.

TIME FRAME: Demonstration period, 1978–79; data collected through 1980; final report, 1983.

TREATMENTS TESTED: The experimental treatment placed subjects in supported work assignments, initially in the public sector, for 35 hours a week. They were paid a subsidized minimum wage while learning skills related to food service, clerical work, mailroom work, maintenance work, housekeeping, and messenger work. Supervisors were assisted by Job Path counselors. Expectations were gradually increased over time, with transfers to more demanding job sites, sometimes going from the public to the private sector. Counseling and supervision were structured to give subjects feedback on how well they were doing, and weekly group meetings for trainees provided mutual support. Controls were returned to the referral agencies from which they had come; six of the controls subsequently were allowed to enter the experimental treatment after the research intake was completed, which complicated the interpretation of some of the research findings.

OUTCOME OF INTEREST: Employment.

SAMPLE SIZE: Experimentals, 60; controls, 60.

TARGET POPULATION: Adults with mental retardation who did not hold unsubsidized employment (many of them worked in sheltered workshops).

NUMBER OF TREATMENT GROUPS: Two (with one control group).

NUMBER AND LOCATION OF SITES: One—New York City.

RESEARCH COMPONENTS:
   Process analysis: Not conducted in the usual sense; this was more like a pilot program. The project report authors stated that extensive job development work had to be performed (2,020 telephone contacts, etc.) to prepare 71 training sites and 34 unsubsidized jobs. They also reported the subjective responses of experimental subjects to the changes in their lives resulting from working in nonsheltered employment.
   Impact analysis: Conducted as a difference in means.
   Benefit–cost analysis: Not conducted.

MAJOR FINDINGS: In general, the authors did not report whether differences were statistically significant.
1. Employment
   Six months after intake: Forty-four percent (24 out of 54) of experimentals had full-time, unsubsidized jobs (usually this was their last Job Path job, and the employer had hired them without subsidy); 20 percent (13 out of 54) of controls had full-time jobs without subsidies; another 24 percent of controls had part-time, unsubsidized jobs.
   Twelve months after intake: Sixty-one percent of experimentals held full-time, unsubsidized positions; 24 percent of controls held such jobs; and another 12 percent had part-time jobs without subsidy.
   Fifteen months after intake: Sixty-one percent of experimentals held unsubsidized jobs (hours unspecified), whereas 30 percent of controls did.
   Eighteen months after intake: Seventy-two percent of experimentals and 42 percent of controls had unsubsidized employment, a difference that is statistically significant.
2. Wages
   Fifteen months after intake: Average weekly earnings of employed experimentals, $146; of employed controls, $117.

3. *Benefits*

Most employed experimentals had private health and dental insurance, paid sick days and vacations, and workman's compensation coverage. Most employed controls did not. Sample sizes declined over time.

TIME TRENDS IN FINDINGS: Given above.

DESIGN ISSUES:

1. Small sample size. Apparently this is the reason the authors generally did not report statistical significance.
2. New York City is a more difficult environment for independent adults with mental retardation than some other areas; on the other hand, there is a larger variety of employers.
3. A deteriorating labor market over the course of the experiment.
4. Pilot project staff were frequently more able or more enthusiastic than staff in regular projects.

REPLICABILITY: Replicable.

GENERALIZABILITY: Not generalizable, because of items mentioned in "Design Issues." But see "Structured Training and Employment Transitional Services Demonstration" (STETS) and "Transitional Employment Training Demonstration" (TETD) summaries.

FUNDING SOURCE: A private foundation. Hillsman does not recall which one.

TREATMENT ADMINISTRATOR: Job Path (of the Vera Institute of Justice). Key personnel: Arlene Silberman.

EVALUATOR: Vera Institute of Justice. Key personnel: Sally T. Hillsman and Janet Weinglass.

ENABLING LEGISLATION: None.

POLICY EFFECTS: Sally Hillsman has stated that this study's treatment and findings have had a powerful impact on policy, and have changed the nature of support services to individuals with developmental disabilities in New York and across the country.

INFORMATION SOURCES: Sally T. Hillsman, Janet Weinglass, and Arlene Silberman, "Fostering Independence in Developmentally Disabled Adults: Supported Work as a Rehabilitative Mechanism," Paper presented at the annual meeting of the American Orthopsychiatric Association, Boston, Massachusetts, April 1983, photocopy; copies can be obtained from Vera Institute of Justice.

PUBLIC-USE ACCESS TO DATA: We have no information about a public-use file for this demonstration.

STRUCTURED TRAINING AND EMPLOYMENT TRANSITIONAL SERVICES DEMONSTRATION (STETS)

SUMMARY: This demonstration, conducted from 1981 to 1984, tested the effects of training, work placement, and follow-up services on a medium-sized sample of young adults with low IQs. Subjects were followed for up to three years.

COST: $2.5 million (1983) for service delivery; research only, $1.2 million (1983) for impact and benefit–cost analysis.

TIME FRAME: Demonstration period, November 1981–June 1984; data collected through October 1984; final report, 1985.

TREATMENTS TESTED: Experimentals received a three-phase treatment of up to 18 months. Phase 1 consisted of initial training and support services in a low-stress work environment, with paid employment of up to 500 hours. Phase 2 was a period of on-the-job training (subsidized or unsubsidized) in local firms and agencies, emphasizing job performance and work stress resembling the demands faced by nondisabled workers in the same types of jobs. Phase 2 jobs were intended to be potentially permanent jobs in which participants would continue after the withdrawal of program support. Phase 3 consisted of up to 6 months of follow-up services to workers who had made the transition into unsubsidized, competitive employment. Controls received no STETS services.

OUTCOMES OF INTEREST: (1) Employment; (2) Earnings; (3) Transfer recipiency; and (4) Payments.

SAMPLE SIZE: Experimentals, 236; controls, 231.

TARGET POPULATION: Young adults aged 18–24 years with IQ scores between 40 and 80, limited prior work experience, and no severe secondary handicaps.

NUMBER OF TREATMENT GROUPS: Two (with one control group).

NUMBER AND LOCATION OF SITES: Five—Cincinnati, Ohio; Los Angeles, California; New York City; St. Paul, Minnesota; Tucson, Arizona.

RESEARCH COMPONENTS:

Process analysis: Conducted. The project report authors believed the evidence suggests that ongoing programs would have an impact greater than that found in the full sample; the employment behavior of experimentals and controls was found to differ most, and the administrative cost per participant was lowest, during the "steady-state period," defined as the five months during which client intake reached its maximum monthly rate and during which operations were relatively smooth.

Impact analysis: Conducted with ordinary least squares (OLS). Probit and tobit were also used where appropriate and did not yield substantively different results than those yielded using OLS.

Benefit–cost analysis: Conducted from participant, taxpayer, and social perspectives.

MAJOR FINDINGS:

		Month 6	Month 15	Month 22
1.	Employment in regular (unsubsidized) job:			
	Experimentals (%)	11.8	26.2*	31.0*
	Controls (%)	10.7	16.8	19.1
2.	Average weekly earnings from regular job (includes zeros):			
	Experimentals ($)	11.81	26.90*	36.36*
	Controls ($)	9.81	16.31	20.55
3.	Average weekly earnings from any job (includes zeros):			
	Experimentals ($)	52.39*	37.91*	40.79*
	Controls ($)	25.93	26.48	28.41
4.	Percentage in any training (including STETS):			
	Experimentals (%)	61.7*	20.6*	16.6*
	Controls (%)	40.6	28.4	29.1
5.	Percentage in any schooling:			
	Experimentals (%)	7.5*	6.2	8.0
	Controls (%)	15.7	10.1	11.4
6.	Percentage receiving any cash transfers (most commonly SSI, SSDI):			
	Experimentals (%)	31.7*	44.5*	49.6
	Controls (%)	43.1	51.5	52.0
7.	Average monthly income from transfers (includes zeros):			
	Experimentals ($)	80.23	114.78	126.53
	Controls ($)	99.98	138.72	136.08

	Month 6	Month 15	Month 22
8. Average weekly personal income			
(including earnings, transfers, and			
other regular sources)			
Experimentals ($)	71.72*	67.22	$71.59
Controls ($)	50.94	59.67	62.39

*Experimental/control difference is statistically significant at the 5 percent level.

Subgroup analysis found that the greater the retardation of the subject (the lower the IQ), the greater the impact, with essentially no impact on those with slight retardation.

From a social perspective, total benefits were predicted to outweigh the costs. The taxpayer investment would be repaid within four and one-half years in lower outlays; from the social perspective, the investment would pay for itself after two and one-half years.

TIME TRENDS IN FINDINGS: Shown above.

DESIGN ISSUES: The subgroup analysis finding that the greater the retardation of the subject, the greater the impact is the opposite of the finding in the "Transitional Employment Training Demonstration" (see summary following). Thornton has explained this as a difference in the sample: IQs in STETS ranged from about 40 to about 80, whereas IQs in TETD were, at worst, too low to test and, at best, somewhat over 70. He noted that higher-IQ individuals who get into this type of program tend to have severe secondary problems inhibiting employment, whereas those with severe retardation are probably unemployable. He contended the intervention is most likely to succeed with those between the extremes; on the other hand, he cautioned that simply using t-tests for the statistical testing of this hypothesis can be misleading.

REPLICABILITY: Replicable.

GENERALIZABILITY: The study findings "are based on only five judgmentally selected urban sites, whose programs were specially designed and implemented for this demonstration. We cannot be certain whether other program operators in other sites who operate ongoing programs under different social, political, and economic conditions would have similar experiences. . . . It is also problematic whether similar programs could be efficiently and effectively operated in rural areas or even in more dispersed labor markets." Findings may be compared with the previous "Job Path" and the subsequent "Transitional Employment Training Demonstration" experiments.

FUNDING SOURCE: U.S. Department of Labor, Employment and Training Administration. Key personnel: None.

TREATMENT ADMINISTRATOR: Manpower Demonstration Research Corporation. Key personnel: Judith M. Gueron.

EVALUATOR: Mathematica Policy Research. Key personnel: Stuart Kerachsky and Craig Thornton.

ENABLING LEGISLATION: None.

INFORMATION SOURCE: Stuart Kerachsky and Craig Thornton, "Findings from the STETS Transitional Employment Demonstration," *Exceptional Children*, vol. 6, April 1987: 515–21.

PUBLIC-USE ACCESS TO DATA: Public-use file does not exist.

TRANSITIONAL EMPLOYMENT TRAINING DEMONSTRATION (TETD)

SUMMARY: This demonstration, conducted from 1985 to 1988, tested the effects of job placement, on-the-job training, and follow-up services on a medium-sized sample of adults with mental retardation. Subjects were followed for up to three years.

COST: Research only: $1,271,307 (1987).

TIME FRAME: Demonstration period, June 1985–June 1987; data collected through December 1988; final report, July 1989.

TREATMENTS TESTED:
1. Experimentals were placed in unsubsidized, potentially permanent jobs; they were provided specialized on-the-job training that was phased out over time; and they received postplacement support and follow-up as necessary. These "core services" were to be provided within one year of intake into the experiment; subsequent services were to be arranged as necessary, but had to be funded from a source other than the demonstration.
2. Controls received none of these services, but were free to seek other services in the community.
   One of the goals of the experiment was to test various approaches to service delivery. Providers were competitively selected to represent different methods and philosophies of service delivery.

OUTCOMES OF INTEREST: (1) Employment; (2) Earnings; (3) Wage rates; and (4) SSI payments.

SAMPLE SIZE: Experimentals, 375; controls, 370.

TARGET POPULATION: SSI recipients with mental retardation. Participants had to apply to enter the experiment, and had to be between 18 and 40 years old. The average IQ score was 57. Prior to random assignment, intake workers excluded persons who had severe emotional problems or who would otherwise not benefit from the treatment.

NUMBER OF TREATMENT GROUPS: Two (with one control group).

NUMBER AND LOCATION OF SITES: Twelve: Dover, Delaware; Harrisburg, Lancaster, Philadelphia, and York, Pennsylvania; Monmouth County, New Jersey; Chicago, Illinois; Boston, Massachusetts; Los Angeles, California; Milwaukee, Wisconsin; Portland, Oregon; and Chippewa, Dunn, Eau Claire, and Pepin Counties, Wisconsin.

RESEARCH COMPONENTS:
  Process analysis: Conducted. It showed that the treatment was substantially implemented as planned, and (among other things) that transportation barriers were often as serious or more serious than the lack of job skills.
  Impact analysis: Conducted with raw means and ordinary least squares (OLS).
  Benefit–cost analysis: Conducted.

MAJOR FINDINGS:
1. Two-thirds of experimentals were placed on jobs. One half of those placed (one-third of experimentals) were "successfully stabilized" on a potentially permanent job. These results were consistent with the initial expectations of the program designers.
2. By the third year after enrollment, 45 percent of experimentals were in unsubsidized jobs, compared with 30 percent of controls. (Experimentals spent 32 percent less time than controls in sheltered workshops.)
3. Estimated treatment effects on earnings over three years ("percentage change" represents the increase over the raw mean of the controls):

Year	Impact (%)	Percentage Change ($)
1	66.5	108
2	90.9	96
3	74.2	63

4. Effects on SSI payments were small, on the order of $240, or 2 percent, over three years. Earnings increased but generally remained below the income disregards in SSI regulations.
5. Earnings impacts varied considerably across sites. The New Jersey project raised earnings by $2,000 a year over three years; it tried to place experimentals in light manufacturing and assembly jobs. Projects in Portland and Los Angeles were exceptions to the general rule of treatment impacts declining over time.
6. Treatment impacts rose with IQ scores. Persons with IQs over 70 had an earnings gain of over 200 percent, whereas those with IQs under 40 had a gain that was not statistically significant.
7. Average treatment costs per person enrolled were $5,600.
8. The treatment raised the net income of experimentals, but SSI savings did not offset the costs from an SSI-budget perspective. From a government-budget perspective, the costs and benefits were about equal, because the program costs were offset by reductions in the use of sheltered (and subsidized) workshops. Targeting services to currently sheltered workers would mean that the program would have a neutral effect on budgets. From a social perspective, the benefits exceeded the costs.

TIME TRENDS IN FINDINGS: Note the impact reductions in "Major Findings," #3; most projects showed impacts declining over time.

DESIGN ISSUES:

1. The training organizations were competitively selected from 80 providers who applied. These agencies were chosen to reflect different treatment approaches; generally, the less-rigid treatment approaches appeared to have the most success. The findings are from a mix of successful and unsuccessful programs, all conducted by the agencies that were judged to offer the best versions of alternative approaches; findings from a mix of agencies offering the same, relatively successful, approach, but with different degrees of competence, might not be the same.
2. In determining benefits and costs, it turned out to be important whether the alternative was sheltered employment or no employment. Budgetary savings were possible if the alternative was sheltered employment, but otherwise did not occur.

REPLICABILITY: The eight treatment providers had different methods and philosophies, each of which could be replicated.

GENERALIZABILITY: The experiment represents a reasonably large-scale national test; the only region excluded was the South. Those enrolled in the experiment represent about 5 percent of those who were sent initial invitation letters; two-thirds of those responding were screened out at intake. Enrollees therefore do not represent the population of SSI recipients with retardation, but that part who volunteered for these services and were thought to have some probability of benefiting from them. In addition, transitional employment (and some of the agencies) were unfamiliar; only the more adventuresome members of the population would have left the well-established, sheltered worksites. As agencies become more established, this will be less true. Findings from the experiment will not necessarily reflect the impacts of the treatment on a less-adventuresome population.

FUNDING SOURCE: U.S. Department of Health and Human Services, Social Security Administration. Key personnel: Aaron Prero.

TREATMENT ADMINISTRATOR: Eight training organizations. Key personnel: Too many to list.

EVALUATOR: Mathematica Policy Research. Key personnel: Craig Thornton.

ENABLING LEGISLATION: Social Security Disability Amendments of 1980.

INFORMATION SOURCE: Craig Thornton and Paul T. Decker, "The Transitional Employment Training Demonstration: Analysis of Program Impacts," Mathematica Policy Research, July 1989.

PUBLIC-USE ACCESS TO DATA: We have no information about a public-use file for this demonstration.

Part Eighteen

FRAIL ELDERLY

INTRODUCTION

Since the 1960s, a number of home and community care studies have been conducted as social experiments. In addition to the criteria set forth in the introduction to this volume, these studies all met four other criteria: (1) they tested the effects of providing a home- and community-based alternative to existing long-term care services (which may have included other home- and community-based services as well as services provided in an institution); (2) they used the individual as their primary unit of analysis; (3) they served primarily an elderly population; and (4) institutionalization (nursing home placement) was one of their outcomes.

We include these experiments with some misgivings. We have tried to exclude experiments with only health status outcomes. Some institutionalization is dictated by health need—the patient might die or suffer grievous harm in its absence. However, some institutionalization is truly a choice for the patient—a choice that may be affected by his or her endowment with community services.

Most of the information contained in the following summaries comes from the paper by Weissert, Cready, and Pawelak (1988, see "Information Sources" in accompanying summaries), who reviewed 13 long-term care studies and discussed many of the cost and targeting issues they contain. Targeting success is measured by the percentage of the control group that was institutionalized during the study, for this is an indication of the number of experimentals who would have been institutionalized had they not received the intervention. The article also noted whether multivariate analysis was used.

Another review has been provided by Susan Hughes (1985), who identified problems with the definitions of both the treatment and the target population in these studies (the latter was very broadly defined and included those with minimal impairment, the acutely ill, and the chronically ill).

Reference

Hughes, Susan. 1985. "Apples and Oranges? A Review of Evaluations of Community-Based Long-Term Care." *Health Services Research* 20(4): 461–88.

SUMMARY: This demonstration, conducted from 1963 to 1971, tested the effects of public health nurse home visits on a medium-sized sample of elderly noninstitutionalized individuals. Subjects were followed for two years.

COST: Cost figures not available.

TIME FRAME: Demonstration periods, 1963–71.

TREATMENTS TESTED: The treatment group received public health nurse home visits. The control group received no demonstration services, but could seek out existing long-term care services.

OUTCOMES: Impact on nursing home use, hospital use, and patient functioning.

SAMPLE SIZE: Treatment, 150; control, 150.

TARGET POPULATION: Elderly patients who had been in a rehabilitation hospital for at least a week before being discharged to a noninstitutional setting.

NUMBER OF TREATMENT GROUPS: Two (including control).

NUMBER AND LOCATION OF SITES: One—Cleveland, Ohio.

RESEARCH COMPONENTS:
    Process: No process analysis information was available.
    Impact: Comparison of means.
    Benefit–cost analysis: Not conducted.

MAJOR FINDINGS:
1. Over the two-year period during which each sample member was followed, only 11 percent of the control group ever entered a nursing home, and about one-third entered the hospital. This is indicative of poor targeting.
2. Treatment group members entered nursing homes less than control group members (-1.1 percent) and spent less time there (-7.3 days per capita). Statistical significance was not reported for the total sample, although in subgroup analyses it was shown that significantly fewer treatment group members who had physical disabilities and were socially deprived used nursing homes than did control group counterparts.
3. Significantly more treatment group members were admitted to hospitals during the study period (9.6 percent) than were control

group members. There was no difference in the number of total days, per capita, in the hospital.

4. There were no significant differences between groups on measures of physical or mental functioning.

TIME TRENDS IN THE FINDINGS: None reported.

DESIGN ISSUES: This project was not very effective at targeting those frail elderly individuals who were most likely to be institutionalized.

REPLICABILITY: Replicable.

GENERALIZABILITY: Weissert, Cready, and Pawelak (1988) did not address this issue. However, given the poor targeting and fairly small sample size, generalizations would be speculative.

FUNDING SOURCE: U.S. Department of Health, Education & Welfare.

TREATMENT ADMINISTRATOR: Case Western Reserve University School of Medicine.

EVALUATOR: S. Katz, Case Western Reserve University.

ENABLING LEGISLATION: None.

INFORMATION SOURCES: Information for this summary came from William G. Weissert, Cynthia Matthews Cready, and James E. Pawelak, "The Past and Future of Home- and Community-Based Long-Term Care," *Millbank Quarterly* 66(1988): 309–88; the source document cited is S. Katz, A.B. Ford, T.D. Downs, M. Adams, and D.I. Rusby, *Effects of Continued Care: A Study of Chronic Illness in the Home,* DHEW Pub. No. (HSM) 73-3010, Case Western Reserve University School of Medicine, 1972.

PUBLIC-USE ACCESS TO DATA: Not available.

BRI PROTECTIVE SERVICES

SUMMARY: This demonstration, conducted from 1964 to 1966, tested the effects of case management and ancillary services on a small sample of elderly individuals with mental disabilities. Subjects were followed for one year.

COST: Cost figures not available.

TIME FRAME: Demonstration period, 1964–66.

TREATMENTS TESTED: Case management plus ancillary services including home aide services, and legal, medical, and psychiatric consultation and evaluation. Control group members received nothing from the demonstration, but could seek out existing long-term care services from the community.

OUTCOMES: Nursing home use and measures of patient functioning.

SAMPLE SIZE: Treatment, 76; controls, 88.

TARGET POPULATION: Elderly individuals mentally incapable of adequately caring for themselves, living in the community without the support of an informal caregiver.

NUMBER OF TREATMENT GROUPS: Two (including control).

NUMBER AND LOCATION OF SITES: One—Cleveland, Ohio.

RESEARCH COMPONENTS:
   Process: Preliminary surveys were used to assist in targeting the population and in sample selection. Other interviews were conducted with participants and referring agencies.
   Impact: Comparison of means.
   Benefit–cost analysis: Not conducted.

MAJOR FINDINGS:
1. Twenty percent of control group members entered a nursing home during the study period.
2. The treatment led to a 14 percent *increase* in nursing home use (treatment versus control). The statistical significance of this finding was not reported.
3. There were no significant impacts on physical or mental functioning between groups. However, significantly more treatment group members reported satisfaction with their care services.

TIME TRENDS IN THE FINDINGS: None reported.

DESIGN ISSUES:
1. Only 50 percent of the treatment group ever received any home health aide service, and no utilization data are reported on the volume of service provided.
2. The sample consisted only of elderly persons with mental impairment. The study did not address the possible effect of services on those with physical impairment.

REPLICABILITY: Replicable.

GENERALIZABILITY: Generalizing from this small sample would be speculative. The sample did represent the target population at the time in Cleveland—generally poor white females over 75 years of age. Men, nonwhites, and married persons are underrepresented compared to the general population of frail elderly.

FUNDING SOURCES: U.S. Social Security Administration; Ohio Welfare Administration, Social and Rehabilitative Services; and A. M. McGregor Home of Cleveland.

TREATMENT ADMINISTRATOR: Benjamin Rose Institute, Cleveland, Ohio.

EVALUATORS: M. Blenkner and M. Bloom, Benjamin Rose Institute.

ENABLING LEGISLATION: None.

INFORMATION SOURCES: M. Blenkner, M. Bloom, and M. Nielson, "A Research and Demonstration Project of Protective Services," *Social Casework* 52 (1971): 483–89; Wiliam G. Weissert, Cynthia Matthews Cready, and James E. Pawelak, "The Past and Future of Home- and Community-Based Long-Term Care," *Millbank Quarterly* 66(1988): 309–88.

PUBLIC-USE ACCESS TO DATA: Not available.

BRH HOME AIDE

SUMMARY: This demonstration, conducted from 1966 to 1969, tested the effects of home aide visits on a small sample of the recently hospitalized elderly. Subjects were followed for one year.

COST: Cost figures not available.

TIME FRAME: Demonstration period, 1966–69.

TREATMENTS TESTED: Home aide visits (escort, health care, housekeeping, leisure and personal care services). The control group did not receive these services.

OUTCOMES: Hospital and nursing home use and measures of client functioning.

SAMPLE SIZE: Treatment, 50; control, 50.

TARGET POPULATION: Elderly patients about to be discharged from a geriatric rehabilitation hospital to a noninstitutional setting and not already receiving organized home aide services from a community agency. These patients were not economically disadvantaged.

NUMBER OF TREATMENT GROUPS: Two (including control).

NUMBER AND LOCATION OF SITES: One—Benjamin Rose Hospital, Cleveland, Ohio.

RESEARCH COMPONENTS:

Process: Services performed by aides were tracked with daily reports.

Impact: Comparison of means.

Benefit–cost analysis: Not conducted.

MAJOR FINDINGS:
1. Control group members spent an average of 53.1 per capita days in a nursing home and 11.4 days in a hospital during the study period.
2. Significantly fewer (20 percent) treatment group members entered a hospital than did control group members. Treatment group members averaged 44.8 fewer hospital days than their control group counterparts.
3. Treatment group members spent an average of 4.6 fewer days in the hospital than did control group members. The statistical significance of this finding is not reported.
4. The treatment had no significant impact on physical or mental functioning. However, significantly more treatment group members reported satisfaction with care than did control group members.

TIME TRENDS IN THE FINDINGS: None.

DESIGN ISSUES:
1. The evaluators claim to have had no prior experience with a more advantaged population and probably provided more services than were necessary. Most clients opted to cancel services at the end of the study period rather than pay fees that were "within their economic capacity."
2. Information regarding cost and level of aide use are not reported, making it difficult to estimate potential policy implications.

REPLICABILITY: Replicable.

GENERALIZABILITY: Generalizing from this small sample would be speculative.

FUNDING SOURCES: A. M. McGregor Home of Cleveland; U.S. Department of Health, Education & Welfare.

TREATMENT ADMINISTRATOR: Benjamin Rose Hospital, Cleveland, Ohio.

EVALUATORS: M. Nielson and M. Blenkner were the likely principal investigators, but they could not be reached to confirm.

ENABLING LEGISLATION: None.

INFORMATION SOURCES: M. Nielson, M. Blenkner, M. Bloom, T. Downs, and H. Beggs, "Older Persons after Hospitalization: A Controlled Study of Home Aide Service," *American Journal of Public Health* 62(1972): 1094–1101; William G. Weissert, Cynthia Matthews Cready, and James E. Pawelak, "The Past and Future of Home- and Community-Based Long-Term Care," *Millbank Quarterly* 66(1988): 309–88.

PUBLIC-USE ACCESS TO DATA: Not available.

CHRONIC DISEASE

SUMMARY: This demonstration, conducted from 1971 to 1976, tested the effects of in-home health care services on a medium-sized sample of elderly subjects. Subjects were followed for one year.

COST: Cost figures are not available.

TIME FRAME: Demonstration period, 1971–76.

TREATMENTS TESTED: In-home services by an interdisciplinary team (a half-time nurse or social worker, a part-time physician, and two full-time health assistants who provided the bulk of in-home care). The control group received nothing from the demonstration, but could seek existing long-term care services.

OUTCOMES: Hospital and nursing home use and health care costs.

SAMPLE SIZE: Treatment, 438; control, 436.

TARGET POPULATION: Elderly patients in an ambulatory care facility or about to be discharged from a hospital, living in a noninstitutional setting, and needing assistance for at least three months.

NUMBER OF TREATMENT GROUPS: Two (including control).

NUMBER AND LOCATION OF SITES: Five communities in Michigan— two urban and three rural.

RESEARCH COMPONENTS:

Process: Information was collected that would allow description and comparison of the participants, description of the use of services, and descriptions of community settings in which services were offered.

Impact: Conducted using multivariate techniques.

Benefit–cost analysis: Not conducted.

MAJOR FINDINGS:

1. The control group members spent an average of 14.5 days per capita in a nursing home and 11.6 days in a hospital. Targeting of at-risk individuals was fairly ineffective.
2. Treatment group members spent fewer days, on average, than control group members in both nursing homes (−5.9 days) and hospitals (−0.6 days). These differences were not statistically significant.
3. Overall average annual per capita cost savings from the treatment was $84 (1988 dollars). This reflects a savings of $630 for inpatient services, −$54 for outpatient services, and −$492 for treatment services.

TIME TRENDS IN THE FINDINGS: Savings occurred only when treatment was short. They were present only after 6 months. By 12 months, continued treatment without additional benefits in terms of reduced institutionalization had turned the savings into losses.

DESIGN ISSUES: Only 43 percent of the treatment group used services, thereby making per capita treatment costs appear artificially low. The low intensity of service may suggest the presence of subjects with fewer or less serious health problems in the sample.

REPLICABILITY: Replicable.

GENERALIZABILITY: Targeting difficulties discourage attempts at generalization.

FUNDING SOURCE: National Center for Health Services Research, U.S. Department of Health, Education & Welfare (now DHHS).

TREATMENT ADMINISTRATOR: Different for each site. Included a hospital, a county health department, two ambulatory clinics, and a clinic in a housing unit for the elderly.

EVALUATOR: Margaret Blenkner was the project director until her death in August 1973. The cited text does not identify her successor.

ENABLING LEGISLATION: None.

INFORMATION SOURCES: Joseph A. Papsidero, Sidney Katz, Sr., Mary H. Kroger, and C. Amechi Akpom, eds., *Chance for Change: Implications of a Chronic Disease Module*, Michigan State University Press, 1979, additional information came from William G. Weissert, Cynthia Matthews Cready, and James E. Pawelak, "The Past and Future of Home- and Community-Based Long-Term Care," *Millbank Quarterly* 66(1988): 309–88.

PUBLIC-USE ACCESS TO DATA: Not available.

WORCESTER HOME CARE

SUMMARY: This demonstration, conducted from 1973 to 1975, tested the effects of case management on a medium-sized sample of the elderly. Subjects were followed for one year.

COST: Cost figures not available.

TIME FRAME: Demonstration period, 1973–75.

TREATMENTS TESTED: Case management and other services not normally covered by Medicaid (escort, linen, special therapies, transportation). The control group received no services from the demonstration, but could seek out existing long-term care services.

OUTCOMES: Nursing home and hospital use and measures of client functioning.

SAMPLE SIZE: Treatment, 280; control, 205.

TARGET POPULATION: Either (1) elderly individuals living in the community with some level of service need who primarily receive services from informal sources or (2) institutionalized individuals with the potential to return to the community.

NUMBER OF TREATMENT GROUPS: Two (including control).

NUMBER AND LOCATION OF SITES: One—Worcester, Massachusetts.

RESEARCH COMPONENTS:
    Process: No process analysis information was available.
    Impact: Comparison of means.
    Benefit–cost analysis: Not conducted.

MAJOR FINDINGS:
1. Control group members spent an average of 49.6 days in a nursing home and 4 days in a hospital over the 12-month period.
2. The treatment had no impact on time spent in either nursing homes or hospitals. However, a subgroup analysis found that those in the treatment group members who were "in danger of institutionalization" experienced significantly less use of nursing homes than their control group counterparts. A specific definition of "in danger" was not provided.
3. Impact on client functioning was mixed. There was a positive, though not significant, impact on activities of daily living, a significantly negative impact on mobility, and a negative, but not significant, impact on mental functioning. Treatment group members more often reported satisfaction than did control group members, although this finding was not statistically significant.

TIME TRENDS IN THE FINDINGS: None.

DESIGN ISSUES: Insufficient information on this study was available to address design issues.

REPLICABILITY: Replicable.

GENERALIZABILITY: Weisert et al. (1988) did not address this issue.

FUNDING SOURCE: Department of Elder Affairs, Commonwealth of Massachusetts.

TREATMENT ADMINISTRATOR: Elder Home Care of Worcester.

EVALUATOR: Unknown.

ENABLING LEGISLATION: None.

INFORMATION SOURCES: Information for this summary came from William G. Weissert, Cynthia Matthews Cready, and James E. Pawelak, "The Past and Future of Home- and Community-Based Long-Term Care," *Millbank Quarterly* 66(1988), 309–88; source document cited is Commonwealth of Massachusetts, *Home Care: An Alternative to Institutionalization: Final Report*, Commonwealth of Massachusetts, Department of Elder Affairs, 1975.

PUBLIC-USE ACCESS TO DATA: Not available.

NCHSR DAY CARE/HOMEMAKER DEMONSTRATION

SUMMARY: This demonstration, conducted from 1974 to 1977, tested the effects of adult day care and homemaker services on a medium-sized sample of the elderly. Subjects were followed for one year.

COST: Cost figures are not available.

TIME FRAME: Demonstration period, 1974–77; data collected, same period.

TREATMENTS TESTED: There were four treatments: (1) an adult day-care program with services including meals, nursing, social services, therapies, and transportation; (2) homemaker services including chores, personal care, shopping, and escort; (3) a combined treatment group; and (4) a control group who received neither adult daycare nor homemaker services from the demonstration.

OUTCOMES: Nursing home and hospital use, health care costs, and client functioning and satisfaction.

SAMPLE SIZE: Day Care treatment, 194; Day Care control, 190; Homemaker treatment, 307; Homemaker control, 323; Combined Services treatment, 59; Combined Services control, 80.

TARGET POPULATION: Elderly individuals needing health care services to restore or maintain functional ability but not 24-hour-a-day supervision. Individuals receiving homemaker services were also required to be post-hospital patients.

NUMBER OF TREATMENT GROUPS: Six (including controls).

NUMBER AND LOCATION OF SITES: There were a total of six sites. Day-Care-only sites: White Plains and Syracuse, New York; Homemaker-only sites: Providence, Rhode Island, and Los Angeles, California; Combined Services sites: Lexington, Kentucky, and San Francisco, California.

RESEARCH COMPONENTS:

Process: Evaluators paid special attention to services and activities offered by the program, to subject characteristics, and to the possibility of bias in the analysis.

Impact: Comparison of adjusted means using multivariate methods.

Benefit–cost analysis: Costs were calculated, but a formal benefit–cost analysis was not done.

MAJOR FINDINGS:
1. Only 21 percent of the control group was institutionalized (hospital or nursing home) during the observation period. This indicates that few patients who used day care and homemaker services were potential beneficiaries.
2. Day Care treatment group members were significantly less likely to enter a nursing home or hospital than were their control group counterparts. Homemaker treatment group members were also less likely to use nursing homes and hospitals than their control group

counterparts, although this finding was not statistically significant. This information is not presented for the Combined Services groups.

3. Both Day Care and Homemaker services cost substantially more than their respective control group health care costs, because treatment costs were added to existing Medicare-covered services rather than substituting for them. Day Care services cost 71 percent more than services for the control group, and Homemaker services cost 60 percent more.

4. Treatment group members in all three service groups had significantly lower mortality rates than their control group counterparts. Other measures of physical functioning yielded mostly nonsignificant results, and there were no significant differences in mental functioning between treatment and control group members (although the Homemaker treatment produced higher levels of client contentment).

TIME TRENDS IN THE FINDINGS: None.

DESIGN ISSUES: There was a fairly high level of contamination in the study. A large number (229) of treatment group members never used the services, and some members of the control group found they were eligible to receive the same or similar services paid for from a non-study source such as Medicaid-covered day-care services in New York. Still other patients dropped out of the study before its completion. For some patients, the assessment teams did not fill in a crucial data item related to activities of daily living, and the patients were classified as missing data. Finally, some patients were accepted without following the randomization procedures. Careful steps were taken in the analysis to compensate for these departures, but conclusions should be drawn cautiously.

REPLICABILITY: Replicable.

GENERALIZABILITY: Generalizability may be hampered because of the heterogeneity of the sample. Better efforts at targeting the elderly who are truly at-risk for institutionalization are needed.

FUNDING SOURCE: National Center for Health Services Research (NCHSR), U.S. Department of Health and Human Services.

TREATMENT ADMINISTRATOR: Services were provided by health care providers at each of the six treatment sites.

EVALUATORS: Thomas Wan, University of Maryland Baltimore County, Department of Sociology; and William Weissert and Barbara Livieratos, NCHSR.

ENABLING LEGISLATION: Commissioned by Congress under Section 222 of the 1974 amendments to the Social Security Act.

INFORMATION SOURCES: Thomas T.H. Wan, William G. Weissert, and Barbara B. Livieratos, "Geriatric Day Care and Homemaker Services: An Experimental Study," *Journal of Gerontology* 35(1980): 256–74; Weissert, William, Thomas Wan, Barbara Livieratos, and Sidney Katz, "Effects and Costs of Day-Care Services for the Chronically Ill: A Randomized Experiment," *Medical Care* 18(1980): 567–84; William G. Weissert, Thomas T. H. Wan, Barbara B. Livieratos, and Julius Pelegrino, "Cost-Effectiveness of Homemaker Services for the Chronically Ill," *Inquiry* 17(1980): 230–43.

PUBLIC-USE ACCESS TO DATA: Available through National Technical Information Service, Springfield, Virginia.

WISCONSIN COMMUNITY CARE ORGANIZATION (CCO)— MILWAUKEE

SUMMARY: This demonstration, conducted from 1975 to 1979, tested the effects of case management and home health services on a medium-sized sample of the elderly. Subjects were followed for up to 16 months.

COST: Cost figures are not available.

TIME FRAME: Demonstration period, 1975–79.

TREATMENTS TESTED: Case management and other services not normally covered by Medicaid (including adult day health care, home-health aide, housing search, personal care, skilled nursing, and transportation). The control group received nothing from the demonstration, but could seek existing long-term health services.

OUTCOMES: Nursing home and hospital use, health care costs, client functioning.

SAMPLE SIZE: Milwaukee only: Treatment, 283; control, 134.

TARGET POPULATION: Elderly persons at risk of institutionalization, as determined by the project administrators.

NUMBER OF TREATMENT GROUPS: Two (including control).

NUMBER AND LOCATION OF SITES: One experimental site—Milwaukee County, Wisconsin. Two other counties, La Crosse and Barron, used a matched comparison design.

RESEARCH COMPONENTS:
   Process: Interviews at the state and federal level and a panel study were conducted to assist in the project design. Special care was taken in defining and targeting the at-risk population.
   Impact: Comparison of adjusted and unadjusted means.
   Benefit–cost analysis: Not conducted.

MAJOR FINDINGS:
1. Of the control group, 13.6 percent entered a nursing home and 14.9 percent were hospitalized. This suggests that the demonstration was fairly ineffective at targeting at-risk individuals.
2. Slightly fewer treatment group members used a nursing home during the observation period (approximately 14 months) than did control group members, although the finding was not statistically significant. On average, treatment group members spent significantly fewer days hospitalized (-8.7) than did control group members.
3. Average annual per capita costs were slightly higher for the treatment group compared to the control group. Inpatient services were $2,027 less for the treatment group and outpatient services were $1,156 less, but treatment services were $3,288 more (total cost savings, $-\$105$).
4. There was a positive, but not significant, impact on client physical functioning.

TIME TRENDS IN THE FINDINGS: None.

DESIGN ISSUES:
1. The project was initially designed to be at one site and of short duration. It expanded beyond this design at the same time that resources for the evaluation were shrinking. This reduced the "tightness of the design and the data collection." Data had to be collected by Community Care Organization (CCO) staff rather than evaluators, and randomization was carried out by service providers. Also, distance costs and staff turnover made training difficult and reliability was less assured.
2. A large portion of the experimental group (71 of the 283) never received services. Some were found to be ineligible after the initial intake, some were subsequently screened out for having "special

needs" (controls were not subsequently screened), some refused services, and some went directly into a nursing home. These 71 were still considered part of the treatment group.

REPLICABILITY: Replicable, though better care needs to be taken in randomization to avoid uneven attrition.

GENERALIZABILITY: Generalizable only to the narrow group of "needy-but-not-too-needy" that were eventually provided services in this project. Further, the mean age of the study sample was at least 10 years younger than the average age at admission of residents of nursing homes nationally.

FUNDING SOURCE: The Kellogg Foundation. Project officer: Barbara Lee.

TREATMENT ADMINISTRATOR: Wisconsin Community Care Organization, Madison.

EVALUATORS: Fredrick Seidl, University of Wisconsin, Madison; Robert Applebaum, Mathematica Policy Research; Carol Austin, University of Minnesota; and Kevin Mahoney, Connecticut Department on Aging.

ENABLING LEGISLATION: None.

INFORMATION SOURCES: Fredrick W. Seidl, Robert Applebaum, Carol Austin, and Kevin Mahoney, *Delivering In-Home Services to the Aged and Disabled: The Wisconsin Experiment*, D. C. Heath and Company, 1983.

PUBLIC-USE ACCESS TO DATA: Not available.

GEORGIA ALTERNATIVE HEALTH SERVICES

SUMMARY: This demonstration, conducted from 1976 to 1980, tested the effects of case management and home care services on a medium-sized sample of the elderly. Subjects were followed for one year.

COST: Cost figures not available.

TIME FRAME: Demonstration period, 1976–80.

TREATMENTS TESTED: Case management and other services not normally covered by Medicaid (adult day health care, adult foster care, home health aide, skilled nursing, medical transportation and social services). The control group received nothing from the demonstration, but could seek existing long-term care services.

OUTCOMES: Nursing home and hospital use, health care costs, and measures of client functioning.

SAMPLE SIZE: Treatment, 819; control, 257.

TARGET POPULATION: Previously institutionalized elderly individuals, eligible for Medicaid-sponsored nursing home care.

NUMBER OF TREATMENT GROUPS: Two (including control).

NUMBER AND LOCATION OF SITES: Ten rural and 7 urban counties in Georgia.

RESEARCH COMPONENTS:

Process: Social and health information was collected by caseworkers and reviewed by a project team. A service provider verified team records and recommendations.

Impact: Comparison of means.

Benefit–cost analysis: Not conducted.

MAJOR FINDINGS:
1. Of the control group, 15.6 percent entered a nursing home and spent an average of four days in a hospital during the 12-month period.
2. The treatment produced a slight decrease in nursing home use (– 1.1 percent less use among the treatment group and an average of seven fewer days compared to the control group). There was a slight increase in hospital use (an average of two more days). The statistical significance of these findings was not reported.
3. Average annual per capita costs were 35 percent higher for the treatment group, compared to the control group, for all categories of service: inpatient services, + $315; outpatient services, + $38; and treatment services, + $2,632. On average, combined services cost $2,985 more for the treatment group than for the control group.
4. Experimental subjects experienced a statistically significant reduction in mortality.

TIME TRENDS IN THE FINDINGS: None.

DESIGN ISSUES: None.

REPLICABILITY: Replicable.

GENERALIZABILITY: The typical AHS client served was a 75-year-old woman with less than nine years of education. This is similar to those who were being admitted to nursing homes nationally.

FUNDING SOURCE: Georgia Department of Medical Assistance.

TREATMENT ADMINISTRATOR: Georgia Department of Medical Assistance.

EVALUATOR: Medicus Systems Corporation.

ENABLING LEGISLATION: None.

INFORMATION SOURCES: Information for this summary came from William G. Weissert, Cynthia Matthews Cready, and James E. Pawelak, "The Past and Future of Home- and Community-Based Long-Term Care," *Millbank Quarterly*, 66(1988): 309–88; source document cited is A. Skellie, F. Favor, C. Tudor, and R. Strauss, *Alternative Health Services Project: Final Report*, Georgia Department of Medical Assistance, 1982.

PUBLIC-USE ACCESS TO DATA: Not available.

HOME HEALTH CARE TEAM

SUMMARY: This experiment, conducted between 1978 and 1981, tested the effects of a team approach to long-term home care on a small sample of homebound chronically or terminally ill patients. Subjects were followed for up to six months.

COST: The evaluators were unable to provide estimates of evaluation costs due to substantial donated time and resources. Further, much of the analysis was completed after the grant had expired.

TIME FRAME: Demonstration period, 1978–81; data collected, same period.

TREATMENTS TESTED: A team approach to home care. The team included a physician, nurse practitioner, and a social worker. The team delivered primary health care in the patients' homes, and were available for 24-hour and weekend care. The team physician attended to the patient during any necessary hospitalization. The control group received existing health and home care services available in the community (i.e., not a team approach; limited availability for home visits).

OUTCOMES OF INTEREST: (1) Health care system utilization and cost; (2) Patient health status; and (3) Satisfaction with health care.

SAMPLE SIZE: Total, 167; treatment, 85; control, 82.

TARGET POPULATION: Homebound, chronically or terminally ill elderly.

NUMBER OF TREATMENT GROUPS: Two (including control).

NUMBER AND LOCATION OF SITES: One—Rochester, New York.

RESEARCH COMPONENTS:

Process analysis: Focused on health care team activities, patient characteristics, intake processes, and attrition.

Impact analysis: Comparison of unadjusted means, as well as multiple regression approaches.

Benefit-cost analysis: Not conducted.

MAJOR FINDINGS:
1. The average cost per day for all services (in-home and out-of-home) recorded for the treatment group patients was $47.83, or 8.6 percent less than the $52.33 for the control group patients. For treatment group patients, out-of-home services were 61.1 percent of what they were for controls, whereas in-home services were 60.9 percent more.
2. The trend toward reduced hospitalization utilization seen among the treatment group is largely related to the considerably higher proportion of treatment than control patients dying at home.
3. Findings fail to demonstrate any program effects on patient status or morale. There were trends toward higher caregiver and patient satisfaction among the treatment group participants.

TIME TRENDS IN FINDINGS: None reported.

DESIGN ISSUES: The control group was not truly without intervention. They kept health utilization diaries and were visited at home by interviewers who sometimes offered advice and support. This may account for an increase in satisfaction among the control group.

REPLICABILITY: Replicable.

GENERALIZABILITY: The sample size was fairly small and the program was voluntary. Roughly 80 percent of those deemed eligible agreed to participate in the study and were subsequently assigned to either the treatment or control group. Thus, these participants (in both groups) were interested in receiving this type of care.

FUNDING SOURCE: National Center for Health Services Research (NCHSR). Key personnel: Julius Pelegrino.

TREATMENT ADMINISTRATOR: Home Health Care Team, an outreach program of the University of Rochester Medical Center's Ambulatory Care Unit. Key personnel: Annemarie Groth-Juncker.

EVALUATORS: James G. Zimmer, research director; Annemarie Groth-Juncker, principal investigator; and Jane McCusker.

ENABLING LEGISLATION: None.

INFORMATION SOURCES: James G. Zimmer, Annemarie Groth-Juncker, and Jane McCusker, "A Randomized Controlled Study of a Home Health Care Team," *American Journal of Public Health* 75(1985): 134–41; James G. Zimmer, Annemarie Groth-Juncker, and Jane McCusker, "Effects of a Physician-Led Home Care Team on Terminal Care," *Journal of the American Geriatrics Society* 32(1984): 288–92.

PUBLIC-USE ACCESS TO DATA: Available through National Technical Information Service, Springfield, Virginia.

PROJECT OPEN

SUMMARY: This demonstration, conducted from 1978 to 1983, tested the effects of case management and home health services on a medium-sized sample of the elderly. Subjects were followed for up to three years.

COST: The HCFA grant for the administrative/research components totaled roughly $1.7 million.

TIME FRAME: Demonstration period, 1978–83.

TREATMENTS TESTED: Case management and other services not normally covered by Medicare (including adaptive/assistive equipment, day health care, drugs, transportation, homemaker, home delivered meals, therapies, and social day care). The control group received existing long-term care services.

OUTCOMES: Nursing home and hospital use, health care costs, and measures of client functioning.

SAMPLE SIZE: Treatment, 220; control, 115.

TARGET POPULATION: Cognitively aware elderly individuals with medical problems and needing assistance to function independently.

NUMBER OF TREATMENT GROUPS: Two (including control).

NUMBER AND LOCATION OF SITES: One—San Francisco, California.

RESEARCH COMPONENTS:
   Process: An advisory committee met regularly during the planning and operation phases of the project to discuss operations, interagency coordination, and related issues.
   Impact: Comparison of means.
   Benefit–cost analysis: Not conducted.

MAJOR FINDINGS:
1. Only 5.6 percent of control group members entered a nursing home (Medicare-covered skilled nursing facility), and 30.3 percent entered a hospital during the project period (up to three years). This provides a measure of the study's effectiveness in targeting at-risk individuals.
2. The treatment had a slight, though not statistically significant, impact on nursing home use (1.7 percent fewer users in the treatment group compared to the control group and an average of 3.6 fewer days). The same can be said for the treatment's impact on hospital use (−4.1 percent and an average of 1.9 fewer days).
3. The treatment produced average annual per capita cost savings of $1,464. This reflects savings in inpatient services ($3,040) and outpatient services ($1,146) and losses in treatment services (−$2,722).
4. Impacts on client functioning were mixed and not statistically significant.

TIME TRENDS IN THE FINDINGS: The greatest impact on the participants' health status, utilization patterns, and costs occurred during the first six months of participation.

DESIGN ISSUES: Cost reductions in hospital and nursing care were based on nonsignificant differences in nursing home and hospital use between treatment and control groups. Inadequate attention may have been paid to pretest differences between the groups as well as to attrition. Since multivariate analytic techniques were not used to adjust for possible pretest of attrition-induced differences, the results should be interpreted cautiously.

REPLICABILITY: Replicable.

GENERALIZABILITY: The evaluation does not specifically address this issue. The typical client of Project OPEN (Organization Providing for Elderly Needs), whether treatment or control, was a 79-year-old, nonemployed, white widow living alone in her own home or apartment, existing on an income of less than $7,000 a year.

FUNDING SOURCE: U.S. Department of Health and Human Services, Health Care Financing Administration (HCFA).

TREATMENT ADMINISTRATOR: Mt. Zion Hospital and Medical Center, San Francisco. Project director: Barbara Sklar.

EVALUATOR: Principal investigator: Lawrence Weiss (now at Scripps Gerontology, Miami University, Oxford, Ohio).

ENABLING LEGISLATION: None.

INFORMATION SOURCES: B. W. Sklar and L. J. Weiss, *Project OPEN (Organization Providing for Elderly Needs): Final report,* Mount Zion Hospital and Medical Center, 1983; additional information came from William G. Weissert, Cynthia Matthews Cready, and James E. Pawelak, "The Past and Future of Home- and Community-Based Long-Term Care," *Millbank Quarterly* 66(1988): 309–88.

PUBLIC-USE ACCESS TO DATA: not available.

SAN DIEGO LONG-TERM CARE

SUMMARY: This demonstration, conducted from 1979 to 1984, tested the effects of case management and home health services on a medium-sized sample of the frail elderly. Subjects were followed for 18 months.

COST: Cost figures not available.

TIME FRAME: Demonstration period, 1979–84.

TREATMENTS TESTED: Case management and other services not normally covered by Medicare (including adult day health care, client/family health education, homemaker/personal care, and transportation). The control group received nothing from the study, but could seek out existing long-term care services.

OUTCOMES: Nursing home and hospital use and measures of client functioning.

SAMPLE SIZE: Treatment, 549; control, 270.

TARGET POPULATION: Elderly individuals unable to maintain themselves at home without assistance, at risk of long-term institutional placement or frequent acute hospital admissions.

NUMBER OF TREATMENT GROUPS: Two (including control).

NUMBER AND LOCATION OF SITES: One—San Diego, California.

RESEARCH COMPONENTS:
Process: No process analysis information was available.
Impact: Comparison of adjusted means.
Benefit–cost analysis: Not conducted.

MAJOR FINDINGS:
1. For control group members, 46.3 percent entered a hospital, but only 7 percent entered a nursing home during the observation period (18 months on average). This indicates that the study was better at targeting those at risk of acute placement than those likely to seek a long-term institutional placement.
2. Slightly fewer treatment group members entered nursing homes (-1.8 percent) or hospitals (-0.4 percent) than did control group members. However, this finding was not statistically significant.
3. Impacts on physical and mental functioning were mixed, and were mostly nonsignificant.

TIME TRENDS IN THE FINDINGS: None.

DESIGN ISSUES:
1. The study was unable to effectively target those most at risk for long-term institutional placement.
2. Aliece Pinkerton feels that this project was terminated before valid outcomes could be obtained.

REPLICABILITY: Replicable.

GENERALIZABILITY: Neither Pinkerton nor Weissert et al. (1988) addressed this issue. Given the targeting problem, findings may not generalize to a population at risk for nursing home placement.

FUNDING SOURCE: Health Care Financing Administration.

TREATMENT ADMINISTRATOR: Allied Home Health Association. Key personnel: Aliece Pinkerton, executive director; and Deborah Hill.

EVALUATOR: Pinkerton believes the principal investigator was Carl Beatty (affiliation unknown).

ENABLING LEGISLATION: None.

INFORMATION SOURCES: Information for this summary came from a conversation with Aliece Pinkerton and William G. Weissert, Cynthia Matthews Cready, and James E. Pawelak, "The Past and Future of Home- and Community-Based Long-Term Care," *Millbank Quarterly* 66(1988): 309–88. The source document cited is Aliece Pinkerton, and Deborah Hill, *Long-Term Care Demonstration Project of North San Diego County: Final Report*, NTIS no. PB85-10391, Allied Home Health Association, 1984.

PUBLIC-USE ACCESS TO DATA: Not available.

FLORIDA PENTASTAR

SUMMARY: This demonstration, conducted from 1980 to 1983, tested the effects of case management and home health services on a medium-sized sample of the at-risk elderly. Subjects were followed for 18 months.

COST: Evaluation costs, approximately $100,000.

TIME FRAME: Demonstration period, 1980–83.

TREATMENTS TESTED: Case management and other services not normally provided by Medicare (including adult day health care, homemaker, skilled nursing, therapies, and transportation). The control group received existing long-term care services.

OUTCOMES: Nursing home use and measures of client functioning.

SAMPLE SIZE: Total, 935, treatment, 723; control, 212.

TARGET POPULATION: Elderly individuals at risk for institutional placement within a year and in need of project services. The sample was further limited to those eligible for Medicaid.

NUMBER OF TREATMENT GROUPS: There were three groups: one treatment and two control groups. Only one of the control groups was randomly assigned; comparisons between this group and the treatment group are presented here.

NUMBER AND LOCATION OF SITES: Five sites in Florida.

RESEARCH COMPONENTS:

Process: There was a fairly extensive process evaluation involving site visits—a survey of service providers and a survey of the non-randomly assigned comparison group. It focused on where the participants were drawn from, staff turnover, and participation patterns.

Impact: Comparison of means, simple and adjusted.

Benefit–cost analysis: Not conducted.

MAJOR FINDINGS:

1. Of the control group 5.7 percent entered a nursing home during the 18-month observation period. This provides a measure of the study's effectiveness in targeting at-risk individuals.

2. A slightly smaller percentage of treatment group members entered a nursing home compared to members of the control group (− 0.6 percent). However, this finding is not statistically significant.

3. On average, the treatment group members scored significantly lower on several measures of physical functioning. There was no significant impact on mental functioning.

TIME TRENDS IN THE FINDINGS: None.

DESIGN ISSUES: None.

REPLICABILITY: Replicable, though quality of case management will vary.

GENERALIZABILITY: Designed to generalize to the population of Medicaid-eligible elderly in the state of South Carolina. The Medicaid-eligible population, as a whole, is less impaired than participants in most of the long-term care studies that have been conducted.

FUNDING SOURCE: Florida Department of Health and Rehabilitative Services, under a federal waiver.

TREATMENT ADMINISTRATOR: Florida Department of Health and Rehabilitative Services, Department of Adult Services.

EVALUATOR: Nancy Ross, Department of Health and Rehabilitative Services, Office of Evaluation.

ENABLING LEGISLATION: None.

INFORMATION SOURCES: Information for this summary came from a conversation with the evaluator and William G. Weissert, Cynthia Matthews Cready, and James E. Pawelak, "The Past and Future of Home- and Community-Based Long-Term Care," *Millbank Quarterly* 66(1988): 309–88. The source document cited is J. M. Maurer, N. L. Ross, Y. M. Bigos, M. Papagiannis, and T. Springfield, *Final Report and Evaluation of the Florida Pentastar Project*, Florida Department of Health and Rehabilitive Services, 1984.

PUBLIC-USE ACCESS TO DATA: Not available.

SOUTH CAROLINA COMMUNITY LONG-TERM CARE

SUMMARY: This demonstration, conducted from 1980 to 1984, tested the effects of case management and home health services on a large sample of nursing home applicants. Subjects were followed for one year.

COST: Cost figures are not available.

TIME FRAME: Demonstration period, 1980–84.

TREATMENTS TESTED: Case management and other services not normally covered by Medicaid (including adult day health care, home-delivered meals, medical social services, personal care, and therapies). The control group received nothing from the demonstration, but could seek out existing long-term care services.

OUTCOMES: Nursing home and hospital use, health care costs, and measures of client functioning.

SAMPLE SIZE: Treatment, 802; control, 789.

TARGET POPULATION: Nursing home applicants certified as eligible for Medicaid-sponsored nursing home care.

NUMBER OF TREATMENT GROUPS: Two (including control).

NUMBER AND LOCATION OF SITES: Three South Carolina counties: Spartanburg, Cherokee, and Union.

RESEARCH COMPONENTS:
   Process: Internal peer review, development of care planning guidelines, and external review by representatives from nursing homes and home health agencies.
   Impact: Conducted using multivariate techniques.
   Benefit–cost analysis: Costs were analyzed, but a formal benefit–cost analysis was not conducted.

MAJOR FINDINGS:
1. South Carolina was quite effective at targeting at-risk individuals, as shown by the high percentage of control group members entering

nursing homes (58.6 percent) and hospitals (38.8 percent) during the observation year.

2. A significantly smaller percentage of treatment group members entered nursing homes than did control group members (-16.1 percent) and they spent significantly fewer days there (on average, 40 fewer days for the treatment group).The impact on hospital use was in the same direction, but was not significant (-5.5 percent and two fewer days for the treatment group).

3. Average annual per capita costs were higher for the treatment group. On average, combined services cost $744 (1988 dollars) more for the treatment group (inpatient services cost $1,175 less; outpatient services cost $413 more; and treatment services cost $1,506 more).

4. There were no significant impacts on client physical or mental functioning.

TIME TRENDS IN THE FINDINGS: None.

DESIGN ISSUES: Because randomization took place prior to screening for eligibility and appropriateness of treatment services, many of those assigned to the treatment group were never real candidates to use the services. Only 42 percent of the treatment group used treatment services.

REPLICABILITY: Replicable.

GENERALIZABILITY: Designed to generalize to the entire state of South Carolina.

FUNDING SOURCE: South Carolina Department of Social Services with federal matching grants.

TREATMENT ADMINISTRATOR: South Carolina Department of Social Services. Key personnel: Tom Brown, project director; and Geraldine Nantz, site supervisor.

EVALUATOR: Berkeley Planning Associates. Key personnel: John Kapitman, Brandeis University.

ENABLING LEGISLATION: None.

INFORMATION SOURCES: Information for this summary came from William G. Weissert, Cynthia Matthews Cready, and James E. Pawelak, "The Past and Future of Home- and Community-Based Long-Term Care," *Millbank Quarterly* 66(1988): 309–88; source document cited is T. E. Brown, Jr., D. K. Blackman, R. M. Learner, M. B. Witherspoon, and L. Saber, *South Carolina Long-Term Care Project: Report of Find-*

ings, South Carolina State Health and Human Services Finance Commission, 1985.

PUBLIC-USE ACCESS TO DATA: Not available.

NATIONAL LONG-TERM CARE
(CHANNELING) DEMONSTRATION

SUMMARY: This demonstration, conducted from 1982 to 1985, tested the effects of two case management models on a large sample of older persons with severe impairments. Subjects were followed for up to 18 months.

COST: Evaluation costs, approximately $13 million.

TIME FRAME: Demonstration period, February 1982–March 1985; data collected, same period; final report, 1986.

TREATMENTS TESTED: Two models of comprehensive case management were tested. The Basic Case Management model included screening, assessment, case planning, service initiation, monitoring, and reassessment. A limited amount of funding was provided to fill gaps and purchase community services. The Financial Control model added several elements to the Basic model, including expanded service coverage, a funds pool, and case manager authorization power in order to provide more financial support for community services. There were expenditure limits and cost sharing by clients. The control group participants received existing community services without the Channeling case management.

OUTCOMES OF INTEREST: Use of community care services, nursing home admissions, hospitalizations, client quality of life, and health care costs.

SAMPLE SIZE: Total, 6,326. For Basic model sites: treatment, 1,779; control, 1,345. For Financial Control model sites: treatment, 1,923; control, 1,279.

TARGET POPULATION: Older persons with severe impairments (minimum age, 65) who required long-term care and were considered at high risk for institutionalization. Several specific criteria relating to disability and unmet needs were applied. Participants resided in the community or were soon to be discharged from a nursing home. Participants needed to be covered by Medicare Part A to be eligible for the Financial Control model sites.

NUMBER OF TREATMENT GROUPS: Four—Basic model; Financial Control model; and a control group for each.

NUMBER AND LOCATION OF SITES: The Basic model operated in five sites: Eastern Kentucky; Southern Maine; Baltimore, Maryland; Middlesex County, New Jersey; and Houston, Texas. The Financial Control model operated in five sites: Miami, Florida; Greater Lynn, Massachusetts; Rensselaer County, New York; Cleveland, Ohio; and Philadelphia, Pennsylvania.

RESEARCH COMPONENTS:

Process analysis: All procedures were reviewed and pretested. Efforts were made to minimize the control group's contact with Channeling services. Interviews were conducted with staff to measure success of implementation.

Impact analysis: Conducted using multiple regression.

Benefit–cost analysis: Conducted.

MAJOR FINDINGS:
1. The increased costs of case management and expanded community services were not offset by reduced nursing home costs. During the evaluation period, total costs under the Basic model increased by 6 percent over the control group costs. Total costs under the Financia Control model increased by 18 percent over control group costs.
2. Nursing home use was lower among the treatment group than among the control group under both models, but the difference was small and not statistically significant.
3. Channeling did not affect longevity, hospital use, or use of physicians and other medical services. It also had no effect on measures of client functioning.
4. Channeling significantly reduced the unmet needs for care reported by clients. Treatment group clients (both models) also reported an increase in confidence and satisfaction with life. Informal caregivers of treatment group clients also reported significantly higher satisfaction with arrangements for care.

TIME TRENDS IN FINDINGS: None reported.

DESIGN ISSUES:
1. Caseload buildup was slower than planned, and it took roughly one year for all projects to reach their planned caseload levels.

2. The baseline interviews for treatment and control participants were conducted by separate staff. Whereas this served to insulate the control group members from the Channeling project, there was some noncomparability of baseline data. Some variables were replaced with screening interview data or were dropped.

3. Proxy respondents were used for 40–45 percent of the follow-up interviews owing to the frailty of some of the sample members. When treatment and control groups are compared, the percentages of proxy respondents are quite similar. Because of this, it is less likely that there was a major distortion of impacts. However, there was an indication that the use of proxies artificially inflated the impact on client satisfaction with life, even after controlling for disability and cognitive impairment. Proxy responses may have indicated their own satisfaction rather than that of the sample member.

4. Existing services in some areas and for some clients provided comprehensive case management similar to that offered by the Channeling treatments. It is estimated that 10–20 percent of the control group members received comprehensive case management.

REPLICABILITY: Replicable.

GENERALIZABILITY: Designed to generalize to the entire nation with the following caveats: (1) Site selection was not a probability sample. Sites were selected based on interest, commitment, capacity to perform the case management functions, and the quality of their proposals; and (2) Channeling clients were younger, slightly less disabled, and more likely to be married than a national sample of nursing home residents. Also, a higher proportion of the Channeling sample was nonwhite (27 percent versus 7 percent nationally).

FUNDING SOURCE: Funding was through a consortium at the U.S. Department of Health and Human Services (DHHS) including the Health Care Financing Administration (HCFA), Office of the Assistant Secretary for Planning and Evaluation (ASPE), and the Administration on Aging (AOA). Key personnel: Mary Harahan and Robert Clark.

TREATMENT ADMINISTRATOR: DHHS had overall responsibility for the demonstration. Within the department, three agencies (and their key personnel) were responsible for design and conduct of the demonstration: HCFA, Linda Hamm; ASPE, Mary F. Harahan; AOA, Barbara Fallon. Temple University Institute on Aging provided technical assistance (key personnel: Barbara Schneider). Frontline administration was handled by the agencies at the state level.

EVALUATOR: Mathematica Policy Research. Co-principal investigators: Peter Kemper and Randall Brown; Project director: George Carcagno.

ENABLING LEGISLATION: None.

INFORMATION SOURCES: Peter Kemper, et al. *The Evaluation of the National Long-Term Care Demonstration: Final Report*, Mathematica Policy Research, 1986. Also, the April 1988 issue of *Health Services Research* 23(1) is devoted to this demonstration.

PUBLIC-USE ACCESS TO DATA: Available through National Technical Information Service, Springfield, Virginia.

NEIGHBORHOOD TEAM EXPERIMENT

SUMMARY: This experiment, conducted from 1983 to 1985, tested the effects of a neighborhood team model of case management on a medium-sized sample of elderly and chronically ill patients. Subjects were followed for up to two years.

COST: Evaluators were unable to provide estimates of evaluation costs owing to substantial donated time and resources.

TIME FRAME: Demonstration period, April 1983–July 1985; data collected, same period.

TREATMENTS TESTED: This experiment compared the neighborhood team model of case management (treatment) with the centralized individual model (control), which was the status quo in Monroe County. In the Team model, team case managers had smaller case loads and were assigned specific geographic regions. They performed client assessments, case planning, some direct services, and reassessment. In the centralized individual model, case management functions were delegated to hospitals and certified home health agencies.

OUTCOMES OF INTEREST: (1) Health care utilization and expenditures; (2) Participant satisfaction; and (3) Health status.

SAMPLE SIZE: Total, 476; treatment, 273; control, 203.

TARGET POPULATION: Elderly and other chronically ill patients who required long-term care. DMS-1 scores (a measure of the level of disability) of 180 or higher were required for eligibility.

NUMBER OF TREATMENT GROUPS: Two.

NUMBER AND LOCATION OF SITES: One—Rochester, New York.

RESEARCH COMPONENTS:
Process analysis: Attrition (due to refusal to participate and mortality) was closely monitored. Patient characteristics and case histories were documented. Health care utilization diaries were kept for each patient. The evaluators also paid close attention to the randomization process.
   Impact analysis: Comparison of means.
   Benefit–cost analysis: Not conducted.

MAJOR FINDINGS: "Old cases"—patients who were receiving services when the project began—and "new cases"—patients who entered the program after its initiation—were analyzed separately and in the aggregate.

1. Among old cases, the treatment group experienced both less hospital utilization (27 percent less, or $6.04 less per patient per day) and less home care utilization (28 percent less, or $12.08 less per day) and expenditures. These findings are significant at the .1 level.
2. Among the new cases, the treatment group experienced less hospital utilization (30 percent less, or $9.78 less per day). However, home care utilization was greater for the treatment group (15 percent more, or $2.29 more per day). The latter finding was not statistically significant.
3. When old and new cases were aggregated, the average day cost was $62.27 for treatment cases and $72.08 for controls. Both hospital and home care estimated expenditures were lower for the treatment cases, but they used more nursing home care and slightly more ambulatory care. Overall, treatment cases averaged 14 percent lower ($9.81 lower) estimated costs than controls, significant at the .084 level.
4. There were no significant differences between groups on a measure of patient and caregiver satisfaction.
5. Patients with either a diagnosis of dementia or high initial assessment ratings on psychobehavioral problems showed the greatest reduction in use and estimated cost for the treatment group as opposed to controls (41 percent lower costs).

TIME TRENDS IN FINDINGS: Treatment group savings were not significant during the first six-month period, were greatest during the second six-month period (29 percent), and continued at roughly half that percentage for the remaining two six-month periods.

DESIGN ISSUES: The fraction of the sample assigned to treatment status changed during the final six months to increase the team case-load, but the assignment procedure remained random.

REPLICABILITY: Replicable.

GENERALIZABILITY: Designed to generalize to a population of frail, elderly patients needing long-term care. The sample had a median age of 76, half were Medicaid eligible, and they were slightly more impaired than the overall U.S. impaired noninstitutionalized population.

FUNDING SOURCES: The Robert Wood Johnson Foundation and U.S. Department of Health and Human Services, Health Care Financing Association (DHHS/HCFA).

TREATMENT ADMINISTRATOR: Monroe County Long-Term Care Program,/ACCESS, Rochester, New York; Gerald Eggert, director.

EVALUATORS: Gerald M. Eggert, James G. Zimmer, W. Jackson Hall, Bruce Friedman, and Patricia Chiverton.

ENABLING LEGISLATION: None.

INFORMATION SOURCES: Gerald M. Eggert, James G. Zimmer, W. Jackson Hall, and Bruce Friedman, "Case Management: A Randomized Controlled Study Comparing a Neighborhood Team and a Centralized Individual Model," *Health Services Research* 26(1991): 471–507; James G. Zimmer, Gerald M. Eggert, and Patricia Chiverton, "Individual versus Team Case Management in Optimizing Community Care for Chronically Ill Patients with Dementia," *Journal of Aging and Health* 2(1990) 357–72.

PUBLIC-USE ACCESS TO DATA: Not available.

TEAM APPROACH TO OUTPATIENT GERIATRIC EVALUATION EXPERIMENT

SUMMARY: This experiment, conducted from May 1983 to October 1985, tested the effects of a team approach to geriatric evaluation on a small sample of frail older persons. Subjects were followed for one year.

COST: Evaluators were unable to provide estimates of evaluation costs due to substantial donated time and resources.

TIME FRAME: Enrollment period, May 1983–October 1984; data collected for one year after enrollment.

TREATMENTS TESTED: An outpatient geriatric consultative service that included a team approach to evaluation. The team could include internists, psychiatrists, nurses, social workers, and/or nutritionists. Aside from evaluation, the team also provided counseling and family support services. The control group received a geriatric evaluation by a qualified internist from the community who was paid his or her usual and customary fee.

OUTCOMES OF INTEREST: (1) Costs of medical care and social services; (2) General health and functioning; (3) Hospitalizations and nursing home placements; and (4) Participant satisfaction.

SAMPLE SIZE: Total, 117; treatment, 58; control, 59.

TARGET POPULATION: The program targeted noninstitutionalized frail older persons aged 65 or older who had changing medical and social needs.

NUMBER OF TREATMENT GROUPS: Two (including control).

NUMBER AND LOCATION OF SITES: One—Monroe County (Rochester), New York.

RESEARCH COMPONENTS:
   Process analysis: Use of health care diaries and intake interviews used to monitor service delivery and participant characteristics.
   Impact analysis: Comparison of adjusted means.
   Benefit–cost analysis: Cost-effectiveness figures are computed, but a formal cost–benefit analysis was not conducted.

MAJOR FINDINGS:
1. At eight months, there was an indication that the treatment group experienced less deterioration in general health and functioning than the control group, although the finding was not statistically significant. Total scores on the functional scales of the Patient Assessment Forms (PAF) increased by 26.3 percent for control subjects and by 5.1 percent for treatment subjects. An increase in PAF scores indicates a decline in functioning.
2. At 8 months, utilization diaries collected over a two-week period showed substantial savings in hospital costs for the treatment group compared with the control (average cost per subject: treatment, $4,297; control, $7,018), but an increase in nursing home

costs (average cost per subject: treatment, $2,288; control, $1,756). The estimated savings in total costs for the treatment group over this two-week interval was 63 percent ($P = .06$). Over the full 12 months, total institutional costs for the treatment group were roughly 25 percent lower than those of the control group.
3. There were no significant treatment–control differences on measures of institutional placement or satisfaction with care.

TIME TRENDS IN FINDINGS: With time, control subjects spent progressively more days in the hospital, whereas treatment subjects experienced a decline in hospital days.

DESIGN ISSUES:
1. The control group received high-quality care from excellent general internists who were paid their customary fee. It was felt that the randomization process should not jeopardize vulnerable older people by leaving medical care for the control group to chance. Thus, findings may underestimate the benefits that might accrue if compared with usual medical practices (i.e., what would occur if patients chose general internists from those available, some of whom might provide less-than-excellent service at a lower price).
2. The levels of utilization were highly variable and very skewed. Fifteen percent of the clients accounted for 75 percent of the costs. One-half incurred costs averaging less than $5 daily, whereas 7 percent incurred costs averaging over $100 daily. This skewed distribution makes any treatment effects difficult to identify.
3. Data from clients, when checked later against institutional records, were frequently found to be in error, though those errors were usually minor and were corrected for in the analysis.

REPLICABILITY: Replicable.

GENERALIZABILITY: The sample was representative of the frail, older, noninstitutionalized population, but the small sample size and implementation issues discourage attempts at generalization.

FUNDING SOURCES: Robert Wood Johnson Foundation and National Institute on Aging.

TREATMENT ADMINISTRATOR: Geriatric Ambulatory Consultative Service (GACS) of Monroe Community Hospital.

EVALUATORS: Mark Williams, University of North Carolina School of Medicine; T. Franklin Williams, James Zimmer, W. Jackson Hall, and Carol Podgorski.

ENABLING LEGISLATION: None.

INFORMATION SOURCES: Mark E. Williams, T. Franklin Williams, James G. Zimmer, W. Jackson Hall, and Carol A. Podgorski, "How Does the Team Approach to Outpatient Geriatric Evaluation Compare with Traditional Care: A Report of a Randomized Controlled Trial," *Journal of the American Geriatric Society* 35(1987): 1071–78.

PUBLIC-USE ACCESS TO DATA: Not available.

Part Nineteen

HEALTH CARE PROVIDERS

NCHSR NURSING HOME INCENTIVES DEMONSTRATION

SUMMARY: This demonstration, conducted between 1980 and 1983, tested the effects of incentive payments on a small sample of proprietary nursing homes. Subjects were followed for 30 months.

COST: The evaluators are unable to separate evaluation and program costs. Total costs, approximately $4.6 million.

TIME FRAME: Demonstration period, May 1981–April 1983. Data collected, November 1980 to end of demonstration period.

TREATMENTS TESTED: The use of incentive payments made to nursing homes for reaching admission, outcome, and discharge goals. Incentives were in addition to Medicaid reimbursement. Control group homes did not receive incentive payments.

OUTCOMES OF INTEREST: Admissions, discharges, and outcome patterns for Medicaid patients in nursing homes.

SAMPLE SIZE: Nursing homes were the unit of analysis. There were a total of 36 homes: 18 experimental and 18 control. The number of individual patients varied by outcome. The total number of individual patients observed was 3,215.

TARGET POPULATION: Proprietary, Medicaid-certified nursing homes in San Diego County.

NUMBER OF TREATMENT GROUPS: Two (including a control).

NUMBER AND LOCATION OF SITES: Thirty-six Medicaid-certified nursing homes in San Diego County, California.

RESEARCH COMPONENTS:
   Process analysis: Special effort went into the definition and classification of all components within the experiment.
   Impact analysis: Conducted using multivariate regression methods, as well as simple comparisons of means.
   Benefit–cost analysis: Not conducted.

MAJOR FINDINGS: For admissions outcomes, the study investigated the number of harder-to-care-for patients who were admitted. Patients were classified as A, B, C, D, or E; C was the "break-even" patient, and disbursements (incentives) were made for D and E patients. There was a negative incentive for B patients.
1. During the first half of the treatment period, there were no statistically significant differences in Medicaid admissions between the experimental and control facilities. During the second half, how-

ever, the experimental facilities were admitting significantly fewer B patients and significantly more E patients. There was no effect on the admission of D patients.

2. Experimental facilities admitted patients with significantly higher average activities of daily living (ADL) scores (a measure of dependency and need for care—a higher ADL score indicates a higher need for care). Experimental facilities also had significantly higher average management minutes than did control facilities.

3. There were no statistically significant differences in patient outcomes, as measured by goal achievement, between experimental and control facilities.

4. Discharge results are less clear than those for admissions and outcomes because there was no comparable discharge planning process in control facilities. Nevertheless, the results suggest that the discharge incentive payment did little to encourage the experimental facilities to identify their patients for possible discharge, but did increase the likelihood of placing appropriate discharge candidates in a lower level of care.

TIME TRENDS IN FINDINGS: Admissions incentives appear to have had a greater impact in the second half of the project period. It may have taken some time for the facilities to adjust some of their admissions policies and practices.

DESIGN ISSUES: Participation in, and the design of, the discharge component of the experiment precluded the generation of meaningful results. Research team nurses felt that little effort was expended on the discharge process. The study requirements for discharge planning and implementation may have been a barrier to participation.

REPLICABILITY: Replicable. The reports furnish detailed information regarding the calculation of incentives and other operations.

GENERALIZABILITY: Designed to generalize to, at least, San Diego County. The sample is representative of those found throughout the state of California. Roughly three-fourths of nursing homes in California are proprietary (rather than nonprofit). Thirty-six of the 41 skilled nursing facilities in San Diego County participated in the study. However, the two-year project duration is an inadequate test of a permanent, widespread change in this system. It is hypothesized that many homes were reluctant to make changes that would affect them for years after the experiment's termination.

FUNDING SOURCE: National Center for Health Services Research, U.S. Department of Health and Human Services.

TREATMENT ADMINISTRATOR: Applied Management Sciences was responsible for data collection, training, and supervising a local field team of nurses, and disbursing incentive payments. Admission, discharge, assessment, goal setting, and care planning of residents remained the responsibility of the nursing homes.

EVALUATOR: National Center for Health Services Research and Health Care Technology Assessment (NCHSR/HCTA). William Weissert was the principal investigator during the design stage of this experiment; Mark Meiners was the principal investigator for later stages.

ENABLING LEGISLATION: None.

INFORMATION SOURCES: William G. Weissert, William J. Scanlon, Thomas T.H. Wan, and Douglas E. Skinner, "Care for the Chronically Ill: Nursing Home Incentive Payment Experiment," Health Care Financing Review 5(1983): 41–49; Mark R. Meiners, Phyllis Thorburn, Pamela C. Roddy, and Brenda Jones, Nursing Home Admissions: The Results of an Incentive Reimbursement Experiment, Long-Term Care Studies Program Research Report, DHHS Pub. No. 86-3397, October 1985; Phyllis Thorburn, and Mark R. Meiners, Nursing Home Patient Outcomes: The Results of an Incentive Reimbursement Experiment, Long-Term Care Studies Program Research Report, DHHS Pub. No. 86-3400, March 1986; Brenda J. Jones and Mark R. Meiners, Nursing Home Discharges: The Results of an Incentive Reimbursement Experiment, Long-Term Care Studies Program Research Report, DHHS Pub. No. 86-3399, August 1986; Norton, Edward C., "Incentive Regulation of Nursing Homes," Journal of Health Economics 11(1992): 105–28.

PUBLIC-USE ACCESS TO DATA: Available through National Technical Information Service (NTIS), Springfield, Virginia.

NATIONAL HOME HEALTH PROSPECTIVE PAYMENT
DEMONSTRATION—PHASE I

SUMMARY: This demonstration, conducted between 1990 and 1994, tested the effects of a prospective per-visit rate for home health visits on a small sample of nongovernmental home health agencies. Subjects were followed for three years.

COST: Evaluation costs, $3.1 million.

TIME FRAME: Demonstration period, October 1990–October 1994; data collected, same period; final report, December 1995.

TREATMENTS TESTED: Home health care agencies were paid a pre-determined per-visit rate for each type of home health visit. There were six types of visit: skilled nursing; home health aide; physical therapy; occupational therapy; speech therapy; and medical/social services. Rates were set at an agency's predemonstration costs per visit times expected inflation rates. Profits and losses were shared with the Health Care Financing Administration (HCFA). Control group agencies continued with the current payment method, paying agencies as services were rendered and reconciling payments to actual costs later.

OUTCOMES OF INTEREST: Principal outcomes were: agency cost per visit; volume of services; quality of care provided; and agency profit-ability. Patient outcomes included functional ability, hospitalizations, and satisfaction with care.

SAMPLE SIZE: A total of 47 health care agencies: 26 treatment; 21 control.

TARGET POPULATION: Nongovernmental home health agencies that had been in operation for at least three years. There were 41 urban agencies in three strata: freestanding proprietary; freestanding voluntary or nonprofit; and facility-based. The 6 rural agencies formed a separate stratum.

NUMBER OF TREATMENT GROUPS: Two (including control).

NUMBER AND LOCATION OF SITES: There were a total of 47 agencies in five states: California, Florida, Illinois, Massachusetts, and Texas.

RESEARCH COMPONENTS:
   Process analysis: Case studies and analysis of primary and second-ary data were used to determine agency response to demonstration incentives. Agency staff at both treatment and control agencies were interviewed.
   Impact analysis: Conducted using fixed effects and other regression models.
   Benefit–cost analysis: Not conducted.

MAJOR FINDINGS:
1. There was no significant difference between groups on costs per visit, on the number of visits that agencies provided, or on patients'

needs for other Medicare-covered services. Thus, total costs to Medicare were unaffected by prospective rate setting.

2. A rapid growth in visits occurred over the period for all agencies, although average total visits for both groups grew at a similar rate (21.3 percent for the treatment group; 23.6 percent for the control group).

3. There was a statistically significant difference in the length of home health aide visits. Average visit lengths were substantially shorter for the treatment group—65 minutes compared to 83 minutes for the control group. The evaluators pointed out that this finding was inconsistent with the finding of no effects on the average costs of aide visits and was probably not due to the demonstration.

4. The subset of treatment group agencies that serve predominantly Medicare patients and were not controlled by hospitals or hospices were significantly more likely than their control agency counterparts to hold their visit cost increases below inflation rates. As a result, net revenues on services to Medicare patients were positive for 77 percent of agency years for the treatment group. Only 40 percent of control group agencies would have earned profits had their actual costs been compared to revenues calculated under demonstration rules. The difference in cost growth was small, however (about 4 percent less for the treatment group). Treatment group agencies on average earned about $197,000 more in net revenues from Medicare than the average hypothetical net revenues for control group agencies.

5. There were no differences between groups on almost all measures of patient outcomes. Quality of care, access to home health care, and patient health and functioning were not significantly affected by the treatment.

TIME TRENDS IN FINDINGS: None reported.

DESIGN ISSUES:

1. There was a skewed distribution of agency size. Demonstration agencies delivered anywhere from 120 to 330,000 visits per year. This disparity led to problems in the analysis of patient level data. Patient observations were weighted to represent agencies equally, sometimes leading to anomalous estimates.

2. A sizable number of observations in the individual-level analyses were lost owing to the inability to link data from the treatment forms, patient intake forms, and Medicare claims files to the dem-

onstration claims files and the survey files. Identification numbers were often recorded incorrectly, and many agencies did not submit all patient intake forms. This reduced precision levels of the analyses.

REPLICABILITY: Replicable. Phase II of this demonstration, with some replication components, is currently being conducted.

GENERALIZABILITY: Designed to generalize to the entire nation, with sites in five large states. However, the sample size was small. Specifically, there were too few observations on facility-based and rural agencies to estimate impacts for each group, separately. Thus, the results are mainly indicative of the effects of prospective rate setting on urban, freestanding agencies. Also, there were a number of differences between the sample agencies and a random sample of home health care agencies nationally. The proportion of for-profit agencies was significantly higher and the proportion of hospital-based agencies significantly lower in the sample than in home health agencies generally. Area characteristics, such as urbanicity, population, and hospital wage index, differed considerably from national averages, mostly because of the small proportion of rural agencies.

FUNDING SOURCE: Health Care Financing Administration (HCFA). Key personnel: Elizabeth Mauser, Office of Research and Demonstration.

TREATMENT ADMINISTRATOR: Abt Associates was the implementation contractor for the demonstration. Key personnel: Henry Goldberg, project director. Actual home health care was administered by the individual agencies.

EVALUATOR: Mathematica Policy Research, Key personnel: Randall S. Brown, project director; Randall S. Brown and Barbara R. Phillips of Mathematica and Christine Bishop of Brandeis University, co-principal investigators.

ENABLING LEGISLATION: Section 4027 of the Omnibus Budget Reconciliation Act of 1987 and Section 4207(c) of the Omnibus Reconciliation Act of 1990.

INFORMATION SOURCES: Randall Brown, Barbara Phillips, Christine Bishop, Amy Klein, Grant Ritter, Craig Thornton, Peter Schochet, and Kathleen Skwara, *The Effects of Predetermined Payment Rates for Home Health Care*, Mathematica Policy Research, December 1995.

PUBLIC-USE ACCESS TO DATA: HCFA has data tapes, but they are not set up for public use.

Part Twenty

HOMELESS PERSONS

HOMELESS EMPLOYMENT PARTNERSHIP (HEP)

SUMMARY: This demonstration, conducted from 1989 through 1992, tested the effects of intensive case management and employment services on a medium-sized sample of homeless men. Subjects were followed for six months.

COST: Approximately $36,000–$45,000.

TIME FRAME: May 1989–December 1992; HHS/OCS report, December 1993.

TREATMENTS TESTED: The Homeless Employment Partnership (HEP) treatment, or case management (CM), group received all normal services available at the Metropolitan Development Council resource center (personal maintenance, job referrals, bus tokens) plus "employment intensive services" (wraparound case management, job development, and housing subsidy). The case management included financial aid for transportation and identity card assistance, job counseling, résumé assistance, and client/employer liaison. The control, or information and referral (I&R), group members received the normal facility services and were eligible for intensive services after a 90-day waiting period. Because very few of these subjects returned to enroll in the CM group after this period, the eligibility of controls for CM had little impact on the analysis.

OUTCOMES OF INTEREST: (1) Employment; (2) Income; and (3) Homelessness.

SAMPLE SIZE: Total, 254; CM group, 127; I&R group, 127.

TARGET POPULATION: Homeless men who were judged to be "employable."

NUMBER OF TREATMENT GROUPS: Two (including control).

NUMBER AND LOCATION OF SITES: One—Tacoma, Washington.

RESEARCH COMPONENTS:
Process analysis: Service delivery data were collected throughout the intervention period. Demographic characteristics and required services of the clients were monitored. This led to a change in intervention focus from training to job search and retention services.

Impact analysis: Analysis varied with outcome being measured. Regression and analysis of variance were used.

Benefit–cost analysis: Not conducted.

MAJOR FINDINGS:

1. CM group members were significantly more likely to have had an employment experience in the week prior to follow-up than were I&R group members (80 percent versus 48 percent). The intervention appears to have a slightly stronger effect on this outcome for the higher-risk client. Further, the CM group's employment was more likely to be permanent, rather than temporary, when compared to the I&R group's employment.
2. The CM group worked significantly more hours in the week prior to follow-up than did the I&R group (28.09 versus 16.16).
3. The CM group members were more likely to have job benefits such as insurance and sick leave than were I&R group members.
4. The CM group members had significantly higher pay than did I&R group members ($159.61/week versus $95.46).
5. The CM group was more likely to be living in a house or an apartment (not homeless) than the I&R group (46 percent versus 23 percent).

TIME TRENDS IN FINDINGS: Long-term follow-up was not conducted. Follow-up at six months suggested that individuals who were more "job-ready" at the start of the program were more likely to retain employment and other benefits at follow-up.

DESIGN ISSUES:

1. After random assignment, there were statistically significant differences between groups on several "barriers to employment" variables. Although the evaluator reported that "painstaking measures were taken to ensure random assignment," he questioned whether the assignment procedure may have been compromised. It is likely that some selection bias was present when one partner (see Appendix I for an explanation of the DPP "partners") had difficulty excluding some of the participants from the control group. This partner was replaced and the intended design was maintained.
2. In a very few cases, intervention services were offered to control group members felt to be "in desperate need." The evaluator feels this deviation is small and not likely to affect outcomes.
3. There was a follow-up rate of only 59 percent. However, a comparison of those with follow-up data and those lost to follow-up shows few significant differences.

REPLICABILITY: Replicable.

GENERALIZABILITY: Design and implementation issues discourage attempts at generalization. In addition, the program was voluntary and a screening process was used to assess educational background, employment history, mental health, drug/alcohol abuse, and financial eligibility. Those admitted to the program were found to be drug/alcohol free, mentally stable, and motivated to find employment. The project report's authors cited several studies showing that roughly 50 percent of the homeless population would not fit these characteristics. The evaluator agreed that the sample "is certainly not representative of all the homeless," but represents "a sizable portion."

FUNDING SOURCE: Demonstration Partnership Program, Office of Community Service, U.S. Department of Health and Human Services (DHHS). Key personnel: John Buckstead.

TREATMENT ADMINISTRATOR: Metropolitan Development Council, Tacoma, Washington. Key personnel: Doug Swanberg, project director.

EVALUATOR: Dennis McBride, Puget Sound Research Associates.

ENABLING LEGISLATION: Demonstration Partnership Program under Section 408 of the Human Services Reauthorization Act of 1986.

INFORMATION SOURCES: U.S. Department of Health and Human Services (DHHS), Administration for Children and Families, Office of Community Services, *Homeless and Youth at Risk: Demonstration Partnership Program Projects—Summary of Final Evaluation Findings from 1990,* 1993.

PUBLIC-USE ACCESS TO DATA: Available through Office of Community Services, DHHS.

Part Twenty-One

MULTIPLE GROUPS

NATIONAL SUPPORTED WORK DEMONSTRATION

SUMMARY: This demonstration, conducted from 1975 to 1980, tested the effects of supported work experience on a large sample of AFDC recipients, ex-offenders, substance abusers, and high school dropouts. Subjects were followed for two years.

COST: $82.4 million (but this includes $10.6 million in sales of goods and services produced), in 1977 dollars; research, $11.1 million.

TIME FRAME: Demonstration March 1975–December 1978; data collected, April 1975–mid-1980; final report, 1981.

TREATMENTS TESTED: (1) Controls received no treatment. (2) Experimentals were offered employment in a structured work experience program involving peer group support, a graduated increase in work standards, and close sympathetic supervision, for 12 to 18 months. Local agencies contracted with Manpower Demonstration Research Corporation to employ the experimentals in a broad range of activities, with pay starting at the minimum wage (or slightly higher, depending on local market conditions), and bonuses and merit increases for workers who met increasing work standards. Agencies maintained a high ratio of supervisors to participants (1:8 to 1:12), and implemented different on-site methods for crew interaction and shared responsibility. Typical work activities were construction, building maintenance, and child day care.

OUTCOMES OF INTEREST: (1) Increases in post-treatment earnings; (2) Reductions in criminal activity; (3) Reductions in transfer payments; (4) Reductions in drug abuse.

SAMPLE SIZE: Experimentals, 3,214; controls, 3,402.

TARGET POPULATION: (1) Long-term recipients of AFDC (30 of last 36 months, no children under age six); (2) Ex-addicts following drug rehabilitation treatment (within past 6 months); (3) Ex-offenders, aged 18 or over, incarcerated within past 6 months; (4) Young school dropouts, aged 17–20, not in school past 6 months, at least 50 percent having delinquent or criminal records.

NUMBER OF TREATMENT GROUPS: Two.

NUMBER AND LOCATION OF SITES: Twelve—Atlanta, Georgia; Chicago, Illinois; Hartford, Connecticut; Jersey City and Newark, New Jersey; New York City; Oakland and San Francisco, California; Philadelphia, Pennsylvania; and several sites in Wisconsin.

Research Components:

Process analysis: Conducted. Results do not, however, appear in the summary volumes but in earlier reports.

Impact analysis: Comparison of means; regressions performed in earlier work produced similar results.

Benefit–cost analysis: Conducted from taxpayer, subject, and social perspectives. Results very sensitive to assumptions about the social costs of criminal activity, somewhat sensitive to extrapolation of earnings effects.

Major Findings:
1. Major positive effect on earnings of AFDC-recipient group.
2. Minor increase in earnings of ex-addicts, and major reduction in criminal activity.
3. No discernible effects on young dropouts.
4. No clear effects on ex-offenders.
5. Benefits exceeded costs for AFDC recipient and ex-addict groups by $8,000 and $4,000, respectively. Costs exceeded benefits for young dropouts. For ex-offenders, the bulk of findings show costs substantially exceeding benefits (experimentals were arrested more frequently), but a small-sample, three-month follow-up shows the reverse tendency.

Time Trends in Findings: Earnings differences showed little decay over time among recipients of Aid to Families with Dependent Children (AFDC); criminal activity differences fell over time among ex-addicts.

Design Issues:
1. Local organizations competed to win these contracts. Some projects were not funded, and one was discontinued for poor performance. Thus, self-selection of sites might bias the results.
2. Displacement effects could occur in two ways. First, the greatest impact seemed to be for AFDC recipients in periods of high unemployment. Second, the agencies competed for local government contracts, they set up small businesses, and so on, and might have displaced other businesses.
3. Both controls and experimentals underreported arrests. A research finding that underreporting seemed to be of the same magnitude between controls and experimentals is critical to results.

Replicability: Treatment seems to require development of entrepreneurial local project management.

GENERALIZABILITY: The large number of sites and subjects adds power to the findings. However, site and contractor self-selection are certainly present.

FUNDING SOURCES: U.S. Department of Labor (DOL), Education and Training Administration; U.S. Department of Justice, Law Enforcement Assistance Administration; U.S. Department of Health and Human Services (DHHS), Office of Planning and Evaluation, National Institute on Drug Abuse (NIDA); U.S. Department of Housing and Urban Development, Office of Policy Development and Research; U.S. Department of Commerce, Economic Development Administration; and the Ford Foundation. Key personnel: DOL—Howard Rosen and Fritz Kramer; DHHS—Mike Barth and Bill Barnes; Ford Foundation—Stan Breznoff; and NIDA—Deborah Hastings Black.

TREATMENT ADMINISTRATOR: Manpower Demonstration Research Corporation. Key personnel: Judith M. Gueron.

EVALUATORS: Primary—Mathematica Policy Research; secondary—Institute for Research on Poverty, University of Wisconsin-Madison. Key personnel: Robinson G. Hollister, Jr., Peter Kemper, David A. Long, and Craig Thornton.

ENABLING LEGISLATION: AFDC sample required waivers to Social Security Act.

INFORMATION SOURCES: Board of Directors, Manpower Demonstration Research Corporation (MDRC), *Summary and Findings of the National Supported Work Demonstration*, MDRC, 1980; Peter Kemper, David A. Long, and Craig Thornton, *The Supported Work Evaluation: Final Benefit–Cost Analysis*, MDRC, 1981.

PUBLIC-USE ACCESS TO DATA: Public-use access file exists; contact Manpower Demonstration Research Corporation.

AFDC HOMEMAKER–HOME HEALTH AIDE DEMONSTRATIONS

SUMMARY: This demonstration, conducted from 1983 to 1986, tested the effects of having AFDC clients work as aides in the homes of the elderly/impaired on large samples of both the elderly/impaired and recipients of Aid to Families with Dependent Children (AFDC). Subjects were followed for two years.

COST: Research only, $8 million (1984).

TIME FRAME: January 1983–June 1986; data collected, same period; final report, 1987.

TREATMENTS TESTED: Experimental elderly/impaired subjects (clients) could receive up to 100 hours per month of homemaker and home health aide services as needed for the duration of the demonstration. These services were free if subjects' incomes were less than two times the AFDC standard of need in their state; persons with incomes above that level were charged on a sliding scale. Control elderly/impaired subjects could not receive these services. Experimental AFDC subjects (trainees) received a four- to eight-week training course to become a homemaker–home health aide, followed by a year of subsidized employment. Wages averaged $3.84 per hour, and hours averaged 75 per month. Controls did not receive this training, nor did they receive subsidized employment.

OUTCOMES OF INTEREST:
    For clients: (1) Changes in other informal or paid in-home care; (2) Changes in survival; (3) Changes in hospital and nursing home utilization; (4) Changes in Medicare and Medicaid reimbursements; (5) Changes in health outcomes. For trainees: (1) Employment; (2) Earnings; and (3) AFDC and food stamp payments and recipiency.

SAMPLE SIZE: Elderly/impaired: roughly 9,500 experimentals, 9,500 controls; AFDC: roughly 4,750 experimentals, 4,750 controls.

TARGET POPULATION: Elderly/impaired subjects had to be elderly or disabled and at risk of institutionalization, and home health aide services could not "reasonably or actually" be available to them. AFDC subjects had to be currently eligible for AFDC and had to have received it for the past 90 days. They could not have been employed as a homemaker–home health aide during that period, and they had to have applied to enter the program.

NUMBER OF TREATMENT GROUPS: This was a two-component experiment. There were two AFDC-recipient groups (one control) and two elderly/impaired groups (one control).

NUMBER AND LOCATION OF SITES: Arkansas, Kentucky, New Jersey, New York, Ohio, South Carolina, and Texas.

RESEARCH COMPONENTS:
    Process analysis: The process analysis was generally limited to observing that the treatments were delivered as planned to the groups for whom they were designed. One salient finding, however, was that

intake workers' ratings of AFDC subjects' potential had little value in selecting applicants who would most benefit from the demonstration.

Impact analysis: Conducted with ordinary least squares (OLS).

Benefit–cost analysis: Conducted from social, taxpayer, client, and trainee perspectives.

MAJOR FINDINGS:

Note: In the tables following, asterisks denote results that are statistically significant at the .05 percent level.

1. Clients

   a. Experimental effect on hours per week of care ("total" is not the sum of formal and informal; effects are estimated from three different regressions):

	Formal	Informal	Total
Arkansas	4.92*	−0.62	4.20*
Kentucky	1.20*	−0.47	0.72
New Jersey	3.47*	−0.55	3.26*
New York	4.21*	0.34	4.83*
Ohio	1.58*	−0.63	1.09*
South Carolina	8.29*	−1.42*	7.05*
Texas	4.02*	−0.19	4.26*

Survival: There was no significant impact on mortality.

Percentage of period spent in hospitals: The only statistically significant effect was in New York and in the wrong direction (clients spent an additional 4.5 percent of their time in hospitals).

Percentage of period spent in nursing homes: There was no significant impact on institutionalization.

   b. Experimental effect on Medicare/Medicaid reimbursement:

	Medicare	Medicaid
Arkansas	−$39	−$40*
Kentucky	+32	+ 1
New Jersey	−240*	− 30
New York	−30	Data not collected
Ohio	−66	+13
South Carolina	+25	−59*
Texas	+26	0

Health and functioning: Clients were slightly less likely than controls to be completely dependent, communicated somewhat better, and their medical conditions were less likely to have worsened during the demonstration period.

2. Trainees

Note: In the tables following, effects are computed per participant, by dividing the effect per experimental by the fraction of assigned experimentals who actually entered training.

   a. Experimental effect on average monthly earnings over 30-month follow-up period (in dollars):

Arkansas	122*
Kentucky	148*
New Jersey	216*
New York	39
Ohio	210*
South Carolina	140*
Texas	141*

Note: In the tables following, postdemonstration-year 1 is the 12 months following the time when the typical trainee left subsidized employment. Year 2 is the next 12 months.

   b. Experimental effect on percentage employed:

	Year 1 (%)	Year 2 (%)
Arkansas	3	31*
Kentucky	0	2
New Jersey	9*	12*
New York	−2	−13
Ohio	6*	13*
South Carolina	3	3
Texas	−3	28*

   c. Experimental effect on hours worked per month:

	Year 1	Year 2
Arkansas	3	24*
Kentucky	3	11
New Jersey	15*	22*
New York	−9	−10
Ohio	14*	25*
South Carolina	4	−2
Texas	1	48*

   d. Experimental effect on earnings per month:

	Year 1 ($)	Year 2 ($)
Arkansas	10	101*
Kentucky	28*	161*
New Jersey	81*	126*
New York	−36	12

	Year 1 ($)	Year 2 ($)
Ohio	68*	105*
South Carolina	26*	22
Texas	8	215*

e. Experimental effect on percentage receiving AFDC or food
stamps (during a typical follow-up period month):

	AFDC (%)	Food Stamps (%)
Arkansas	−13*	−1
Kentucky	−28*	−3*
New Jersey	−26*	−11*
New York	−3*	5*
Ohio	−27*	−15*
South Carolina	−39*	−8*
Texas	−11*	−1

f. Experimental effect on dollars received monthly per participant:

	AFDC (%)	Food Stamps (%)
Arkansas	−31*	−16*
Kentucky	−52*	−17*
New Jersey	−106*	12*
New York	−2	6*
Ohio	−84*	−28*
South Carolina	−68*	−42*
Texas	−18*	−8*

TIME TRENDS IN FINDINGS: Shown above for trainee earnings. Savings
in AFDC and food stamps drop sharply over time.

Benefit–cost analysis: The unit of analysis chosen is dollars per
hour of service. The analysis is dominated by the failure of the treatment to reduce the usage of hospitals and nursing homes. Trainees
and clients are net gainers by the treatment, but taxpayers are worse
off.

Net social benefit in dollars per hour of service:

Arkansas	−$9.67
Kentucky	−4.47
New Jersey	+15.75
New York	−40.00
Ohio	+13.47
South Carolina	−0.39
Texas	−3.68

DESIGN ISSUES: Orr has stated that there are several reasons why New York was an extreme outlier. The first is turnover at the upper management level, with half a dozen persons holding the project director position at one time or another. The second is that contract negotiations with local providers took too long, and implementation was too slow; in some respects, the demonstration never properly got off the ground. The third is that New York has a heavy turnover in its AFDC population; controls would catch up to experimentals more quickly there than elsewhere for other interventions as well (Orr, personal communiction, 1990).

REPLICABILITY: Replicable.

GENERALIZABILITY: This is a massive demonstration, but the sites are not a representative sample of the United States. States were selected for their strong interest in home care. In some ways, this makes the negative results on the client side more striking.

FUNDING SOURCE: Health Care Financing Administration. Key personnel: Kathy Ellingson-Otto.

TREATMENT ADMINISTRATOR: Social service agencies in seven states. Key personnel: Joann Barham (Arkansas); Darlene Goodrich (Kentucky); Sybil Stokes (New Jersey); Joe Capobianco (New York); Ruth Ann Sieber (Ohio); Mary Frances Payton (South Carolina); and David Chavez (Texas).

EVALUATOR: Abt Associates. Key personnel: Larry L. Orr, Stephen H. Bell, and Nancy R. Burstein.

ENABLING LEGISLATION: Omnibus Budget Reconciliation Act of 1980.

POLICY EFFECTS: Larry Orr has stated that this is one of several studies that dampened enthusiasm for home care. Although the findings suggest positive effects from the component that trained and employed AFDC recipients, the findings have not been utilized at the federal level, perhaps because the funding agency for the experiment is not the agency with responsibility for AFDC.

INFORMATION SOURCE: Stephen H. Bell, Nancy R. Burstein, and Larry L. Orr, "Overview of Evaluation Results," Abt Associates, December 1987.

PUBLIC-USE ACCESS TO DATA: Public-use file exists; contact Abt Associates.

APPENDIX I: THE DEMONSTRATION PARTNERSHIP PROGRAM (DPP) PROJECTS

THE DEMONSTRATION PARTNERSHIP PROGRAM (DPP) PROJECTS

The Demonstration Partnership Program (DPP), under Section 408 of the Human Services Reauthorization Act of 1986, authorizes a demonstration program to operate in conjunction with the Community Services Block Grant Program with the unique purpose of developing and implementing new and innovative approaches to address the needs of the poor.

This program was to stimulate eligible entities (mainly Community Action Agencies) to develop new approaches to provide self-sufficiency for the poor, to test and evaluate those approaches, and to disseminate project results and evaluation findings so that new approaches could be replicated.

DPP grants were made for projects that were innovative and could be coordinated with a grantee's ongoing programs. Projects were to involve new combinations of resources, especially partnerships with other community agencies (called "partners" throughout this *Digest*'s summaries), and were to be evaluated by a third party.

Some of these third-party evaluations were conducted as social experiments.

APPENDIX II: ONGOING SOCIAL EXPERIMENTS AS OF FALL 1996

LIST OF ONGOING SOCIAL EXPERIMENTS

Alabama Avenues to Self-Sufficiency through Employment and Training Services (ASSETS)

STARTING YEAR/YEAR FINAL REPORT EXPECTED: 1990/1997.

INFORMATION SOURCE: Alan Werner and David Rodda, *Evaluation of the Alabama Avenues to Self-Sufficiency through Employment and Training Services (ASSETS) Demonstration: Interim Impact Report*, Abt Associates, July 1994. This quasi-experimental welfare reform demonstration is sponsored by the Alabama Department of Human Resources; Gudrun Hanson, project officer. It is being evaluated by Abt Associates; Alan Werner, project director.

PRINCIPAL INTERVENTIONS: (1) Consolidates the Food Stamp and AFDC programs with standardized and simplified rules and provision of a single cash grant; (2) Broadens the participation requirements for employment and training services; (3) Extends requirements to cooperate with child support enforcement officials; (4) Case management.

TARGET POPULATION: Recipients of AFDC and food stamps.

OUTCOMES OF INTEREST: Welfare participation and receipt of welfare benefits.

The JOBS Evaluation

STARTING YEAR/YEAR FINAL REPORT EXPECTED: 1991/2000.

INFORMATION SOURCE: Gayle Hamilton and Thomas Brock, *The JOBS Evaluation: Early Lessons from Seven Sites*, Manpower Demonstration Research Corporation, 1994.

PRINCIPAL INTERVENTIONS: JOBS provides an array of education, training, and employment services. Each state determines the exact sequence and content of program services. Services can include adult education; job skills training; job readiness activities; job placement services; job search assistance; on-the-job training; and/or community work experience. Child care, in the form of direct services or payment to providers, is also offered.

TARGET POPULATION: Recipients of AFDC. Those with children ages three and above or, at the state's option, ages one and above, are required to participate.

OUTCOMES OF INTEREST: The outcomes addressed by the key evaluation questions include participation rates; welfare caseloads; welfare receipt; employment; earnings; educational attainment; and cost-effectiveness.

New Jersey Family Development Program

STARTING YEAR/YEAR FINAL REPORT EXPECTED: 1992/1998.

INFORMATION SOURCE: No written source. This welfare reform demonstration is sponsored by the Kaiser Foundation and the State of New Jersey, Department of Human Services; Rudy Myers, project officer. It is being evaluated by Rutgers University; Michael Camasso, principal investigator.

PRINCIPAL INTERVENTIONS: (1) A family cap (additional children do not automatically increase the amount of the AFDC grant); (2) A higher earned-income disregard for noncustodial spouses; and (3) Stiffer sanctions for nonparticipation in designated work activities.

TARGET POPULATION: Recipients of AFDC.

OUTCOMES OF INTEREST: Fertility, earned income, and consumption of AFDC benefits.

To Strengthen Michigan Families (TSMF)

STARTING YEAR/YEAR FINAL REPORT EXPECTED: 1992/2000.

INFORMATION SOURCE: Alan Werner and Robert Kornfeld, The Evaluation of To Strengthen Michigan Families: Fourth Annual Report— Third-Year Impacts, Abt Associates, June 1996.

PRINCIPAL INTERVENTIONS: (1) A social contract (under which participants agree to engage in "personally and/or socially useful activities for at least 20 hours/week"); (2) A larger earned-income disregard than under AFDC; (3) Broadened AFDC eligibility for two-parent families; and (4) Allowing children to earn and save without affecting benefits. In 1994, a new job search requirement, a new sanctions policy, and a requirement for the immunization of preschool children were added to the program.

TARGET POPULATION: Low-income families (recipients of AFDC and/ or State Family Assistance).

OUTCOMES OF INTEREST: Employment, earnings, welfare participation, and receipt of benefits.

Georgia Preschool Immunization Project (PIP)

STARTING YEAR/YEAR FINAL REPORT EXPECTED: 1993/1999.

INFORMATION SOURCE: No written source. PIP is a welfare reform demonstration sponsored by the Georgia Department of Human Resources; Diane Simms, project officer. It is being evaluated by Abt Associates; Larry Kerpelman, project director; David Connell, principal investigator.

PRINCIPAL INTERVENTIONS: A sanction applied to clients who do not have their preschool children up-to-date on their immunizations.

TARGET POPULATION: Recipients of AFDC with preschool children.

OUTCOMES OF INTEREST: Immunization rates. Secondary outcomes include economic burdens on the family and on the agency for administering the program and the dollar benefits of the program.

Illinois Work Pays Initiative

STARTING YEAR/YEAR FINAL REPORT EXPECTED: 1993/1998.

INFORMATION SOURCE: No written source. This welfare reform project is sponsored by the Illinois Department of Public Aid; Peggy Powers and Dave Gruenenfelder, project officers. It is being evaluated by the Center for Governmental Studies, Northern Illinois University.

PRINCIPAL INTERVENTION: Lower benefit reduction rates on earned income. For every three dollars of gross earnings, a client's AFDC grant is reduced by one dollar. Clients remain eligible for a grant until the sum of earned and unearned income reaches the poverty level.

TARGET POPULATION: Recipients of AFDC.

OUTCOMES OF INTEREST: Welfare participation and benefit receipt, employment, and earnings.

Iowa Family Investment Program

STARTING YEAR/YEAR FINAL REPORT EXPECTED: 1993/1999.

INFORMATION SOURCE: Anne R. Gordon, Carol Prindle, and Thomas M. Fraker, Initial Findings from the Evaluation of the Iowa Family Investment Program. Paper prepared for presentation at the annual meeting of the Association for Public Policy Analysis and Management, Washington, D.C., November 4, 1995. The evaluation is funded by the Iowa Department of Human Services.

PRINCIPAL INTERVENTIONS: A variety of revisions to the program rules for both the AFDC and Food Stamp programs, including: a complete disregard of earnings for the first four months of employment and continued liberalization of the earnings disregards after four months; extending eligibility for Transitional Child Care from one year to two years; a required goal-oriented Family Investment Agreement; fewer JOBS exemptions; and stronger sanctions for noncompliance.

TARGET POPULATION: All ongoing AFDC cases in October 1993 and new applicants to both AFDC and Food Stamp programs after that date.

OUTCOMES OF INTEREST: Employment, earnings, and welfare receipt.

Maryland's Primary Prevention Initiative (PPI)

STARTING YEAR/YEAR FINAL REPORT EXPECTED: 1993/1998.

INFORMATION SOURCE: *PPI Evaluation: Maryland's Primary Prevention Initiative—An Interim Report.* Schaefer Center for Public Policy, School of Public Affairs, University of Baltimore, November 1995.

PRINCIPAL INTERVENTIONS: Requires AFDC recipients with school-age children to verify that their children attend school. Recipients with preschool children must verify that their children receive preventive health care. Sanctions (grant reductions) are used for noncompliance. Cash allowances are provided for preventive health care and prenatal nutritional needs of pregnant recipients. One-day problem-solving workshops (which were later discontinued) and targeted case management are also part of the program.

TARGET POPULATION: Recipients of AFDC.

OUTCOMES OF INTEREST: Program costs, recipient perceptions, preventive health care visits, and the overall effectiveness of PPI-related disallowances.

Utah Single Parent Employment Demonstration Program

STARTING YEAR/YEAR FINAL REPORT EXPECTED: 1993/1998.

INFORMATION SOURCE: *Utah Single Parent Employment Demonstration Program: It's about Work—Three Year Report,* Office of Family Support, Utah Department of Human Resources, May 1996. This welfare reform project is being evaluated by the Social Research Institute, University of Utah, Salt Lake City; Fred Janzen, principal investigator.

PRINCIPAL INTERVENTIONS: For the treatment group, self-sufficiency planning occurs before eligibility determination, and there is an option of receiving a one-time diversion payment of up to three times the regular monthly grant level, rather than entering the ongoing AFDC caseload; universal and mandatory participation in employment-related activities; an emphasis on child support; a higher disregard level for earned income; and a simplification of AFDC, Medicaid, Food Stamp, and Child Care rules.

TARGET POPULATION: Recipients of, and applicants for, AFDC benefits.

OUTCOMES OF INTEREST: Employment, earnings, and welfare receipt, as well as participation rates and cultural change.

Wyoming New Opportunities/New Responsibilities

STARTING YEAR/YEAR FINAL REPORT EXPECTED: 1993/1997

INFORMATION SOURCE: No written source. This welfare reform project is sponsored by the Wyoming Department of Family Services; Ken Kaz, project officer. It is being evaluated by Mary Byrnes, an independent evaluator.

PRINCIPAL INTERVENTION: The project is employment-focused and is operated with the cooperation of the state Department of Employment. New AFDC applicants must register at the job service office at application. If found to be job-ready, they are assigned to Department of Employment case management. Otherwise, their case is handled by the welfare office.

TARGET POPULATION: Recipients of AFDC, especially new applicants.

OUTCOMES OF INTEREST: Employment, earnings, welfare participation and benefit receipt, completion rates of educational and training programs.

Arkansas Welfare Waiver Demonstration Project

STARTING YEAR/YEAR FINAL REPORT EXPECTED: 1994/2000.

INFORMATION SOURCE: No written source. This welfare reform demonstration is sponsored by the Arkansas Department of Human Services; Roy Kindle, Jr., project officer. It is being evaluated by the University of Arkansas at Little Rock; Brent Benda, principal investigator.

PRINCIPAL INTERVENTIONS: A family cap: no additional AFDC benefits for children conceived after July 1994. The project was also intended to test the effectiveness of family planning support (in the form of informational pamphlets and case manager encouragement), but it has been shown that the control group is also receiving this service.

TARGET POPULATION: All recipients of AFDC.

OUTCOMES OF INTEREST: Birthrate, employment, earnings, and welfare receipt.

California's Work Pays Demonstration Project (WPDP)

STARTING YEAR/YEAR FINAL REPORT EXPECTED: WPDP started in 1994, replacing the Assistance Payment Demonstration, which began in 1992. Final report expected in 1998.

INFORMATION SOURCE: No written source. This welfare reform project is sponsored by the California State Department of Social Services; Lois Van Beers, project officer. It is being evaluated by the University of California–Los Angeles (UCLA); Rosina Becerra, principal investigator.

PRINCIPAL INTERVENTIONS: A variety of work incentives: (1) Elimination of the 100-hour rule for two-parent families; (2) Extension of the 30 and a third income disregard from several months to indefinitely; (3) "Fill-the-gap" budgeting; (4) Restricted accounts that are exempted from income and a higher vehicle asset limit; and (5) Extended transitional child care and Medicaid benefits.

TARGET POPULATION: AFDC cases with an adult who is able to work.

OUTCOMES OF INTEREST: Employment, earnings, AFDC participation, benefit receipt, and total family income.

Colorado Personal Responsibility and
Employment Program (CPREP)

STARTING YEAR/YEAR FINAL REPORT EXPECTED: 1994/2000.

INFORMATION SOURCE: Unpublished excerpts from the CPREP Evaluation Plan. Center for Public-Private Sector Cooperation, University of Colorado at Denver. Undated.

PRINCIPAL INTERVENTION: (1) Consolidates AFDC, Food Stamps, and Child Care Assistance into a single benefit structure providing cash to the client paid in two checks monthly; (2) Provides a more generous disregard of earnings in calculating benefits than the current AFDC system and also increases the gross income limit and the asset limit; (3) Provides for additional JOBS case managers; (4) Provides a cash incentive for high school graduation or its equivalent; (5) Stipulates stronger sanctions for noncompliance (including sanctions for non-immunization of preschool children).

TARGET POPULATION: AFDC-Basic recipients who are not currently employed.

OUTCOMES OF INTEREST: Employment, earnings, educational achievement, immunization rates, and AFDC receipt and recidivism among clients leaving the rolls.

Florida Family Transition Program (FTP)

STARTING YEAR/YEAR FINAL REPORT EXPECTED: 1994/2002.

INFORMATION SOURCE: No written source. FTP is a welfare reform demonstration sponsored by the Florida Department of Health and Rehabilitative Services; Don Winstead, project officer. It is being evaluated by Manpower Demonstration Research Corporation; Dan Bloom, project director.

PRINCIPAL INTERVENTIONS: (1) Time limit of either two or three years (depending on welfare and employment history); (2) More-generous earned-income disregards than in the existing AFDC system; (3) Enhanced employment-related services such as job search activities, job clubs, and computer assisted instruction; (4) Parental responsibility mandates such as a requirement of school attendance for school-age children, parental involvement in school, and proof of immunization for preschool children.

TARGET POPULATION: AFDC recipients with no children under six months of age.

OUTCOMES OF INTEREST: Employment, earnings, and welfare receipt, and measures of child well-being.

Georgia Personal Accountability and Responsibility

STARTING YEAR/YEAR FINAL REPORT EXPECTED: 1994/1999.

INFORMATION SOURCE: No written source. This is a welfare reform demonstration project sponsored by the Georgia Department of Human Resources; Nancy Meszaros, project officer. An outside evaluator for the demonstration has not yet been contracted.

PRINCIPAL INTERVENTIONS: A family cap: no incremental increase of AFDC benefits to a child conceived while his or her family is enrolled in this program. Medicaid and Food Stamp benefits are not reduced. A second intervention applies sanctions toward recipients who refuse to accept, or who quit, full-time employment at or above the minimum wage and have children at least 14 years of age. However, this intervention has not often been applied.

TARGET POPULATION: Recipients of AFDC.

OUTCOMES OF INTEREST: The principal outcome is birthrate, although earnings, employment, and welfare receipt will also be measured.

Oklahoma Learnfare

STARTING YEAR/YEAR FINAL REPORT EXPECTED: 1994/1999.

INFORMATION SOURCE: No written source. This welfare reform demonstration is sponsored by the Oklahoma State Department of Human Resources; Ann Kent, project officer. It is being evaluated by the University of Oklahoma, Department of Sociology; Harold Gramsick and Peter Wood, principal investigators.

PRINCIPAL INTERVENTION: Provides for financial sanctions and incentives based on the school attendance of children in AFDC families.

TARGET POPULATION: Recipients of AFDC.

OUTCOMES OF INTEREST: Welfare participation and benefit receipt, employment, family income, and measures of child well-being.

Postemployment Services Demonstration (PESD) Evaluation

STARTING YEAR/YEAR FINAL REPORT EXPECTED: 1994/1998.

INFORMATION SOURCE: Anu Rangarajian, Stuart Kerachsky, Joshua Haimson, Alan Hershey, and Rita Stapulonis, *Postemployment Services to Promote Job Retention among Welfare Recipients*, Mathematica Policy Research, February 1996. The PESD Evaluation is funded by the State of Illinois Department of Public Aid. It is being evaluated by Mathematica Policy Research; Stuart Kerachsky and Anu Rangarajian, project directors.

PRINCIPAL INTERVENTIONS: Extended case management and transitional financial support (work expenses, transportation assistance) and employment services such as job search assistance.

TARGET POPULATION: People who have participated in JOBS (primarily nonexempt clients) and have since found employment. They may or may not remain recipients of AFDC, and they may or may not retain the same employment over the life of the project. Demonstration sites include Chicago, Illinois; Portland, Oregon; Riverside County, California; and San Antonio, Texas.

OUTCOMES OF INTEREST: Employment, earnings, welfare participation, and welfare receipt.

The Strengthening of South Dakota Families

STARTING YEAR/YEAR FINAL REPORT EXPECTED: 1994/1999.

INFORMATION SOURCE: No written source. This is a welfare reform demonstration sponsored by the South Dakota Department of Social Services; Judy Thompson, project officer. It is being evaluated by the Business Research Bureau of the University of South Dakota; Steve Tracy, principal investigator.

PRINCIPAL INTERVENTIONS: The waiver includes five components: (1) A time limit of 24 months for individuals in the job-ready track and 60 months for those in the education track; (2) A Teen Work Incentive savings account that is not counted toward family resources; (3) A Teen Work Incentive vehicle asset waiver; (4) Transitional employment allowance of one month; and (5) A sanction imposed if the recipient voluntarily leaves employment.

TARGET POPULATION: AFDC recipients, excluding two-parent families (AFDC-U), as well as those with disabilities, and children not in the care of their parents.

OUTCOMES OF INTEREST: Employment, earnings, welfare receipt, and measures of child well-being.

Vermont Welfare Restructuring Project

STARTING YEAR/YEAR FINAL REPORT EXPECTED: 1994/2002.

INFORMATION SOURCE: No written source. This project is a welfare reform demonstration sponsored by the Vermont Department of Social Welfare; Donna Jenckes, project officer. It is being evaluated by the Manpower Demonstration Research Corporation; David Butler and Dan Bloom, project directors.

PRINCIPAL INTERVENTIONS: A time limit, after which AFDC recipients must begin working. If not working, the case is reviewed and benefits may continue if the recipient can demonstrate good cause for continued unemployment. There are also more generous earned-income disregards and expanded transitional benefits than are found in the existing AFDC system.

TARGET POPULATION: Recipients of AFDC.

OUTCOMES OF INTEREST: The principal outcomes of interest are employment, earnings, and welfare receipt.

Wisconsin AFDC Two-Tier Demonstration Project

STARTING YEAR/YEAR FINAL REPORT EXPECTED: 1994/1998.

INFORMATION SOURCE: *Wisconsin Welfare Reform: A History of Progress—A Plan for the Future*, Wisconsin Department of Health and Human Services. April 1996. This project is being evaluated by Maximus; Philip Richardson, project director.

PRINCIPAL INTERVENTION: Applicants to AFDC, within six months of moving to Wisconsin, receive a payment similar to the AFDC level in their prior state. Payments may be higher or lower than the Wisconsin benefit level.

TARGET POPULATION: Applicants to AFDC who have recently moved to Wisconsin from another state, with some exclusions.

OUTCOMES OF INTEREST: Welfare participation and benefit receipt, and interstate migration.

Arizona EMPOWER

STARTING YEAR/YEAR FINAL REPORT EXPECTED: 1995/2003.

INFORMATION SOURCE: No written source. This welfare reform demonstration is sponsored by the Arizona Department of Economic Security; Ellen Konrad, project officer. It is being evaluated by Abt Associates; Greg Mills, project director. The process study is subcontracted to Arizona State University, School of Justice Studies; Dennis Palumbo, principal investigator.

PRINCIPAL INTERVENTIONS: Two demonstrations comprise EMPOWER. The first has eight main components: a 24-month time limit for AFDC benefits; a family cap (no incremental increase in AFDC benefits for new children); a requirement that unwed teen parents must live with a responsible adult to receive benefits; stronger JOBS participation requirements; stricter sanctions for noncompliance with JOBS rules; easier access for two-parent families (an elimination of the 100-hour rule); extension of transitional child care and Medicaid to 24 months; and the establishment of individual development accounts that are exempt from asset limits if earmarked for specific purposes. The second demonstration, called JOBSTART, cashes out AFDC and Food Stamp benefits and pays employers a wage supplement.

TARGET POPULATION: Recipients of, and applicants to, AFDC.

OUTCOMES OF INTEREST: Employment, earnings, welfare receipt and participation, marital stability, child well-being, and health and nutritional outcomes.

Delaware—A Better Chance

STARTING YEAR/YEAR FINAL REPORT EXPECTED: 1995/2000.

INFORMATION SOURCE: No written source. This welfare reform project is sponsored by the Delaware Department of Health and Social Services, Division of Social Services; Mary Ann Daniels, project officer. It is being evaluated by Abt Associates; David Fein, project director.

PRINCIPAL INTERVENTIONS: A comprehensive welfare reform project including: a four-year lifetime maximum for AFDC benefits (with a two-year period of employability services and up to two years of pay-for-performance work activities); and a family responsibility contract that includes a family cap and requirements for immunization and school attendance.

TARGET POPULATION: Recipients of AFDC.

OUTCOMES OF INTEREST: An array of self-sufficiency and family structure measures. Among these are employment, earnings, welfare receipt, and measures of child well-being.

Illinois Get a Job Initiative

STARTING YEAR/YEAR FINAL REPORT EXPECTED: 1995/2001.

INFORMATION SOURCE: No written source. This welfare reform project is sponsored by the Illinois Department of Public Aid (IDPA); Peggy Powers and Dave Gruenenfelder, project officers. An evaluator has not yet been selected.

PRINCIPAL INTERVENTION: Mandates six months of job search activities for newly approved AFDC clients as a condition of eligibility. IDPA staff conduct job search meetings and teach clients job-related skills (applying, interviewing, keeping a job). Clients must make 20 employer contacts per month. Unsuccessful clients will be reassessed and assigned to a work experience or training program.

TARGET POPULATION: Newly approved AFDC clients with children ages 5 to 12, with monthly earnings less than $255, and who are job-ready (have high school diploma or equivalent or recent work history).

OUTCOMES OF INTEREST: Welfare participation and benefit receipt, employment, and earnings.

Illinois Targeted Work Initiative

STARTING YEAR/YEAR FINAL REPORT EXPECTED: 1995/2001.

INFORMATION SOURCE: No written source. This welfare reform project is sponsored by the Illinois Department of Public Aid; Peggy Powers and Dave Gruenenfelder, project officers. An evaluator has not yet been selected.

PRINCIPAL INTERVENTION: Over the course of a two-year time limit, clients must be involved in job search activities. Clients with less than a high school education have the option to participate in job training or a general equivalency diploma (GED) program while they participate in job search. If a job does not develop, the client is placed on a subsidized job assignment and is required to continue job search. There are sanctions for noncompliance.

TARGET POPULATION: AFDC clients with no children under age 13.

OUTCOMES OF INTEREST: Welfare participation and benefit receipt, employment, and earnings.

Massachusetts Welfare Reform '95

STARTING YEAR/YEAR FINAL REPORT EXPECTED: 1995/2006.

INFORMATION SOURCE: *Welfare Reform '95*, Commonwealth of Massachusetts, Executive Office of Health and Human Services, Department of Transitional Assistance, March 1995.

PRINCIPAL INTERVENTION: A comprehensive package of welfare reform. Including: 20-hour-per-week work requirement; time-limited AFDC benefits; higher earned-income disregards; increased allowable asset levels; a family cap; and requirements for child support orders, school attendance, and child immunization.

TARGET POPULATION: Recipients of AFDC.

OUTCOMES OF INTEREST: Employment, earnings, total family income, receipt of welfare benefits, and a number of family and child well-being outcomes.

Missouri Families Mutual Responsibility

STARTING YEAR/YEAR FINAL REPORT EXPECTED: 1995/2001.

INFORMATION SOURCE: This welfare reform project is sponsored by the Missouri Department of Social Services; Tom Jones, project officer. It is being evaluated by the University of Missouri–Columbia; Sheila Watson, project director.

PRINCIPAL INTERVENTIONS: (1) A time-limited self-sufficiency agreement of 24 months (benefits do not end after 24 months if the participant has complied with all components of the agreement, although participants are sanctioned if they do not comply); (2) An increase in the allowable asset level; (3) Exemption of one automobile (the second automobile is subject to the existing asset limit); (4) Waiving of the 100-hour rule for AFDC-UPs under age 21; (5) A child development plan that includes referrals to appropriate service agencies; and (6) A requirement that minor parents return home.

TARGET POPULATION: AFDC participants who are JOBS mandatory; nonmandatory participants may volunteer for the program.

OUTCOMES OF INTEREST: Employment, earnings, welfare participation and benefit receipt, and measures of child well-being.

Nebraska Welfare Reform Demonstration Project

STARTING YEAR/YEAR FINAL REPORT EXPECTED: 1995/2003.

INFORMATION SOURCE: No written source. This welfare reform demonstration is sponsored by the Nebraska Department of Social Services; Dan Cillessen, project officer. It is being evaluated by the University of Nebraska at Omaha; Jerry Deichert, principal investigator.

PRINCIPAL INTERVENTIONS: An increase in the resource limit for participants; vehicle asset waiver; more generous earned-income disregards; a 24-month time limit on ADC (AFDC) benefits; and an extension of transitional Medicaid and child care to 24 months.

TARGET POPULATION: All ADC (AFDC) recipients and all new applicants.

OUTCOMES OF INTEREST: Employment; earnings; participation in ADC, Food Stamp, and Medicaid programs and the costs of those programs; family structure and stability; and measures of child well-being.

North Dakota Early Intervention Project

STARTING YEAR/YEAR FINAL REPORT EXPECTED: 1995/2003.

INFORMATION SOURCE: No written source. This is a welfare reform project sponsored by the North Dakota Department of Human Resources; Carol Cartledge, project officer. The evaluator for this experiment has not yet been chosen.

PRINCIPAL INTERVENTIONS: The treatment is a requirement to participate in the JOBS program. There is a four-month exemption after childbirth. Supportive services such as child care are provided.

TARGET POPULATION: AFDC recipients who are single women with their first child or no other children in the household and who are in their first or second trimester of pregnancy.

OUTCOMES OF INTEREST: Employment, earnings, and welfare participation and benefit receipt.

Ohio Children of Opportunity

STARTING YEAR/YEAR FINAL REPORT EXPECTED: 1995/2000.

INFORMATION SOURCE: No written source. Children of Opportunity is one component of Ohio's *A State of Opportunity* welfare reform program. It is sponsored by the Ohio Department of Human Services; Tom Hutter, project officer. It is being evaluated by Macro International; Joann Kuchek, project director.

PRINCIPAL INTERVENTIONS: Part of this project is "Learnfare"—AFDC benefit grant reductions for poor school attendance. Children must comply with state school attendance regulations. In addition, there is enhanced case management to work with families to avoid these sanctions.

TARGET POPULATION: Recipients of AFDC with children ages 6–19.

OUTCOMES OF INTEREST: School attendance and achievement and other child well-being outcomes, employment, earnings, welfare participation, and benefit receipt.

Virginia Independence Program (VIP)

STARTING YEAR/YEAR FINAL REPORT EXPECTED: 1995/2004.

INFORMATION SOURCE: No written source. VIP is a welfare reform project sponsored by the Virginia Department of Social Services; Barbara Cotter, project officer. An evaluator for this project has not yet been chosen.

PRINCIPAL INTERVENTIONS: A comprehensive package of welfare reform components, including: a child cap; a time limit for benefit receipt of 24 months within a five-year period; stricter sanctions for noncooperation; and an expansion of the AFDC-U (two-parent families) program. There is also an employment program, VIEW, which involves an agreement of personal responsibility; subsidized and unsubsidized employment; community work experience; and higher earned-income disregards. (Note: not all features of VIP are in the experimental research design and subject to random assignment.)

TARGET POPULATION: Recipients of AFDC.

OUTCOMES OF INTEREST: Employment, earnings, welfare participation and benefit receipt, and measures of child well-being.

Wisconsin AFDC Special Resource Account (SRA) Demonstration Project

STARTING YEAR/YEAR FINAL REPORT EXPECTED: 1995/2001.

INFORMATION SOURCE: Wisconsin Welfare Reform: A History of Progress—A Plan for the Future, Wisconsin Department of Health and Human Services, April 1996. SRA is being evaluated by Maximus; Philip Richardson, project director.

PRINCIPAL INTERVENTION: Once eligible for AFDC, recipients are allowed to open an SRA. The account is separate from other accounts that the recipient may have. Up to $10,000 in the SRA is exempt from the asset limitation. Money from the SRA can only be used for designated purposes (e.g., education, expenditures related to employability, emergency needs).

TARGET POPULATION: Recipients of AFDC.

OUTCOMES OF INTEREST: Welfare participation and benefit receipt. Will also measure participation in employment and employment-related training activities and family income.

Wisconsin Vehicle Asset Limit (VAL) Demonstration Project

STARTING YEAR/YEAR FINAL REPORT EXPECTED: 1995/2001.

INFORMATION SOURCE: *Wisconsin Welfare Reform: A History of Progress—A Plan for the Future*, Wisconsin Department of Health and Human Services, April 1996. VAL is being evaluated by Maximus; Philip Richardson, project director.

PRINCIPAL INTERVENTION: Raises the federal AFDC vehicle asset limit. The first $2,500 of combined equity value of all vehicles owned is exempt. Excess equity value is applied to the AFDC $1,000 asset limit.

TARGET POPULATION: Recipients of AFDC, especially two-parent families.

OUTCOMES OF INTEREST: Welfare participation and benefit receipt, participation in employment and employment-related training activities, and family income.

Achieving Change for Texans

STARTING YEAR/YEAR FINAL REPORT EXPECTED: 1996/2003.

INFORMATION SOURCE: No written source. This welfare reform project is sponsored by the Texas Department of Human Services; Kent Gummerman, project officer. An evaluator has not yet been chosen.

PRINCIPAL INTERVENTIONS: (1) Requires AFDC clients to sign a personal responsibility agreement. The resource limit is raised, child income is exempt, and eligibility for two-parent families is expanded; (2) Imposes time limits for AFDC benefits, which vary dependent on work experience (one-, two-, or three-year limits); (3) Provides AFDC applicants the option of taking a $1,000 cash payment if they stay off welfare for one year; (4) Establishes voluntary individual development accounts that are exempt from asset limits and can be used for specified purposes.

TARGET POPULATION: Recipients and applicants of AFDC.

OUTCOMES OF INTEREST: Employment, earnings, welfare participation and benefit receipt, and measures of child well-being.

Connecticut Reach for Jobs First (RFJF)

STARTING YEAR/YEAR FINAL REPORT EXPECTED: 1996/2003.

INFORMATION SOURCE: No written source. RFJF is a welfare reform demonstration project sponsored by the Connecticut Department of Social Services; Mark Heuschkel, project officer. It is being evaluated by Manpower Demonstration Research Corporation; Barbara Goldman and Dan Bloom, project directors.

PRINCIPAL INTERVENTIONS: A 21-month time limit on the receipt of cash assistance (AFDC), with more generous earned-income disregards and expanded transitional benefits for child care and Medicaid.

TARGET POPULATION: Recipients of AFDC.

OUTCOMES OF INTEREST: Employment, earnings, and welfare receipt. Other measures include the types of jobs found and measures of child well-being.

Illinois Six-Month Paternity Establishment

STARTING YEAR/YEAR FINAL REPORT EXPECTED: 1996/2001.

INFORMATION SOURCE: No written source. This welfare reform project is sponsored by the Illinois Department of Public Aid; Peggy Powers and Dave Gruenenfelder, project officers. An evaluator has not yet been selected.

PRINCIPAL INTERVENTION: Clients have six months from the point of intake, redetermination, or adding a child to an existing case to establish paternity. If paternity is not established within this time, and the client is not cooperating with the child support process, the child's portion of the AFDC grant is removed.

TARGET POPULATION: Recipients of AFDC.

OUTCOMES OF INTEREST: Rate of paternity establishment and amount of child support collected.

Indiana Manpower Placement and Comprehensive Training Program (IMPACT)

STARTING YEAR/YEAR FINAL REPORT EXPECTED: 1996/1999.

INFORMATION SOURCE: No written source. IMPACT is a welfare reform project sponsored by the Indiana Family and Social Services Administration, Division of Family and Children; Brian Noss, project officer. It is being evaluated by Abt Associates; David Fein, project director.

PRINCIPAL INTERVENTIONS: IMPACT is a comprehensive welfare reform project emphasizing transitional assistance. It features intensified job training and placement services, as well as stronger work incentives; and it promotes responsible parenting behaviors.

TARGET POPULATION: Recipients of AFDC.

OUTCOMES OF INTEREST: Among outcomes measured are employment, earnings, welfare receipt, children's immunization, and school attendance.

Ohio Community of Opportunity

STARTING YEAR/YEAR FINAL REPORT EXPECTED: 1996/2004.

INFORMATION SOURCE: No written source. This project is one component of Ohio's *A State of Opportunity* welfare reform program. It is sponsored by the Ohio Department of Human Services; Tom Hutter, project officer. It is being evaluated by Maximus; Philip Richardson and Julie Beaver, project directors.

PRINCIPAL INTERVENTION: A voluntary subsidized wage program. Recipients can trade food stamp and AFDC benefits for a job paying at least $8/hour. A 50 percent subsidy is paid to the employer during the first year and 25 percent the second year. Employers agree to hire participants permanently. Participants are followed with intensive case management.

TARGET POPULATION: Recipients of AFDC who live in federally designated empowerment zones and enterprise communities (economically disadvantaged communities). There are four participating counties in Ohio.

OUTCOMES OF INTEREST: Employment, earnings, total family income, employee benefits, AFDC participation and benefit receipt, and measures of child well-being.

Wisconsin AFDC Benefit Cap Demonstration Project

STARTING YEAR/YEAR FINAL REPORT EXPECTED: 1996/2002.

INFORMATION SOURCE: *Wisconsin Welfare Reform: A History of Progress—A Plan for the Future*, Wisconsin Department of Health and Human Services, April 1996. The demonstration is being evaluated by Maximus; Philip Richardson, project director.

PRINCIPAL INTERVENTION: Eliminates automatic increases to AFDC grants when additional children are born. First applies to children born to recipients in November 1996 who were receiving benefits on January 1, 1996. Children will receive Medical Assistance, food stamps, and other social service assistance.

TARGET POPULATION: Recipients of AFDC.

OUTCOMES OF INTEREST: Welfare participation and benefit receipt, family income, employment, and measures of family and child well-being.

Wisconsin Pay for Performance (PFP)

STARTING YEAR/YEAR FINAL REPORT EXPECTED: 1996/2001.

INFORMATION SOURCE: Wisconsin Welfare Reform: A History of Progress—A Plan for the Future, Wisconsin Department of Health and Human Services, April 1996. PFP is being evaluated by Maximus; Philip Richardson, project director.

PRINCIPAL INTERVENTIONS: There are two components: (1) Self-Sufficiency First (SSF)—an interview with a financial planning resource specialist; immediate referral to the JOBS program as an applicant; a minimum of 60 hours of JOBS participation, 30 hours of which must include direct employer contact; and (2) Pay for Performance (PFP)—increased AFDC eligibility for two-parent families; a minimum of 20 weekly hours of JOBS activities; monetary sanctions for missed activities.

TARGET POPULATION: SSF—AFDC applicants; PFP—AFDC recipients.

OUTCOMES OF INTEREST: Employment, earnings, welfare participation and benefit receipt; participation in JOBS activities; family income.

Hawaii Pursuit of New Opportunities (PONO)

STARTING YEAR/YEAR FINAL REPORT EXPECTED: 1997/?.

INFORMATION SOURCE: No written source. This welfare reform project will be sponsored by the Hawaii Department of Human Services; Kris Foster, project officer. An evaluator for the project has not yet been chosen.

PRINCIPAL INTERVENTION: More lenient earned-income disregards, increased asset limits, and expanded eligibility for two-parent families.

TARGET POPULATION: Recipients of AFDC, especially two-parent families.

OUTCOMES OF INTEREST: Outcome measures have not yet been finalized.

AFDC, FOOD STAMPS

Mississippi New Direction

STARTING YEAR/YEAR FINAL REPORT EXPECTED: 1995/2000.

INFORMATION SOURCE: No written source. New Direction is a welfare reform demonstration sponsored by the Mississippi Department of Human Services; Zenotha Robinson, project officer. It is being evaluated by the Center for Applied Research, Millsaps College (Jackson, Mississippi); Bill Brister, principal investigator.

PRINCIPAL INTERVENTIONS: (1) Extensive job search by AFDC and food stamp recipients—includes sanctions for noncompliance (100 percent of benefit); (2) A subsidy paid to an employer who hires a Workfirst participant, for the first six months of employment.

TARGET POPULATION: Recipients of both AFDC and food stamp benefits. Recipients of one or the other, but not both, are exempt.

OUTCOMES OF INTEREST: Earnings, employment, and welfare receipt, as well as social variables such as nutrition and school attendance.

AFDC-U

Illinois Family Responsibility Initiative

STARTING YEAR/YEAR FINAL REPORT EXPECTED: 1993/1998.

INFORMATION SOURCE: No written source. This welfare reform project is sponsored by the Illinois Department of Public Aid; Peggy Powers and Dave Gruenenfelder, project officers. It is being evaluated by the Jane Addams College of Social Work, University of Illinois, Chicago Campus.

PRINCIPAL INTERVENTION: Increases AFDC eligibility for two-parent families. Lack of work experience or working more than 100 hours per month do not affect income-eligible families.

TARGET POPULATION: AFDC two-parent households.

OUTCOMES OF INTEREST: Employment, earnings, and welfare participation and benefit receipt.

West Virginia Opportunities for Independence (JOIN)

STARTING YEAR/YEAR FINAL REPORT EXPECTED: 1995/2001.

INFORMATION SOURCE: No written source. JOIN is a welfare reform project sponsored by the West Virginia Department of Health and Human Services; Jim Shaffer, project officer. An evaluator for this experiment has not yet been chosen.

PRINCIPAL INTERVENTIONS: Places individuals in employment positions with private or public employers to provide full-time experience. The employment is 34 hours per week, and there is an additional 6 hours of job search assistance per week in the local welfare office. The program is mandatory for those who are eligible.

TARGET POPULATION: Recipients of AFDC-U, that is, two-parent households where both parents are unemployed. Only one person per family is required to participate.

OUTCOMES OF INTEREST: Employment, earnings, and welfare receipt, plus a number of family outcomes.

AFDC—TEEN PARENT

Ohio's Learning, Earning, and Parenting Program (LEAP)

STARTING YEAR/YEAR FINAL REPORT EXPECTED: 1989/1997 (new LEAP: 1996/2004).

INFORMATION SOURCE: David Long, Judith M. Gueron, Robert G. Wood, Rebecca Fisher, and Veronica Fellerath, *LEAP: Three-Year Impacts of Ohio's Welfare Initiative to Improve School Attendance among Teenage Parents*, Manpower Demonstration Research Corporation, April 1996. This welfare reform project is sponsored by the Ohio Department of Human Services.

PRINCIPAL INTERVENTIONS: LEAP is mandatory for all those who are eligible. The treatment consists of financial incentives and penalties to promote school attendance. Participants who provide evidence of school enrollment receive a bonus of $62 plus an additional $62

monthly for meeting attendance requirements. Those who do not attend an initial LEAP interview, or who fail to enroll in school, have $62 deducted from their AFDC grant each month until they comply. They are also sanctioned for exceeding the allowed number of unexcused school absences. LEAP itself provides no other service.

TARGET POPULATION: All pregnant women and custodial parents under 20 years of age (during LEAP's first year, participation was not mandatory for pregnant women and the age limit was 19) who are receiving AFDC and do not have a high school diploma or its equivalent. This includes both teens who head welfare cases and those who receive assistance on someone else's case.

OUTCOMES OF INTEREST: High school graduation, college enrollment, employment, earnings, and welfare receipt.

Note: A new version of LEAP was started in 1996 and is to end in 2004. It is basically the same program, although it has an enhanced case management component, and some performance incentives have been changed. An evaluator for this program has not yet been chosen.

Cal-Learn

STARTING YEAR/YEAR FINAL REPORT EXPECTED: 1994/1999.

INFORMATION SOURCE: No written source. This welfare reform demonstration is sponsored by the California Department of Social Services; J. Oshi Ruelas, project officer. It is being evaluated by the University of California–Los Angeles (UCLA), and data collection is being conducted by UC Data at UC-Berkeley; Rosina Becerra, principal investigator.

PRINCIPAL INTERVENTIONS: Bonuses and sanctions directly linked to school report cards. Case management and supportive services are also provided.

TARGET POPULATION: Pregnant or parenting teens receiving AFDC.

OUTCOMES OF INTEREST: High school graduation, subsequent pregnancies, employment, earnings, and welfare receipt.

Wisconsin Parental and Family Responsibility (PFR) Demonstration Project

STARTING YEAR/YEAR FINAL REPORT EXPECTED: 1994/1999.

INFORMATION SOURCE: *Wisconsin Welfare Reform: A History of Progress—A Plan for the Future,* Wisconsin Department of Health and Human Services, April 1996. PFR is being evaluated by Maximus; Philip Richardson, project director.

PRINCIPAL INTERVENTIONS: Increased eligibility for AFDC and incentives to work. Participants can keep the first $200 and one-half of their earnings each month with no time limit. The size of the grant increase is limited when a second child is born, and is not increased at all for subsequent children. The program also has required case management services that provide assessment, planning, and training.

TARGET POPULATION: AFDC recipients under the age of 20 whose first child was born on or after July 1, 1994, or who are pregnant for the first time.

OUTCOMES OF INTEREST: Employment, family income, welfare participation and benefit receipt, subsequent pregnancies, and other family and child outcomes.

Illinois Home Visitor Demonstration

STARTING YEAR/YEAR FINAL REPORT EXPECTED: 1995/2000.

INFORMATION SOURCE: No written source. The experiment is sponsored by the U.S. Department of Health and Human Services. It is being evaluated by the University of Pennsylvania.

PRINCIPAL INTERVENTION: A comprehensive service package for teenage parents and their families. JOBS services are supplemented with weekly home visits by specially trained paraprofessionals.

TARGET POPULATION: First-time AFDC mothers under age 20.

OUTCOMES OF INTEREST: Incidence of repeat pregnancy, educational achievement, improved parenting skills, employment, and earnings.

AFDC—YOUTH

Illinois Youth Employment and Training Initiative (YETI)

STARTING YEAR/YEAR FINAL REPORT EXPECTED: 1993/1998.

INFORMATION SOURCE: No written source. This welfare reform project is sponsored by the Illinois Department of Public Aid; Peggy Powers and Dave Gruenenfelder, project officers. It is being evaluated by the Department for Social Work, Illinois State University, Normal, Illinois.

PRINCIPAL INTERVENTIONS: Intensive vocational training, drug education and avoidance counseling, pregnancy prevention education, and life skills training.

TARGET POPULATION: At-risk children of AFDC clients attending three Chicago high schools.

OUTCOMES OF INTEREST: Student graduation rates, teenage pregnancy, substance abuse, and welfare participation.

Wisconsin Learnfare

STARTING YEAR/YEAR FINAL REPORT EXPECTED: Learnfare, 1987/1996; Learnfare expansion, 1994/1999.

INFORMATION SOURCE: *Wisconsin Welfare Reform: Learnfare*, Wisconsin Department of Health and Human Services, 1996. Learnfare is being evaluated by the Wisconsin Legislative Audit Bureau; Judy Fry, project director.

PRINCIPAL INTERVENTION: Learnfare reduces the monthly AFDC benefit for the families of teenagers aged 13 through 19 who do not attend school regularly. The Learnfare expansion includes children from age 6. In addition, child care and transportation is available for teenage parents; alternative education is an option; and there is case management to facilitate improved school attendance.

TARGET POPULATION: Recipients of AFDC ages 13 through 19 (Learnfare) and ages 6 through 19 (Learnfare expansion).

OUTCOMES OF INTEREST: School attendance and completion, as well as family income, welfare participation, and other child well-being measures.

School Attendance Demonstration Project (SADP)

STARTING YEAR/YEAR FINAL REPORT EXPECTED: 1996/2000.

INFORMATION SOURCE: No written source. SADP is a welfare reform project sponsored by the San Diego Department of Social Services; Lynn Titalii, project officer. It is being evaluated by San Diego State University, School of Social Work; Loring Jones, project director.

PRINCIPAL INTERVENTION: Participants must maintain 80 percent attendance in each month. If they do not meet this requirement, they must report to an orientation meeting where they are given three options: accept services (normally an assessment by a social worker and referral to appropriate community services); improve attendance the following month; or demonstrate good cause for the absences. If participants do not attend the orientation or do not follow through with any other requirements, they are removed from the family's AFDC grant.

TARGET POPULATION: Recipients of AFDC age 16 through 18.

OUTCOMES OF INTEREST: Attendance rates, school completion, receipt of AFDC benefits.

PUBLIC ASSISTANCE RECIPIENTS—ALL CATEGORIES

Minnesota Family Investment Program (FIP)

STARTING YEAR/YEAR FINAL REPORT EXPECTED: 1994/1999.

INFORMATION SOURCE: Virginia W. Knox, Amy Brown, and Winston Lin, *MFIP: An Early Report on Minnesota's Approach to Welfare Reform. The Minnesota Family Investment Program,* Manpower Demonstration Research Corporation, November 1995.

PRINCIPAL INTERVENTIONS: Consolidation of AFDC, Food Stamps, and the state's Family General Assistance into one set of rules, with (1) A package of financial incentives, including: expanding the earned income disregard; increasing asset limits; expanding eligibility for two-parent families; and cashing-out Food Stamp benefits; (2) Mandatory JOBS activities for a targeted group of individuals. There are two experimental groups: one receives the financial incentives, but remains in JOBS voluntarily; the other group receives the incentives and is JOBS mandatory.

TARGET POPULATION: Recipients of AFDC, food stamps, and Family General Assistance who are age 18 or over.

OUTCOMES OF INTEREST: Employment, earnings, welfare receipt, total family income, poverty rates, and measures of child well-being.

Families Achieving Independence in Montana (FAIM)

STARTING YEAR/YEAR FINAL REPORT EXPECTED: 1996/2005.

INFORMATION SOURCE: No written source. FAIM is a welfare reform package sponsored by the Montana Department of Public Health and Human Services; Sue Skinner, project officer. It is being evaluated by the University of Montana; Richard Offner, project director.

PRINCIPAL INTERVENTIONS: Comprehensive welfare reform that integrates and standardizes eligibility requirements for all state benefit programs (AFDC, Medical Assistance, and Food Stamps). Includes: a Job Supplement Program that offers a cash benefit in lieu of welfare assistance; a mandatory Family Investment Agreement; a community service requirement after two years; an increase in the resource limit to $3,000 for all assistance programs; and increased eligibility for two-parent families.

TARGET POPULATION: All recipients of state benefit programs (AFDC, Medical Assistance, Food Stamps).

OUTCOMES OF INTEREST: Employment, earnings, welfare participation and benefit receipt, and measures of family and child well-being.

LOW-INCOME CHILDREN AND THEIR FAMILIES

Comprehensive Child Development Program (CCDP)

STARTING YEAR/YEAR FINAL REPORT EXPECTED: 1990/1996.

INFORMATION SOURCE: No written source. CCDP is funded by the U.S. Department of Health and Human Services, Administration on Children, Youth, and Families; Mike Lopez, project manager. It is being evaluated by Abt Associates; Robert St. Pierre, principal investigator.

PRINCIPAL INTERVENTIONS: A case management model designed to ensure the delivery of services to enhance parents' ability to contribute to the overall development of their children and to ensure continuous services until children enter elementary school. Services are provided by existing resources whenever possible, although CCDP case managers provide some services directly. Services are wide-ranging and include: early childhood education; health screenings and treatment; immunizations for children; and employment counseling and vocational training for parents. There are 34 CCDP projects throughout the United States.

TARGET POPULATION: Low-income families (below the poverty level) who have children younger than one year old or have a pregnant woman in the family.

OUTCOMES OF INTEREST: Cognitive development; social and emotional development; physical health; and birth outcomes. Maternal outcomes include: employment; earnings; welfare receipt; education level; participation in training; and birth antecedents/risk factors.

Family Service Centers for Head Start Families

STARTING YEAR/YEAR FINAL REPORT EXPECTED: 1991/1996.

INFORMATION SOURCE: No written source. The evaluation is being conducted by Abt Associates.

PRINCIPAL INTERVENTIONS: Case management home visits by a Family Service Center case manager who helps in coordinating social services.

TARGET POPULATION: Families with one or more children involved in Head Start.

OUTCOMES OF INTEREST: Employment, literacy, and substance abuse.

Memphis Nurse Home-Visitation Program

STARTING YEAR/YEAR FINAL REPORT EXPECTED: 1990/1998.

INFORMATION SOURCE: David L. Olds, Jann Belton, Robert Cole, Howard Foye, June Helberg, Charles R. Henderson, Jr., David James, Harriet Kitzman, Charles Phelps, Patrick Sweeney, and Robert Tatelbaum, *Nurse Home-Visitation for Mothers and Children: A Research Proposal*, New Mothers Study, Department of Pediatrics, University of Rochester, 1989, Photocopy. David L. Olds and Harriet Kitzman, "Review of Research on Home Visiting for Pregnant Women and Parents of Young Children," *Future of Children*, vol. 3, no. 3, 1993, 53–92.

PRINCIPAL INTERVENTIONS: Test of two programs: Nurse visits during pregnancy for group 1; nurse visits until child is two years of age for group 2. Both groups also receive referrals to services and encouragement to resume school or work.

TARGET POPULATION: Disadvantaged first-time mothers; women under age 18 will be over-represented.

OUTCOMES OF INTEREST: Maternal education, employment, welfare receipt, food stamps, fertility, health habits, infant care, and service use.

PUBLIC ASSISTANCE—CANADA

Canadian Self-Sufficiency Project (SSP)

STARTING YEAR/YEAR FINAL REPORT EXPECTED: 1992/2000?.

INFORMATION SOURCE: David Card and Philip K. Robins, *Do Financial Incentives Encourage Welfare Recipients to Work? Initial 18-Month Findings from the Self-Sufficiency Project*, Social Research and Demonstration Corporation (Vancouver, British Columbia), February 1996.

PRINCIPAL INTERVENTIONS: There are three key elements to SSP: (1) A financial incentive for work relative to nonwork; (2) A relatively low reduction of benefits, compared to Income Assistance (IA), based on earnings; and (3) A "full-time" work requirement (at least 30 hours/week). Those assigned to the treatment group have one year from the date of notification of eligibility to obtain a full-time job and initiate the first supplement payment. The earnings supplement is equal to half the difference between a participant's gross earnings and a "benchmark" level ($37,000 in British Columbia and $30,000 in New Brunswick).

TARGET POPULATION: Long-term single-parent recipients of Income Assistance (Canada's primary welfare program). Participants are over age 18 and have received IA for at least one year prior to recruitment.

OUTCOMES OF INTEREST: Employment, earnings, and welfare receipt.

LOW-INCOME

Moving to Opportunity for Fair Housing Demonstration

STARTING YEAR/YEAR FINAL REPORT EXPECTED: 1994/2004.

INFORMATION SOURCE: *Expanding Housing Choices for HUD-Assisted Families: First Biennial Report to Congress—Moving to Opportunity for Fair Housing Demonstration,* U.S. Department of Housing and Urban Development, Office of Policy Development and Research, April 1996. Design, setup, and initial data collection are by Abt Associates. An evaluator for this project has not yet been selected.

PRINCIPAL INTERVENTIONS: (1) Rental housing vouchers that may only be used in low-poverty (i.e., middle-class) neighborhoods, with search assistance to find appropriate units; and (2) Rental housing vouchers without locational restrictions.

TARGET POPULATION: Very low-income families with children who live in public housing or Section 8 project-based housing located in central-city neighborhoods with high concentrations of poverty in Baltimore, Boston, Chicago, Los Angeles, and New York City.

OUTCOMES OF INTEREST: Evaluation hopes to answer two questions: (1) What are the impacts of the treatment on families' location choices and on their housing and neighborhood conditions? and (2) What are the impacts of neighborhood conditions on the employment, income, education, and social well-being of the demonstration families?

New Hope

STARTING YEAR/YEAR FINAL REPORT EXPECTED: 1994/1997.

INFORMATION SOURCE: Fred Doolittle and Irene Robling, *Research Design for the New Hope Demonstration,* Manpower Demonstration Research Corporation, June 1994.

PRINCIPAL INTERVENTIONS: A wage supplement (similar to an expanded Earned Income Tax Credit), creation of temporary jobs, affordable health coverage, and child care services.

TARGET POPULATION: Low-income (largely recipients of public assistance) urban families in Milwaukee, WI.

OUTCOMES OF INTEREST: Employment, earnings, and income, as well as a benefit–cost analysis from several standpoints.

Bridges to Work

STARTING YEAR/YEAR FINAL REPORT EXPECTED: 1996/2001.

INFORMATION SOURCE: U.S. Department of Housing and Urban Development (HUD), *The Bridges to Work One-Page Summary* and *The Bridges to Work Fact Sheet*, September 1996. This experiment is being evaluated by Public/Private Ventures; Beth Palubinsky and Joseph Tierney, co-directors. It is funded by HUD and Dept. of Transportation. HUD project officer: Jim Hoben.

PRINCIPAL INTERVENTIONS: Provides job placement, transportation, and supportive services such as child care and counseling in order to place participants in suburban jobs. This demonstration will operate in five sites: Baltimore, Chicago, Denver, Milwaukee, and St. Louis.

TARGET POPULATION: Work-ready, low-income, inner-city residents.

OUTCOMES OF INTEREST: Earnings, employment, and dependence on government support.

YOUTH

Alternative Schools Evaluation

STARTING YEAR/YEAR FINAL REPORT EXPECTED: 1988/1996.

INFORMATION SOURCE: Mathematica Policy Research, *The Alternative Schools Random Assignment Evaluation Project Summary*, 1996. Photocopy. This project is sponsored by the U.S. Department of Labor and is being evaluated by Mathematica Policy Research; Mark Dynarski, project director.

PRINCIPAL INTERVENTIONS: Replicates in seven sites the High School Redirection program model from Brooklyn, New York. The model emphasizes the acquisition of basic reading and mathematics skills in a comfortable setting of small class sizes, extensive student–teacher contact, and strong peer support. The program also offers an on-site child-care center for students with children.

TARGET POPULATION: Students at risk for dropping out of school.

OUTCOMES OF INTEREST: Academic participation and performance; employment and earnings; and household and family income.

School Dropout Demonstration Assistance Program (SDDAP)

STARTING YEAR/YEAR FINAL REPORT EXPECTED: 1991/1997.

INFORMATION SOURCE: Mark Dynarski, Alan Hershey, Rebecca Maynard, and Nancy Adelman, *The Evaluation of the School Dropout Demonstration Assistance Program—Design Report: Volume I*, Mathematica Policy Research, October 1992. The project is sponsored by the U.S. Department of Education, Planning and Evaluation Service; Audrey Pendleton, project officer.

PRINCIPAL INTERVENTIONS: SDDAP will evaluate "Targeted Projects" in secondary schools. Targeted projects include: (1) An emphasis on accelerated, context-rich learning; (2) Culturally sensitive outreach to assist parents; (3) Systematic monitoring of attendance; (4) Counseling; and (5) Increased linkages among schools, the business community, and other community agencies. Sixteen diverse targeted projects are being evaluated using an experimental design.

TARGET POPULATION: Dropouts and youth at risk of dropping out.

OUTCOMES OF INTEREST: A wide array of outcomes are being measured. These include: school participation and completion; school performance; employment; and social behavior.

Upward Bound

STARTING YEAR/YEAR FINAL REPORT EXPECTED: 1991/1997.

INFORMATION SOURCE: No written source. This ongoing program is being evaluated by Mathematica Policy Research for the U.S. Department of Education.

PRINCIPAL INTERVENTIONS: Upward Bound, begun in 1966, provides summer and academic year experiences that may last one to four years. The summer program, which is usually six weeks long, is generally a residential program in which participants receive academic instruction, tutoring, counseling, and cultural enrichment (e.g.

field trips, concerts). During the school year, they receive instruction, tutoring, and counseling approximately once a week.

TARGET POPULATION: Economically disadvantaged youth entering the 9th, 10th, or 11th grades, with a need for academic support in order to pursue a successful program of education after high school. There are two federal criteria: (1) students' families must be at or below 150 percent of the poverty level; and (2) neither parent has received a college degree. Two-thirds of the participants must meet both criteria, and one-third can meet one or the other.

OUTCOMES OF INTEREST: The ultimate program goal is to prepare the students, academically and emotionally, for college. Principal outcomes are college enrollment, courses taken in high school and academic performance, attitudes and educational expectations, career plans, and, in some cases, employment and earnings.

Conservation and Youth Service Corps

STARTING YEAR/YEAR FINAL REPORT EXPECTED: 1993/1996.

INFORMATION SOURCE: JoAnn Jastrzab, Julie Masker, John Blomquist, and Larry Orr, *Evaluation of National and Community Service Programs. Impacts of Service: Final Report on the Evaluation of American Conservation and Youth Service Corps*, Abt Associates, August 1996.

PRINCIPAL INTERVENTION: The standard youth corps is a nonresidential program employing teams of 5 to 10 young people in community service projects. Corps members work for between $100 and $170 per week, doing mainly unskilled physical labor such as cleaning graffiti, clearing park trails, and painting cabins. Nationwide, 91 corps programs operate in 197 sites. The 8 programs selected as the focus for the evaluation are intended to be representative of all corps.

TARGET POPULATION: Young people between 18 and 23 years old. Most are from a disadvantaged background, although the program is not restricted to low-income youth.

OUTCOMES OF INTEREST: Measures include personal development outcomes; involvement in community and other social service; education and training achievements; involvement with risk behavior; and employment and earnings.

National Job Corps Evaluation

STARTING YEAR/YEAR FINAL REPORT EXPECTED: 1993/2001.

INFORMATION SOURCE: John Burghardt, Todd Ensor, Mark Gritz, Russell Jackson, Terry Johnson, Sheena McConnell, Charles Metcalf, and Peter Schochet, *Evaluation of the Impacts of Job Corps on Participants' Postprogram Labor Market and Related Behavior: Study Design Report*, Mathematica Policy Research, report to U.S. Department of Labor, August 1994.

PRINCIPAL INTERVENTIONS: Comprehensive basic education and vocational training, primarily in a residential setting (though outcomes will also be measured for trainees who reside in their home community while they participate in Job Corps).

TARGET POPULATION: Disadvantaged young men and women, between the ages of 16 and 24, who applied for and were found eligible to participate in Job Corps between November 17, 1994, and December 16, 1995.

OUTCOMES OF INTEREST: Employment, earnings, participation in education and job training, welfare receipt, involvement with the criminal justice system, and use of drugs.

Center for Employment Training (CET) Replication

STARTING YEAR/YEAR FINAL REPORT EXPECTED: 1995/2000.

INFORMATION SOURCE: No written source. The evaluation is being conducted by Manpower Demonstration Research Corporation and is funded by the U.S. Department of Labor, Employment and Training Administration.

PRINCIPAL INTERVENTIONS: This experiment tests whether the CET model (which is highlighted in both the "JOBSTART" and "Minority Single Female Parent" experiments) can achieve success at other sites. The model focuses on occupational training and offers training for a selection of occupations based on area employer demand. Basic skills needs of the clients are linked to the occupational training classes. The program is full-time, with peer training and behavioral expectations that reflect the workplace. There is an emphasis on job placement, and clients are considered to have graduated when they have found employment.

TARGET POPULATION: Job Training Partnership Act (JTPA) Title II-C eligible youth. These youth are economically disadvantaged and are not currently attending school (though some may have already graduated).

OUTCOMES OF INTEREST: Along with the primary outcomes of employment, earnings, and welfare receipt, evaluators will also estimate program impacts on training credentials received, health factors, household status, and involvement in the criminal justice system.

Quantum Opportunities Program Demonstration (QOP)

STARTING YEAR/YEAR FINAL REPORT EXPECTED: 1995/2000.

INFORMATION SOURCE: No written source. QOP is sponsored by the U.S. Department of Labor; Eileen Pederson, project officer. It is being evaluated by Mathematica Policy Research, with Berkeley Planning Associates and the Educational Testing Service; Myles Maxfield (Mathematica), project director.

PRINCIPAL INTERVENTIONS: A four-year comprehensive program of: basic education; LifeSkills and cultural enrichment; community service; mentoring; summer activities (including a part-time job and summer school for those who need it); and financial incentives (a stipend for participation and a bonus for completion of major blocks of activities).

TARGET POPULATION: High school students from low-income families (receiving public assistance).

OUTCOMES OF INTEREST: High school graduation, postsecondary attendance, academic achievement (grades and test scores), involvement in community service, teenage pregnancy, and employment.

EMPLOYED, MATURE

Lifelong Learning Demonstration

STARTING YEAR/YEAR FINAL REPORT EXPECTED: 1995/1999.

INFORMATION SOURCE: Stephen Bell, Suzanne Reyes, Jane Kulik, Terry Johnson, and Mark Gritz, *The Lifelong Learning Demonstration: Evaluation Design*, Abt Associates, 1996. Larry Orr, at Abt Associates, is the current project director. There is one experimental site for this project—Baltimore, Maryland. There are also two saturation sites.

PRINCIPAL INTERVENTIONS: A public information campaign promoting worker investment in education and skill training at local postsecondary schools, using direct mail marketing. Two brochures are mailed to treatment group members. The brochures contain a tear-off post card that can be sent in for further information.

TARGET POPULATION: Mature incumbent workers, defined as individuals 25 and older with steady work histories in the past two years.

OUTCOMES OF INTEREST: Application, enrollment, course participation and completion, and degree attainment at postsecondary institutions; applications for and use of student financial aid; and long-term employment and earnings.

UNEMPLOYED

Maryland Unemployment Insurance (UI) Work Search Demonstration Project

STARTING YEAR/YEAR FINAL REPORT EXPECTED: 1992/1997.

INFORMATION SOURCE: Terry R. Johnson and Jacob M. Benus, Design of the Maryland Unemployment Work Search Demonstration Project, Abt Associates, September 1992. The project is sponsored by the Maryland Department of Economic and Employment Development; Lucy Smith, project officer.

PRINCIPAL INTERVENTIONS: There are four treatment groups in the demonstration, each altering only one policy element as compared to existing UI services and requirements. (1) An increase in the work search requirement from two to four employer contacts per week; (2) Eliminating the requirement to report work search contacts; (3) Requiring claimants to attend a job search workshop; (4) Increased verification of claimants' reported work search contacts.

TARGET POPULATION: UI claimants filing an initial claim. There are several exclusions, such as: interstate claimants; members of union hiring halls; and claimants on temporary layoff.

OUTCOMES OF INTEREST: Duration and amount of UI benefits paid to claimants; employment and earnings of claimants; labor force participation; and UI benefits exhaustion.

Job Search Assistance Demonstration

STARTING YEAR/YEAR FINAL REPORT EXPECTED: 1993/1999.

INFORMATION SOURCE: No written source. The project is being funded by the U.S. Department of Labor and is being evaluated by Mathematica Policy Research with Battelle Memorial Institute; Walter Corson (Mathematica), project director.

PRINCIPAL INTERVENTIONS: There are three experimental treatments: (1) Structured job search assistance, wherein all participants are expected to participate in services and workshops; (2) Individualized job search assistance; and (3) Individualized job search assistance plus training through the Title III program.

TARGET POPULATION: Permanently separated unemployment insurance (UI) recipients with a high probability of exhausting benefits.

OUTCOMES OF INTEREST: Principal outcomes are the number of weeks and the dollar amounts of UI receipt, employment, and earnings.

UNEMPLOYED—CANADA

Canadian Earnings Supplement Project (ESP)

STARTING YEAR/YEAR FINAL REPORT EXPECTED: 1996/?.

INFORMATION SOURCE: Howard Bloom, Barbara Fink, Susanna Gurr, and Wendy Bancroft, *The Canadian Earnings Supplement Project (ESP): Subsidizing Reemployment Instead of Subsidizing Unemployment.* Paper prepared for the 17th Annual Research Conference of the Association for Public Policy Analysis and Management, Washington, D.C., November 2–4, 1995. The project is commissioned by the Innovations Branch of Human Resources Development Canada and is being conducted by the Social Research and Demonstration Corporation of Canada.

PRINCIPAL INTERVENTION: A reemployment incentive, referred to as a reeemployment earnings supplement, that will offset a portion of the earnings loss experienced by unemployment insurance (UI) claimants who become reemployed within a specified period in a job that pays less than the one they had lost.

TARGET POPULATION: There are two separate target populations. Four sites will target displaced workers who have lost stable, well-paid jobs through no fault of their own. Another four sites will target "UI-repeaters" who experience a regularly repeating cycle of employment followed by receipt of UI benefits.

OUTCOMES OF INTEREST: Employment, earnings, and UI costs.

ELDERLY

Expanded Medical Care in Nursing Homes for Acute Episodes

STARTING YEAR/YEAR FINAL REPORT EXPECTED: 1993/1998.

INFORMATION SOURCE: James G. Zimmer, *The Expanding Role of Nursing Facilities in the Continuum of Care*, Department of Community and Preventive Medicine, University of Rochester School of Medicine and Dentistry, 1996, Photocopy; James G. Zimmer, "Needed: Acute Care in the Nursing Home," *Patient Care* 27(November 30, 1993): 59–68. Sponsored by a Health Care Financing Administration grant to the Monroe County Long Term Care Program (ACCESS); Gerald Eggert, principal investigator; James Zimmer, research director.

PRINCIPAL INTERVENTIONS: Incentives to reduce hospitalizations among nursing home residents. The incentive is an acute-care Medicare benefit that allows reimbursement of nursing homes and physicians for the extra care that acutely ill residents require. The acute care provided in the skilled nursing facilities (SNFs) includes medical workup, skilled nursing care, and therapy.

TARGET POPULATION: Medicare eligible, non-HMO, nursing home residents with a high likelihood of hospitalization within 24 hours.

OUTCOMES OF INTEREST: Hospitalizations, cost of health care, patient health outcomes, and patient/family satisfaction.

Primary- and Consumer-Directed Care for People with Chronic Illnesses

STARTING YEAR/YEAR FINAL REPORT EXPECTED: 1994/1998.

INFORMATION SOURCE: Gerald M. Eggert, and Brenda R. Wamsley, "Medicare Consumer Choice Benefits: Options for HMOs," *Current Concepts in Geriatric Managed Care* 2(1996):8A–14A. Supported by a grant from the Health Care Financing Administration to the Monroe County Long-Term Care Program and to the Center for Aging and Healthcare in West Virginia; Gerald Eggert, principal investigator; Brenda Wamsley, co-principal investigator; James Zimmer, research director.

PRINCIPAL INTERVENTIONS: Two optional benefits that could be incorporated into a managed-health-care plan: (1) A consumer choice "account" or voucher enabling subjects to purchase home and community-based long-term care services from the provider of their choice; (2) Use of a health promotion nurse to assist the physician in providing primary-care practice-based risk management.

TARGET POPULATION: Community-residing, impaired, medically vulnerable HMO Medicare enrollees.

OUTCOMES OF INTEREST: Quality of life, satisfaction with health care, Medicare and overall health-care costs, hospitalizations.

HEALTH CARE PROVIDERS

National Home Health Prospective Payment Demonstration: Phase II

STARTING YEAR/YEAR FINAL REPORT EXPECTED: 1994/2000.

INFORMATION SOURCE: No written source. This demonstration is being funded by the Health Care Financing Administration; Elizabeth Mauser, project officer. It is being evaluated by Mathematica Policy Research; Barbara Phillips, principal investigator.

PRINCIPAL INTERVENTIONS: Home health agencies are paid a per-episode payment for all visits rendered for up to 120 days of care to a given patient under a Medicare home health plan of care. If care exceeds 120 days, the agency receives per-visit payments for each "outlier" visit rendered. The per-visit payment rates vary for each of six disciplines covered by Medicare: Skilled Nurse; Physical Therapy; Occupational Therapy; Speech Therapy; Medical Social Work; and Home Health Aide. In the demonstration, both the per-episode and the per-visit payments for a given agency are based on that agency's cost experience in the year preceding the demonstration, adjusted in each successive demonstration year for inflation in the prices of inputs.

TARGET POPULATION: Medicare-certified home health agencies and their patients receiving services under a Medicare home health plan of care. Agencies are randomly assigned to receive per-episode payment or to continue on cost-reimbursement.

OUTCOMES OF INTEREST: The cost and use of Medicare home health services, quality of care, patient satisfaction, access to care, the use and cost of other Medicare services, the use and cost of non-Medicare services, and agency revenues and profits.

PERSONS WITH DISABILITIES—SSDI AND SSI BENEFICIARIES

Project NetWork

STARTING YEAR/YEAR FINAL REPORT EXPECTED: 1992/1998.

INFORMATION SOURCE: Rupp, Kalman, Stephen A. Bell, and Leo A. McManus, "Design of the Project NetWork Return-to-Work Experiment for Persons with Disabilities," Social Security Bulletin 57(1994):3–20. This experiment is sponsored by the U.S. Department of Health and Human Services, Social Security Administration. It is being evaluated by Abt Associates.

PRINCIPAL INTERVENTIONS: A case management model offering rehabilitation services, job training, employment assistance, and removal of Disability Insurance work disincentives.

TARGET POPULATION: All Social Security Disability Insurance beneficiaries in eight sites nationwide; all Supplemental Security Income applicants and recipients who are blind and have disabilities.

OUTCOMES OF INTEREST: Employment, earnings, disability benefits, health status, and functional abilities.

HOMELESS PERSONS

HUD/VA Supported Housing Program

STARTING YEAR/YEAR FINAL REPORT EXPECTED: 1991/1998.

INFORMATION SOURCE: No written source. The project is funded by the Department of Veterans Affairs (VA) and the Department of Housing and Urban Development (HUD). Principal investigator is Robert Rosenheck, Dept of Psychiatry, School of Medicine, Yale University, and New Haven VA Hospital.

PRINCIPAL INTERVENTIONS: There are three treatment groups: (1) Housing vouchers (which provide subsidies that allow tenants to move into housing units of their choosing) with intensive case management; (2) Intensive case management alone; and (3) Standard VA treatment (outpatient referral and treatment).

TARGET POPULATION: Homeless veterans with serious psychiatric or substance abuse disorders.

OUTCOMES OF INTEREST: Housing (number of days in housing— where participants have lived during the previous 90 days), mental health status, employment, health service utilization, income, and satisfaction with services.

INDEX

INDEX OF INTERVENTIONS

This index references the various types of policy intervention that have been tested by completed experiments. It should be used with care. Interventions with similar names may differ in many ways; interventions with different names may be similar. It is common for demonstrations to give idiosyncratic titles to activities that are known by other names elsewhere. We have listed at most four interventions per experiment; the evaluators and administrators might believe we have missed or misnamed the most important ones. Only the first page of the summary is shown.

ABOUT THE AUTHORS

David Greenberg is professor of economics at the University of Maryland–Baltimore County. He has been involved in social experimentation for many years. During the 1970s, he was a project officer at the U.S. Department of Health and Human Services for the Seattle-Denver and the Gary Income Maintenance Experiments. In the early 1980s, Dr. Greenberg worked on the Seattle-Denver Experiment as an employee of SRI International, the major contractor for this experiment. Dr. Greenberg has assisted in the design of Milwaukee's New Hope Experiment and Canada's experimental Self-Sufficiency Project.

Mark Shroder is an economist at the Office of Policy Development and Research of the U.S. Department of Housing and Urban Development. Dr. Shroder's publications in the *Review of Economics and Statistics*, the *National Tax Journal*, and *Economic Design* test and extend the theory of public assistance provision in a federal system of government. At HUD he has contributed to the design of the Moving to Opportunity for Fair Housing experiment and to other major research programs.